Armed Force
Personal Financial Planning

Strategies for Managing Your Budget, Savings, Insurance, Taxes, and Investments

---

5th Edition

Maj. David C. Trybula, Ph.D.
Lt. Col. Richard A. Hewitt, CFP

Contributing Associates, Department of Social Sciences, U.S. Military Academy, West Point, New York:

Prof. Dean Dudley, Maj. Sonya Finley, Maj. Blaire Harms, Maj. Paul Kucik, Maj. Joel Levesque, 2nd Lt. Felisa Lewis, Maj. J. Christopher Lover, Maj. Stephen Mannell Jr., Col. Gregg Martin, Maj. Steven Miska, Maj. Joanne Moore, Maj. James O'Connor, Maj. Carlos Perez Jr., Maj. Michael Peters, Maj. Gary Pieringer, Capt. Paul Ritkouski, and Maj. Michael Wright.

STACKPOLE
BOOKS

Published by
STACKPOLE BOOKS
5067 Ritter Road
Mechanicsburg, PA 17055
www.stackpolebooks.com

The ideas and opinions expressed in this volume are those of the authors and do not represent official policies of any governmental agency, the United States Military Academy, or the U.S. Army.

Printed in the United States of America

10 9 8 7 6 5 4 3 2 1

Cover design by Wendy A. Reynolds

Library of Congress Cataloging-in-Publication Data

Trybula, David C., 1967–
Armed Forces guide to personal financial planning : strategies for managing your budget, savings, insurance, taxes, and investiments.—5th ed. / by David C. Trybula, Richard A. Hewitt.
p. cm.
"Contributing associates ... Dean Dudley ... [et al.]."
Rev. ed. of: Armed Forces guide to personal financial planning / Michael J. Meese and Bart Keiser. 4th ed. c1997.
Includes bibliographical references and index.
ISBN 0-8117-3014-X (alk. paper)
1. Finance, Personal. 2. Soldiers—United States—Finance, Personal. I. Hewitt, Richard A., 1962– II. Meese, Michael J. Armed Forces guide to personal financial planning. III. Title.

HG179 .P55 2002
332.024'355—dc21 2002020501

Dedicated to
Brig. Gen. Daniel J. Kaufman

Dean of the Academic Board, 2000–Present
Professor and Head of the Department of Social Sciences, 1996–2000
Academy Professor, 1983–2000
United States Military Academy
West Point, New York

His great wisdom, leadership, enthusiasm, and teaching excellence have educated and inspired a generation of cadets, faculty, and Army leaders and continue to do so.

Contents

PART III: BIG-TICKET ITEMS

PART IV: BUILDING YOUR NEST EGG

PART V: PLANNING FOR RETIREMENT AND LATER

APPENDIXES

Tables

Figures

Introduction

We have written the fifth edition of the *Armed Forces Guide to Personal Financial Planning* to present the most essential topics military members and retirees need to know in a concise, readable manner. The purpose of this book is to enhance the satisfaction associated with military service by improving the financial decisions servicemembers make so that military families can enjoy the most from their income, purchases, investments, and financial planning.

Personal financial planning can be intimidating. As the options and complexity of spending, investing, and insurance increase, so does the challenge of managing personal finances. New financial services and investment and insurance programs seem to appear daily. In addition, federal and state laws, tax rates, health coverage, military pay, and retirement programs are constantly changing. While finances are growing more complex, the time available to servicemembers to understand them has decreased, and leaders are increasingly responsible for not only their financial statuses but also those of their subordinates.

The objective of this book is not to provide a prescription for servicemembers to get rich fast. Most of us remain in the military because of the opportunity it provides to serve with others in a profession that prides itself on the values of duty, honor, and country—not because we seek financial reward. Our hope is that by following the advice in this book, servicemembers can achieve their military career goals and provide a quality standard of living for their family. Then they can remain in the military for the right, nonmonetary reasons. Far too many good officers and noncommissioned officers leave the military early in the hopes of earning more money, but they lose the intrinsic value of service that called them to join the military in the first place.

This book is also a valuable guide for leaders as they counsel soldiers, sailors, airmen, and marines on their financial readiness. With increasing stress on families, more no-notice deployments, and rapidly changing financial conditions, the financial readiness of servicemembers is an important component of their combat readiness. Following the concepts throughout this book will help families to be financially prepared, so that servicemembers can concentrate on their vital military duties.

This book is organized by the order in which servicemembers encounter financial circumstances throughout their careers. You can read them straight through or skip to the chapters that most address your current financial situation. Chapters 1 through 4 cover basic financial concepts and military pay. This is a good place to start if you need to review financial terms and principles, understand the details of pay and allowances, and establish a family budget. You should at least skim this section first and refer to it as you have questions throughout the rest of the book.

Chapters 5 through 7 discuss the basics that everyone must face: bank accounts, credit, and taxes. These seem simple, but servicemembers can waste a great deal of money if they choose banks, credit unions, checking accounts, credit cards, or loans that charge excessive interest rates, fees, or expenses. Taxes are particularly important for servicemembers because of special laws that pertain to the military, especially when servicemembers move or deploy to imminent danger areas. Servicemembers will want to read these chapters to ensure they are paying no more than necessary in bank costs or taxes.

Chapters 8 through 13 provide strategies for large expenses such as buying cars, insurance, housing, health care, and college education. You should read these chapters well before incurring those expenses and update your financial plan accordingly. Chapters 8 and 9 concern the second largest expense most servicemembers have—their car. By carefully reading these chapters before buying or insuring your car, you may save hundreds of dollars. Chapter 10 explains the latest details on the military's continually changing medical and dental care systems. Servicemembers often take their family's health and medical care for granted and then make costly mistakes when a health-care crisis occurs. Servicemembers should scan this chapter now and then read it carefully with their spouses before they have to make health-care decisions. Chapters 11 and 12 explain the details of housing and property insurance. They begin by discussing the basic decision of whether to rent or buy, especially considering the number of times that military families move. Chapter 13 provides advice on saving for college and discusses the details of college financial aid formulas. By developing a plan early and sticking to it, college and other large expenses can be within the reach of most servicemembers.

Chapters 14 through 18 concern investments and are the best source of information about how to manage your long-term savings program. Many professional financial advisors will also give you advice—for a fee or a commission. You will be a much more informed consumer, however, after reading these chapters—for free. Chapter 14 provides a concise overview of investing and a way to develop a personal investment strategy that meets your family's needs. It may be the most important chapter for any investor to read. Chapter 15 explains stocks, bonds, and commodities, and it gives important information on all types of investing. Chapter 16 explains mutual funds, a must for most servicemembers, in detail. Chapter 17 is a new addition that focuses on the different retirement savings options currently available to servicemembers, including a section on the new Thrift Savings Plan (TSP). And finally, chapter 18 discusses real estate as an investment; this may be appropriate for some to consider.

In the final section, chapters 19 through 23 discuss issues servicemembers must face now because they affect future finances—life insurance, retirement, Social Security, veterans benefits, estate planning, and the Survivor Benefit

Plan. Families can save a great deal of money by reading chapter 19 before they meet with an insurance agent; then they will know the facts and can decide what is truly in their best interest. Chapter 20 explains military retirement benefits, which may seem far off now, but it is important to understand what you will have after you retire. Wills, powers of attorney, and trusts are discussed in chapter 21. Scanning this chapter is important to everyone to ensure that they have a will, a letter of instruction, and other provisions for their families if they die unexpectedly. Chapters 22 and 23 explain the details of Social Security, veterans benefits, and the Survivor Benefit Plan. These will significantly affect your family's well-being, even after you die.

Readers of previous editions will notice that, along with incorporating the most current personal finance information, we have made a few major changes in this book. First, we have rewritten several chapters in their entirety and have added a new chapter, "Retirement Savings Options" (chapter 17). Second, we have an updated comprehensive list of Internet sites in Appendix A so you can get the latest up-to-date information. This list will be continually updated on the Armed Forces Personal Finance Website, which complements this book and supports the cadets' instruction at the United States Military Academy (USMA). That site is *http://www.dean.usma.edu/sosh/econ/persfin/default.htm.* Finally, each chapter concludes with tips on how to make the most from that chapter. These are general principles that apply to most servicemembers and can serve to pique your interest before reading the chapter. By scanning them after reading it or before making an important financial decision, you can remember some of the principles the book explains. However, the tips are necessarily short, so if you need more information, refer to the detailed explanations within the chapters.

All the discussions, advice, and recommendations in this book need to be carefully applied to your particular situation. Among the nineteen editors and authors, who have a combined 229 years of service, we have made over 120 moves, have bought at least 60 cars and 25 houses, and have achieved nearly every success and made almost every mistake discussed in this book. Our recommendations are our best opinions, but they may not necessarily be right for you.

There is no such thing as a one-size-fits-all financial plan. This book needs to be an important part of the plan you develop for yourself. You are your best personal financial manager and you need to adapt the information in this book to your family's needs. You should consult with friends and co-workers or seek professional assistance as necessary to make the best decisions. By learning the terms, concepts, and lessons discussed on these pages, you will better understand the value of their advice. Then you can make informed decisions.

This book has been written by a number of officers and a civilian associate professor who either are or have been assigned to the Department of Social Sciences at USMA. With graduate degrees from many of the nation's leading universities, our mission is to provide instruction in the economics, politics, finance, and management courses offered at West Point. As important as graduate education is, much of our best experience is from our role as leaders. All but one of the authors has commanded at least one battery, company, or troop of America's finest soldiers. We bring to these pages the experience of counseling scores of military families on personal finance and of teaching cadets, officers, soldiers, and family support groups the basics of personal financial planning.

This book continues a series of publications on personal finance by associates in the Department of Social Sciences that has spanned the last three-and-a-half decades. Former contributors include Brig. Gen. Herman Beukema, Brig. Gen. George A. Lincoln, Lt. Gen. William S. Stone (USAF), Brig. Gen. Robert F. McDermott, Maj. Norbert Frische (USAF), Capt. Lloyd Briggs, Brig. Gen. James R. Golden, Lt. Col. Robert Baldwin, Col. Hobart Pillsbury, Lt. Col. Michael Edleson, Maj. Kevin Berner, Lt. Col. Thomas Daula, Lt. Col.(P) Michael Meese, and Lt. Col. Bart Keiser. We hope this edition continues in the great tradition of these exemplary soldier-scholars.

Of course, any discussion of products, services, or strategies does not imply endorsement by the authors or any government agency. The opinions expressed are based on our experience and research and do not reflect the opinions of USMA, the Army, or the Department of Defense.

We hope this book will provide you with the information that you need to improve your own financial decisions and to assist you in counseling your subordinates.

PART I

Personal Financial Planning

1

Assessing the Situation

As members of the military, we plan continuously as part of our job. Few of us, however, put the same effort into our personal financial planning. If we did, we'd more likely be able to avoid those "peanut butter and jelly" months that occur when unexpected expenses pop up.

TABLE 1-1
A COMPARISON OF MILITARY AND FINANCIAL PLANNING

Military	Financial
Situation	Balance sheet/net worth
Objective	Financial goals
Plan	Creating the budget
Execution	Implementing the budget
Consolidate/redistribute	Review/revise the budget

Table 1-1 shows a comparison between military and financial planning. Understanding the current situation is the first step in personal financial planning. In this chapter, we will help you create a balance sheet to assess your situation. The next few chapters will give you a quick introduction to some basic financial concepts and to setting financial goals. Once you know where you are and where you are going, all you need is a means to get there. Your budget is a plan that enables you to achieve your goals. As with any plan, you must provide for contingencies and periodically review to check your progress. In all cases, you will need to revise your plan as your financial situation changes.

THE BALANCE SHEET

A balance sheet is nothing more than a snapshot of your financial situation at a specific point in time. As you can see in Table 1-2, the balance sheet has two

TABLE 1-2
A FAMILY BALANCE SHEET: DETERMINING YOUR NET WORTH

ASSETS*	
LIQUID ASSETS	
Cash	$
Savings Accounts	
1.	
2.	
Checking Accounts	
1.	
2.	
Money Market Fund	
Total Liquid Assets	
REAL PROPERTY	
Primary Residence	$
Autos/Recreational Vehicles	
1.	
2.	
Recreation Equipment	
Other	
Total Real Property	
PERSONAL PROPERTY	
Furniture & Appliances	$
Stereos, TVs, Computer, etc.	
Clothing	
Jewelry	
Other	
Total Personal Property	
INVESTMENTS	
CDs	$
Bonds	
Mutual Funds	
Stocks	
Rental Property	
Cash Value of Life Ins. Policy	
Other	
Total Investments	
TOTAL ASSETS	

LIABILITIES & NET WORTH	
SHORT-TERM DEBT	
VISA	$
MasterCard	
American Express	
Discover	
Store Cards	
1.	
2.	
3.	
Signature Loan	
Overdraft Protection Loan	
Total Short-Term Debt	
LONG-TERM DEBT	
Auto/Recreational Vehicle Loan	
1.	
2.	
Appliance/Furniture Loan	
Bank Loan	
Finance Company Loan	
College Loan	
Loan from Family/Friends	
Primary Residence	
Second Home	
Rental Property	
Total Long-Term Debt	
TOTAL LIABILITIES	
NET WORTH	
TOTAL LIABILITIES & NET WORTH	

*Assets should be listed at "market value" (i.e., what you could get for them today if you had to sell them), not "cost."

sides. In order for it to "balance," the two sides must be equal; assets must equal the sum of liabilities and net worth.

Assets are simply the things that you own. They are listed at their "fair market value," which is the amount of money that a willing buyer would pay a willing seller for a particular item today. In some cases, the fair market value is significantly lower than the price you paid for the item. A car is a good example. Once you drive across the exit ramp leaving the dealership, the amount you could get for the car is considerably less than the check you just wrote. On the other hand, some of your assets should appreciate in value, and the amount you list on the balance sheet will be more than what you paid.

Assets are generally broken into two major categories. The first category includes liquid assets, and the second category includes fixed or long-term assets. The difference between the two categories is your ability to quickly convert the asset into cash and to do so at or near market value. This distinction is often called liquidity. For example, stocks are very liquid because you can trade them at a moment's notice and you will get the going market value for those stocks traded. An old car or a home that is located in an undesirable neighborhood is probably not "liquid." It may take a long time to sell, or if you need the money right away, you will probably have to steeply discount the car or the home to sell it quickly.

Your debts, or liabilities, are listed on the right-hand side of the balance sheet. This is simply a list of all your creditors and the amount you owe them.

The other section on the right-hand side of the balance sheet represents your net worth. This is an important number because it shows how much money you would have left over if you had to sell all your assets and pay all your creditors. Net worth is equal to assets minus liabilities. Many young couples, especially those with school loans and a car loan, will find that they have a negative net worth until they pay off some of the debt they owe. A negative net worth is not a sustainable financial situation. If your net worth is negative, the financial plan that we are developing should help get you out of this situation. On the other hand, as your net worth becomes positive and grows larger, you may find that you are actually capable of living off the interest that your assets generate. The name of the game is to maximize your net worth.

Once you total the liabilities and the net worth, the right-hand side will equal the left-hand side, and the balance sheet will balance. Remember, the focus of the balance sheet is to give you a picture of your current financial situation. You may or may not like that picture. The purpose of this book is to help you order your personal finances and, over time, improve your balance sheet. The chapters in this book will help you understand some of the many aspects of personal finance. With some work on your part, some sacrifice in the near term, and some luck, you can improve your bottom line, set and achieve financial goals, and reduce the number of "peanut butter and jelly" months that you and your family have. As usual, we must begin with training in the basics.

Tips on How to Get the Most from This Book

- Skim the table of contents to see what you are most interested in.
- Skip between chapters, depending on your financial situation.
- Review the basics in part I (chapters 1 through 4) so that you are grounded in the fundamentals.
- Use the Internet addresses and other references in Appendix A to keep abreast of the latest information.
- Skim the long-range chapters, such as buying a house, providing for college, and planning for retirement, so that you know what to plan for in the future.
- Read the tips at the end of the chapters for lessons you should know, and then go back to read the chapter if you need more information.
- Remember, the one who best has your financial interests in mind is you!

2

Financial Basic Training

Most readers can digest most of this book without any special training or tools in economic or financial analysis. While this makes individual topics easily accessible, the old saying that "a little knowledge is a dangerous thing" can prove to be true. Really understanding insurance, investments, mortgages, and car leases requires a basic understanding of a few simple principles of finance and economics. Five of these concepts are before-tax versus after-tax income; inflation (real versus nominal values); opportunity cost; time value of money; and the relationship between risk and reward. You don't need an MBA to develop a rudimentary understanding of these concepts sufficient to aid in making solid financial decisions. This brief chapter provides the financial basic training you need to identify key issues, avoid confusion, and separate the gimmicks from the good ideas in the vast supermarket of financial products.

Many people say, "Why worry about learning financial concepts? I can always ask a professional if I don't understand something." Unfortunately, professional advice costs money—money that can't go into your investment plan. Actually, the problem is that there are too many professionals out there willing to give you advice—financial salesmen, advisors, planners, counselors, brokers, and consultants, all hoping to share in a piece of your portfolio. They are as wide ranging as you can imagine in terms of qualifications, motivation, products offered, and sales tactics. There are many good professionals who are truly professional and worth their fees. But the less you know about financial basics, the more likely you are to fall prey to high-pressure salesmen more interested in a sizable commission than your welfare. A skilled salesman can make any financial product look enticing, regardless of its true merits. You must defend your wealth by arming yourself with enough basic knowledge to sort out the ridiculous from the rewarding.

WHAT DETERMINES BEFORE-TAX AND AFTER-TAX INCOME?

Taxes enter into every investment, saving, and spending decision so regularly and routinely that we often ignore them completely. But simply knowing the difference between before-tax and after-tax income can be a major help in budget and investment decision making. An entire chapter later in this book is dedicated to personal tax issues.

A few everyday examples affecting servicemembers come immediately to mind. For illustration purposes, we'll consider a captain in the 27 percent tax bracket, with no state taxes. You probably know that the Basic Allowance for Housing (BAH) and Variable Housing Allowance (VHA) are not taxable. Receiving $654 in a combined BAH and VHA allowance (after-tax income) is equivalent to receiving $1,000 in pay (before-tax income). Why? Because if you had received $1,000 in pay, $280 ($1,000 × 0.27 = $270) would come out for federal taxes, and about $76 more would be deducted for Social Security tax. These differences (particularly state income tax and Social Security tax) are often ignored, causing servicemembers to underestimate their effective income. The true value of any out-of-pocket savings, such as lower commissary prices, is also underestimated.

The bottom line is that $1 in after-tax income is better than $1 in before-tax income. Seven dollars in coupon savings is better than $10 of additional pay (which only provides $654 after taxes to our captain above). This is particularly important information when you are budgeting. In actuality, a penny saved is not a penny earned: It is far more than a penny earned, because the taxing authority gets a big chunk of every penny you earn.

As a result of this, work that you (or your family) do for yourself can pay off in a bigger way than you think. Paying a neighborhood kid $10 to mow the lawn really costs our captain $15.30 of his salary (he had to earn $15.30 to have $10 left over after taxes). By cutting it himself, he would effectively "earn" $15.30 of before-tax income.

To fully understand the impact of taxes, maybe it would be better if we received our gross pay and then had to dole out, a dollar at a time, all of the tax payments so that we would treat the few remaining after-tax dollars with the respect they deserve.

Once you've earned income, paid taxes on it, and then saved and invested some, it gets taxed again. Although this time it is not your investment (or principal) that is taxed, but the earnings (dividends, interest, capital gains) on your investment that are taxed. So by some measure, you have to worry about taxes twice with investments—once going into the investment and once coming out of it. In general, the most powerful tax savings are on the front end, if you can get them. Unless you face much higher tax rates in the future, you are far better off investing all your before-tax dollars (before the IRS gets hold of some of them) than investing only those dollars left after taxes. But how can you invest before-tax dollars, since the IRS taxes your earnings before you get a chance to invest them? The most common way to do this is with an Individual Retirement Account (IRA). As long as you are married and your adjusted gross income is under $50,000 (or single and under $25,000), you have the opportunity to put at least some before-tax dollars to work in an IRA investment without losing them to the tax man. Additionally, the Thrift Savings Plan (see chapter 17) is also funded with before tax dollars. Also, if you have a spouse working in the civilian sector and any retirement plan is offered (401k is the most common), money can be deducted from salary before taxes are paid to fund a retirement investment. Similar options exist for anyone with a sideline business or self-employment income. These are phenomenal opportunities that are passed up by many servicemembers (see chapters 7, 14, and 17).

Tax savings are also available on the back end of your investment, depending on the investment vehicle you choose. Just remember that there may be a difference between what you earn on an investment before and after taxes. Though Social Security taxes do not apply to investment income, other taxes do. A major who thinks her earnings on a bond are 10 percent will get only 7.3 percent after taxes. The range of tax strategies is far too varied to cover here and in the tax chapter, but there are a few brief points that are often overlooked and must be mentioned.

Retirement plans not only allow front-end tax savings, but also allow investment income to compound tax-free within the fund. (Actually, all these tax savings are really only tax deferrals, because the money is taxed when it is withdrawn. Even so, such tax deferrals are valuable to the individual.) Money grows much faster this way, particularly over long periods of time. The advantages are so overwhelming that if you had some money you could do without for at least a few years, you would need a pretty convincing reason not to fill up your IRA or other retirement fund. See chapters 7, 14, and 17 for more information.

Other general strategies concern the fact that capital gains are not taxed until they are realized (sold). A capital gain is the difference between the price at which you sell an asset and the price at which you bought it. If held until your death, capital gains are totally untaxed. Thus, it makes sense to put investments that generate interest income (bonds and CDs) into your tax-deferred retirement funds and to have equity investments (stocks, which are usually held for their capital gain potential) outside your IRA. Many people have it backward, for whatever reason. Also, don't carelessly sell a long-term stock investment, as you'll have to pay taxes on the full capital gain now, instead of deferring the taxes until later or avoiding them completely.

If you are in a high-income tax bracket, it might be to your advantage to purchase the stocks of companies that retain earnings for financing future growth instead of paying high dividends. This makes sense because dividend income is taxed immediately, whereas capital gains are not taxed until you have realized them by selling your stocks. If you concentrate on stocks that will appreciate in market value, you can defer payment of taxes on your investment income. As you will see in the "Time Value of Money" section later in this chapter, it is always advantageous to speed up receipts and defer payments of money as much as possible.

Also remember that college expenses for children generally get paid out of after-tax income. That is, your college fund investments are generally taxed on both ends. But this need not be the case. Chapter 13 discusses income-shifting strategies and other options to keep investment income from being taxed, or at least have it taxed at a lower rate.

Although some of these strategies may appear obvious, many military families fail to take advantage of them. Such failures probably result from a lack of understanding of the substantial difference between before-tax and after-tax income.

HOW DOES INFLATION AFFECT FINANCIAL PLANNING?

We're all aware of inflation; we just do a poor job of working it into our financial planning. Since purchasing power tends to decline over time, we need more dollars to purchase the same level of goods. This raises the important distinction between real and nominal values. If we speak in terms of nominal dollars, we mean whatever a dollar can buy at a given time, even if it's a head of lettuce today and a single pinto bean in the year 2010. Thus, if we set our financial goals in nominal dollars, it's extremely important to make sure we account for inflation properly. It wouldn't make much sense basing our 2005 budget on the same figures we used in 1998, because we would need more nominal dollars due to inflation, and our income, in nominal dollars, is likely to increase with inflation as well. If we speak in terms of real dollars, we refer to their purchasing power in a base year. Thus, if at some point in the future you expect to purchase something that costs $100 in 2002, you'll need more than $100 to purchase it. If the inflation rate is 4 percent in 2002, you will need $104 in nominal 2003 dollars to have the purchasing power that $100 nominal dollars had in 2002.

Although this is a bit confusing, it is not terribly difficult. Problems often arise, however, when there is an inconsistency in planning, such as ignoring inflation altogether or somehow getting real and nominal figures mixed up. Many whole life insurance policies and investment contracts have been using projections of a million nominal dollars sometime in the future. The salesman is talking in nominal dollars (when a Yugo might cost a quarter million!), while you are dreamily thinking in real dollars (gosh, if I could have a million dollars, just think what I could buy!). Another problem is failing to forecast projected numbers consistently. In evaluating a rental property investment, you could figure that your rents would increase 5 percent a year but make no adjustment to expenses for inflation, causing you to overvalue the deal. Or you could make no adjustment for any inflation at all and undervalue the deal. Be careful to treat inflation correctly when analyzing any investment situation.

Just as there are real and nominal dollars, there are also real and nominal rates of return on investments. If you purchase a $1,000 one-year bond that pays 8 percent interest, you will have $1,080 next year. But if inflation was 3 percent over the year, it takes $1,030 nominal dollars to buy what could be bought with $1,000 real dollars. Although your nominal rate of return on this investment was 8 percent, your real rate of return was only 5 percent. Your purchasing power increases at the real rate of return, not at the nominal rate. It is easy to convert the nominal rate of return to a real rate of return by simply subtracting the inflation rate. (*Note:* This is an approximation that works well only over short periods of time, about one to two years.) It is possible to have a negative real rate of return if the inflation rate is larger than the nominal rate of return. When this happens, your purchasing power declines.

Because inflation erodes purchasing power, it is important to protect your savings against inflation. Some investments, like savings accounts and life insurance policies, provide relatively low nominal rates of return, at times even negative real rates of return, and therefore provide inadequate protection against inflation. Stocks and tangible assets such as real estate, precious metals, and art objects have historically performed better in protecting purchasing power. If you expect inflation to be high in the future, you should consider investing in some of those assets.

WHAT IS OPPORTUNITY COST?

The opportunity cost of any action or decision is simply the value of the best alternative that was forgone. Cost in this sense may not be purely monetary, but may also include your time or even something intangible. The opportunity cost of getting an MBA degree is not just the $40,000 or so you will pay in tuition and fees, but would also include the two years of lost wages, two years of forgone seniority, perhaps the cost of two moves, and some additional stress.

Opportunity cost is a concept best understood in conjunction with the saying "There is no free lunch." You will be confronted with many situations that claim to offer something for free, at least monetarily. "Free" financial advice often comes with hidden or even explicit commissions or fees. Be on guard, and use your common sense when offered a deal that seems too good to be true.

Whole life insurance provides an excellent example of the opportunity cost idea. Some insurance agents will proudly show how you can buy their insurance product and ten years later get all of your premium money back, making it sound like free insurance! But if you stop to analyze the opportunity cost, you see that the money you spent on whole life premiums could have bought cheaper term insurance with no cash value. You could have invested the difference and possibly had even more cash to show for it than with the whole life policy. In fact, the savings in premium payments that term insurance affords is one of the places you should look when trying to find funds to set aside for your financial goals.

HOW DOES THE TIME VALUE OF MONEY AFFECT YOUR FINANCES?

Would you rather pay your $200 grocery bill right at the store or pay the $200 a month later? Would you rather receive a $1,000 gift right now or wait a year? Of course, we like to get money as soon as possible and delay giving it up as long as possible. This actually has more to do with interest rates than it does with any human quality like greed or impatience. With a bank account paying you 3 percent interest (that's 0.25 percent per month), all you would need is $199.50 in the bank right now to cover the delayed $200 grocery bill next month. That's better than paying $200 right now. The $1,000 gift received right now will grow to $1,030 by next year; that beats getting $1,000 next year. In fact, the interest rate is the opportunity cost of money, reflecting its time value.

At this time, it would be a good idea for you to read through Appendix D, which gives a more detailed treatment of the time value of money and the related concept of present value. An example of this has already been given: The present value of $200 received a month later is $199.50 if the interest rate is 3 percent. The $200 future value is said to be "discounted" to the present at a discount rate of 3 percent per annum, or 0.25 percent for the one-month period in question. Present value techniques are quite useful in analyzing such problems as which mortgage or car loan to take, whether or not to buy property, and how much a particular financial contract is worth.

Specific applications of interest rates and present values are given throughout this book. It's a good idea to understand the techniques and even be able to replicate them. You should have an inexpensive ($10 to $20 range) financial calculator that will easily and quickly solve complicated formulas with little work. Most computer spreadsheet or financial management software will also perform these calculations. But unless you know what a present value is, or how to use it once it's calculated, this technology will be useless.

A conceptual application of the importance of the time value of money involves contract funds, which are explained in chapter 16. Basically, you sign a contract to purchase an investment on a periodic basis, but you pay most of your fees to the salesman in the first twelve months (and very little in the way of fees in later months). Though on average, you pay 8.5 percent of your gross investment to the salesman in fees over the entire contract period, the reality is far worse. Because most of the fees you pay are up-front, their present value is extremely high. The fee "savings" in later years have a present value that is extremely low. By using present value techniques, you can calculate that the commission you are effectively paying the salesman is more than 12 percent in present value, even though it looks like only 8.5 percent on paper. With an understanding of the concept of the time value of money, you could have figured out that this type of fee structure is a bad deal for you, without calculating any numbers at all.

HOW RISK AND REWARD AFFECT YOUR FINANCIAL DECISIONS

We all take risks when we invest our money. You may need the money in a certificate of deposit before it matures; your money market fund could dip in value; your house, stock, and bond prices will fluctuate constantly. Even a "risk-free" investment like a Treasury bill is subject to some price risk while you own it, as the price at which you could resell the T-bill varies from day to day. Risk is the amount of uncertainty or variance in your possible future returns on investment over some holding period. Investments vary greatly in the amount of risk involved. You get to choose your own risk level for your investment program.

Most investors would prefer less risk, everything else held equal. Thus, if an investment is risky, investors are not likely to purchase it at the same rate of return as a safe investment. In the late 1980s, when Treasury bonds were yielding about 9 percent, investors avoided purchasing corporate bonds also yielding 9 percent, because the chance that a corporation will default on its debt is significantly greater. At 10 percent, however, investors were willing to purchase the bonds of very solid corporations. And at 15 to 20 percent, they were even tempted to invest in very risky bonds that came to be known as "junk bonds." Because the typical investor doesn't like risk, market returns on risky investments are higher to compensate investors for incurring the "cost" of that risk.

As a rough guideline, historical returns over the past several decades show this relationship at work. The very long-run average return on nearly riskless T-bills is just barely over inflation. Long-term T-bonds are riskier (more volatile in their price movements, not at risk of default) and have averaged a 1 percent real rate of return. Assuming the additional risk of corporate bonds earns an average real return of almost 2 percent. But common stocks, which have the most price uncertainty, have returned more than 9 percent over inflation on average over the past seven decades. Based on a rough estimate of expected inflation of 3 to 4 percent annually, you might expect an average return in the stock market of about 12 percent per year in the long run. That's quite a reward, but then the risk has been fairly substantial as well-stock prices move fairly wildly, even if you hold a diversified portfolio.

Don't confuse the long-run averages with what actually happens on a year-to-year basis. Market returns have an annual standard deviation of about 20 percent. As a general rule, you can expect results within a standard deviation of the average about two-thirds of the time. This means that most of the time, your returns in the market will range between losing 8 percent of your value and gaining a sizable 32 percent. About one year in six you could expect to do better than a 32 percent gain, but the bad news is that you will just as frequently have a year where you lose even more than 8 percent, perhaps a lot more. And although the 1980s were far better than average for market performance, there were still some particularly bad years. The high risk inherent in stock investments means that you are less likely to be able to predict future performance with any confidence or accuracy. So, to earn the returns on the stock market, either you must be willing to subject your annual outcome to substantial uncertainty and even to occasionally lose money, or you must have a rather long time horizon (such as in retirement planning or college funding) to let these year-to-year gyrations average out. Over a four-year time frame, the risk in your average annual return on stocks is cut approximately in half, so two-thirds of the time your annualized return over the entire four-year period will fall in a range between roughly a 4 percent gain and a 24 percent gain. Remember, though, there is still some likelihood that you might lose money over even a four-year period.

From the discussion so far, it might seem that there is a definite relationship between risk and reward—as you take more risk, your expected (long-run average) reward goes up as well. That's a good general sense to have, but it is not quite accurate. Unreasonable and unnecessary risk is generally not rewarded. Risk in a well-crafted, diversified portfolio (a collection of investments in different financial assets) is usually rewarded, although not every year, of course. This is a finer point, but one that is crucial particularly for the small investor to grasp.

Someone who invests in a single risky stock, XYZ, and nothing else, may experience returns with a standard deviation of 40 to 50 percent per year. That's a lot of risk. It is also a lot of unnecessary risk. The typical investor in XYZ stock holds a little bit of it (perhaps through a mutual fund) in conjunction with several other stocks and bonds. That investor has a diversified portfolio of investments. The risk of wild movements in XYZ stock is absorbed and averaged out with the differing movements of the many other investments in the portfolio; some go up, others go down, but on average the overall return is positive. Diversification reduces risk, but it does not eliminate risk. Even a diversified portfolio of investments experiences price risk, and it is this nondiversifiable risk that the market rewards. If you do not diversify your portfolio, then the market assumes that either you have a high tolerance for risk or you are ignorant of the benefits of diversification. The market will reward you only for the risk that you must bear. It will not reward you for excessive risk tolerance or ignorance.

A purer example of this is gold-mining stocks. By themselves, they are incredibly risky; almost no investors would choose to hold only gold stocks. Yet for all this incredible risk, gold stocks actually return, on average, several percentage points lower than the average stock. The reason for this is a little complex but quite instructive. Gold stocks' price movements seem to be completely unrelated to those of other stocks: When most stocks are moving down, there's no telling what a gold stock will be doing; it could easily be going up. By taking a little of this individualistic gold stock and putting it in a portfolio with a lot of "typical" stocks, you might actually reduce the overall risk of the portfolio's return. Because of the rebel movements of the gold stock, a bad day for the market now won't be quite as bad for your portfolio, but a good day for the market won't be quite as good either. This risk reduction is a nice quality for which diversified investors are willing to "pay" by accepting a slightly lower average return on the gold stock. This may seem ironic, given the outrageous level of risk in the gold stock by itself, but market returns are not driven by the needs of a few irrational and overly risky holdings of a few investors.

So in this seemingly contradictory world of "risk gets rewards" but "unreasonable individual risk gets no rewards," what is a small investor to do? First, determine the level of risk with which you are comfortable. You're never going to make enough on a moderate portfolio to make it worth losing sleep over. Then, pick a diversified portfolio of investments that will achieve your risk target. If you hold only one or two stocks or bonds, either you will give up a sizable return to achieve your risk goal, or else you will accept much more risk than you were comfortable with to achieve a return goal. With a diversified portfolio, you get to have your cake and eat it too.

But do not include too many securities in your portfolio: You incur a brokerage fee every time you buy or sell, and the benefits from diversification decrease rather quickly. Academic research has shown that as a portfolio is expanded from one to five securities, the gain in diversification is substantial. Further additions to the portfolio, until it contains ten securities, will still yield significant gains, but beyond ten securities the improvement is slight. Also remember that the more securities you include in your portfolio, the more time you will have to spend tracking their performance as you manage your portfolio. For investors who are willing to spend time managing their portfolios, picking five to ten securities in which to invest may be the best choice.

For those who do not want to manage their portfolios, a mutual fund may be the appropriate instrument for achieving their goals. More information on investing in financial assets, mutual funds, retirement savings plans, and real assets is available in chapters 14 through 18.

SUMMARY

Saving and investing is certainly not an easy task for most of us. In a complex world of investment bankers, convertible subordinated debentures, and put options on commodities futures, you cannot be blamed for feeling a bit overwhelmed sometimes. But you don't need to learn everything at once; just master a few basic concepts as you think about your personal financial options. This will help you avoid misunderstanding financial products and buying products you don't want or need. Many financial products that servicemembers buy are overpriced and oversold, and should be avoided. We're not stupid, and we're certainly not more stupid than the next guy. Bad or mediocre products are usually distorted by a skilled seller to look better than they are. How is this done? In almost all cases, the "magic" is a simple twisting around or violation of one of the five basic concepts presented above. It is easy to make a deal seem too good to be true when you confuse present and future values; ignore taxes, inflation, and the time value of money; ignore the opportunity cost; or avoid risk analysis and comparison. Once you understand these concepts, it is easier to sort out the truth from exaggeration or even misrepresentation. You may not be able to convince an eager salesman of your more accurate point of view, but at least you'll know when to shut the door or hang up the phone. Just remember, it's your money, and no one (except the IRS) can tell you what you ought to do with it.

Tips on How to Get the Most from Financial Principles

- Save as much as possible early to allow for compounding returns over time.
- Defer taxes whenever possible through IRAs, income shifting, or working for yourself.
- Consider inflation to ensure that your calculations are consistently made in real dollars.
- Defer payments and accelerate receipts as much as possible, because the interest rate reflects the opportunity cost of holding money.
- To achieve higher returns, generally you will have to accept greater risk.
- The effect of volatility can be reduced with a long time horizon and a diversified portfolio.
- Using mutual funds or picking five to ten securities is an effective way to diversify risk.

3

Military Pay, Allowances, and Benefits

Determining your income is one of the initial steps toward establishing a personal financial plan. Total income includes your service pay and allowances, returns from savings and investments, part-time work, and the earnings of other family members. This chapter focuses on your military income, including pay, allowances and other benefits available to you as a servicemember.

WHAT ARE THE COMPONENTS OF YOUR MONTHLY PAY?

All branches of the Armed Forces provide a Leave and Earnings Statement (LES) that lists your pay, allowances, allotments, and collections made each month. Whether or not you receive midmonth pay, you should also receive a midmonth Military Net Pay Advice. If you are away from your duty station at the end of the month, any military pay office can provide you with a duplicate statement from its records, and you can also access your LES online at *www.dfas.mil/emss.* You should be able to identify the following sections on your LES:

- Entitlements: pay and allowances you received.
- Deductions: federal and state taxes, FICA, Social Security and Medicare, collections from your pay for overpayments or advance pay, fines, or forfeitures.
- Allotments: portions of your entitlements paid at your direction to family members, financial institutions, or charities.
- Summary: take-home pay paid to you or sent to your bank (end-of-month pay).
- Leave Information: your leave days accrued during the current fiscal year and your current balance.
- Tax Information: a summary of federal, FICA, and state income taxes withheld.

First we will focus on the entitlements section of your LES. The *Department of Defense Financial Management Regulation,* which can be found at your local finance office or on the Defense Finance and Accounting Service website *(www.dfas.mil),* provides a more detailed description of all available pay and allowances. There is a key distinction between military entitlements identified as "pay" and those identified as "allowances." By law, federal and state taxes are deducted from pay, whereas allowances are generally tax exempt. There are certain exceptions, such as CONUS COLA, described below. When comparing military and civilian pay, you will frequently see "tax advantage" adjustments for allowances to show how much one actually shields from taxes.

What Determines Your Basic Pay?

Basic pay can be received twice a month (midmonth and end-of-month) or once at the end of the month. The twice-a-month option provides you with half of your pay on the fifteenth of each month and the remaining pay at the end of the month. Take advantage of this option because it allows you more flexibility in paying bills. Even if you don't need it to pay bills, you can earn two weeks' interest on half your pay every month.

Appendix C shows monthly basic pay rates for officers and enlisted personnel by pay grade and length of service as of January 2002. Pay rates are reviewed annually, and changes are usually made effective on 1 January. For pay purposes, length of service includes all periods of active and inactive service as a commissioned officer, warrant officer, flight officer, or enlisted person in any regular or reserve component of any of the uniformed services. It does not include time served as a cadet, midshipman, or ROTC student. Length of service is determined by the number of years since the pay date listed on the top line of your LES. It is reported in the "YRS SVC" block. If your pay date is incorrect, contact your finance office to change it.

What Are You Paid for Housing and Higher Costs of Living?

Servicemembers are authorized a Basic Allowance for Housing (BAH) according to pay grade, family composition, and geographic location when government quarters are not available or when government quarters are leased by a private contractor. BAH rates change annually and from place to place. Generally, married servicemembers receive BAH at the "with dependents" rate, while single members receive BAH at the "without dependents" rate. If you reside in government quarters considered substandard because of its size or condition, you may be paid BAH at the "partial" rate. BAH is designed to cover approximately 80 percent of housing expenses for a typical servicemember at a particular pay grade and family composition. To calculate the BAH rate you would receive, go to the Defense Finance and Accounting Service website *(www.dfas.mil);* you will need a zip code for the duty station you are inquiring about.

If You Are Living in the United States. Within the United States, you may receive CONUS COLA (cost-of-living allowance) if you live in a high-cost area. COLA is a partial compensation for higher living expenses, including housing. It is payable to you whether or not you occupy government housing. CONUS COLA is a taxable payment paid to servicemembers living in areas having costs that exceed the average cost of living by more than 9 percent. Servicemembers are expected to pay the first 9 percent of the higher cost; CONUS COLA will compensate them for the remainder.

If You are Living Overseas. Overseas, you will receive Overseas Housing Allowance (OHA) if you do not live in government housing and the cost of lodging "on the economy" exceeds your BAH. The government will pay you for the cost of rent, up to a ceiling specified for your grade and your area, plus the average cost of utilities. You will also receive a Move-In Housing Allowance (MIHA) in addition to other payments when you first move into quarters off base. These allowances are not paid if you move into government-leased quarters and do not pay rent. If you live in a high-cost area, you will receive OCONUS COLA, which is calculated by comparing the cost of living in an overseas location with the cost of living in CONUS (excluding housing). It is still paid to you if you live in government housing, but is less than the rate for servicemembers living on the economy. The amount of this COLA varies based on changes in the exchange rate so that the amount in local currency is roughly constant. When you see the payment on your LES, it will normally be labeled COLA and will include a figure for rent and utilities (OHA) and cost of living. The OHA and COLA rates for nearly every location in the world are online at the Internet site listed in Appendix A.

What Are You Paid for Clothing and Food?

Subsistence and Clothing Allowances are paid to help defray the cost of food and uniforms. As of 1 January 2002, all officers receive a Basic Allowance for Subsistence (BAS) at a fixed rate of $166.37 per month. Enlisted members are paid BAS only when meals are not provided by the government. Rates for BAS for enlisted members can be found in Appendix C.

Clothing allowances are paid annually to enlisted personnel to help defray the cost of clothing repair and replacement. Payment amounts vary with branch of service, length of service, and gender and are paid annually on the anniversary of your date of entry. Check the finance regulation online or with your finance office for specifics.

How Do Contingency Deployments Affect Your Pay and Allowances?

With increasing short-term deployments to places like Bosnia and Kuwait, it is important to know what happens to your and your soldiers' pay and allowances. This section briefly describes what you can expect, using Operation Joint Guard as an example. In each deployment, however, you should check with your finance office to see what conditions or rules may apply to your situation.

First, all of the normal pay and allowances continue. It is critical that servicemembers have a check-to-bank (direct deposit) pay option that provides accessible funds to their families when they are deployed. Family members need to have access to accounts, proper powers of attorney, and instructions on how to take care of their finances when the military member is deployed. Fortunately, family income generally increases during a deployment in several ways:

Imminent Danger Pay. Servicemembers are paid $150 per month for any month in which they are present in or flying over a designated "imminent danger area" (previously known as a hostile fire area). If wounded in an imminent danger area, members are entitled up to three months imminent danger pay while hospitalized. Aircrews flying off carriers and entering airspace above the designated areas would receive the pay; ship crewmembers would not. However, if a naval vessel were fired upon, the crew would then receive imminent danger pay.

Family Separation Allowance. Married members whose assignments separate them from their families for thirty or more consecutive days receive a monthly allowance of $100. (This is true even if the thirty days are part of a routine training deployment.) If members are not assigned to government quarters while separated from their families, they may also be entitled to draw an extra monthly BAH at the "without dependents" rate to defray the cost of maintaining two homes.

Foreign Duty Pay. Foreign duty pay is payable to enlisted members assigned to locations deemed particularly arduous by the Secretary of Defense (for example, Bosnia). It ranges from $8 a month for E-1 to $22.50 a month for E-9. See Appendix C for the specific amounts for each grade.

Per Diem Rate. Soldiers may be authorized the incidental part of the per diem rate. (The government provides mess and lodging.) In Bosnia, this is $105 per month. BAS payments will stop and be replaced by the appropriate per diem rate for the length of the duty.

Tax Advantages. If an enlisted member is serving in a "qualified hazardous duty area" (Bosnia is one example) for at least one day of a month, all of his or her military pay for that month is nontaxable. Commissioned officers may exclude up to the maximum enlisted amount per month (currently $4,060.40).

This tax advantage has important implications if you contribute to an IRA account and military pay is your only source of taxable income. Current IRS (June 2001) rules state that your IRA contribution cannot exceed your total tax liability or $5,000, whichever is greater. You will need to withdraw any excess contributions and the dividends they earned to avoid an excise tax. (For more details concerning IRAs, see chapter 7 and IRS Publication 590.) Fortunately, servicemembers have an extension on filing tax returns, paying taxes, and fixing IRA accounts until 180 days after they leave the qualified hazardous duty area. The extension does not accrue interest on monies owed to the government; however, like a normal extension, the servicemember must still file a request for it.

Filing a form with the phone company or filing IRS Form 8849, "Claim for Refund of Excise Taxes," can help you avoid even the federal excise tax on calling card calls from Bosnia.

What Other Pay and Allowances May You Receive?

In addition to payments for deployments, many servicemembers receive pay and allowances based on categories such as special skills and type of duty. The following listings summarize the most important categories. Your local finance office will have complete details.

Hazardous Duty Incentive Pay. Servicemembers who qualify for hazardous duty incentive pay as noncrewmembers in the following areas will receive $150 per month:

- Duty involving parachuting.
- Duty involving frequent participation in flight operations on the decks of ships from which aircraft may be launched.
- Duty inside a high- or low-pressure chamber.
- Duty as a human acceleration or deceleration experimental subject.
- Duty involving the demolition of explosives, including training for such duty.
- Duty as a human test subject in thermal stress experiments.
- Duty involving handling of chemical munitions.

Hazardous duty incentive pay for crewmembers is based on rank. See Appendix C for details.

Sea Pay. Some officers and enlisted members receive sea pay as an incentive for service on ships at sea. The rates vary with pay grade and cumulative years of sea duty and are shown as of 1 January 2001 in Appendix C.

Submarine Duty Pay. Naval personnel who meet certain submarine duty qualifications receive monthly submarine duty pay. Rates as of 1 January 2001 are in Appendix C.

Nuclear Duty Pay. Officers who have nuclear qualifications and are performing duties involving nuclear operations and equipment are authorized special pay. There are three general categories of nuclear duty pay:

1. New accessions to nuclear specialties receive a bonus of up to $8,000.
2. Members extending their obligations in nuclear specialties for three, four, or five years may receive bonuses of up to $12,000 per year of extension.
3. Members serving in nuclear specialties beyond an obligated extension may receive an incentive bonus of up to $10,000 per year.

Diving Duty Pay. Members assigned to diving duty are entitled to special pay for periods of actual diving performance. A master diver can receive up to $300 a month.

Flight Pay. Servicemembers who participate in regular and frequent aerial flights as crewmembers or noncrewmembers are entitled to flight pay. The monthly amount of pay depends upon a number of factors; see Appendix C for details.

Foreign Language Proficiency Pay. Members who have proficiencies in certain foreign languages will receive a monthly allowance of $25 to $100.

Special Pay for Health-Care Professionals. Several types of special pay are authorized for dentists, medical doctors, and other health-care professionals, depending on rank, years of service, and qualifications. Details are given in Appendix C.

TRAVEL PAY AND ALLOWANCES

Permanent-change-of-station (PCS) and temporary duty (TDY) travel can be very expensive. Fortunately, you are entitled to financial assistance to help defray the cost of travel. For a complete reference, see the *Joint Federal Travel Regulations* (JFTR), *Volume 1, Uniformed Service Members*, commonly called the JFTR, available at your finance office or online at the Internet address listed in Appendix A.

How Much Are You Paid When You Move (PCS)?

Moving yourself, your family, and your household goods will be easier if you know what type of assistance the government will provide. Not all costs are covered—make the best use of what the government offers.

Travel Pay. The pay you receive will depend on whether the government provides the transportation (either using a government vehicle or a commercial carrier) or you provide your own privately owned vehicle (POV). If you provide your own transportation, you are entitled to a Monetary Allowance in Lieu of Transportation (MALT) of 15 cents per mile for yourself, 17 cents per mile if one family member is traveling with you, 19 cents with two family members, or 20 cents with more than two family members. If you are transporting a second POV within CONUS, you are eligible for an additional 15 cents per mile for the second vehicle. The official distance between permanent duty stations, including travel to TDY locations en route to the new duty station, will be used to calculate your mileage allowance. In addition, the servicemember receives a flat rate of $50 per diem, family members twelve years and older receive $37.50 per diem, and those under twelve receive $25 per diem. When a spouse travels separately from the servicemember, the spouse receives $50 per day.

You are authorized one travel day for every 350 miles between duty stations. If you take less than the maximum number of authorized days, you will not be paid the per diem for the days you did not use. For example, if you move the 2,408 miles from Fort Lewis to Fort Polk, you are authorized seven days' travel. If you complete it in only four days, you may lose three days' per diem (with a spouse and three children under twelve that would be a loss of $487.50). You may be better off taking the full seven days if you keep your travel expenses below the per diem rate.

Government or commercial carrier accomplishes most overseas moves. You can also request "transportation-in-kind" (a government ticket) when moving within the United States. You will not receive the mileage allowance when you use transportation-in-kind, but you will be paid per diem for those days that you are traveling. In addition, certain expenses, such as cab fares, tips to porters, visa fees, and even the fee for travelers' checks, are reimbursable. Keep a good record of such costs and report them when you arrive at your next duty station.

Transportation of Household Goods. The government will pay to move your belongings to your next duty station, within certain weight limitations that depend on your grade and length of service. The government will use the lowest-cost mode of transportation that provides the required service. Your local transportation office will make all the necessary arrangements. You can find your weight allowance in the following table.

TABLE 3-1
HOUSEHOLD GOODS WEIGHT ALLOWANCE

Rank	Without Dependents	With Dependents
O-6 to O-10	18,000	18,000
O-5, W-5	16,000	17,500
O-4, W-4	14,000	17,000
O-3, W-3	13,000	14,500
O-2, W-2	12,500	13,500
O-1, W-1	10,000	12,000
E-9	12,000	14,500
E-8	11,000	13,500
E-7	10,500	12,500
E-6	8,000	11,000
E-5	7,000	11,000
E-4 (over 2 years' service)	7,000	8,000
E-3	2,000	5,000
E-2	1,500	5,000
E-1	1,500	5,000
Cadets	350	n/a

DITY Moves. You may also elect to move yourself under the voluntary "Do-It-Yourself" (DITY) program. This program provides a way to earn extra money by moving yourself using your own truck, van, SUV, or a rented vehicle, but not a passenger car. If you want to do a DITY move, apply for it at your transportation office. You must complete a counseling form and have the empty vehicle weighed before making this type of move. The government will pay you 80 percent of what it would cost to move you commercially, with 60 percent paid up front if you are renting a vehicle. The government will usually withhold some portion of the final settlement for federal, state, and local taxes and provide a Form W-2 for income tax purposes.

You can also make a "partial DITY" move, in which you move some of your household goods and the government moves the rest. This is particularly popular among servicemembers who own a truck or minivan, because it enables them to load up their own vehicles when they move and be paid for it. The government saves money too, because it does not have to pay professional movers to move those goods. The same requirements regarding vehicle type, mandatory counseling, and weighing your vehicle apply. Check with your local transportation office for details.

Household Goods Storage. If your PCS orders limit you to less than your normal weight allowance, the government will pay for nontemporary storage of what you must leave behind. (The weight shipped plus the amount stored cannot exceed your weight allowance.) When you arrive at your new duty station, you are authorized temporary storage of your goods for up to ninety days, regardless of whether the government shipped them or you did a full or partial DITY move. At your request, the transportation office at your new duty station may extend storage for an additional ninety days. For overseas moves, each servicemember may ship one privately owned vehicle (POV) at government expense. Certain restrictions apply for specific destinations, so check with you transportation office.

Mobile Home. If you own a mobile home, the government will pay for all or part of the cost of moving it to your next duty station within the continental United States and Alaska. The following three conditions must be met:

1. You bought the home on or before the effective date of the orders.
2. The home will be your residence at your new duty station.
3. The body and chassis, including tires, are in fit condition to the satisfaction of the government.

Moving your mobile home will, in most cases, substitute for shipping your household goods. If the move costs more than it would cost to move your household goods, you must agree in writing to pay the difference. This can be a fairly common added expense of several hundred or thousands of dollars. To ensure that you will have a place to set your home, reconnoiter your new duty station. Many areas no longer allow mobile homes. Additionally, you are not entitled to Dislocation Allowance (discussed below) when moving a mobile home. One final note: Mobile homes do not always arrive undamaged from the journey, so there may be some additional expenses if the repair costs exceed the amount of government insurance.

What Other Help Can You Get? DLA, TLE, and Advance Pay

Except for moving to your first duty station and upon separation, you are authorized a Dislocation Allowance (DLA) equal to two months' BAH when you relocate your household. You may not receive more than one DLA per fiscal year. Also, if you are a member without dependents and are assigned government quarters at your new duty station, DLA will not be authorized. Single servicemembers are eligible for DLA only if they are not assigned to government quarters. If you are moving overseas and not moving into government quarters, you may be eligible for a Move-In Housing Allowance to help defray the additional cost of setting up a household overseas.

Servicemembers are authorized to receive a Temporary Lodging Expense (TLE) for CONUS moves of up to $110 per day for a maximum of ten days ($1,100). These ten days can be taken at either location, but they normally have to be while you are signed in to either your old or new duty station and quarters are not reasonably available. (Finance and transportation offices usually use the day that your household goods are packed or shipped as the day TLE can start and the date that they arrive at your new home as the day TLE should end.) TLE pays for the actual cost of lodging plus per diem for the servicemember and his or her family (after subtracting BAH and BAS payments), not to exceed $110 per day. This per diem is reduced if kitchen facilities are available, such as those in a government guesthouse. You should consider the trade-off of convenience and reduced rent of a guesthouse with the higher per diem payment if you stay in a hotel. You may need to get a statement of nonavailability to stay in a local hotel instead of the guesthouse. Overseas, you may also receive TLE, with a modified maximum rate and length of payment (up to sixty days) based on the specific conditions at the overseas location. Check with your finance office for details.

Your travel pay and the allowances described above are payable in advance. In addition, you may receive one month's base pay in advance and two months' base pay once you arrive at your new duty station, with your commander's approval. Be forewarned, however, that you will be required to repay any excess travel and relocation allowances in addition to a monthly deduction for the advance on your base pay.

What Pay Do You Receive While on Temporary Duty (TDY)?

Generally, local transportation facilities provide tickets for TDY travel, and your finance office authorizes per diem allowances to cover food, lodging, and incidentals. Your TDY payment will be for the actual cost of lodging (which must be documented by receipts) and a per diem expense for meals and incidentals. Both have maximum amounts that vary by location. Your per diem will be based on one of three formulas, based on the extent to which government meals are available:

1. If government meals are available, you will be paid the lowest amount because your costs are lower. As of 2001, the rate is $8 per day in CONUS.
2. If government meals are not available, you will be paid the maximum meals and incidentals per diem for the area. As of 2001, the rate is between $22 and $44 in CONUS.
3. If some government meals are available (either because you can eat some meals in a mess hall or the trip includes some meals as part of a conference fee), you will be paid the proportional rate, which is computed to be the average of the cost of less expensive government meals and more expensive nongovernment meals. As of 2001, the rate is between $18 and $26 in CONUS.

For the day you start or end TDY, you are paid a partial per diem equal to 75 percent of the appropriate amount listed above. Check with your finance office or use the Internet location listed in Appendix A to determine the TDY rate for any location.

WHAT OTHER IMPORTANT FINANCIAL BENEFITS DO YOU HAVE?

Medical and Dental Care

As a servicemember, you are entitled to any medical and dental care you require while on active duty. Medical and dental care for your family, however, will be provided on a space-available basis. See chapter 10 for further information regarding family health care.

Department of Veterans Affairs Benefits

The VA offers a number of programs for your benefit while you are on active duty and after you have resigned or retired. Chapter 22 contains a detailed discussion of the most significant benefits. For complete information, visit, call, or write to your nearest VA facility, which you can find listed in you local phone book under U.S. Government, Department of Veterans Affairs. You can also visit their website, listed in Appendix A.

Servicemembers Group Life Insurance

All members of the Armed Forces are automatically insured under Servicemembers Group Life Insurance (SGLI) for $250,000, unless they elect in writing not to participate or to be covered for a lesser amount. Premiums are automatically dedicated from your pay. SGLI represents a low-cost method of providing some excellent term life insurance coverage. Additional insurance you need depends on your family situation. You can convert SGLI to Veterans Group Life Insurance (VGLI) without a medical exam when you leave the service. VGLI is a renewable five-year term policy with a premium based on your age when you leave the service.

Additionally, your spouse is also automatically enrolled in SGLI for $100,000 worth of coverage or the amount of your SGLI, whichever is less. Each dependent child is also covered for $10,000 with no fee. Fees for spouses are age based and vary dramatically. See chapter 19 for more details on insurance.

WHAT MILITARY BENEFITS ARE PAID AT DEATH?

Survivor Benefits

If you die while on active duty, your family or other designated beneficiaries may be entitled to lump-sum payments, monthly benefits, and funeral and burial rights. Chapters 21 through 23 discuss planning financial support for your loved ones in the event of your death. This section identifies the types of payments your family may be authorized if you die while on active duty.

Lump-Sum Benefits

The following benefits are paid on a one-time basis, at the death of the servicemember:

- Death Gratuity: A payment equal to six months' pay of the deceased, but not more than $6,000, is paid as soon as possible.
- Social Security Lump-Sum Death Benefit: A one-time payment of $255 made by the Social Security Administration. It is payable only to the surviving spouse if living with you at the time of death.
- Pay for Accrued Leave: Survivors will receive the deceased's basic pay for up to sixty days of earned but unused leave.
- Arrears of Pay: All pay due but unpaid up to the date of death will be paid to the designated beneficiary of the deceased.

Monthly Payments

- Dependency and Indemnity Compensation (DIC): A payment of $991 is provided by the VA to the surviving spouse of a deceased active-duty servicemember. An additional payment of $229 is provided for each dependent child.
- VA Dependents' Education Allowance: Your surviving spouse and children between the ages of eighteen and twenty-six (extended up to age thirty-one in some cases) may be eligible for up to forty-five months of education benefits. Spouses must use the benefits within ten years of your death. Training may be in any approved vocational or business school, college, professional school, or establishment providing apprentice or on-the-job training. Current rates (2001) are $588 for full-time attendance and lesser amounts for part-time attendance. Need-based college tuition loans are also available for amounts up to $2,500 per semester. Some states may also offer additional assistance (tuition, loans, or grants) for the survivors of deceased servicemembers who were legal residents of the state.
- Social Security Survivor Benefits: Eligible beneficiaries may get Social Security Survivor Benefits depending on the amount of your average monthly earnings. Computations of the payment are complex. See chapter 22 for a discussion of Social Security benefits.
- Survivor Benefit Plan. Upon reaching twenty years of service and, thus, eligibility for retirement, active-duty personnel are automatically covered by the Survivor Benefit Plan (SBP). SBP is essentially a life insurance plan that extends your retirement pay to your family in the event of your death. See chapter 23 for a full discussion of that SBP program.
- Death Pension: The surviving spouse and dependent children of a veteran with wartime service may be eligible for a death pension on a need basis. All other annual income sources, including Social Security benefits, are considered when setting the pension rates. The maximum allowable pension for a surviving spouse is $6,237 with an additional $1,586 per child. Check with the Veterans Administration for details.

Tips on Making the Most from Your Military Pay

- Check your LES monthly to verify its accuracy.
- Select the midmonth pay option to get half your pay two weeks earlier.
- If serving on a contingency deployment, check whether you are receiving imminent danger pay, family separation allowance, foreign duty pay, or the incidental portion of TDY, and have some or all of your income excluded from taxes.
- Use all authorized days for PCS moves, and claim both cars if you are moving with two cars.
- Consider a partial DITY move in your own vehicle if you own a minivan or truck.
- When moving, time the pickup and arrival of household goods so that you do not exceed the maximum TLE amount ($110 per day for ten days in CONUS and up to sixty days overseas).
- If some government meals are not available on TDY, ask for the proportional per diem rate; if no government meals are available on TDY, ask for the maximum per diem rate.
- Ensure that your family knows what benefits you have, in case you should die on active duty.

Funeral and Burial Benefits

If you die while on active duty, the government will bury you in any national cemetery (if space is available) designated by your next of kin. Burial of your spouse, minor children, and in some restricted cases, adult children in the same grave as the servicemember may also be authorized. The nearest national cemetery can provide details. Arlington National Cemetery is under the jurisdiction of the Department of the Army. For information, write to Superintendent, Arlington National Cemetery, Arlington, VA 22211, or call (703) 695-3250 or DSN 225-3250.

The government will provide headstones and markers for all persons buried in national cemeteries. For servicemembers on active duty, the government will arrange for shipment and preparation of remains and provide a burial flag. If death occurs near a military installation and the next of kin makes the funeral arrangements, reimbursements may not exceed what the government would have had to pay for preparation of the remains. A maximum reimbursement of $1,750 will be paid for a death occurring away from a military installation's contracting area.

A servicemember buried in a private cemetery will receive a maximum of $3,100 in addition to preparation costs to help defray other expenses. If you are buried in a national or post cemetery and the next of kin contracts for a funeral director to conduct the burial, a maximum of $2,000 will be paid in addition to reimbursement for preparation of the remains. For burial in a national or post cemetery with government preparation of the remains, a maximum of $300 is paid to cover other expenses incidental to burial.

All benefits apply whether remains are cremated or interred.

SUGGESTED REFERENCES

Army Times, Navy Times, and *Air Force Times* all contain current information on military pay and allowances, and any anticipated changes.

The Handbook for Military Families is published each year as a newspaper supplement to the various *Times* during the first week in April.

Joint Federal Travel Regulations, Volume 1, Uniformed Servicemembers (JFTR).

Websites

www.dfas.mil: Pay and allowances.
www.dfas.mil/emss: LES online.
www.va.gov: Death and burial benefits.

4

Financial Planning and Budgeting

Armed with your balance sheet, basic training in financial topics, and an understanding of military pay, you are ready to undertake the basic tasks of financial planning: setting financial goals and establishing a budget to achieve those goals.

HOW DO YOU SET FINANCIAL GOALS?

While most of us have thought about financial goals, few have probably taken the time or effort to calculate just how much achieving these financial goals will actually cost. A key part of the goal-setting process is determining how much money you need to set aside, either now or each month, to achieve these goals. Clarifying your objectives and deciding exactly how much to save are important first steps in your personal financial planning. Establishing specific goals can provide the motivation necessary to achieve them.

When calculating what it will cost to achieve your goals, you can use either nominal or real values. The first three rows of Table 4-1 show the projected nominal cost of sending a child to college in 2007, 2012, and 2017. The nominal cost increases from year to year for two reasons. First, inflation erodes the purchasing power of the dollar, so $1 in 2017 will buy less than $1 in 2007. Second, providing a college education in the future may require an increasing amount of real resources, as would be the case if, over time, colleges built new science laboratories and had to charge more for the better educational experience that results. Predicting such real price changes is difficult; for personal financial planning purposes it is sufficient to ascribe all of these price increases from year to year to inflation. That is, we assume that if we could pay for a year of education at a four-year public college in 2017 with "real" 2007 dollars, the real price would be $9,649. Due to the effect of inflation, however, the nominal price will be $15,717. (Chapter 13 examines how to plan for and pay those looming college bills in great detail.)

TABLE 4-1
NOMINAL AND REAL FUTURE COLLEGE COSTS

Average Annual College Expenses (in Year)*	Public College 2-Year	Public College 4-Year	Private College 2-Year	Private College 4-Year
2007	$5,910	$9,649	$13,074	$20,361
2012 (nominal 2012 dollars)	7,543	12,315	16,686	25,986
2017 (nominal 2017 dollars)	9,627	15,717	21,296	33,166
2017 (real 2007 dollars)	5,910	9,649	13,074	20,361

* Annual college expenses represent the sum of annual tuition, fees, room, board, books, supplies, transportation, and other charges.
Source: Calculations from *College Board Online,* October 2001.

Just as there are nominal and real prices, so too there are nominal and real interest rates. Because we earn interest on our investments, interest rates are often referred to as a "rate of return." We earn interest at the nominal rate of return. That nominal interest rate consists of two parts: the real rate of return, which is compensation for not consuming our income but saving it instead, and an inflation premium that protects the purchasing power of the investment. Stated differently, the nominal rate of return is equal to the real rate of return plus the inflation rate. Table 4-2 shows average nominal and real rates of return over five-year periods, dating back to 1965, earned by short-term Treasury securities.

TABLE 4-2
REAL AND NOMINAL RATES OF RETURN

5-Year Period Ending December	Nominal Rate of Return	Inflation Rate	Real Rate of Return
1965	3.16%	1.24%	1.92%
1970	5.54	4.17	1.37
1975	5.84	6.54	-0.70
1980	7.80	8.53	-0.72
1985	10.08	5.34	4.74
1990	6.82	3.89	2.93
1995	4.34	3.07	1.27
2000	5.01	2.60	2.41

Rates are 5-year averages; interest rates are from 3-month Treasury bills.
Source: Calculations from *Economic Report of the President,* 2001, online.

In personal financial planning, it is easiest to work with real prices and real interest rates. Working with nominal prices and nominal interest rates requires making predictions about inflation, a task that is difficult even for professional economists. If we have a goal of sending a child to a four-year private college in 2012, and if it costs, on average, $20,361 per year in 2007, we will want to set a goal of having $20,361 real dollars (that is, $20,361 dollars with 2007 purchasing power) in each year from 2012 to 2015. We will then choose a savings plan and investments that earn the real rate of return necessary to achieve our goal.

Now we are ready to determine the cost of our financial goals. Use the financial goals worksheet in Table 4-3 as a guide. The following seven-step process will complete the table and help you develop your financial plan.

Step 1: Brainstorming. List your financial objectives. If you are married, discuss them with your spouse. Achieving these objectives will require that you save some amount each month, and it will be much easier to do this if you and your spouse agree that the objective is worth the sacrifice. Decide which objectives must be achieved in the short term, the medium term, and the long term. An example of a short-term goal would be an emergency fund (if you don't already have one). Most financial planners recommend three to six months' after-tax income for such a fund. Depending on your circumstances, that sum may be too large. Think about the types of emergencies for which you want to save, and then set aside an appropriate amount. Deductibles on your insurance policies or the cost of buying last-minute airline tickets to get your family home in case of an emergency might be typical uses. As you get closer to leaving the service, you should consider increasing your emergency fund.

Medium-term goals might include paying cash for a new car, refurnishing a room in your home, or replacing that old television set. Medium-term goals are often in conflict with more important long-term goals. In the long term, most families are concerned with putting children through college and planning for retirement. Since our military pension will not be enough for us to live on, we should plan to save an additional amount to supplement our pension.

The reason you should separate the goals by time period is that the suitable types of investments and their expected rate of return vary with your planning horizon. It is often possible to achieve longer-term goals by making riskier investments that earn a higher rate of return. We will use an example of sending a child for a year at a four-year private college in 2017. This is a long-term objective that requires saving enough each month to have $20,361 in real 2007 dollars in 2017 and a similar amount for each of the final three years of college.

Step 2: Determine Today's Cost of Your Goals. As explained above, one of the advantages of using real values is that you do not have to try to predict the future cost of your goal. All you need to know is what it would cost you today. From Table 4-1, you know that, on average, a year's tuition, fees, room, board, books, supplies, transportation, and other charges at a four-year private college costs $20,361 in 2002. Enter that value in the column for today's cost in Table 4-3.

TABLE 4-3
FINANCIAL GOALS WORKSHEET

Expected Annual Before-Tax Rates of Return (Table 4-4)		Marginal Income Tax Rates		Expected Real After-Tax Rates of Return	Annual	Monthly
Short-term:	______	Federal:	______	Short-term:	______	______
Medium-term:	______	State:	______	Medium-term:	______	______
Long-term:	______	Combined:	______	Long-term:	______	______

	Today's Cost	Date Required	# of Months	Lump Sum	Monthly Amount to Meet Goal
Short-term goals (within 1 year)					
Emergency fund	______	______	______	______	______
Major purchase	______	______	______	______	______
Christmas gifts	______	______	______	______	______
Other	______	______	______	______	______
Medium-term goals (1 to 5 years)					
Major purchase	______	______	______	______	______
Down payment on home	______	______	______	______	______
Education	______	______	______	______	______
Other	______	______	______	______	______
Long-term goals (over 5 years)					
Education	______	______	______	______	______
Business start-up	______	______	______	______	______
Retirement income	______	______	______	______	______
Care for dependent parents	______	______	______	______	______
Other	______	______	______	______	______

Step 3: Set a Target Date. Make your objective more concrete by setting a deadline. Determine the amount of time until the target date. Because most military families are paid monthly and will save some amount each month, you want the number of months until the money is needed. For the purposes of the example, it is ten years, or 120 months, until you need the annual tuition, room, and board to send your child to college. Enter the date required and the number of months in the appropriate column in Table 4-3.

Step 4: Calculate the "Lump Sum." The lump sum represents the amount of money that you would have to invest today at your expected real rate of return to achieve your financial goal by the target date. To calculate this value, you must be able to fill in the top of Table 4-3 (that is, the expected real rates of return on short-, medium-, and long-term investments consistent with your tolerance for risk, as well as your income tax bracket).

Rates of return depend on the level of risk that you are willing to accept (see chapter 2 for a discussion of financial risk). Although this risk tolerance varies for each individual or family, Table 4-4 should provide some assistance in determining an expected real rate of return (that is, after deducting inflation) for your goals. This table shows the historical average real rate of return for several investment alternatives. Since many people do not invest in individual securities, we have included the corresponding categories of mutual funds. (These investment instruments are explained in more detail in part IV of this book.) The expected rate of return increases with the amount of risk that you are willing to accept. For short-term goals, you may be unwilling to take on as much risk as for longer-term goals. As your long-term goals become your medium-term goals and your medium-term goals become your short-term goals, you may want to change the investment vehicle you have chosen so that you can protect yourself from the greater risks associated with longer-term investments.

TABLE 4-4
HISTORICAL AVERAGES FOR REAL RATES OF RETURN (1926–2000)

Investment Alternatives	Rate of Return*	Corresponding Mutual Funds
Small capitalization stocks	102%	Aggressive growth funds
		Sector or international funds
Large capitalization stocks	38.4	Growth funds
		Growth and income funds
		Equity-income funds
		Balanced or income funds
Long-term corporate bonds	2.7	Bond funds
Long-term government bonds	2.3	Government funds
U.S. Treasury bills	1.2	Money market funds

*Approximate historical rates of return are "real," that is, after deducting inflation. The returns shown are "pre-tax," that is, with no adjustment for taxes.
Source: Ibbotson Associates, updated annually.

The other bit of information you will need is your combined marginal income tax rate, which is the tax rate that applies to the last or next dollar of taxable income you earn. Look at your most recent federal income tax returns to determine your taxable income, which is the total income you earn that is subject to taxation minus itemized or standard deductions and the value of your exemptions (see chapter 7). Find the column in Table 4-5 that corresponds to your filing status, then find the row that contains your taxable income. Your federal income tax bracket is in the left-most column of that row. You can find your state income tax bracket from last year's state income tax return. Enter your federal and state tax brackets in Table 4-3 as decimals (e.g., a 15% tax bracket is 0.15). Add your state and federal income tax brackets to get your combined marginal tax rate.

TABLE 4-5
INCOME TAX BRACKETS FOR 2001
(ADJUSTED ANNUALLY FOR INFLATION)

Taxable Income Range, Based on Filing Status

Tax Rate	Married (Filing Jointly)	Head of Household	Single
15%	$45,200	$36,250	less than $27,050
27.5	$109,250	$93,650	$65,550
30.5	$166,500	$151,650	$136,750
35.5	$297,350	$297,350	$297,350
39.1	over $297,350	over $297,350	over $297,350

Source: IRS Publication 17 or Schedules X, Y-1, or Z in Form 1040 instructions.

Now you are ready to do the necessary calculations. First, you need to calculate the expected, real after-tax rate for the investment period. Begin by adding the expected real return and the expected rate of inflation to get the expected nominal return for each investment period. Next, subtract your combined marginal tax rate from 1, then multiply the result by each of the before-tax nominal rates of return to get the after-tax nominal returns. Finally, subtract the expected rates of inflation for each period to obtain the after-tax real returns. An example of these calculations is shown in part 1 of Table 4-6. We'll use a 6.5 percent expected real rate of return and a 4 percent expected rate of inflation for our example, but you should use the rate of inflation you expect to occur over the investment period and the expected real rate of return that corresponds to the amount of risk that you are willing to take.

This gives you an annual after-tax real rate of return, but you need a monthly rate to correspond to the monthly time periods you will use in your calculations. Always ensure that the interest rate and the time period are for the same length of time (annual rate and years or monthly rate and months). To convert the annual rate to a monthly rate, simply divide by 12 as shown in part 2 of Table 4-6, and enter these real after-tax monthly rates of return in Table 4-3. Now you can calculate the lump sum required to achieve each goal as shown in part 3 of Table 4-6.

Today's cost is the cost of your goal in today's dollars, or $20,361 in this example. The expected real after-tax rate of return, *r*, is 0.00408 (approximately 0.41 percent) per month, and the number of months, *n*, is 120 months. The lump sum of $12,491 is the present value of the $20,361 that you need in ten years. Stated differently, investing $12,491 at a real interest rate of 6.5 percent per year will yield $20,361, after taxes, in ten years. It is important to remember that this is $20,361 in 2007 purchasing power. Actually, the money will accrue interest at the nominal rate, which is higher than the real rate, and in 2017, you will have considerably more than $20,361. Due to inflation, however, you will need to have more than that to buy what you could have bought in 2007 with $20,361.

TABLE 4-6
CALCULATING THE REQUIRED LUMP-SUM INVESTMENT

[1] Calculate the annual after-tax real rate return.

$$r^{\text{after tax}} = [(r^{\text{before tax}} + \text{inflation rate}) \times (1 - \text{tax rate})] - \text{inflation rate} =$$
$$[(0.065 + 0.04) \times (1 - 0.15)] - 0.04 = 0.049 = 4.9\%$$

[2] Convert the annual rate of return to a monthly rate of return.

$$r^{\text{monthly}} = r^{\text{after tax}} \div 12 = 0.049 \div 12 = 0.00408 \cong 0.41\% \text{ per month}$$

[3] Calculate the lump-sum amount you would have to invest today to achieve your financial goal as planned.

$$\text{lump sum} = \frac{\text{today's cost}}{(1 + r)^n} = \frac{\$20{,}361}{(1 + 0.00408)^{120}} = \$12,491$$

Table D-1 contains discount factors for several rates of return and time periods. These discount factors replicate the calculations described above for specific interest rates and may be used instead of the formulas in Table 4-6 to obtain lump-sum amounts that are approximately correct. To calculate the lump sum using the discount factors, merely multiply the future real amount by the discount factor that applies to the real after-tax annual rate of return you are assuming. In the above example, we calculated the real after-tax annual return to be 0.049. Because Table D-1 reports discount factors only for certain real rates, you would either interpolate or use the nearest rate to obtain your discount factor. If you decided that 0.05 is sufficiently accurate, the discount factor would be 0.614 and the lump sum would be $12,502 ($12,502 = 0.614 × $20,361). Because the discount factor is based on an approximate interest rate, the lump sum we calculate using the factor is only approximately correct. Also, the factors in Table D-1 are based on annual and not monthly compounding. Therefore, we recommend that you use the formulas in Table 4-6 if you have a financial calculator available.

Although this material may appear to be somewhat technical, it is important that you attempt to work through it to understand the concepts. Once you understand the principles, you can perform these operations quickly using a financial calculator or spreadsheet program.

Step 5: Calculate the Monthly Allotment. Since most of us will not have the lump sum available to invest to meet our goals, we will need to chip away at the cost of our goal by setting aside a certain amount of money each month. Table 4-7 shows the calculation for our example. The complicated expression in the denominator is called the annuity factor. An annuity is a series of payments at fixed intervals, invested at the same rate of return. An allotment from your monthly paycheck to a mutual fund is an example of an annuity. (Actually, it is not quite an annuity, because the rate of return available through mutual funds changes over time. But for our purposes, it is close enough.) Dividing the lump sum by the annuity factor converts it into an equivalent monthly amount. Investing $131.85 each month for 120 months at a real rate of return of 6.5 percent per year is equivalent to investing $12,491 at a real before-tax 6.5 percent annual rate of return for ten years.

TABLE 4-7
CONVERTING THE LUMP SUM
TO AN EQUIVALENT MONTHLY INVESTMENT

Using the figures from Table 4-6, convert the lump sum into an annuity of equivalent value:

$$\text{allotment} = \frac{\text{lump sum}}{\left(\frac{1}{r}\right) - \frac{1}{r \times (1+r)^n}} = \frac{\$12{,}491}{\left(\frac{1}{0.00408}\right) - \frac{1}{0.00408 \times (1 + 0.00408)^{120}}} = \$131.85$$

r = rate of return

Saving $132 each month is a lot of money, but it is considerably easier than finding $12,491 to invest all at once. And this is only for one year's college expenses! If we invested for eighteen years instead of only ten years, it would cost us only $87 per month, which is 33 percent less. That is why it is important to begin saving early for long-term financial goals like putting children through college.

Table D-2 contains annuity factors that approximate the calculations shown in Table 4-7, just as the discount factors in Table D-1 approximated a portion of the calculations in Table 4-6. Using 0.05 to approximate 0.049, we see that the annual annuity factor is 7.722. If we divide our lump sum by this factor, we obtain the annual amount to be saved ($12,491 ÷ 7.722 = $1,607). If we divide this annual amount by 12, we obtain the amount we would have to set aside each month. In our example, this would be $137 ($1,607 ÷ 12 = $134). Once again, we see that using a published factor provides an answer that is only approximately correct. Therefore, we recommend that you perform the calculations shown in Table 4-7. Remember to compute the total savings per month for a full four-year college education, just as you did to arrive at $12,491. Although the tuition will be due a year later for each year, the amount should be almost four times as large as the amount for just one year.

Step 6: Set Priorities. If you sum the monthly allotments required to meet all your future spending goals, you will probably find that you cannot possibly afford to set aside that much money each month and still meet your monthly living expenses. So, you must choose among your savings goals and living expenses according to your priorities. If you do not have an adequate emergency fund, establishing one should be your top priority. Once you have an emergency fund, you can begin to set aside money toward your other goals. Remember, though, that if you do not make contributions to your long-term goals until they become short-term goals, it will be impossible to set aside the monthly allotment to meet them.

Step 7: Determine the Appropriate Investment. Determine the investment vehicle you will use for each goal. It is important that the mutual fund that you select has the performance characteristics that you assumed in your calculations. Again, see part IV for more information on investing.

HOW DO YOU DEVELOP A FAMILY BUDGET?

Now that you have established where you are and where you want to go, you need to develop a plan that will enable you to achieve your financial goals. That plan is the budget. Budgets allocate your income against your expenses in a way that is consistent with your priorities. In the typical family, the result of a budget will be to reduce your spending to satisfy your current consumption desires to save some of your income each month for longer-term financial goals. Because it involves current sacrifice, even the mention of budgets can conjure up resentment in some families. It does not have to be that way if you follow a few simple principles in developing a budget. We will discuss these important principles before we delve into the mechanics of the budget using Table 4-9.

TABLE 4-8
GETTING RICH SLOWLY

Year in Service Rank	0 O-1	2 O-2	4 O-3	6	8	10 O-4	12
Pay (2001 rate)	$1,997	$2,620	$3,489	$3,656	$3,839	$4,409	$4,629
1/2 of each raise per month		$311	$434	$83	$91	$285	$110
Savings each month	$200	$511	$945	$1028	$1119	$1,404	$1,514
Savings each year	$2,400	$6,132	$11,340	$12,336	$13,428	$16,848	$18,168
Cumulative saved	$4,800	$17,064	$39,744	$64,416	$91,272	$124,968	$161,304
Savings with 10% interest paying 15% taxes	$5,225	$18,937	$45,936	$79,798	$121,937	$178,676	$248,222

Year in Service Rank	14	16 O-5	18	22 O-6	24	26
Pay (2001 rate)	$4,781	$5,481	$5,637	$6,791	$6,967	$7,309
1/2 of each raise per month	$76	$350	$78	$577	$88	$171
Savings each month	$1,590	$1,940	$2,081	$2,658	$2,746	$2,917
Savings each year	$19,080	$20,902	$24,972	$31,896	$32,952	$35,004
Cumulative saved	$199,464	$241,268	$291,212	$355,004	$420,908	$491,916
Savings with 10% interest paying 15% taxes	$331,996	$434,414	$563,470	$729,834	$927,884	$1,165,311

This assumes the officer saves $200 per month plus half of all promotion and longevity raises (it does not include saving any cost-of-living raises). It assumes a 10% return paying 15% in taxes and promotions in the years indicated, roughly according to current due course promotion timelines.

Budget Principles

Gain Consensus. If you are married, then the budget *must* be a family project. Without the cooperation of everyone involved, your plan is doomed to failure. Once you have completed the budget, consider it a family contract to which *all* members are dedicated.

Pay Yourself First. Any financial planner will tell you this. If you wait to see how much you have left after monthly expenses, you will not have any money to set toward your financial goals. Set a minimum percentage of your income that you want to dedicate to achieving financial goals. Set up an automatic withdrawal or deposit program to invest regularly in a mutual fund. By paying yourself first, you will not be tempted to spend that money. Then, see how many of your goals you can work toward, given that amount. Also, when you get a raise, try to set aside at least half of it to put toward your financial goals. If you were meeting your expenses before the raise, you should be able to save a significant portion of it. Table 4-8 demonstrates the wealth-building power of such an approach. Do not forget those expensive long-term goals for which you need to start saving. It demonstrates that if a newly commissioned officer saved $200 per month and then increased his savings by half of each pay raise for promotion or longevity, earned 10 percent interest, and was in the 15 percent tax bracket, he would have over $1.2 million dollars retiring as a colonel or Navy captain (O-6) at the end of twenty-six years.

Make the Big Payments Little Ones. Most of us cannot afford to write a check for several hundred dollars out of our monthly paycheck to meet the large expenses that must be dealt with periodically. Christmas comes every December, and our Christmas spirit is reflected in our generosity toward our family and friends and the credit card bills that arrive in January. You can make a large expense even larger because of the interest and fees charged on credit cards.

Why not take those big payments that come up every year and divide them by twelve, setting aside that much each month? Then, when expenses arise, you will have the money in your savings account to write out the check and will save the interest charge in the bargain.

Minimize Unanticipated Expenses. The budget format in Table 4-9 may seem extremely long and cumbersome, but it is helpful because it focuses on the principle of minimizing unanticipated expenses. If you can avoid unexpected expenses, you can avoid those "peanut butter and jelly" months.

Budget Mechanics

If you know how to use a spreadsheet on a personal computer, this is the time to turn your computer on and start up your spreadsheet program. Family budgets are easiest to make on a spreadsheet because it permits you to make the entries while the machine calculates totals and recalculates them every time you adjust an entry. There is a fair amount of iterative work in developing a budget. Let the machine make it easy for you. Alternatively, several personal finance software packages have budget programs built into them.

TABLE 4-9
BUDGET WORKSHEET

	Preliminary	Revised
Monthly Income		
Salaries, wages, commissions, tips, etc.	________	________
Interest earned on savings accounts	________	________
Interest earned on bonds	________	________
Dividend income	________	________
Other investment income	________	________
Social Security and VA cash benefits	________	________
Pensions and annuities received	________	________
Other income	________	________
	________	________
Total monthly income	________	________
Fixed Monthly Expenses		
Taxes due or withheld	________	________
Mortgage payment or rent	________	________
Automobile loans	________	________
Bank or finance company loans	________	________
Automobile insurance premiums	________	________
Health insurance premiums	________	________
Life insurance premiums	________	________
Other insurance premiums	________	________
Minimum payments for credit cards	________	________
Local service phone bill	________	________
Other fixed monthly expenses	________	________
	________	________
	________	________
	________	________
Total fixed monthly expenses	________	________
Variable Monthly Expenses		
Food	________	________
Transportation	________	________
Clothing	________	________
Utilities bill	________	________
Long-distance phone bill	________	________
Recreation	________	________
Babysitting	________	________
Church donations	________	________

Charitable contributions	________	________
Gifts for birthdays, Christmas, etc.	________	________
Personal allowances:	________	________
Husband	________	________
Wife	________	________
Child	________	________
Child	________	________
Child	________	________
Other variable monthly expenses	________	________
	________	________
	________	________
Total variable monthly expenses	________	________
Cumulative Monthly Expenses		
Long-term goal	________	________
Long-term goal	________	________
Medium-term goal	________	________
Medium-term goal	________	________
Medium-term goal	________	________
Short-term goal	________	________
Total cumulative monthly expenses	________	________
Total monthly expenses	________	________
Total monthly income (compare)	________	________
Amount to be allocated/reallocated	________	________

If you do not know how to use a spreadsheet, do not worry. The budget involves only addition and subtraction, operations that are still easy to do with a calculator or by hand.

Step 1: List Income Sources. List the amounts for each source of income. We will learn more about investments and the income they generate in part IV, and about sources of retirement income in part V.

Step 2: List Expenses. Although the list in Table 4-9 is extensive, you may have expenses not listed there. Be sure to include them. Estimate an amount for each expenditure, and write it in the column for preliminary estimates. You can use any record of previous expenditures to develop these estimates.

Notice that we have divided the expenses into three categories: fixed, variable, and cumulative. Fixed expenses are those that occur every month and that you cannot readily influence (such as rent or insurance). Variable expenses are those that depend directly on the amount of use (for example, your long-distance phone bill). Cumulative items are those big expenses or financial goals that you chip away at each month by setting aside some money for when the bill comes due.

Step 3: Determine the Amount Remaining to Be Reallocated. When all of your income is allocated to an expense and your income exactly equals your expenses, you have a workable budget. You almost certainly will have some reallocation to do to make this happen. If your expenses are greater than your income, you will have to reduce some of your expenses or you will have to find some way to earn extra income. If your expenses are less than your income, then you have the happy task of increasing the amount you can spend on one or more of your expenditure categories.

Step 4: Allocate or Reallocate Income and Expenses. Often your income is less than your desired expenditures. Having classified your expenditures as fixed, variable, or cumulative, you can more easily determine where to cut. Surprisingly, we recommend that you should examine some of your "fixed" expenditures first. They are not always "fixed" at the level that best suits your needs. For example, many military families are overinsured or improperly insured, and it is possible to obtain equal or better insurance protection for a smaller premium. (See chapters 12 and 19 for a discussion of insurance.)

Examine your variable expenses next. These expenses are variable in that if you use less of them, then your expenditures fall. This clearly requires that your entire family agrees to change its behavior to achieve the desired result. For example, you might want to reduce your long-distance telephone bill by $20 per month or reduce your utilities bill by $30 per month.

Finally, avoid trimming money set aside for cumulative goals. The whole point of this exercise is to make room for them in the monthly budget.

When you have allocated your entire income to monthly expenditures and there is nothing left over, you are finished. Write the final estimates of income and expenditure in the column for your revised numbers.

Step 5: Establish Budget Item Accounts and Method of Payment. This step and the next are primarily bookkeeping functions intended to help you with implementing your budget. You pay for most of your regular monthly expenses with cash or a check, so you will want the money for those items readily accessible in your checking account. On the other hand, many of your cumulative expenses occur only occasionally, so you do not need the accessibility that a checking account provides. In fact, you will want to put that money to work earning interest either in a money market fund or in a savings account. When such occasional bills come due, you can charge them and then write a check out of your money market account to pay for them before interest starts coming due. Once you have decided where the expense money should be held, you can divide your paycheck appropriately to match your expenses.

Tips on Making the Most from Financial Planning and Budgeting

- Avoid consumer debt. Pay off credit cards and consumer loans that are a drag on your budget.
- Set financial goals.
- Develop a budget to live within your means in order to meet those goals. Your expenses must be less than your income.
- Set up a program to get rich slowly. You won't get rich fast in the military, but you can amass a lot of money if you set up a solid plan and stick with it.
- Pay yourself first through an allotment or automatic deposit program. You will be less tempted to spend this money and will slowly but surely build wealth.
- When you receive a pay increase, invest half of the raise and spend the other half.
- Maintain at least a ninety-day cash reserve for emergencies.
- Use tax-deductible and tax-deferred savings plans such as Individual Retirement Accounts.
- Consistent with your risk tolerance, invest for the highest possible rate of growth. Low-risk investments generally mean lower growth. Higher returns generally require more risk.
- Monitor your budget regularly and conduct a thorough review and analysis at least every six months, after each pay raise, and after any big event.
- Stick to your plan.

Step 6: Implement. There are as many ways to implement and monitor a budget as there are people. The key is to find a way that works for you and stick with it. At a minimum, you need to track your expenses. Fixed and cumulative expenses usually occur only monthly, so a journal of accounts with a page for each expense is perfectly adequate. The more frequent expenses, like food and entertainment, require closer scrutiny. An inexpensive and easy way to track these expenses is to keep a record of them in a pocket notebook. Just title a page to correspond to each of the variable expenses and record transactions as they occur. Then, at the end of the month, total the amount and post it to the journal of accounts. Then post the monthly total to a ledger that shows all of your accounts on one page. The ledger gives you a mechanism to quickly see how well you are doing at sticking to your budget.

If you find it difficult to track actual expenses for a month using a pocket notebook, you could use your checking account statement and credit card bills. Examining them for the same month will give you a general idea of your expenses and which category they fall into. This method is not as accurate, especially with the prevalence of automatic teller machine (ATM) withdrawals (you may not keep track of what you spent that cash on), but it will give you a good approximation.

Step 7: Review Periodically. Just as you must routinely check on the implementation of any plan, so too you must check on your budget. Look at the ledger to see whether you are consistently over or under budget in any of the accounts. If so, make adjustments. You will also have to make adjustments each time you get a raise or one of your fixed expenses changes. The budget is not locked in concrete.

At a minimum, you should review and analyze your budget every six months, each time you receive a pay raise, after each move, and after a big event such as the birth of a child. Reapportion as necessary.

There you have it—the basics of a financial plan. With a little discipline and determination, you should be well on your way to achieving your financial goals. But do not stop reading here. The rest of this book will show you how to be an educated consumer of financial products and services, to get the most from your investments, and to plan for your retirement.

PART II

Financial Basics

5

Banking Smart

An effective and convenient relationship with a bank is especially important to military families. Military duties often take us away from home and make family separations necessary. Servicemembers also need ready assets they can draw upon away from home and must be able to provide for the needs of the family members left behind. Deciding which bank will receive your hard-earned dollars is up to you to choose. Therefore, you need a framework to compare services offered at different banking institutions. This chapter is dedicated to helping you select the bank that suits you best.

WHAT BANKING SERVICES DO YOU NEED?

Most commercial banks, savings and loans, and credit unions now offer most of the primary services that households will use. Consumers can usually find all the banking services they require at a single institution. Though it's possible to find all the services you will want under one roof, to find the best deal on all your needs you may need to shop carefully and use several institutions.

In a general sense, banking institutions provide the following services:

1. Traditional bank services.
   - Checking accounts.
   - Savings accounts.
   - Time deposits (certificates of deposit).
   - Credit cards.
   - Safe deposit boxes.
   - Consumer and business loans.
2. New banking services.
   - Stock and bond brokerage services.
   - Mutual fund sales.
   - Financial planning services.
   - Tax preparation and advice.

Differentiators between banks will be based on their rates and fees, online banking capabilities, and convenience (banking hours, location of ATMs, and branches).

Households require a variety of banking services to meet their varied financial needs. First, you need a transactions account for paying your recurring bills. Second, you need emergency funds that are quickly and easily available to meet short-term emergencies. Third, you need to save for your medium-term goals, such as major purchases, upcoming college tuition, or buying a home. Additionally, you need a source from which to borrow funds to purchase certain big-ticket items too large to be purchased directly from savings.

Transactions Account

Most people are paid once or twice a month but must be able to make payments for purchases throughout the month. The ideal method to manage your pay is to deposit funds in a transactions account for use whenever you need them. A checking account or a share draft account (a checking account at a credit union) is a transactions account. It is an excellent way of ensuring the immediate availability of cash. You can write checks to anyone who will accept them. You have a written document to help you record where you spent your money. Debit cards and traditional charge cards are additional services offered by banks that can be used to pay for purchases. Whether you prefer checks, share drafts, debit cards, or charge cards, you'll find that banks and their close relatives offer the only convenient services that meet this need.

Emergency Fund Account

The second crucial piece of your financial plan is an emergency fund. The emergency fund provides immediate cash if a disaster or adverse event occurs. You must first determine the size of this fund. Most financial advisors suggest between two and six months' pay. Two months' base pay may be sufficient if you have quick and easy access to credit, unless you anticipate voluntarily leaving the service. Ask yourself what emergencies might arise that would require immediate payments. Certainly you would want a fund large enough to buy a plane ticket home for the entire family. Even though you may purchase the tickets with a credit card, you need access to emergency funds to pay off the credit card balance immediately. In another case, you would want to be able to cover the deductible on your automobile insurance in case of an accident and be able to pay for a significant automobile repair. You may need much more if you anticipate a loss of income due to illness or lost employment.

Savings accounts paying money market rates (money market deposit accounts) and money market funds with check-writing privileges are ideal for emergency funds. With emergency funds, you are much more concerned with the ability to use your money quickly than in the interest such funds receive. You should be willing to trade away higher rates of interest for liquidity (the ability to spend it quickly, if necessary) and safety. If you can't manage to accumulate an emergency fund, you should have a credit card with a sufficient line of credit to provide you with the peace of mind that you can pay for your family's immediate emergency requirements.

Savings Account

The third piece of your financial plan is savings. Each of us has a need to accumulate funds to support future goals. When you made your budget in chapter 4, you forecast the amounts of money needed at certain times in the future. Some of this money, such as for retirement or college tuition, may not be needed for quite some time. Other needs will be sooner, such as saving for new furniture or the down payment on a home. This chapter will concentrate on saving money that you intend to spend within five years. Chapters 14 through 18 deal with longer-term saving and investing.

Banks are one of several sources competing for your short- and medium-term savings dollars. Another option for a savings account is with a brokerage house that offers a brokerage account with check-writing privileges.

Loans

Most people find it necessary to borrow money from time to time. You may not have the cash available to pay for big-ticket items like major appliances or cars, and certainly will need to borrow money to buy a house. It often makes sense to spread the cost over the period of time you anticipate using the purchase and to do so you must borrow and pay interest for that convenience. A credit card is a type of loan. Banks are just one type of institution that issue credit cards. You should make comparisons among different credit card companies before you select one. Chapter 6 will help you evaluate the credit services offered by banks and other credit card companies.

HOW SHOULD YOU SELECT A BANK?

There are three primary factors to consider when selecting a bank. The first and most important is whether the institution is in sound financial condition. A second factor is convenient access to your deposits. Finally, the cost of the services is also important. Each of these factors will be examined in detail.

Bank Safety

Operating a bank is a risky business. Banks lend your deposits to other people, businesses, or countries. If these loans are not paid back, this may jeopardize the safety of your deposit. When choosing a bank, consider foremost the safety of your deposits. The good news is that ensuring that your bank is safe is relatively easy. The federal government insures deposits up to $100,000 in participating institutions through the Federal Deposit Insurance Corporation (FDIC) and the National Credit Union Share Insurance Fund (NCUSIF). Actually, more than $100,000 of deposit insurance is available, because the limit applies to the amount in a single account.

All you really need to do is make sure that your bank or credit union is a member of one of the federal insurance programs mentioned. Most institutions participate in these programs, but not all. There is no reason to use a bank or credit union that is not covered by federal deposit insurance. Eliminate them from consideration—accept no substitutes for federal insurance. Even though some banks are state insured rather than federally insured, depositors have experienced significant delays in gaining access to their funds after their state-insured banks failed. Once you've narrowed your search for banking services to federally insured institutions, turn your attention to the convenience and cost of the services offered and to the interest rates paid on deposits.

Convenience

We use banks because we want to make purchases conveniently and because we want to ensure that our money is quickly available. Since convenience is a major reason for using a bank, it's a major factor to consider when choosing a bank.

When most of us need money, we use a twenty-four-hour automatic teller machine (ATM). The better ATM networks share sites and allow you to obtain cash from machines far removed from your individual bank; many include international access. Look for a bank that has the option of ATM service and that has ATM access convenient to your home or workplace. Keep in mind that there is normally a fee charged for using an ATM that is not associated with your bank.

Another way to get money is to write a check. A check is simply a note to our bank telling it to transfer some money in our account to someone else. In this function, most checking or share draft accounts differ little, if at all. There is a major difference, however, when you need to convert that check to cash. It may be difficult for you to get currency close to work or home and after bank operating hours.

For servicemembers, post and base exchanges almost always cash checks; so do most officers and noncommissioned officers clubs. For check cashing, these facilities are often closer and easier to use than a bank, but they offer only a limited solution to the problem of getting cash after working hours. A more convenient method to make purchases is to use a debit card. A debit card looks exactly like a traditional credit card and is used in the same manner. The fundamental difference is that the use of a credit card is a loan—a loan that must eventually be paid back. A debit card acts much like a check in that it draws against a current balance in either your savings or checking account.

One of the most important convenience features banks offer servicemembers is direct deposit of military and federal government paychecks into checking or savings accounts. A direct deposit arrangement sets up a direct link between the military or governmental pay system and your bank. On payday, your pay is automatically sent to the bank and deposited in your account; you simply receive a Leave and Earnings Statement telling you exactly what was deposited. The important consideration is that your paycheck is deposited and your money is made available even if you are away from your duty station on leave, TDY, or deployment. The convenience and security of this feature are hard to overestimate.

Many military families maintain bank accounts in the locality where they are assigned. If this is the only account they keep, they close out accounts in the area they are leaving and open new ones at their new duty station. Some also maintain a permanent or hometown bank so that they can continue to write checks and maintain savings balances while in transit from one assignment to the next. To say the least, closing and opening bank accounts and shopping for the best banking services are time-consuming and unpleasant chores. It's worth asking, then, if a local bank is really necessary. With the recent advances in computer online banking, it may be more convenient to have one permanent bank that you can use regardless of where you are stationed than to have a local bank. If you have a good permanent bank with which you can easily deal by computer, phone, and mail, you may not need a local bank. To determine whether you need a new local bank at each duty station, ask yourself these questions:

- Do you use credit cards instead of checks for local retail purchases?
- Can you easily and conveniently get cash with an out-of-state account?
- Is your bank a member of a national ATM network?
- Does your bank offer online banking and do you have a computer to access the Internet?
- Does your permanent bank offer convenient loan service by mail or phone?
- Can you easily move savings balances into your checking account by phone in your permanent bank?

If you can answer most of these questions with a yes, you may not need a local bank at all. Establish a relationship with a bank offering the services you want, and do all your banking by phone or mail. Minimizing the number of accounts you have can simplify your life and hold down the cost of your financial services. Additionally, if you have established a long history of reliable credit during a long relationship with a single bank, it may be easier to qualify for a large loan, such as for a home.

Today, most banks offer some form of computer banking that provides the convenience of twenty-four-hour banking. For this you need to have an Internet-connect PC. With Internet banking, you can:

- View your account balance and verify if specific checks have cleared.
- View, print, and download your current account statement to your PC where you can track your income and expenses. Most banks allow you to download your statements into money management software such as Quicken or Microsoft Money.
- Transfer money between accounts.
- Reorder checks.
- Apply for loans.
- Pay bills electronically using an electronic bill-paying service. You can pay your mortgage, credit card payments, and utility bills and send checks to anyone online.

At most banks, online banking is free. However, there is usually a monthly fee for online bill payment, but considering its convenience and that you would not have to pay for postage, it is a valuable service. Judge a bank with computer banking just like you would any other bank; the fundamental analysis remains the same. Remember, you are trying to find the bank that meets your banking needs at the lowest cost.

Cost of Services

There are vast differences in the cost of and interest earned on bank accounts. Banks are allowed to compete head to head in both price and service. In developing a price strategy, most banks try to attract the most profitable customers. In doing so, their pricing schemes encourage or discourage specific types of customers. You should understand these pricing schemes and seek a bank desiring accounts like yours.

Even when two banks claim to offer or charge the same interest rate, the amount of interest received depends on the method used to calculate interest. You need to understand how banks compute interest and charges if you are to choose the best bank and get the most value from its services.

TYPES OF BANK ACCOUNTS

Now let's explore the three major services banks offer to meet your three basic needs: checking and share draft accounts for transactions; savings accounts or money market deposit accounts for emergency funds; and certificates of deposit for short- and medium-term savings. Investment vehicles for long-term savings will be discussed in chapters 14 through 18.

Checking Accounts

No banking service meets your need for transactions as well as a checking or share draft account. Checking accounts come in two basic varieties: noninterest-bearing and interest-bearing. As their name implies, noninterest-bearing accounts offer no interest on the deposited funds. Since there is no interest cost to the bank, these accounts are cheaper to run. Banks generally encourage depositors who plan to keep very small balances (less than $500 or $1,000) to use noninterest checking accounts.

Several varieties of interest-bearing checking accounts are offered. The most common of this type are called negotiable order of withdrawal (NOW) accounts. NOW accounts pay a modest rate of interest. They are best for medium-size consumer deposits having typical balances of $1,000 to $2,500. When the account balance falls below a specified amount, banks often pay no interest or charge a service fee.

Banks also offer Super-NOW accounts. Typically, these accounts pay a money market rate of interest, the rate of interest available to the largest and most sophisticated investors in short-term government securities. Since the bank's interest cost on Super-NOW accounts is relatively high in comparison with other checking accounts, large average balances (generally $2,500 to $5,000 or more) are normally required.

Some banks charge a per-check fee along with a service fee for a checking account. Per-check fees are levied on each check written on the account; they are intended to cover the expenses involved in processing and clearing checks. Typical fees are in the range of 15 to 25 cents per check, but you may find them as low as 10 cents and as high as 50 cents. Service fees, designed to compensate the bank for the costs of maintaining small accounts, are levied every month on some checking accounts. Many banks will waive these fees for direct-deposit customers. Most credit unions associated with the military do not have them at all. These fees can really add up, so it's worth shopping around.

You will often see advertisements for "free" checking accounts, with no per-check or service fees. The catch on most free checking accounts is that the fees are waived only if the average balance in the account is greater than a minimum amount, sometimes $1,000 or more. In other cases, free checking is offered if the depositor has savings accounts or time deposits greater than a required minimum, which again could be $1,000.

The key ingredient in measuring value in an interest-bearing checking account is the cost and interpretation of the minimum balance requirement. We will examine common methods used to compute the minimum balance and then look at an example of the costs and benefits of an interest-bearing account.

Computing Minimum Balance. Your minimum balance determines whether service and check fees are charged or if the account earns interest. You must understand the specific method your bank uses to compute this balance. The two most common methods are the average daily balance and the largest continuous balance.

The average daily balance (ADB) method takes the balance in the account each day of the month, adds them all up, and divides by the number of days in the month. With the largest continuous balance (LCB) method, the bank simply determines the largest amount that has remained in the account for the entire month. Of course, this will be the smallest balance on any day during the month. The largest continuous balance method thus yields a much smaller balance (meaning less interest and/or higher fees) than the average daily balance method. For example, if you had $1,000 in your account for twenty-nine days during the month and withdrew $500 on the thirtieth day, the ADB calculation would put your average balance at about $983 [{(29 days × $1,000) + (1 day × $500)} ÷ 30 days]. The LCB calculation would give you credit for only $500, because only that amount was continuously on deposit for the entire month.

Clearly, the method used to figure the balance in the account and the required minimums are important. They affect whether you are charged for checking services. If you fail to maintain the required minimum balance and are charged per-check and service fees, you could easily wind up paying $5 to $20 or more a month for your checking account. Read the fine print about checking account operations before opening an account and ask if you don't see a clear explanation of fees, minimum balances, and interest rates.

It is not unusual to see checking accounts paying interest and charging fees if the minimum balances are not maintained. In such cases, it may pay to investigate a noninterest-bearing account because the maintenance fees may be lower. In other cases, banks will pay interest on the checking deposit only if the minimum balance is maintained.

Overdraft Protection. It is essential that all military personnel have overdraft protection on their checking accounts. If you write a check for more than the balance of your account, you are said to have bounced a check. A bounced check, or a check presented for insufficient funds, can be detrimental to a military career. Good money management and fiscal responsibility are attributes of good military officers and noncommissioned officers. The military chain of command will generally view a bounced check as an irresponsible or careless act. Bouncing a check is also expensive. Your bank will generally charge you $15 to $25 for the administrative cost of handling the check, and the retailer where you wrote the check will likely charge $25 as well.

All this can be avoided, however, with overdraft protection. Overdraft protection is simply a money transfer and/or a short-term loan. For example, if you write a check for $100 but have a balance of only $50 in your checking account, with overdraft protection, the bank would immediately transfer $50 from your savings account to your checking account and then process the check. Some banks require you to get a bank-issued credit card from them in order to qualify for overdraft protection. They would then link your checking account to your credit card and cover any overdrafts. Although the credit card will charge you interest on this "loan," the cost will be minimal compared with the charges associated with bouncing a check. Simply put, do not bank without overdraft protection.

Interest-Bearing Accounts. Your objective with a checking account is to enjoy convenient checking at the lowest possible cost. Earning interest is nice, but it's not your primary concern. It may be financially wise to obtain an interest-bearing account, but not necessary. If the balance in your account is larger than you need for transaction purposes, you incur an opportunity cost, because the excess funds could be invested elsewhere at a higher rate of return. If the balance is too small, you may incur a service charge for the privilege of quick access to your money. Both costs should be considered when selecting an interest-bearing checking account.

As mentioned earlier, some banks offer free or interest-paying checking if a customer keeps a minimum balance in another account, such as savings. For example, the bank might agree to pay 3 percent interest on the average checking balance and levy no fees on the account if the average balance in checking and savings accounts together is more than $2,500. These arrangements are usually best for most servicemembers, because they keep savings and checking deposits separate while allowing for checking services at the lowest possible cost. Although it may be cheaper to consolidate savings into a checking account, only the disciplined consumer should do so to get free checking. It's too easy to spend money in a checking account. In summary, a basic financial goal should be to find a bank that offers overdraft protection along with free checking; the best bank may also pay interest on larger balances.

Savings Deposits

The liquidity offered by checking accounts makes them ideal for handling your frequent financial transactions. Giving you immediate access to your funds makes the bank's job harder, so the bank charges you for that privilege. One of the purposes of your financial plan is to save some of your income and invest it to achieve your financial goals. You do not need as much access with these funds, and the banks are happy to oblige by providing two basic types of savings deposits: savings accounts and certificates of deposit (CDs). These noncheckable deposits are relatively low-risk instruments for achieving your short- and medium-term financial goals.

Savings Accounts. Increasingly, banks are offering products with easier access to funds in savings accounts (competing directly with checkable accounts) and with higher rates of return (competing directly with money market mutual funds).

Competitive savings accounts, often called money market deposit accounts (MMDAs), offer rates of interest close to the money market rate. Frequently, the rates are tied to those currently prevailing in the money markets. The rates earned in savings accounts are not guaranteed for any length of time, but are adjusted up and down with market rates. *Money* magazine will occasionally list banks with the most competitive interest rates. In addition, *Bank Rate Monitor* publishes information about the best savings accounts and trends in banking. The easiest way to access this data is at the Internet site listed in Appendix A.

Much of what we said about checking account minimum balances also applies to savings accounts. It's common for banks to require a minimum balance—at least $1,000 to $2,500 or even higher—before the money market rate of interest is paid. As with checking account balances, the method used to compute the average balance is most important. In savings as in checking, the average daily balance (ADB) method is much better than the largest continuous balance (LCB) method, and for the same reason. The amount of interest credited is calculated by multiplying the average balance by the interest rate, so the larger your average balance, the more interest you will earn. Be sure you understand the method used in calculating the balance on which interest will be paid. Bank advertising generally emphasizes the interest rate paid on savings deposits, while the method used to compute the average balance is relegated to the fine print. An account paying a lower interest rate using the ADB method can pay more interest than an account with a higher interest rate using the LCB method.

Accounts using the LCB method aren't necessarily to be avoided. Many credit unions use the LCB method on their share draft accounts. A typical credit union may offer 3 percent annual interest compounded quarterly on the LCB. Since 3 percent may be an attractive rate in comparison with that of bank savings accounts, the credit union may have a better deal for you than the bank. Be careful, however, when making deposits and withdrawals from an LCB account. For example, if your share account credits interest quarterly on the LCB and you withdraw $1,000 on the next-to-last day of the quarter, you could lose interest on $1,000 for the entire quarter. At 3 percent annual interest, that loss amounts to $7.50. Similarly, if you deposited $1,000 two weeks before the end of a quarter, you would not be paid any interest on it for that quarter, even though it was on deposit for two weeks. However, many credit unions give a full month's credit for deposits made by the tenth of the month. If you deposit and withdraw funds frequently, you are probably better off with an account using the ADB method. Whatever your situation, know the rules and play by them.

Another important factor to consider is the compounding method used. Compounding refers to the payment of interest on interest earned previously. Bank advertisements usually note how the interest rate is compounded. Some banks pay interest on the balance once a quarter, some once a month, and still others every day. Most banks will also state the annual percentage yield (APY), which automatically accounts for the differences in compounding periods by determining the result of the interest rate over a one-year period. It is easy to compare different banks by looking at the APYs of the different savings accounts; you should choose the savings account that pays the highest APY.

Use the following general principles when evaluating savings accounts:

1. Accounts using the ADB rather than the LCB method will pay more in interest given the same stated interest rate. The difference is important only if deposits and withdrawals are made during a compounding period. If none are made, both methods result in the same number. You can usually identify ADB accounts as those promising to pay daily interest or to use the day of deposit to day of withdrawal method.
2. Look for the account with the highest annual effective yield.
3. Avoid savings accounts with service fees or maintenance charges. These fees are sometimes levied if the required minimum balance is not maintained. In accounts of this type, it's possible that the fees could be larger than the interest credited, so the balance in the account can actually decline. Be sure to read the fine print carefully for any applicable fees.
4. You should be able to find a savings account paying money market rates on a reasonable balance ($1,000 to $2,500). Since your emergency savings should equal at least two months' pay, your account balance should be large enough to qualify. If banks in your area don't offer money market interest rates on deposits of the size you want to maintain, look at credit unions.

Certificates of Deposit. For your medium-term investments, you might want to consider certificates of deposit. (See chapters 14 through 18 for longer-term investments.) Certificates of deposit (CDs) pay higher interest rates than regular savings accounts but levy an early withdrawal penalty if the funds are taken out before the maturity date. Generally, you should use CDs when you have funds in excess of your requirements for emergencies and short-term

Tips on Choosing a Bank

- Find a bank that has telephone access, Internet access, or convenient operating hours.
- Only use federally insured banks, savings and loans, or credit unions.
- It's best to have direct deposit to the bank or credit union where you have your checking account to ensure constant availability of funds.
- It's generally more cost effective to have free checking than to earn interest on your checking account.
- Be sure to have overdraft protection on your checking account.
- Your savings account should pay a competitive interest rate.
- Invest your emergency savings (two to six months' pay) in a money market savings account.
- It's a good idea to have an ATM card so that you'll have access to funds twenty-four hours a day.

needs. For example, if you have already established an emergency fund with a balance two times your monthly pay and you have no other short-term need for the excess funds, a CD paying higher interest than the savings account is one way to save.

It is impossible to generalize about which CD offerings are best among the many available. Interest rates are usually higher for longer maturity periods. A great advantage of CDs is that the interest is guaranteed for the entire life of the certificate, so a CD enables you to "lock in" an attractive rate of interest for a known amount of time. Savings accounts don't offer this advantage, typically paying very low interest rates or money market rates that fluctuate up and down weekly or monthly. Being able to lock in a rate of interest for several years is a double-edged sword, however. You can't tell what will happen to money market rates in the future. For example, a CD rate of 4 percent guaranteed for five years (and locking your deposit in for five years) may seem attractive today if savings deposits are paying 3 percent. If money market rates go to 6 percent next year, however, your guaranteed 4 percent rate is much less attractive.

Don't worry about your money being locked up in a CD, however. If you really need the money or if interest rates shoot way up, you can always get your deposit out of the CD by paying the withdrawal penalty. The penalty may take away some interest earned, but the principal remains intact. As with all bank deposits, it's important to understand fully the terms of a CD before you invest in it. Chapter 14 discusses how a CD may fit into a portfolio of financial assets, and chapter 15 provides some helpful hints about obtaining the best interest rates available.

6

Using Credit Wisely

Borrowing to finance the purchase of durable goods such as cars, furniture, and appliances has long been a prominent feature of American life. This chapter discusses the wise use of consumer credit, the operation of traditional bank-loan services, and some of the different types of loans available to consumers. It concludes with a review of the uses, abuses, and costs of consumer credit and debit cards.

HOW DOES CONSUMER CREDIT FIT IN A PERSONAL BUDGET?

Today, consumer credit is easy to get—so easy that many families find themselves in financial distress. The danger in taking on too much debt is that there is not enough income both to pay off the debt and to provide for the basic needs of food and shelter, much less save for future needs. As emphasized in chapter 4, success in personal financial management requires planning and perseverance. An absolute requirement for any family is a regular savings plan. If large monthly installment debt payments make regular saving impossible, take immediate steps to reduce the amount you owe. Although this situation is easier to prevent than to cure, it is never beyond hope.

This is not to say that military families should never borrow. Virtually everyone, at one time or another, needs to borrow money to finance major purchases, such as automobiles and furniture, or to pay educational expenses. Additionally, very few people can afford to buy a house with cash alone. Without credit, a family could not buy some of these costly items at all unless they had saved enough money to pay for these purchases outright. If you do have the money available to cover such purchases from your own resources (even if intended for some other long-range goal), it is usually more advantageous to use your own funds ("borrowing from yourself") than to borrow from a lending institution. The interest rate you lose on savings is generally lower than the interest rate a lender would charge you on a loan. It is even possible, using Appendix D, to calculate the "loan payment" you need to repay yourself each month.

It is inappropriate to use consumer credit to finance routine day-to-day needs. A good practice is to ensure that any item you finance has a useful life at least as long as the time it takes to repay the debt (for example, durable goods such as cars and furniture and long-lasting assets such as education). You should not routinely carry unpaid credit card balances for purchases of clothes, entertainment, groceries, and other such nondurable items. Cover this spending with current income. Using credit to finance routine purchases or to splurge on extras is a sure sign of personal financial mismanagement.

Since not everyone reading this book will likely adhere to this strict view of consumer credit, the following paragraphs offer some guidance on how much consumer debt is too much. Consumer debt refers to all debts incurred to finance purchases, including car loans and credit card debt but excluding real estate mortgages. One useful rule of thumb is that monthly payments on consumer debt should be no more than 20 percent of monthly disposable income (income after subtracting mortgage or rent, food, utilities, and taxes). Another guideline is that the total outstanding consumer debt should be less than one-third of your annual disposable income. The important point is that you must carefully plan for consumer debt as one component of a monthly budget that includes adequate provisions for regular savings and an emergency reserve. To see how to apply these guidelines, consider the following examples.

Debt-Payment Guideline Example. A family that occupies government quarters has after-tax take-home pay of approximately $2,500 per month. If the family has no utilities or other housing expenses, we need only estimate spending for food to find disposable income. Let's assume that the family's food costs are $500 per month. This means that the family has $2,000 a month in disposable income. According to the first guideline, installment debt payments should not exceed $400 per month (20 percent of $2,000). How much debt could the family carry for $400 per month? If the debt had an average maturity of three years, $400 would be adequate to service about $12,000. (The total debt amounts were derived by multiplying the monthly payment by the annuity factor. See Table 4-7 for the formula and Appendix D for a table of annuity factors.)

Total-Debt Guideline Example. This rule is a bit stricter than the debt-payment guideline. Continuing with our example, the family living in government quarters with an annual disposable income of $24,000 should not owe more than one-third, or $8,000, in consumer debt. Either method of figuring will provide a ballpark figure for the maximum debt you should carry.

WHAT IS INVOLVED IN A CONSUMER LOAN?

The most common type of consumer loan arrangement is the installment loan, in which consumers repay the amount borrowed, plus interest, over a predetermined period in equal monthly payments. Automobile loans and home mortgages are common examples of installment loans. Some lenders also use single-payment loans, but much less commonly. In a single-payment loan, borrowers must repay the full amount plus interest at the loan's maturity date. A loan with a combination of periodic payments and a large repayment at the end is called a balloon loan. This section will primarily focus on installment loans because they are much more common.

What Is the "True Interest Rate?"

Consumers shopping for installment loans should compare three features: the interest rate (the annual percentage rate, or APR), the term (length) of the contract, and any prepayment penalties or other fees. The APR's effect on a loan contract is straightforward: The higher the APR, the higher the monthly payment (for a given term of the loan) and the more total interest you will pay over the loan's life. The impact of the loan's term is more subtle. The longer the period for installment payments, the lower the required monthly payments. However, the total interest you pay will be higher because you are using the money longer. In loan contracts, the total amount of interest over the life of the loan is called the total finance charge, and it is one of the items, along with the APR, that lenders must disclose in every loan agreement, as required by the Truth in Lending Act.

Lenders use several different methods to compute the monthly payment on an installment loan. Two loans that appear to be the same (they are for the same amount, duration, and interest rate) can have different monthly payments, finance charges, and APRs, depending on how the lender calculates the interest. Consumers typically must choose among loans with different durations, different lengths until the first payment is due, and any number of other variables. The APR is a standardized calculation that allows consumers to compare the true interest rate for different loans and know which loan has the lowest cost of borrowing.

Tables 6-1 and 6-2 illustrate the differences between the monthly balance and the add-on interest methods of charging interest on a loan for $2,000 at 12 percent interest per year, repaid in twelve equal monthly payments. These two loans sound identical, but they are not. The monthly balance method is the usual way that loans are repaid. When interest is computed using the monthly balance method, the monthly payments are $177.70 and the APR is 12 percent per year. The add-on interest method charges interest on the entire amount borrowed over the whole year, even though some of the principal is being repaid each month. When interest is computed using the add-on interest method, the monthly payments are $186.67 and the APR is 21.3 percent per year.

Tables 6-1 and 6-2 show two different formulas for the APR, and there are many others (one for every type of consumer loan). Every APR formula is an approximation of the same thing: the true interest cost of the loan. The bottom line is that all APR formulas are very good approximations of the true interest cost of the loan. Consumers don't have to calculate the APR; they need only compare the APRs that the law requires lenders to reveal.

For the most common installment loans (loans in which interest is computed using the monthly balance method), the monthly payment is determined as illustrated in Appendix D. With a careful reading of that section and some practice with a calculator or home computer, you should be able to compute the monthly payments on common loans.

TABLE 6-1
MONTHLY BALANCE INTEREST METHOD
$2,000 AT 12% FOR 1 YEAR, 12 MONTHLY PAYMENTS

Month	Payment	Interest	Principal	Outstanding
				$2,000.00
1	$177.70	$20.00	$157.70	1,842.30
2	177.70	18.42	159.28	1,682.02
3	177.70	16.83	160.87	1,522.15
4	177.70	15.22	162.48	1,359.67
5	177.70	13.60	164.10	1,195.57
6	177.70	11.96	165.74	1,029.83
7	177.70	10.30	167.40	862.43
8	177.70	8.62	169.08	693.35
9	177.70	6.93	170.77	522.58
10	177.70	5.23	172.47	350.11
11	177.70	3.50	174.20	175.91
12	177.70	1.79	175.91	0.00
	$2,132.40	$132.40	$2,000.00	$1,103.08*

*Average outstanding balance (sum of last column divided by 12).

$$\text{APR} = \frac{\text{finance charge}}{\text{average balance}} = \frac{\$132.40}{\$1{,}103.08} = 0.12\ (12\%)$$

TABLE 6-2
ADD-ON INTEREST METHOD

Add-on interest = F = (r × L) = 0.12 × $2,000 = $240
Total to be repaid = L + (r × L) = $2,000 + $240 = $2,240
Monthly payment = total to be repaid ÷ number of monthly payments (n)
= $2,240 ÷ 12 = $186.67

$$\text{APR} = \frac{n \times F \times (95T + 9)}{12T \times (T + 1) \times (4L + F)} = 0.213\ (21.3\%)$$

r = annual interest rate
n = number of payments per year (12)
T = total number of payments over life of loan (12)
F = total finance charge ($240)
L = principal amount of loan ($2,000)

The point of the example in Tables 6-1 and 6-2 is to show how much difference the method of computing interest can make. Do not look only at the advertised interest rate in a loan contract. Find the APR in the Truth in Lending section. Compare the APR the lender is offering you to typical loan rates reported in the "Money Rates" section of either the *Wall Street Journal* or *Barron's,* or in frequent surveys published in *Money, Consumer Reports,* or *Changing Times.* It pays to shop around for various loan terms.

Not knowing the market for consumer loans can cost you a lot of money. It is common today for auto loans to offer very low APRs, but as shown in chapter 8, the low-rate loans are often available only if other purchasing conditions are met. To determine whether the offered interest rate is attractive, identify the costs, if any, of purchasing conditions placed on the loan.

The loan conditions of particular banks may also be important criteria in the selection of the financial institution to which you deposit your paycheck. Loan approval and repayment options will often be easier in conjunction with the bank that receives your direct deposit. This includes the ability to establish monthly automatic deductions from your account (although this is often possible with many financial institutions simply by providing a voided check and signing an agreement to allow such automatic deductions). Such methods save both you and the lender from monthly hassles and add credibility to your repayment commitment.

What Are Prepayment Penalties?

You should also investigate loan contracts for any prepayment penalties. Strangely enough, if you decide you want to pay off your loan in a shorter period than the contract specifies, you may have to pay more interest on the loan than originally stated in the terms. Some lenders use the "sum-of-the-digits" method (also called the Rule of 78) to determine how much of the original finance charge you will have to pay if the loan is repaid before maturity. Your lender should be able to tell you, in writing, how much it will cost you to pay off your loan early. Seek loans without prepayment penalties.

How Does Collateral Affect a Loan?

For many loans consumers use to finance major purchases, the item purchased becomes the collateral for the loan. That is, the bank takes a lien against the item, so that if repayment is not made as agreed, the bank may repossess the property and sell it for cash. Remember that banks are lending their depositors' money and want to have some protection if a borrower fails to repay. Collateral for loans can also include other property, such as stocks and bonds, equity in a home, and sometimes even jewelry. In some cases, as with stock and bond certificates, the bank will insist on taking physical possession of the collateral.

Collateralized, or secured, loans are less risky for banks because they offer some protection in the event the borrower defaults. As a result, the interest rate on a secured loan tends to be lower than for an unsecured, or signature, loan.

This is worth remembering if you want to borrow for some purpose (such as a child's education) where the asset you are financing cannot be used as collateral. It may be worthwhile to use some of your other assets to secure a loan in such cases. Also consider selling the assets for cash, since this may be cheaper than borrowing.

What are Home-Equity Loans?

A popular form of collateralized borrowing involves second mortgages and lines of credit secured by the borrower's equity in a home. Equity in a home is the difference between the value of a home, as determined by an appraiser, and what the homeowner still owes the mortgage holder. Second mortgages and home-equity lines of credit allow homeowners to borrow money at interest rates lower than those of normal consumer loans. The interest on home-equity loans is also usually tax deductible. (Current IRS rules state that the loans must be less than $100,000 and the total mortgages on your home must be less than the appraised value.) Another advantage of home-equity loans is that relatively large amounts of money can be borrowed for long periods of time, often up to fifteen years.

Home-equity loans have several disadvantages, however. They can be fairly expensive to set up, because the closing costs involved in real estate lending can run into several hundreds of dollars. In addition, lenders can charge points (a point is 1 percent of the amount borrowed) on second mortgages, further adding to the cost. Finally, the interest rate on a second mortgage will be a few percentage points higher than the going rate on first mortgages.

If you need to borrow a large amount of money with a reasonably long period to repay (for example, to finance college education costs for children), a second mortgage on your home may be a good alternative. For smaller amounts and shorter repayment periods, shop carefully for more conventional loans before committing yourself to a second mortgage. Weigh the tax and interest rate advantages against the sizable up-front closing fees.

Home-equity lines of credit are similar to second mortgages in that the borrowing is secured by the equity in a home and there are closing costs when the credit line is established. However, once you establish the credit line, there is a great deal of flexibility for use of the credit. In most cases, you can draw cash against the credit line by simply writing a check and can repay on any schedule that is convenient. Borrowers pay interest monthly on the outstanding credit, but some institutions make the interest rates fairly attractive. The closing costs and other fees on a home-equity line of credit will be lower than on a second mortgage for most lending institutions. Some consumers use home-equity credit lines to finance cars, appliances, educational expenses, and many other needs that have traditionally been financed by conventional bank loans. An obvious potential danger in using your home's equity as a source of funds is that you risk losing your home if you default on your loan obligation.

What Are the Sources for Consumer Loans?

Banks are often the first source of credit that comes to mind. However, banks are not the only source of consumer credit. As mentioned in chapter 5, the financial sector of the economy is becoming increasingly competitive as different kinds of institutions enter the market for consumer financial services. Therefore, you should also consider credit unions, savings and loan associations, and mutual savings banks. Many of these institutions are consumer-oriented and may offer better loan rates than banks in your area. In addition, some stockbrokers will lend money using your stocks, bonds, or other qualifying assets as collateral. These "margin loans" are usually used by aggressive investors to leverage their stock portfolios when they believe stock prices are about to rise, but in some cases they may be used for other purposes, too. The rate of interest on broker loans is generally very close to the short-term Treasury bill rate. A loan from your broker may be cheaper than a loan from any other institution. In addition, the repayment terms on loans from brokers are typically flexible: You repay when you want to but pay interest on the amount borrowed as long as you have it.

As discussed in chapter 3, the military provides servicemembers a loan in the form of an advance on future pay. This is available only in conjunction with a permanent-change-of-station (PCS) move. With appropriate justification and command approval, servicemembers can obtain up to one month's advance pay from the departing station and up to two months' advance pay at the new assignment location. Repayment by payroll deduction will take place over a twelve- to twenty-four-month period. Servicemembers are not charged interest for advance pay transactions.

Finally, if you own permanent life insurance (whole life), you can borrow against the cash value of your policy at very attractive rates. If you already own a whole life policy with a substantial cash value, this may be your best alternative for borrowing small amounts cheaply. See chapter 19 for details on borrowing against a whole life policy.

HOW SHOULD YOU USE CREDIT AND DEBIT CARDS?

One of the most familiar and popular forms of consumer credit is the credit card. Banks, credit unions, and thrift institutions usually offer either MasterCard or VISA, and sometimes both. Most military credit unions and USAA offer these cards with no annual fee and very low interest rates. Today, bank credit cards are available to a broad range of consumers. Oil companies, major department stores, and financial service conglomerates such as Sears also offer credit cards. American Express, Diner's Club, and Carte Blanche offer travel and entertainment cards that offer credit but under quite different terms than banks, stores, and oil companies. Most of the long-distance phone companies now offer combination credit and calling cards. Additionally, most financial institutions offer automatic teller machine (ATM) cards that provide access to savings and checking accounts from machines throughout the world. Often these ATM cards are also debit cards that can be used anywhere a credit card is accepted.

The term *credit card* comes from the nature of the arrangement between the lender and the holder of the credit card. When you make a purchase with a credit card, the lender, in effect, makes a loan to you. The lender agrees to pay the merchant quickly for the goods you bought and to bill you later for the purchase. Credit cards represent preapproved lines of credit, up to a specified limit.

From the cardholder's perspective, the credit card is a very effective substitute for cash or checks in making routine purchases. The insecurity and inconvenience of carrying currency and the uncertainty about the acceptance of personal checks are eliminated, since so many retail establishments (including post or base exchanges) accept the nationally known credit cards. Use of a credit card allows the cardholder to make a single payment for all the small purchases made during the month. A cardholder could buy nearly everything needed during the month with credit cards and pay them off right after payday.

One of the best features of credit cards is that they represent a reserve of purchasing power that can be tapped immediately in an emergency. When applying for a credit card, ask for a credit limit that is high enough to allow you to finance airline tickets and other emergency expenditures. Remember that only the unused portion of your credit line serves as an effective source of reserves. This is a good reason to pay off the balance on the card each month.

Credit cards can also prove particularly useful during international travel. They reduce the need for converting currency because they are so widely accepted. Furthermore, the exchange rate used by the card companies to convert foreign currency charges into dollars is generally at least competitive and often better than the exchange rate you would receive at a bank or exchange office.

What Is the Cost of Credit Cards?

Most credit cards provide credit free as long as the cardholder pays the entire balance of the account within a grace period—usually twenty-five days from the end of the monthly billing period. However, if the cardholder fails to pay off the full amount, the lender charges interest on the unpaid balance. Although credit cards offer great utility to consumers, their misuse costs cardholders many millions of dollars in needless interest expenses. Accumulating credit card debt is an easy trap for an undisciplined consumer and a sure sign that he or she has become dangerously overextended on credit. It's best to pay off the entire balance during each billing cycle.

While the convenience and free credit feature of credit cards make them potentially useful to everyone, many consumers run up large unpaid balances on their card accounts and continually make sizable interest payments. The card issuers make this easy by asking that the cardholder make only a minimum monthly payment, which is usually far less than the unpaid balance. This minimum payment can be little more than enough to cover the finance charge of the previous month and 1 or 2 percent of the principal. Making only the minimum payment ensures that it will take a long time to repay the debt and guarantees the card companies a hefty return in interest payments. Occasionally, often right after Christmas, credit card companies encourage consumers to "take a payment holiday" and skip a month's payment. The interest charges, of course, accrue on the unpaid balance, making it a very expensive holiday for the consumer when he or she eventually has to pay the bill with additional interest.

Lenders are eager to have cardholders keep unpaid balances, because the interest rate on these balances is typically much higher than lenders earn on regular loans and investments. Typically, credit card agreements specify that interest on the unpaid balance will be 1.5 percent per month. This may seem like a low rate, but consider that if you maintained a $1,000 unpaid balance on your credit card for a year, you would pay more than $195 in interest. Thus the effective annual interest rate exceeds 19.5 percent, which is much higher than you would pay for even an expensive signature loan. Even worse, if the unpaid balance reaches the credit limit, the card is essentially worthless. At that point all you have is a very expensive loan.

If you find yourself in this situation, consider getting a signature loan from your bank or another financial institution and consolidating your debts at the lower signature loan rate. Such a loan adds the discipline of fixed monthly installment payments. Banks will consider the credit limits of all your active credit cards—even if the intent is to pay them down to zero balance—when they decide whether to approve a loan. After all, there is nothing that stops you from immediately going out and running up new charges on a credit card once you've used the signature loan to pay off the balance.

How Balances Are Computed. When comparing cards, keep in mind that you cannot simply compare the interest rates charged. Card issuers use different methods to determine the balance on which they charge interest. As with bank deposits and loans, the method used to calculate the outstanding balance can have an important effect on the total interest expense. The most common method used by card issuers is the average daily balance (ADB) method, identical to the approach used in savings and checking accounts (see chapter 5). This method applies the daily interest rate to the average of your daily balances during the billing cycle.

Two other methods are frequently used. In the "previous balance" method, finance charges are levied on the previous due balance as of the beginning of the billing period. The "adjusted balance" method levies the charge on the amount of the previous balance minus any payments made during the billing period. Thus, the adjusted balance method results in the lowest finance charge, the previous balance method has the highest charge, and the ADB method falls somewhere in between.

One other method of billing that has come to light recently is a two-cycle billing method. This is a more costly method than the others. This method takes the average of your balance over the previous two billing cycles (two months) and applies the finance charge to that. Using this method, it is even possible to carry no unpaid balance for a month and still be charged interest based on the balance of the previous month.

Credit cards also allow cardholders to get cash advances from any bank around the world that services the card. Most cards also allow you to get a cash advance by writing a check on your account or using your card in a participating ATM machine. This service can be a real convenience for travelers who run short of cash. However, lenders assess finance charges on the cash advances even when the balance is fully paid within the twenty-five-day grace period. Usually, interest is charged from the day of withdrawal at the normal credit card rate. Many cards also charge a sizable fee, often 3 percent of the cash advance, along with the finance charge. Some cards apply a higher interest rate to cash advances than they do to purchases (this appears to be a common feature for cards issued under attractive introductory offers). Because of the high additional cost of cash advances, you should use this service only in emergencies.

If you have to use a credit card to help you through a tough time, such as emergency leave or unexpected major car repairs, pay off the balance as soon as possible. In most cases, it's more cost effective to use savings you have to pay off credit card debt, since the APR of the credit card is likely to exceed the return on the savings you have available.

If you do not have adequate savings available to pay off a credit card balance after the emergency, figure out a way to pay it off at a rate greater than the minimum requirements established by the lenders. To help discipline yourself, consider establishing your own repayment goals to pay down the balance on credit card charges. For example, treat a particular credit card balance as a closed-end loan (like those a bank might approve) and establish a time period for repayment. A quick way to figure out a payment plan is to determine how much time is reasonable for repayment and then divide the balance on the card by the number of months you will allow yourself for repayment. Every month when you receive your credit card bill, pay the amount you came up with plus the finance charge of the previous months. For example, to pay off a $2,000 balance in ten months requires that you pay $200 of the principal each month. This means that you need to add $200 to the finance charge for the previous month to come up with the appropriate payment. It's also generally wise to use any leftover funds from other parts of your budget to pay down credit cards further. In summary, avoid carrying a balance on credit cards, but if you do end up carrying a balance, make it a priority to pay it down. If you have more than one credit card carrying a balance, pay the minimum on the cards with the lowest APR and concentrate on eliminating each credit card, one at a time, starting with the card with highest APR.

Credit Card Theft. Credit card fraud and theft are increasing problems. Mail-order firms will ship merchandise from telephone orders based on a credit card number. Though such services are convenient, they do present the danger of some unauthorized person using your credit card number to order goods by phone. Carbon copies of credit slips are routinely stolen and used for this purpose. There is also the risk that a lost or stolen card may be used directly. Cardholders have the responsibility to notify the card issuers as soon as they realize a card is missing. A number of firms and automobile clubs now offer a service of registering all of a customer's credit card numbers and notifying all issuers on behalf of the cardholder if the cards are lost or stolen. This is a useful service that you should take advantage of if it is free.

Credit Card Insurance. Occasionally, credit card issuers will push you to buy credit card insurance. There really is little reason to pay for such insurance, because your liability for unauthorized use of your cards is limited to $50, and as a practical matter, few issuers actually attempt to get their cardholders to pay even that. Just make sure that you report any loss within twenty-four hours. One technique to keep track of your cards in case your purse or wallet is lost or stolen is to empty its contents onto a copy machine and make a copy. Do this now and on each birthday. Put the copy in a safe place at home. This provides a quick and convenient record in case of a loss or theft.

Whose Credit Card Should You Get?

Today, virtually anyone in the military who wants a credit card can get one, and many servicemembers have more than one. This has changed the competition among card issuers from one of simply reaching new credit users to one of trying to lure credit card customers away from one another. A common technique for lenders is to offer a low introductory APR (such as 0.9 percent) for a six-month to one-year period. At the end of the introductory period, the APR often will jump several percentage points. It's common for lenders to exclude cash advances from these introductory rates and to convert to the higher, "regular" APR if cardholders exceed the credit limit or have a late payment.

Credit cards with no annual fee are common today. Better-educated consumers caused many financial institutions to offer credit cards with no annual fees and to compete for credit card holders in other ways. Many banks offer free credit cards for a brief period as a competitive offer to lure new customers. It's common for a credit card issuer to change its terms or rates and even to change a no-fee card to one with an annual fee. Since there is really no reason to have your credit card issued by your regular bank, feel free to shop for the best deal. There are so many no-fee cards available to servicemembers that you should never pay an annual fee without a very good reason. If you pay off your balance nearly every month, you should almost certainly select a card with no annual fee and no charges if you pay off your balance within the grace period. Among credit cards with no annual fee and a long (twenty-five days) grace period, select the one with the lowest regular interest rate (as opposed to introductory interest rate). Many military credit unions have cards with lower rates, often some of the lowest rates in the nation.

If for some reason you have to carry a credit card balance for a while (because of an emergency or other high-cost event), consider taking advantage of low introductory rate offers and, if necessary, transferring any remaining balance to another low-rate introductory offer when the original introductory period expires. With the competition among lenders, such offers will generally show up in your mailbox with little or no effort on your part. You should also maintain a card whose regular APR is generally lower than the rate that takes effect after the introductory period of other cards expire. *Money, Barron's, Kiplinger's,* and other financial magazines, as well as the addresses and Internet sites listed in Appendix A, are the best source of credit card interest rate information.

To obtain information about credit card offers, contact one of the agencies that will sell lists of institutions and their comparative credit card offers. A list is available for a nominal fee from *myvesta.org* or from RAM Research, Box 1700, Frederick, MD 21702.

Other Specialty Cards

Debit Cards. Debit cards may look like conventional bank credit cards and may even sport the VISA or MasterCard logo, but their purpose is quite different. A debit card is an alternative way for a checking-account holder to draw upon deposits in order to make purchases. When a debit card holder makes a purchase using his card, his checking account is electronically debited. Since use of a debit card affects the account balance, be very careful to record each transaction in your checkbook ledger. Debit cards are becoming more universally accepted, and many retailers now offer this service in addition to cash, check, and credit transactions.

Travel and Entertainment Cards. The travel and entertainment (T&E) cards issued by American Express, Diner's Club, and Carte Blanche are used just like credit cards but differ in a very important way from credit cards such as VISA or MasterCard. Issuers of the T&E cards expect you to use the cards only for the convenience of eliminating cash and check purchases—not for revolving credit. That means you must pay the full balance when it is due. Failure to use the cards as prescribed may result in very stiff penalties, including interest rates of up to 2.0 percent per month and probable cancellation of the agreement. Use these cards only if you will pay off the entire balance each month.

Since these cards are most useful to those who travel and entertain away from home frequently, most military people will not find much extra benefit from having one if they already have a conventional bank credit card. Besides the requirement that the balance be paid in full each month, the annual service or membership charges are rather high ($50 to $75 per year). American Express also has marketed a regular credit card with revolving credit, the Optima Card, along with its traditional travel and entertainment card.

Government Travel Cards. For servicemembers who travel often on temporary duty, the government has arranged for VISA to provide government cards for official travel. Rather than provide cash advances, servicemembers are encouraged (and in most cases required) to apply for the government travel card through appropriate channels. Contact your unit finance office to learn how to get the official card. The restriction on the card is that it may be used only for official purchases and expenses in conjunction with official orders. Upon completion of temporary duty, you must still file your TDY claim and then use the proceeds from the reconciliation to pay off the travel card balance.

Premium Credit Cards. Another service that has been growing in prominence is the premium credit card. Card issuers market "gold," "platinum," and sometimes even "titanium" VISAs, MasterCards, and American Express cards to customers as signs that an individual has achieved a high economic standing. The premium cards are usually tied to a larger line of credit ($5,000 to $100,000 or more) and offer a variety of other services to cardholders. The main allure of these cards is their snob appeal, but the primary disadvantage is their high annual cost, which can be $50 or more. Although issuing financial institutions may offer expanded services to premium cardholders, you should determine whether the additional services are worth the extra cost. The competition by card issuers to obtain more customers has led to a tremendous proliferation of gold cards, many of which do not have annual fees, and to relaxation of the criteria for their issue. If you need to obtain the higher credit limits associated with a gold card, a little comparative shopping goes a long way.

WHAT SHOULD YOU DO IF YOU HAVE CREDIT PROBLEMS?

Credit and some people just do not mix. Through bad luck, bad management, or just lack of willpower, some people either cannot get credit or cannot handle it once they do.

If you can't get either a VISA or MasterCard, it is probably because your credit is bad. This could mean about a dozen different things, from having a history of bankruptcy or unpaid bills to just being too young or inexperienced to be offered a credit card. This does not happen much anymore, since issuers are trying hard to get new card customers. If you can't get a card and you don't have any credit history, then take some measures to build a credit history. Start with an oil company credit card—practically anyone can get one. Use it and pay it off immediately. Then work your way up to a department store card and eventually to a bank card. Try your bank or credit union—most military credit unions will start you up with a low credit limit, even if you have no credit history.

If all else fails and you just can't wait, you can get a secured credit card, which is usually very expensive and operates more like a debit card. If you have destroyed your credit rating and have exhausted your other options, there are about twenty-five banks that will issue you a card secured by a sizable deposit. If you prove that you can use this for a while, you could "graduate" to a normal credit card. A list of banks with secured cards is available from *myvesta.org* or from RAM Research's Cardtrak, Box 1700, Frederick, MD 21702.

You may be tempted by an offer (for a fee, of course) from some direct mailer to check your credit rating. You shouldn't pay for something like this. If you are ever turned down for credit, you can get your credit rating information for free (see point 9 under Borrowers' Rights, below).

If you get out of control with high, unpaid credit card balances, you have a serious problem. Each service has trained financial counselors (such as Army Community Service) to help structure a way out. There are also other agencies in the civilian community (such as the National Foundation for Consumer Credit, telephone 800-388-2227) that can assist with personal budgeting and debt management. Moreover, the sooner you get some help working on your problem, the easier it will be to get out of it.

WHAT ARE BORROWERS' RIGHTS?

When considering whether to take advantage of any of the various forms of consumer credit outlined in this chapter, know your legal rights as a borrower. Over the years, the U.S. Congress has passed two major pieces of legislation that protect the borrower's rights: the Consumer Credit Protection Act of 1968 (better known as the Truth in Lending Act) and the Fair Credit Billing Act of 1975. Under these two acts, you, as a borrower, have the following rights:

1. You have the right to know the true interest rate (in APR terms) and total finance charges before signing any loan agreement.
2. Credit card issuers must advertise the true interest rate (in APR terms) charged on their cards.
3. You must be given at least fourteen days from the postmark on your credit card statement to pay off your balance and avoid paying any interest.
4. When considering your application for a loan or a credit card, a financial institution cannot ignore income from child support, alimony, or a pension.
5. In the event that you purchased goods or services in excess of $50 with your credit card and you are dissatisfied, you have the right to cancel the charges if you make a genuine effort to settle matters with the seller and the purchase was made in your home state or within one hundred miles of your home.
6. In the event that your credit card is used against your will or without your permission (that is, it is stolen or lost), your liability for the unauthorized purchases is limited to $50. If you are able to notify the credit card issuer of the loss or theft of the card before anyone tries to purchase something with it, you will not be liable for any unauthorized purchases.
7. In the event that a debit card is stolen or lost, you must notify the bank within two business days in order to limit your liability to $50. If you fail to do so, you can be liable for the first $500 taken from your account. If sixty-one days pass after the mailing date of your first bank statement showing unauthorized withdrawals, you may be liable for all the money taken from your account.
8. In the event you are applying for a credit card or loan on your own for the first time (in other words, you have no credit record of your own), you have the right to have your spouse's unblemished credit record considered as your own.
9. Should you ever be denied a loan or a credit card, you have the right to be told the specific reasons why you were turned down. You cannot be denied access to what has been reported about you to a credit bureau. If the credit

Tips on Using Credit Wisely

- Do not use consumer credit to finance routine day-to-day needs.
- Limit consumer debt payments to 20 percent of monthly disposable income and total debt to one-third of annual disposable income.
- Shop for loans carefully. Compare interest rate (APR), term (length) of the contract, prepayment penalties, and other fees.
- Try to get a loan without a prepayment fee.
- Consider a home-equity loan as an alternative to high consumer credit for large loan needs.
- Find credit cards with low or no annual fees, especially if you have a low monthly balance.
- Pay off credit card balances each month during the grace period whenever possible.
- If you must carry a credit card balance, select cards with lower APRs.
- Carry no more than three different cards: a low-interest credit card with no annual fee for major purchases or emergencies; a travel and entertainment card to be paid off each month; and a debit card issued by your bank for everyday, cash-free transactions.
- Read the fine print!

bureau's report was instrumental in your being rejected for a loan or a credit card, you must be provided access to your file at no charge. If you wish to find out what is in your credit record without having been rejected for a credit application, you can contact the three major credit bureaus: Experian (formerly TRW), Equifax, and Trans Union. Any or all may have a file on you, and your report may be accurate at one and inaccurate at another. Therefore, you should check your credit report at all three bureaus. To find out how to get your credit report, contact credit bureaus listed in Appendix A.

SUGGESTED REFERENCES

See the Internet sites listed in Appendix A.

"House of Cards." *Consumer Reports* 61, no. 1 (January 1996): 31–34.

"A Question of Money: Dealing with Debt." *Consumer Reports* 61, no. 9 (September 1996): 63.

Singletary, Michelle, and Albert B. Crenshaw. "When Credit Is Due: Card Issuers Flood Consumers with Solicitations Leaving Behind a Sea of Debt." *The Washington Post National Weekly* 14, no. 5 (December 2–8, 1996): 6–7.

7

Paying Your Taxes

Military compensation has peculiarities that distinguish it from typical civilian pay systems. Many military allowances are exempt from income taxation by all three levels of government: federal, state, and local. Considering the housing (BAH) and subsistence (BAS) allowances alone, about one-fourth of military compensation is tax exempt. In addition, the 2000 presidential election highlighted that many states, like Florida, either have no state income tax or allow military incomes to forgo state income taxes. This could be worth up to 9.5% of your income in California. Thus, by exempting military income from taxation, the tax code raises the value of military compensation by providing a "tax advantage" to servicemembers. Like civilians however, basic military pay, investment income, and your spouse's income are fully taxable by all levels of government. As a result, you need to understand tax laws so you can ensure compliance, incorporate tax considerations into your financial planning decisions, and understand the value of your military compensation. In this chapter, we discuss the military member's personal tax responsibilities and the peculiarities of federal, state, and local taxation that apply to servicemembers. You will learn how to prepare your tax returns and how to tackle the myriad of roadblocks that discourage many Americans from preparing their taxes themselves. We also provide some general tax planning guidance that should be useful in your overall financial plan and help you avoid overpaying.

The information provided in this chapter is by necessity general in nature. Each individual family's financial situation is different and tax law is complex. In addition, many of the dollar values for exemptions, credits, exclusions, and deductions change annually and are subject to political forces. To help, all military installations have legal assistance offices that provide tax forms and offer professional help in tax matters at no charge to you and your family. In addition, the Volunteer Income Tax Assistance (VITA) program at each base provides unit-level volunteers with training to assist with simple tax preparation. Finally, the Internal Revenue Service (IRS) maintains local offices around the country, a toll-free phone number, and assistance over the internet. You can consult the IRS when you need advice or tax forms. For additional information on the specifics of your tax situation, consult the references listed in Appendix A.

FEDERAL INCOME TAX

In this section, we will provide a summary of the general provisions of the complicated federal tax code. We start here because federal income taxes are the largest tax burden on the average American. These taxes are based upon the Internal Revenue Code, official rulings, and the decisions of the tax and federal courts. Luckily, every IRS form has detailed instructions, and the federal tax computations for the typical servicemember are relatively straightforward. You should be able to calculate your federal income tax liability without professional assistance, although experts say it may take you up to twenty hours to gather the appropriate information and complete the forms. Besides completing Form 1040, you may also have to tackle many other schedules and other forms, depending on whether or not you itemize deductions, receive investment or rental income, or are eligible for various credits.

Prior to covering the mechanics of completing the actual tax return, we will try to answer some basic questions to alleviate some of these complexities. Common questions include the following: How many exemptions should I have? What is my filing status? Do I even have to file a federal tax return? Which forms do I use? As a military member, do I have to pay state and military taxes? Should I itemize deductions or take the standard deduction? All of these are valid questions and taxpayers must understand their answers to them prior to preparing their tax return.

Tax Basics

One of the first things to do in the military is to file Form W-4 with your local finance office. This form basically records your marital status and the number of exemptions you wish to claim for withholding purposes. An exemption frees a specified amount of income ($2,900 in 2001) from taxes based on the idea that a taxpayer with a small amount of income should be exempt from taxes. Thus, the greater the number of exemptions, the more income we can "exempt" from being taxed. Tax codes provide one personal exemption for the taxpayer and an exemption for the spouse if a joint return is filed. In addition, a taxpayer may claim an exemption for each dependent (i.e., child). Thus, a married soldier with two children is allowed four exemptions if he or she files a joint return with his or her spouse. An unmarried soldier without responsibility for children would be allowed one exemption. There are many situations where it is not clear whether or not a person is a soldier's dependent. Some servicemembers care for elderly parents, have stepchildren, or are the primary caregiver for nephews and nieces. In general, a dependency exemption may be claimed for each individual for whom the following five tests are met:

- Support test: Dependent receives at least half of his or her support from the taxpayer.
- Relationship or member of the household test: Dependent must be a blood relative or a member of the taxpayer's household.

- Gross income test: Dependent's income must be less than the exemption amount ($2,900 in 2001).
- Joint return: A parent cannot claim a married child as a dependent if that child filed a joint return with his or her spouse.
- Citizenship or residency test: Dependent must be a resident or citizen of the United States.

There are many nuances of each of these rules. Servicemembers should consult their tax office before claiming an exemption because failure to meet the criteria for any of these tests results in the disallowance of an exemption. If the IRS determines you inappropriately claimed an exemption, you will be subject to back taxes, interest, and possibly penalties.

Filing status is a much more straightforward issue. There are five categories of filing status: single, married filing joint return, married filing separate return, head of household, and qualifying widower. Each filing status carries different tax rate schedules and standard deductions and hence has a significant effect on tax liabilities. In general, if you are legally married by a state law, you have the choice to file a joint return or a separate return. If you are separated from your spouse by a degree of divorce or separate maintenance and do not qualify for another filing status (i.e., head of household or dependent), you must use the rates for single taxpayers. A single parent who chooses not to live with his or her spouse should consult with the IRS to see if he or she qualifies as a head of household under the abandoned spouse provisions. Marital status is determined as of the last day of the tax year, except when a spouse dies during the year.

TABLE 7-1
STANDARD FEDERAL INCOME TAX DEDUCTION

Filing Status	2001 Standard Deduction
Single	$4,550
Married Filing Jointly	$7,600
Surviving Spouse	$7,600
Head of Household	$6,650
Married Filing Separately	$3,800

This brings us to questions about itemizing deductions or taking the basic standard deduction. You should itemize only if your deductions exceed the standard deduction shown in Table 7-1. Given the large standard deduction, itemizing typically applies only if you own a home because the interest paid on the mortgage debt is deductible. (This feature is explained in more detail in chapter 11.) If you decide to itemize, be sure to include all possible deductions, many of which are listed in Table 7-3. Common deductions include mortgage interest, contributions to charities, special uniform costs, employee business expenses, tax preparation fees, and investment expenses. Besides mortgage interest and charitable contributions, servicemembers often try to deduct unreimbursed moving expenses. According to IRS Publication 3, *Tax Information for Military Personnel,* servicemembers can deduct expenses that exceed dislocation and travel allowances. Most servicemembers do not qualify, however, because the Army normally reimburses legitimate moving expenses. If you do qualify, you will need to file Form 3903, "Moving Expenses." Remember, you may only deduct unreimbursed expenses. As is required with all deductions, be sure to save receipts, canceled checks, and mortgage records as evidence to support your deductions.

Finally, almost all soldiers have to file a federal income tax return each April. The general rule is that a tax return is required for every individual who has a gross income equal to or exceeding the sum of his or her exemptions amount plus the applicable standard deduction. For example, a single taxpayer under age sixty-five was required to file a tax return in 2001 if his or her gross income equaled or exceeded $7,450 ($2,900 exemption plus $4,550 standard deduction). Unless you are a private who entered the service in the second half of a given year, then you almost certainly earned more income than this amount and hence must file a tax return.

How Do I Prepare My Tax Return?

Now that we have an understanding of filing status, standard deductions, and how to determine the number of dependents, we are ready to began calculating taxable income as shown in Figure 7-1. During January of each year, you should receive a Form W-2 from the Defense Finance and Accounting Service, which documents your taxable income, income tax withheld, and Social Security (FICA) tax withheld for the prior calendar year. You should also receive Form 1099-Div for dividend and capital gains income from your investments and Form 1099-Interest for interest income from your banks. If you are using the married filing jointly status, ensure you have the W-2s for your spouse as well. Next, choose the correct filing status and number of exemptions. You must provide the IRS with the Social Security numbers for all exemptions, so make sure you have obtained these for dependents. Use the long Form 1040 unless you are single and cannot claim any dependents or have a taxable income of less than $50,000 and are not itemizing. Then, follow the four steps below:

1. Tally all income that is subject to taxes. Do not include income not subject to taxes, such as inheritances, life insurance proceeds, or military allowances, outlined in Table 7-3.

2. Reduce that total by the proper legal methods—adjustments, deductions, and exemptions.

Figure 7-1
Form 1040 Process

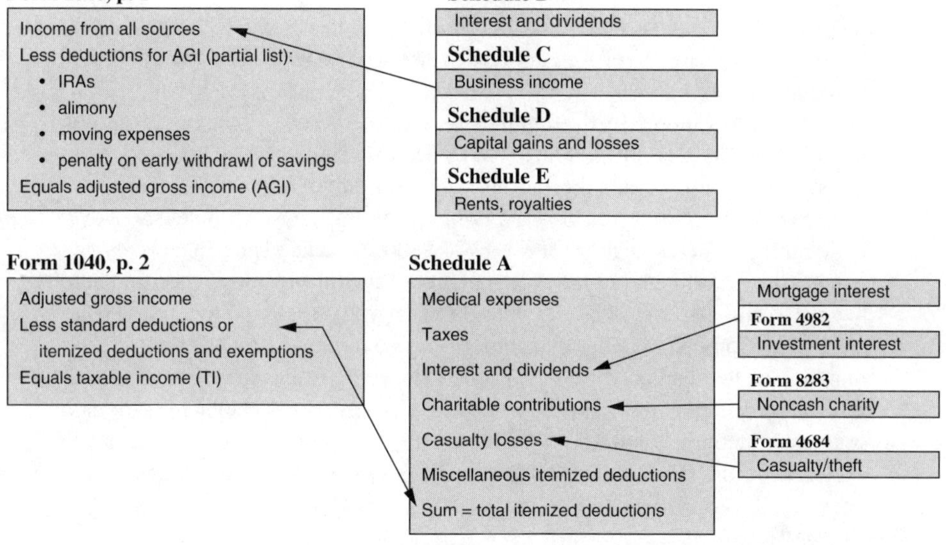

TABLE 7-2
FEDERAL INCOME TAX BRACKETS

2001 Tax Bracket	Married Filing Jointly	Single
10% income tax bracket (based on taxable income)	\$0–\$12,000	\$0–\$6,000
15% income tax bracket (based on taxable income)	\$12,001–\$45,200	\$6,001–\$27,050
Beginning of 27.5% bracket	\$45,201	\$27,051
Beginning of 30.5% bracket	\$109,251	\$65,551
Beginning of 35.5% bracket	\$166,501	\$136,751
Beginning of 39.1% bracket	\$297,351	\$297,351

3. Then figure the lowest possible tax by choosing the right filing status and apply the correct tax rates to the marginal income. Table 7-2 outlines the marginal tax rates for 2001 for the married filing jointly and single filing statuses. These are the most common filing statuses but the other income levels can be easily obtained at the IRS website. Also, the tax change of June 2001 reduces these rates through the year 2006. In 2002 and 2003, the 27.5, 30.5, 35.5, and 39.1 percent rates will be reduced to 27, 30, 35, and 38.6

percent, respectively, and by 2006, the final rates of 25, 28, 33, and 35 percent will be reached.

4. After calculating your federal income tax, reduce it by any tax credits you may have. We will discuss common credits later in the chapter.

Figure 7-1 summarizes these steps and how to complete the long Form 1040. Once we have discussed tax credits, we will do an example to help illustrate the process.

Do not be alarmed by the complexity of the diagram. Remember to start by listing all income from all sources in order to calculate your adjusted gross income. You must include the various schedules only if you draw income from sources outside of your military pay. For example, you must complete Schedule B if you have interest income in excess of $400, Schedule D if you have capital gains from investments (mutual funds), and Schedule E if you receive rental income. You must complete Schedule B only if you choose not to take the standard deductions. Remember that it makes sense to itemize only if your deductions are greater than your standard deductions. To assist you in determining your income and deductions, Table 7-3 summarizes some of the more common sources of income, itemizable deductions, and nonreportable income that can be excluded from your taxable income (step 2), as well as the most common deductions.

What Are Tax Credits and How Do I Use Them?

Now we are ready to attack step 4 of our process—reducing your tax by the appropriate credits. Besides merely raising revenue, our tax system is used to obtain equity and social and economic goals. Tax credits in particular have been enacted to make tax burdens more equitable across income levels. A tax deduction reduces your taxable income, and hence its benefit depends on your filing status and tax rate. A tax credit, on the other hand, reduces your taxes on a dollar-for-dollar basis. Ignoring tax credits is like tearing up a paycheck because each dollar of credit equals a dollar of tax savings. Still, lots of Americans ignore tax credits because they involve filling out extra forms and making calculations. Spending the few minutes to do this, however, could save you hundreds of dollars.

Many servicemembers can take advantage of tax credits. The most common is the earned income credit (EIC). Many younger servicemembers can take advantage of the EIC. It is intended to provide tax equity for those of modest means. For example, in tax year 2000, a family with two dependent children earning less than $31,152 in earned income would still qualify for a tax credit. This income situation could apply to many E-5s and below.

The earned income credit is computed by multiplying a maximum amount of earned income by the appropriate credit percentage listed in Table 7-5. For example, SPC Moore receives military wages of $14,000 and has no other income. She has one qualifying child. Her earned income credit is $2,428 ($7,150 × 0.34) reduced by $144 [($14,000 – $13,100) × 0.1598]. Thus her earned income credit is $2,284.

TABLE 7-3
TAXABLE AND NONTAXABLE INCOME AND DEDUCTIONS

Taxable Income

1. Basic pay, including longevity pay
2. Special pay
3. Incentive pay for hazardous duty
4. Special pay
5. Military retirement pay
6. Accrued leave and separation pay
7. Armed services academy pay (cadet and midshipman pay)
8. Personal money allowances
9. Bonuses (enlistment, reenlistment, overseas extension)
10. A portion of DITY—move incentive payment (you will receive a separate W-2 form that details the taxable income and taxes withheld)
11. CONUS cost-of-living allowance (COLA)
12. Spouse's income (if filing a joint return)
13. Interest received on investments
14. Dividends
15. Capital gains (requires a Schedule D)
16. Rental income (requires a Schedule E)
17. Royalties
18. Alimony
19. Prizes, awards, and gambling winnings
20. Gains realized on the sale of assets*

Nontaxable Income

1. Basic Allowance for Housing (BAH)
2. Subsistence allowance
3. Value of quarters and subsistence received in kind
4. Overseas COLA
5. Uniform, travel, and family separation allowances
6. Dividends on veterans insurance
7. Death gratuities
8. Dislocation Allowances (DLAs)
9. Combat zone pay (when combat zone exclusion applies)
10. Sick pay (after the first thirty days not combat connected)
11. Forfeiture/detention of pay
12. Professional education (paid by U.S. government)
13. Evacuation/interment allowance
14. Medical benefits (including dental)
15. Veterans benefits
16. ROTC allowances
17. Moving and storage (in kind)
18. Group term life insurance
19. Medal of Honor pension payments
20. Child support payments you receive
21. Value of scholarships and grants

Deductions

1. Medical and dental expenses in excess of 7.5% of AGI
2. City and state taxes
3. Charitable contributions (cash or property)
4. Home loan interest
5. Investment margin interest
6. Student loans
7. Fees for investment advice and management
8. Fees for administration
9. Subscriptions to publications on investing
10. Unreimbursed business expense in excess of 2% AGI.

Realized gain (or loss) on asset = amount realized from the sale - adjusted basis of the property.
Adjusted basis of property = cost + capital additions = depreciation property.

TABLE 7-4
TAX EXAMPLE

	Abby	Bill	Carmen
Tax benefit if a $250 credit is allowed	$250	$250	$250
Tax benefit if an itemized deduction is allowed	$150	$396	$0

TABLE 7-5
EARNED INCOME CREDIT

Number of Qualifying Children	Maximum Earned Income	Credit Percentage	Phaseout Begins	Phaseout Percentage	Phaseout Ends
None	$4,610	7.65%	$5,950	7.65%	$10,710
One	7,150	34%	13,100	15.98%	28,281
Two or more	10,050	40%	13,100	21.06%	31,121

Obviously, computing the EIC is complicated but worth the effort. It is recommended that you consult the Post Tax Assistance Office if you suspect you might qualify, given the maximum amount of earned income in Table 7-5. The table and example are intended for illustrative purposes only. The information will be obsolete by 2002 because the phaseout limits and maximum income will change. Also, listing all the exact percentages for credit determination would take pages of tables. Servicemembers and their leaders should be aware of the EIC and have a general idea of the income range. From there, they should consult the IRS web page. Each year, the IRS issues an Earned Income Tax Credit Table for determining the appropriate amount of credit. Claim the EIC on Form 1040, line 60a. If you have a qualifying child, you must attach Schedule EIC.

Credit for Child and Dependent Care Expenses. If you paid for someone to take care of your children under age thirteen so you can work, you can claim a credit for child-care expenses of up to $3,000 for one child and $6,000 for two or more children. The credit will range from 20 percent to 30 percent of these qualifying expenses (0.20 × $3,000) depending on your adjusted gross income. The maximum credit therefore ranges from $480 to $720 for one child under thirteen. Be careful. You do not qualify for this credit if you are married and your spouse does not work. It is intended to help mitigate only necessary child-care expenses. In addition, you must supply the name and Social Security number of your care provider and fill out Form 2441, "Child and Dependent Care Expenses." Be careful if you hire an in-home care provider (e.g., nanny). Form 2441 alerts the IRS that you may owe a nanny tax. If this applies to you, visit the IRS website for more information on this tax.

You may also qualify for this credit if you incur expenses taking care of any other dependent who is physically or mentally unable to care for him or herself (e.g., an elderly or disabled parent). Again, to take advantage of the credit the person must pass the dependency tests described earlier in this chapter.

Foreign Tax Credit. If you invest in international mutual funds, it is likely that you paid foreign taxes last year. These foreign taxes will show up on Forms 1099-Div and 1099-Interest, which must be provided to you by all mutual funds at the end of the calendar year. If your foreign taxes come to less than $300 ($600 if filing jointly), you simply claim this as credit on line 43 of Form 1040. If you paid more in foreign taxes, you must file Form 1116, which is a very complicated form.

If you or your spouse receive income from a foreign country and pay income taxes to that country, you will be excused from being taxed by the United States. An example of this is a U.S. servicemember living in Germany whose spouse is a German citizen with a job earning income on the German economy. If the spouse pays taxes in Germany, the U.S. servicemember will have to declare that income on the United States Form 1040. However, filling out Form 1116 will relieve the servicemember from paying taxes to the United States government if the spouse can prove income taxes were paid to Germany.

Child Tax Credit. This allows a credit for each dependent child under age seventeen. From 2001 to 2004 this is a generous $600 credit per child, rising to $700 in 2005, $800 in 2009, and $1,000 in 2010. This is perhaps the easiest credit to include on your tax return. Assuming you have dependents under age seventeen, there is no form to fill out. All you have to do is provide the Social Security number for each dependent under age seventeen on the front of your Form 1040.

Tax Questions

Should I Withhold Too Much or Too Little? The proportion of your income that is withheld as tax payment from your wage statements is determined by the number of withholding allowances you claim when you file a statement (Form W-4) with your finance office. A very rough estimate of the effects of one additional allowance is $25 (in the 15 percent tax bracket) or $50 (in the 27.5 percent tax bracket) less withheld from your pay each month.

There is good reason not to have too much withheld each month. In effect, you are extending an interest-free loan to the government—the government holds your excess tax payments until you get your refund, but pays you no interest for the use of your funds. If you consistently receive a large refund, you may want to file a new W-4 form. This will allow you to match your monthly tax withholding to your tax liability. As a result, you will have more take-home pay to use or invest as you see fit. While this approach offers the potential for additional investment income, you should be careful not to underwithhold. Specifically, the tax code requires a pay stub tax withholding sufficient enough to meet 100 percent of your previous year's tax liability or 90 percent of the current year's tax liability. If you fall beneath the minimum required withholding amount, you expose yourself to the risk of an IRS penalty that undoubtedly would exceed the investment return you received on the amount you under-withheld. To avoid this penalty, you should ensure withholdings cover 100 percent of your previous year's tax liability.

What About Extension for Filing Tax Returns? Income tax returns and final payments become due on 15 April. Military personnel and government employees living outside the United States and Puerto Rico get an automatic extension until 15 June. This rule also applies even if only one spouse is out of the country and files a joint return with the one who is not. You must attach a statement to your return showing that you met the requirement for the extension. *Remember, this extension only prevents the assessment of penalties for a late filing and payment of tax; interest will be charged on any taxes still unpaid after 15 April.*

Along with the automatic extension for persons serving overseas, any individual may apply for an extension to file (IRS Form 4868). In these cases, however, the extensions apply only to filing the return. To avoid interest and penalties, you must estimate your total tax liability and pay any shortfall between the taxes you will own and the amount of taxes withheld by 15 April.

What if I Served in a Combat Zone? There is special consideration for military pay earned in a combat zone, such as Operation Desert Storm and currently southwest Asia and Balkan rotations. If you are serving in an imminent danger area designated by an Executive Order for any part of a month, then your pay for the entire month falls under the exclusion. It differs for enlisted members and officers, as described below. It will be hard to be sure about whether or not you are serving in an imminent danger area. In general, if you are receiving hazardous duty pay, then you are in one.

Enlisted Members and Warrant Officers. For enlisted members and warrant officers, all basic pay received in a combat zone is nontaxable. Specifically, if you were in a combat zone for any portion of a month, your pay for the entire month is nontaxable. For example, a sergeant earning $2,000 a month would accrue a tax savings of $300 per month (0.15 × $2,000). Over a six-month rotation in Kosovo, this would mean a pay increase of $1,800.

Officers (after March 1996). In March 1996, Section 112 of the Internal Revenue Code was amended to raise the dollar amount of the exclusion for officers serving in a designated combat zone. Officers may now deduct their monthly pay up to the maximum enlisted amount. Before March 1996, if you served in a designated combat zone for any part of the month, the first $500 received monthly was nontaxable.

An Example

Let us make Figure 7-1 and the tables a little clearer. SFC Smith and his working wife, Janice, earned $69,200 in 2001, ignoring military allowances. They have two children under age thirteen, paid $8,000 in mortgage interest, donated $400 to charity, had a rental loss of $200, and have a dependent child-care credit of $800. They received a Form 1099-Div from their mutual fund company stating they had $500 in long-term capital gains in 2001, although they did not cash in any part of their mutual funds. Their Form 1099-Div also reports that they paid $50 in foreign taxes. Their filing status is married filing jointly.

First, we have to calculate the Smiths' adjusted gross income (AGI). This would be the sum of their salaries, capital gains on their investments (Schedule D), and the loss on their rental property (Schedule E). This comes to an AGI of $69,500. Next, they should subtract their deductions and exemptions. They are a family of four, so $11,600 (4 × $2,900) will be exempted from taxes, leaving them with $57,900. Next, given that their $8,000 in mortgage interest and $400 in donations to charity exceeds their standard deduction for married filing jointly ($7,600), the Smiths should fill out a Schedule B and subtract $8,400 from their AGI. This leaves them with a taxable income of $49,500. Next, they have to determine their tax liability using 2001 tax rates from Table 7-2. This is done as follows:

($49,500 – $45,000) × 0.275 =	$1,238
($45,000 – 12,001) × 0.15 =	$4,950
$12,000 × 0.10 =	$1,200
Total	$7,388

Now, we have to apply the appropriate tax credits (step 4 in our process). We can reduce the Smiths' tax bill of $7,388 by $1,200 by applying the $600 care credit for each of their two children under age thirteen. Next, we reduce that by $800 for the child-care expense credit. Finally, we deduct another $50 for the foreign taxes paid by their mutual fund company in 2001. This leaves them with a tax bill of $5,338 ($7,388 – $2,050). Of course, the more talented tax expert would search for more deductions for the Smiths. This might include professional association membership fees (AUSA), uniform pressing costs, unreimbursed moving expenses, or job search costs for SFC Smith's spouse. These deductions should not be added to the Schedule B haphazardly, but rather only after consulting with a tax professional.

If this looks difficult, do not worry. For $20, you can buy a software package such as TaxCut or TurboTax that will do the calculations for you. In addition, you can deduct the cost of this software if you are itemizing your deductions. Or, you can try some of the tax calculators on the Internet sites listed in Appendix A. Hopefully, this section and the example have made you more familiar with how one goes about determining the tax bill of a typical soldier and how the income sources, deductions, and credits come into play in Figure 7-1.

What Taxes Are Due if I Die in a Combat Zone? The Internal Revenue Code provides tax forgiveness for any member whose death results from service in a terrorist or military action. This tax forgiveness applies to income for the taxable year in which the member dies and for prior years that ended on or after the first day served in a combat zone. Furthermore, any tax liability outstanding against such a member at the time of death will be canceled or reduced. Make sure your spouse knows to check out this provision with the legal assistance officer in case of your death by including a note to this effect in the letter of instruction that should accompany your will (see chapter 21).

What if My Joint Return Is Due, and My Military Spouse Is Deployed to a Hazardous Duty Area? You still have to file by 15 April. In this case, you should have prepared a power of attorney prior to the deployment so that you could sign your spouse's name on the joint return. If you failed to do this, IRS Publication 3 states that you should simply attach a signed statement stating that your spouse cannot sign the joint return because he or she is serving in a combat zone or qualified hazardous duty area.

What Are the Tax Implications of IRA Savings? An Individual Retirement Account (IRA) is an individual savings plan that also offers unique tax benefits. Congress has introduced several types of IRAs over the years, but three types are of importance to military members: the traditional IRA, introduced in the early 1980s; the Roth IRA, introduced in 1997; and the education IRA. If you meet certain criteria of filing status and income level, then you may qualify to deduct part or all of your traditional IRA contribution from your taxable income. In a sense, a $2,000 contribution costs you only $1,400 if you are in the 15 percent tax bracket. When you withdraw the money, usually at retirement, some or all will be taxable. Unfortunately, this IRA is very inflexible and can only be used, in most cases, for retirement.

The Roth IRA is more flexible and a better choice for most military members. It is not tax deductible, meaning you do not reduce your taxable income by the contribution. You can, however, take your contributions out for first-time home purchases and to meet educational expenses. More importantly, your contributions grow tax deferred, which is the real benefit of contributing to a Roth IRA. In other words, you do not pay taxes on the interest, dividends, or capital gains income that your account generates during the year. Although this does not sound like much, as Figure 7-2 shows, the benefit can be significant. In the 15 percent tax bracket, an individual who invests $2,000 per year in an IRA will have nearly $1 million dollars by the age of sixty-two, compared to only $500,000 for the individual who did not invest in an IRA. (This assumes $2,000 invested per year with a 10 percent annual return.) When the Roth IRA funds are withdrawn, no taxes are paid since you funded the Roth with after-tax dollars.

The education IRA is tax deferred like the Roth IRA. Funds are contributed to this IRA for a designated minor (beneficiary) for the single purpose of saving money for college and graduate or professional schooling. The funds grow tax deferred but are not tax deductible. They must be used by the age of

Figure 7-2
Benefit of IRA Tax Deferred Growth

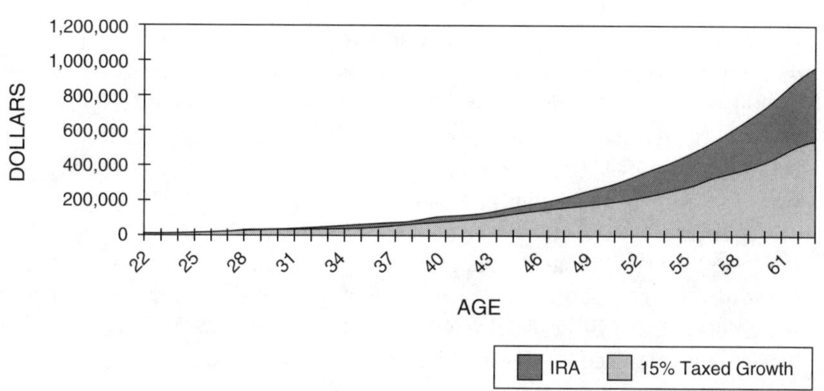

thirty by the beneficiary, or the education IRA balance will be taxed at the individual's normal tax rate. Prior to June 2001, $500 could be given each year to each beneficiary. The contribution maximum was raised to $2,000 per year at that time.

You may contribute to an IRA if you have taxable compensation during the year and are under the age of 70½. Prior to 2001, you were limited to contributing $2,000 per year or your annual income if it is less. In the same legislation that changed tax rates and repealed the estate tax in June 2001, Congress changed the rules to increase the IRA contribution maximums. You can contribute $3,000 per year from 2002 to 2004, $4,000 per year from 2005 to 2007, and $5,000 per year afterwards. Put these numbers into Figure 7-2, and you see that simply contributing the maximum to your Roth IRA over a lifetime will leave you fairly comfortable in your old age. Perhaps the only drawback to all versions of the IRA is that the Internal Revenue Code places a 10 percent penalty on top of normal taxes on early withdrawals. The earliest you can begin withdrawals is age 59½, except for the limited withdrawal reasons mentioned.

As an added incentive to save, your spouse may also contribute to a separate IRA, even if he or she does not work. Since 1997, the maximum contribution ($2,000 prior to June 2001) can be placed into each spouse's IRA annually, although your combined contributions can not exceed your combined taxable compensation for the year. This stipulation is in place only because some taxpayers manage to itemize deductions worth more than their annual income and avoid all federal taxes. Still, under the current rules, the IRAs are a tremendous way to reduce your tax liability or save for your future.

What about Additional Income? Servicemembers (or family members) running a business or earning nonwage income "on the side" will most likely have to report that income on Schedule C and pay a "double" Social Security tax on it (with Schedule SE). As a general rule, if you receive any income (except investment or rental income) on which taxes have not been withheld, you should check on the likely requirement to report it here. Failure to do so could result in serious consequences.

How Long Should I Keep the Old Returns? You should keep a copy of your tax return for a minimum of seven years. Along with your tax return, you should keep copies of any supporting documents. These include W-2 forms, 1099 forms, receipts, and mortgage records. If you make nondeductible contributions to your IRA, you should keep page 1 of Forms 1040 and 8606 until you withdraw those contributions beginning after age $59^1/_2$.

In this section, we have provided an overview of the rules governing federal taxes. However, our coverage has not been exhaustive. If you still have questions, your legal assistance officer, unit tax advisor, community services representative, and IRS officials can help you. Also, refer to the income tax aids listed in the references at the end of this chapter.

STATE TAXES

State tax codes change constantly, and they can be as complicated as the federal code. Before preparing your state taxes, you should check with your local legal assistance office or taxation authority in your state of legal residence. Contacting your state is now easier because most states have Internet sites that offer specific information and the necessary tax forms (see Appendix A).

Each state treats military compensation differently (see Figure 7-3). Seven states have no income tax. If you are a legal resident of one of these states, your income from any source will not be taxed. Many other states provide special breaks to servicemembers. For example, some do not tax military compensation at all while other states do not tax military pay if the servicemember is serving outside the state. The remaining states levy some form of tax on military income.

May I Change My Legal Residence? Military personnel can legally reduce state income tax by establishing their domicile of choice in a state that does not have an income tax. The servicemember must be able to show evidence of certain criteria for a change in domicile to be persuading to state tax authorities. If you are able to provide such evidence without extreme difficulty or large expenses, then you might want to consider doing so. However, tax authorities are alert for fraudulent domicile changes. Therefore, you should seek advice at your installation legal assistance office to ensure that your actions meet all of the legal requirements. They will discuss legal terms with you, including the definitions of *domicile* (or *legal residence*) and *residence.*

Residence. *Residence* is established in a state by residing in that state. Residence involves your physical presence or the presence of your living quarters for a period of time. When you are assigned to a service installation, you are usually a temporary resident of that state.

Domicile. *Legal residence,* which is synonymous with *domicile* and *home of record* for tax purposes, refers to the individual's permanent home for legal

Figure 7-3

State Tax Treatment of Military Compensation

No state income tax

Special breaks on military pay

Tax military pay

Source: *Military Tax Guide*, Supplement to the *Army Times*.

purposes. According to the Soldiers and Sailors Relief Act, servicemembers are subject to the tax laws in the state of their domicile. Everyone has only one legal residence at any given time. This legal residence may be in the state where a person was born—domicile of origin—or it may be a place he or she has chosen—domicile of choice. Once established, legal residence continues until legally changed. Legal residence changes only by a voluntary and positive action. A mere attempt or desire to make a change is not sufficient. As a rule, to acquire a domicile of choice you must meet the following three conditions concurrently:

1. Be physically present in the new state.
2. Have the intention of abandoning the former domicile.
3. Have the intention to remain in the new state indefinitely.

Once a person has established a legal residence in a particular state, a temporary absence does not cause that legal residence to change. Thus, it is possible for you to have a domicile in one state and a temporary residence in another.

Servicemembers can use some of the following as evidence of intent to establishing domicile of choice:

1. Place of birth.
2. Permanent place of abode.
3. Payment of state income taxes or intangible personal property taxes.
4. Registering to vote and voting by absentee ballot.
5. Obtaining a driver's license.
6. State from which you entered the military service.
7. Filing with state authorities an approved certificate or other statement indicating legal residence.

Once you have legally changed your domicile of choice using this information, contact your finance office. The finance office must adjust your state tax withholding and pay it to the proper state.

What Are Common Rules on State Tax Liabilities?

1. Your state of domicile may tax your service income and other income (such as dividends and interest), no matter how or where it is earned.

2. Your state of temporary residence may not tax military pay. However, your state of temporary residence (because of military orders) may tax any other income you or your family members derive from working or investing in that state.

3. Your state of temporary residence cannot tax your personal property located in the state. Your state of domicile could tax your personal property, but typically states do not tax personal property that is not physically in the state. Real estate is taxed where it is located.

4. For retirees, the state may tax your military pension only if it taxes other pensions in the same manner.

5. If you obtain your state automobile license tags from the state in which you are temporarily residing, check with your local legal assistance office. You may be exempted from paying certain fees.

What about Military Spouses?

Under current tax law, a spouse does not become a legal resident of the servicemember's state of domicile at the time of marriage. A spouse's income is normally taxed in the state in which it is earned—the state of residence. Consequently, military spouses will often have to file nonresident state income taxes with the state in which the family is stationed. Since the servicemember's state of domicile taxes the military income, it is possible for many military families to file tax forms in two or three states:

1. For the servicemember's income in the state of domicile.
2. For the spouse's income in state of temporary residence.
3. For the spouse's income in the spouse's state of domicile.

What Tax Savings Should I Always Look For?

Although each state's tax code is unique, here are some rules to look for that might reduce your tax burden. (Read the rules carefully because these are not offered in all states!)

1. Deduct your federal tax liability.
2. Deduct your property taxes.
3. Deduct interest and dividend income depending on the source of these earnings.

LOCAL TAXES

Typically, you will pay local taxes in a state of temporary residence only if you own real estate in the state. However, servicemembers may also be subject to local income or property taxes levied by town, county, or other local governments in whose jurisdiction their legal residence lies. If you are unsure, contact

Tips to Legally Save the Most on Your Taxes

- If you consistently receive large tax refunds, file a new W-4 to reduce withholding to match your tax liability and increase your monthly disposable income.
- Invest in an Individual Retirement Account annually to gain the benefit of tax-deferred growth and possibly a deduction on your income tax return.
- Make sure you take advantages of legitimate credits to reduce your tax bill.
- If you itemize deductions, be especially familiar with deductible items such as professional expenses (uniform pressing and AUSA), investment advice, charitable contributions, and mortgage interest. If these do not total more than 2.5 percent of your income, pay your dues and fees in advance every other year so you can deduct then.
- Pay attention to the capital gains on your mutual funds. Even though you do not cash in shares of your mutual fund, you may owe capital gains taxes on the fund even if your net asset value has decreased.
- If you owe taxes, file by 15 April to avoid paying the interest charges, even if you can get an automatic extension.
- If you will receive a refund, file as soon as possible.
- Keep your tax records for at least seven years.
- If you plan to change your state of domicile, seek advice at your installation legal assistance office to ensure that your actions meet all legal requirements.

local government clerks for information on income taxes that may be due while you are on active duty.

SUGGESTED REFERENCES

See the Internet sites listed in Appendix A.

The following IRS publications (available free from IRS publications centers and electronically from the Internet site) are particularly helpful:

- IRS Publication 3, *Tax Guide for Military Personnel.*
- IRS Publication 17, *Your Federal Income Tax.*
- IRS Publication 552, *Recordkeeping for Individuals.*
- IRS Publication 553, *Highlight of Tax Changes.*

Annual income tax supplement to the *Army, Navy,* and *Air Force Times,* published annually (typically in mid-February). It contains useful tax tips and information, including detailed information on state taxes.

Numerous personal finance periodicals such as *Money, Kiplinger's,* and the *Wall Street Journal* have special editions concerning taxes.

Software packages for preparing taxes include most forms for printing and transmitting returns directly to the IRS. These include Quicken, Turbotax, and Kiplinger's TaxCut.

Tax guides are also published by the J. K. Lasser Tax Institute, Prentice-Hall, Commerce Clearing House, and accounting firms such as Arthur Young and Price, Waterhouse.

PART III

Big-Ticket Items

8

Buying a Car

Most people in the United States consider an automobile a necessity. Your automobile is most likely one of the largest purchases you will ever make. Transportation is second only to housing in most household budgets. Therefore, making wise decisions when buying a car is critical to sound financial planning.

You are faced with a staggering array of vehicles and options from which to choose. Hundreds of models and thousands of option combinations are available. Finance, insurance, and maintenance decisions increase the complexity of your automobile purchase decision. Dealers' and manufacturers' sales incentives, rebates, price discounts, cut-rate financing, option bundles, and other enticements may confuse your purchase decision. Many consumers, bewildered by the available choices, make impulse buying decisions. The result is often a vehicle that destroys the household budget without meeting household needs. However, if you conduct research prior to shopping for an automobile, you will be more successful in selecting the car that is right for you and your lifestyle.

This chapter offers practical advice and identifies helpful references in your quest for an automobile, whether new, used, or leased. It will help you negotiate the maze of automobile decisions and devise a systematic plan to guide you through your automobile purchase choices. If you use the information in this chapter, you will be an informed consumer with the ability to get a good deal on an automobile that fulfills your transportation requirements and helps you toward your financial goals.

As you approach your automobile purchase, remember that the goal of all business is profit. It is every salesperson's goal to sell you something. Almost every decision you make in buying a new car will affect the amount you ultimately pay. Selecting options, negotiating the purchase price, determining the trade-in value, and financing and insuring your new car are all separate steps you must take *and understand* in order to get the best deal for you. Therefore, taking the time to systematically identify what is important to you, do some homework, and arm yourself with information before you visit the dealers' lots will pay off in this major purchase! (See Appendix A for useful guides and Internet sites referenced within this chapter.)

HOW MUCH CAN YOU AFFORD?

It is very important to begin your car-buying process with a solid idea of how much you are willing to spend each month for transportation, realizing your monthly payments are only a portion of the total monthly cost. Insurance, operating expenses, and maintenance add to the total bill. A good rule of thumb is to spend no more than 15 percent of your pretax income for transportation. To estimate your monthly transportation expenses, you must make estimates for the various expenses associated with automobile ownership. Therefore, your first step should be determining the amount of your monthly budget to allot to transportation expenses. You should always consider the opportunity cost of your purchase decisions (see chapter 2). Your household budget (see chapter 4) is a useful tool to test how increased spending on transportation affects your consumption of other goods. The automobile you buy will be the result of many trade-offs.

Gathering Cost Information

Payments. Automobile payments will be the largest outlay in most transportation budgets. Table 8-1 shows the monthly payments per $1,000 financed at various interest rates for twenty-four, thirty-six, forty-eight, and sixty months. To use these tables, 1) determine the amount you plan to finance after making your down payment; 2) select a payment period shorter than the time you expect to own the automobile; and 3) select the interest rate corresponding to that which banks or credit unions offer for car loans. The amount below the interest rate will be very close to your monthly payments per $1,000 financed. Multiply this number by the amount, in thousands of dollars, you plan to finance. This will give you a close estimate of your monthly automobile payment. For example, to finance a $15,000 automobile purchase for four years at a 10 percent interest rate (assuming no down payment) would result in a monthly payment very close to $380 (15 × 25.36 = $380.40).

Your monthly payment consists of two components: principal and interest. The principal portion of the payment is really paying for the car; the interest portion is paying for the loan. This process of paying off the loan is known as amortizing the loan. That is, the bank charges you interest each month, at a stated rate, for the amount of money you still owe. The rest of your payment goes to "pay down" the amount of the loan, called the principal balance.

In the above example, we borrowed $15,000 from the bank at a 10 percent interest rate with monthly payments of $380. Determining how much of this monthly payment is interest versus principal is simple. First, calculate the interest portion by multiplying the amount you owe the bank by the monthly interest rate (annual interest rate ÷ 12 months). In our example, a 10 percent annual interest rate divided by twelve months equals a monthly interest rate of 0.008333 (0.10 ÷ 12 = 0.008333). For our first month's payment, multiplying 0.008333 by the $15,000 that you borrowed from the bank shows that you must pay $125 in interest. The remaining $255 of your monthly payment is applied toward the principal. Subtracting $255 from the original $15,000 loan balance, leaves a new balance of $14,745. In the second month, $122.87 (0.008333 times the principal balance of $14,745) is paid in interest and $257.13 is applied toward the principal. The portion of your payments dedicated to interest decreases over time, while the portion dedicated to principal increases. Table 8-2 illustrates the principal and payments for each month. A loan calculator, spreadsheet program, and some financial software packages also can create a loan payment table that reflects principal and interest payments for each month to help you better understand your payments.

TABLE 8-1
MONTHLY PAYMENTS (PER $1,000) FOR A 24-MONTH LOAN

Rate	4%	5%	6%	7%	8%	9%	10%	11%	12%
24 months	$43.42	$43.87	$44.32	$44.77	$45.22	$45.68	$46.14	$46.61	$47.07
36 months	29.52	29.97	30.42	30.88	31.34	31.80	32.27	32.74	33.21
48 months	22.58	23.03	23.49	23.95	24.41	24.89	25.36	25.85	26.33
60 months	18.42	18.87	19.33	19.80	20.28	20.76	21.25	21.74	22.24

TABLE 8-2
MONTHLY PAYMENTS (INTEREST VS. PRINCIPAL)
FOR A $15,000 LOAN AT A 10% ANNUAL INTEREST RATE

Month	Payment	Interest	Principal	Remaining Principal
First	$380	$125.00	$255.00	$14,745.00
Second	380	122.87	257.13	14,487.87
Third	380	120.73	259.27	14,228.60
Fourth	380	118.57	261.43	13,967.17
Twelfth (1 year)	380	100.62	279.38	11,795.73

Insurance. Insurance costs vary significantly depending on several factors, including the age and driving record of the person insured, the age of the automobile, automobile safety characteristics, insurance coverage limits, use of the automobile, miles driven per year, and automobile location. The USAA Foundation publishes (at no charge) *The Car Guide,* which compares the safety features of most models, as do other companies. This guide helps identify automobiles that have desirable insurance characteristics such as passenger safety in accidents, less damage in accidents, and lower theft rates. *Consumer Reports* also publishes two annual buying guides in April, the *New Car Buying Guide* and the *Used Car Buying Guide,* that review reliability records and safety test reports, or you may subscribe online. Your insurance company will gladly give you quotes on the two or three models you are considering buying so that you can accurately estimate your total monthly transportation expenses. A monthly insurance payment of $100 could be (but may not be) a realistic estimate for full insurance coverage on a new $15,000 car. You must be aware that most lenders require full coverage (comprehensive and liability) on cars that you have financed. The next chapter explains in more detail the various types of automobile insurance available and coverage guidelines.

Operation. Operating expenses consist primarily of fuel charges. Annual operating expenses will vary significantly depending on the gas mileage of the car you choose. The typical automobile owner in the United States drives 1,000 miles each month. Calculate your operating expenses by dividing the number of miles you expect to drive by the miles per gallon (MPG) rating of your automobile. This gives you the number of gallons of fuel you will use each month. Multiply the number of gallons you expect to use monthly by the price you expect to pay per gallon to get an estimate of your monthly operating expenses. For example, if you plan to drive 1,000 miles per month, get 25 MPG, and expect to pay $1.50 per gallon for gas, monthly operating expenses would be $60 ([1,000 miles ÷ 25 MPG] × $1.50 = $60). New cars include an estimated annual fuel expenditure that can serve as a general basis for comparison.

Other annual costs for most car owners are the annual vehicle registration and inspection fees. Many states require an annual automobile emissions inspection in order to have a valid vehicle registration for that year. Costs vary widely within the United States from $50 to over $100, depending on where you live.

Maintenance. Maintenance expenses include the cost of scheduled maintenance, such as fluid changes, as well as replacing worn-out and damaged parts. Maintenance costs vary depending on the items covered under warranty or coverage bought under a separate maintenance contract. For the first several years, monthly maintenance costs for a new car should be low. Annual maintenance costs during the fifth year, however, are expected easily to triple those in the first year. The average maintenance costs over a five-year period are likely to be about $20 per month or more. Actual repair costs, of course, will vary depending on the specific model and your use of the car. The *Consumer Reports Annual Buying Guide* makes current estimates for average maintenance expenses and provides useful information concerning specific problems with various models.

Depreciation. The average consumer keeps a car for approximately thirty-four months. Depreciation is how much resale value a car loses each year. In other words, it is the decrease in the value of an automobile due to time and use. It is an implicit cost of automobile ownership. Many automobile owners ignore depreciation because they do not write a monthly check to pay for it, yet it is one of the largest expenses of automobile ownership. Table 8-3 provides one example of a typical depreciation schedule. It shows that a $15,000 automobile depreciates by over 60 percent in five years. For example, the owner could sell the car for $8,128 after three years, but after four years he could sell it for only $6,909. In essence, the owner has paid $1,219 to use the car during that year. Notice that with depreciation a one-year-old car is worth $11,250; however, according to Table 8-2, you would still owe approximately $11,796 principal on your loan. If you were to have a wreck or decide to trade in your car for a new one, you would owe more to your bank than the insurance payoff or trade-in value.

TABLE 8-3
DEPRECIATION SCHEDULE/RESALE VALUE

Automobile Age	Value	% Change	Annual Depreciation
New	$15,000		
One year old	11,250	25	$3,750
Two years old	9,562	15	1,688
Three years old	8,128	15	1,434
Four years old	6,909	15	1,219
Five years old	5,872	15	1,037
Total depreciation (years 0–5)			9,128
Remaining depreciation (years 6–?)			5,872

Depreciation varies considerably across makes and models. New automobiles depreciate much faster than used automobiles; thus, depreciation expenses decrease as automobiles get older. As a rule of thumb, automobiles lose 25 percent of their purchase value in the first year and 15 percent of the remaining value each following year. Models with excellent maintenance and resale records will generally hold their value better than average cars. *Kelley's Blue Book* and the *NADA Official Used Car Guide* are good sources for determining depreciation, providing average resale values by model, make, condition of the vehicle, year, and location (see their Internet sites listed in Appendix A). *Kelley's Blue Book* is more liberal in its quotes; therefore, most dealers will utilize the *NADA Official Used Car Guide* when determining the value of a trade-in vehicle.

An often overlooked aspect of depreciation concerns the time during the model year when consumers buy their new car. Base car wholesale prices change little over a model year, which usually runs from 1 October to 30 September. The used-car market, however, bases depreciation on calendar years.

Therefore, in 2002, a new 2001 automobile bought in the fall of 2000 will be worth very nearly the same as the same automobile bought late in 2001 (if their mileage and condition are similar). An automobile bought late in a model year depreciates much more rapidly than the same automobile bought early in that model year. Dealers will typically offer sizable discounts on "old" models to make room for the new models on their lots. Keep this point in mind, especially if you are considering the purchase of last year's model after new car models have been introduced. If you plan on owning the car for the entire length of the loan, then buying at the end of the model year may be a wise economical decision. However, if you plan on selling or trading in the car within a couple of years, then you should be aware of the effects of depreciation on your long-term financial planning.

Total Expenses

Having determined your transportation budget and gathered the cost data for owning an automobile, you can now determine the price of a car that you can afford. For example, assume your monthly transportation budget is $450, based on 15 percent of a $3,000 pretax income (0.15 × $3,000 = $450), you have about $2,500 for initial costs, and you can finance your car at a 10 percent interest rate for forty-eight months. You have made the following expense estimates for the model you are considering:

Transportation budget	$ 450
Less insurance	– $ 100
Less operation	– $ 60
Less maintenance	– $ 10
Maximum payment	$ 280

This leaves you $280 per month for automobile payments. From Table 8-1, you see that it will cost $25.36 for each $1,000 financed over a forty-eight-month period. You can thus afford to finance $11,041 ([$280 ÷ $25.36] × $1,000 = $11,041).

With your $2,500 available cash and the knowledge that you can afford to finance $11,041, you may erroneously believe you can afford a car valued at $13,541 ($2,500 + $11,041). Before you make any decision, first you must consider the "hidden" automobile purchase expenses of tax, title, and registration. These costs differ according to the location (county and state) where you reside; however, in most cases this initial expense will be at least $1,000. No matter where you buy your car, you will pay the tax rate of the county/state where you register your car and receive your license plate. You can estimate these costs more accurately by calling your local vehicle registration/tax assessor office and asking for a quote.

Therefore, subtracting $1,000 from your available $2,500, leaves you $1,500 to make a down payment. You could afford a car that retails for about $12,541 ($11,041 + $1,500). Your actual expenses will obviously vary from this example, but as you can see, a $450-a-month transportation budget will not finance a new $30,000 car. Be realistic about how far your limited transportation budget will take you.

Should You Buy a Used Car?

Should you consider a used car rather than a new car? You have undoubtedly noticed that in most cases new cars are much more expensive to own and operate than used cars (when accounting for all costs discussed above). Buying a used car can be an economically sound decision and help contribute to your long-term financial future. If you are unwilling to make a large down payment or a large monthly payment, a used car may be for you. Often a good bet is to buy a used car that is one or two years old. In this case the bulk of the depreciation has already occurred and yet the car mileage (and subsequent wear and tear on the car) is relatively low. Previously leased cars whose mileage was restricted during the lease may be good candidates for purchases. This may also be attractive to buyers who prefer up-to-date models and styling, but otherwise cannot afford the latest models.

TABLE 8-4
TYPICAL AUTOMOBILE OPERATING COSTS*

	1st Year	2nd Year	3rd Year	4th Year	5th Year
Depreciation	$3,750	$1,688	$1,434	$1,219	$1,037
Insurance	1,200	1,100	1,000	900	800
Interest costs	1,500	1,125	956	813	691
Operation	720	720	720	720	720
Maintenance	80	110	190	240	280
Total costs	$7,250	$4,743	$4,300	$3,892	$3,528

*Based on a new purchase price of $15,000 and borrowing at 10%.

There are basic expense trade-offs between new and used cars. Depreciation and insurance are more expensive for newer cars; maintenance is more expensive for older, higher-mileage cars. Consider your maintenance aptitude and your tolerance for car trouble when making this decision. Table 8-4 illustrates these trade-offs, but it does not account for the inconvenience or major repairs that a used car may entail.

If you are considering buying a used car, you should compare the costs of new and used cars by constructing a table similar to Table 8-3. Estimate the depreciation and operating costs using the techniques previously described in this chapter. Insurance costs (see chapter 9) will decline as the appraised value of the automobile declines. For these comparisons, annual interest costs should be based on the amount you will owe each year, assuming that you are financing your purchase. The car's market value times the interest rate is a good proxy for your annual interest cost. For example, if you borrow at 10 percent, the interest cost for the first year is $1,500 (0.10 × $15,000). The interest cost for the second year is $1,125 (0.10 × $11,250 [$15,000 less $3,750, or 25 percent depreciation the first year]). To get a more exact interest cost for each year, you can use a spreadsheet or financial calculator, or contact a bank or other lender.

To estimate the cost of a used car, simply use the column that represents the age of the used car. For the example shown in the table, a three-year-old car would have annual costs of about $4,300. The annual operating expenses for a three-year-old car are 59 percent ($4,300 ÷ $7,250 = 0.59, or 59 percent) of those for a similar new car. Differences of this magnitude between the costs of owning new and used cars are typical.

Once you have made these calculations to compare the cost of buying a new versus a used car, you will probably find that on an exclusively financial basis, a used car will be less expensive. Consider your budget, preferences, lifestyle, and uses for your car to determine whether the added expense of a new car is worth it for you. The point is not that you should necessarily always buy a new or a used car, but that you should use the financial tools available to you to accurately determine the cost of your decision.

HOW SHOULD YOU FINANCE THE CAR?

Once you've decided how much you can afford and whether to purchase a new or used car, the next decision is how to finance your purchase. Most servicemembers have three choices: self-financing (paying cash), borrowing (getting a loan), or leasing. Your choice will depend primarily on your personal financial situation.

You should research financing arrangements before you begin to car shop. Arranging your financing in advance serves a threefold purpose. First, it helps you determine the car price range that fits your transportation budget. Second, it gives you more control over your purchase decision. You will have a financing alternative rather than being dependent on the financing arrangements offered by the automobile dealer. And third, you'll be able to recognize a good deal if the dealer offers one.

Self-Financing

You are to be congratulated if you have saved enough to pay cash for your new car. Even if you plan to pay cash for your car, there is still a financing cost of sorts. This financing cost is the opportunity cost (forgone interest) of the money you spend. If your money was in a money market account earning 7.5 percent interest and your marginal tax rate is 15 percent, your opportunity cost (financing cost) is 6.375 percent (0.075 × [1 – 0.15]). Self-financing is an excellent method of buying an automobile; it is very difficult to get a consumer loan at a lower rate of interest than the opportunity cost of your investments. Self-financing is an even better method if you have the discipline to pay yourself back. To do this, you should calculate payments that include both principal and interest. Select a reasonable loan period and make monthly payments back to your savings. With self-financing, it is hard to go wrong.

Car Loans

Most Americans borrow money to pay for their cars. As discussed in chapter 6, car loans are a correct use of credit since you pay off the debt as you use the bought asset. Financing your automobile purchase involves several decisions. Having determined the amount you will borrow, you must decide the source and duration of the loan. Your decisions in each of these areas will affect your credit costs, both the total interest you will pay and the amount of your monthly payments. Careful evaluation of various sources of auto loans will help you reduce credit costs while making monthly payments that fit your budget. Financing sources often have loan terms that obscure the actual cost of borrowing money. When shopping for financing, your actual cost of borrowing money is an important consideration. By law, all lenders must provide you with a rate of interest based on a standardized calculation. This rate of interest is the annual percentage rate (APR). Keep your eye on the APR. Without making your own detailed calculations, it is the most useful method of comparing the cost of different loans.

The two primary sources for borrowing money are dealer financing or a third-party loan. Dealer financing is when the car manufacturer lends you money to buy its car. Car dealers often advertise below-market-interest-rate loans or cash-back rebates to attract customers to their products. Timing is often a factor in these promotions. At the end of a model year, dealerships must move the old inventory to make room for the new models. Some American automobile manufacturers have even offered 0 percent financing and $0 down payment in recent years. If you are debating between the rebate offer and a lower interest rate, you should consider the long-term financial implications of a lower interest rate. Dealer financing can be a good deal, but check with banks or credit unions to see if you can get the same interest rate. If this is possible, you can choose the cash-back rebate from the dealer and finance through a third party for the same low interest rate. Be aware that dealers often are less willing to negotiate prices when they offer attractive financing.

A third-party loan is when you borrow money from a bank or credit union to buy your car. These institutions are potentially excellent sources from which to secure automobile financing. First, your credit institution should treat you well. Car loans are one of their primary businesses, and they want to maintain good relationships with their customers. Second, it is convenient to have your car loan directly paid from your allotment or direct deposit. Some banks and credit unions offer a discounted loan rate if you have your car payment automatically deducted from your military pay. Third, they are more likely to explain your credit options in detail. Finally, they can provide you with detailed value estimates (wholesale and retail) for both your used car and the new car you plan to buy. You should apply to your bank or credit union for a loan at least seven days before you begin to shop for your automobile. This allows adequate time to process your loan application and will ensure that the money is ready when you need it.

Another alternative for homeowners is using a home equity line of credit. Homeowners who have enough equity in their home can borrow against their equity rather than taking out a third-party loan or using dealer financing. The advantage of this financing option is that the interest on this loan may be tax deductible when filing your federal income taxes.

Having decided the source of financing, the next major decision is the term, or duration, of the loan. Most lending institutions finance new cars for thirty-six, forty-eight, or sixty months. Most lenders finance used cars for twenty-four months and occasionally for thirty-six months. The trade-off is clear. Longer-term loans have lower monthly payments, but you will ultimately pay more in interest. Shorter-term loans have higher monthly payments, but you pay the loan down faster, thus paying less in interest.

Consider the following example. You want to borrow $10,000 of your new-car purchase. After shopping around, the best deal you can find is a bank that offers the following loan schedule: thirty-six months at 8 percent, forty-eight months at 10 percent, or sixty months at 12 percent. Your payments under the various terms are shown in Table 8-5.

TABLE 8-5
FINANCING UNDER VARIOUS LOAN TERMS

	Loan Duration		
	36 Mo.	**48 Mo.**	**60 Mo.**
Monthly payments	$313	$254	$222
Total principal payments	10,000	10,000	10,000
Total interest payments	1,281	2,174	3,347
Total payment to bank	11,281	12,174	13,347

As you can see, your monthly payments are smaller, but you end up paying the bank an additional $2,066 in interest for the privilege of stretching out the payments from thirty-six to sixty months.

Another consideration when deciding the loan duration is the value of the car in relationship to the amount owed on the loan. The longer the loan period, the slower the loan is amortized. Because automobiles depreciate very rapidly when they are new, cars may depreciate faster than a long-term loan is amortized. As a result, it is possible for you to receive less on a trade-in (or from insurance if your car is stolen or destroyed) than the outstanding balance on your loan. In the automobile business this is called being "upside down" or "financially inverted."

For example, assume you borrow $10,000 for forty-eight months at 10 percent interest to buy an automobile, but you have a wreck after one year and the car is totaled. On average, the car would have been worth $7,500 after one year, and you could expect the insurance company to pay you that amount. However, the principal balance on the loan would be $7,830.18, so you would have to write the bank a check for $330.18 to clear the loan. If you had financed the car for thirty-six months, the remaining principal would be only $6,992.57. In this case the check from the insurance company would allow you to pay off the loan and still apply $507.43 toward a new car. The lesson here is that besides costing you less in interest over the period, loans of shorter duration reduce the risk of having the value of your asset fall below the loan principal. You should shop for automobile financing as diligently as you shop for your automobile. If you ignore financing alternatives, you can easily squander the money you saved through careful research of dealer cost information and skillful negotiations.

Leasing

In recent years, leasing an automobile has become an increasingly popular way to meet transportation needs. Leasing can be an attractive option because it allows you to "drive more car for your money." Leasing is similar to renting a car on a long-term basis. Monthly payments are lower than they would be for buying the same car because you are paying not for any equity in the car. You are paying only for the depreciation you use and the interest for the "loan," since you do not pay the entire depreciation up front. Although monthly payments are lower, the disadvantage of leasing is that at the end of the contract you own nothing. Over the long run, leasing will invariably be more expensive than buying a car. With leasing you drive newer cars, more often, when cars depreciate most rapidly.

Car manufacturers have been aggressively marketing leases for the last several years. You often see advertisements for "$299 a month with no money down." This is not necessarily the case. You will normally pay a security deposit equal to the first and last monthly payments. There could be an additional "acquisition fee" ranging from $250 to $700 for the financing whether you use dealer financing or a bank loan. You must also pay taxes and title and registration fees either up front or as an addition to your monthly payments. The actual check you write to cover a "$299 a month" payment may be well over $450. Protect yourself by reading the fine print. Be careful to understand all expenses, including additional insurance requirements, before signing a leasing agreement.

Leasing an automobile can be a sound financial choice for some people. Whether or not you are a good lease candidate depends on your car preferences, personal driving habits, and financial situation. A lease candidate is someone who fits the following profile:

- Wants to drive a new car every two to four years.
- Drives less than 12,000 miles per year.
- Wants a smaller monthly payment.
- Takes good care of his or her car.
- Wants to drive a more expensive car than he or she could afford to buy.
- Does not want the hassle of selling or trading in a used car.

Depending on the terms of the lease, you are responsible for all scheduled maintenance during the lease period. Most leases have a stipulation stating the maximum number of miles the lessor allows during the lease period. If you exceed the limit, you must pay a penalty of perhaps 15 cents per mile.

Today, lease contracts are closed-ended. Closed-ended leases are those for which you have no financial responsibilities other than scheduled maintenance and monthly payments. At the end of the lease, you return the automobile to the leasing company. Normal wear and tear is acceptable; however, excess mileage and/or wear and tear on the vehicle may be an additional expense to the consumer.

Depending on your budget, preferences, and personal situation, leasing can be a sound decision. As with all major purchases, careful research will help you get the most for your money.

WHAT CAR SHOULD YOU BUY?

After determining your monthly transportation budget, you can eliminate automobiles that are too expensive. A good strategy is to reduce your transportation alternatives to two or three before you visit a dealer's lot and become wowed by all of the showroom glitter and the new car smells! Today you can do research almost exclusively on the Internet or at your local library on car types, safety records, options, financing, and insurance to make you an informed consumer.

Transportation Requirements

Your most important transportation decisions revolve around function, economy, comfort, and style. You should select your automobile not only on your current needs, but also based on your projected needs while you expect to own the vehicle. Allow for possible relocation and changes in family size. The previous discussion of new-car depreciation shows that it is very expensive to sell a new car after only a year or two.

Comparative analysis is a useful technique for comparing the overall benefits of several automobiles with different features and for analyzing your purchase decision in advance. A simple but effective comparative analysis technique is to create a simple table listing the automobile features important to you. Table 8-6 identifies several features that are important to many buyers and illustrates a possible range of weights across features. The USAA Automobile Pricing/Auto Purchase Service (800-531-8905) offers a free brochure titled *How to Buy a Car,* which identifies important functional areas. *Consumer Reports Auto Guides* also explains and ranks automobiles in these categories to give you an idea of what these categories entail. Evaluate your three final candidates with regard to each feature and rank order them (3 to 1 from best to worst). Multiply the rank by the weight, and record the result on the chart. Total the column for each candidate. The model with the highest sum is the one that comes closest to meeting your overall transportation requirements.

TABLE 8-6
AUTOMOBILE COMPARATIVE ANALYSIS

Feature or Characteristic	Weight*	Car A	Car B	Car C
Matches functional needs	3			
Depreciation history	2			
Fuel efficiency	2			
Insurance costs	1			
Model maintenance history	1			
Manufacturer reputation	1			
Comfort	2			
Handling	1			
Performance	1			
Style	1			
Safety record	3			
Low price	3			
Total				

*You should adjust these weights based on your preferences.

The nice thing about this method is that it forces you to compare the characteristics of your top three models. You should set up your own comparative analysis system by determining and weighing the characteristics that are important to you. The key is to set up and use a comparative analysis that reflects your personal automobile preferences. Remember: Analyze your automobile needs before you begin to shop. Your analysis will help you navigate through the myriad of automobile choices and select one that best satisfies your transportation desires.

Optional Equipment. Carefully selecting optional equipment for your new automobile helps ensure that the automobile meets your functional, economical, comfort, and style needs. You should decide what options are important to you before you ever visit a dealer's lot. Again, the Internet is an excellent source for comparing options. Most automobile manufacturers have websites that allow you to compare and price options. Options increase the cost, utility, style, and resale value of an automobile. Your most important option choices include engine, transmission, air conditioning, and power windows, doors, and locks. An automatic transmission and air conditioning add to the resale value of an automobile. Thus, you are able to recoup some of your costs when you sell the vehicle. Air bags, antilock brakes, and security alarms will decrease your insurance costs. Most other options do little to enhance the utility, style, or resale value of your automobile. The more options your automobile has, the more likely it will require frequent minor repairs. Today, 90 percent of the cars sold in the United States have automatic transmissions, and 75 percent have air conditioning, power brakes, power steering, and stereos. Some simple guidelines can help you make your option selections:

- Select only the options you want. Make your option decisions before you visit a dealer.
- Consider options that increase convenience, durability, and resale value. Shop for a model that includes most of the options you want as standard equipment. Most models have various versions (i.e., LT, LS, LX) with different standard equipment. Manufacturer websites often illustrate and compare the standard equipment and available options. Standard equipment will decrease your overall cost, because dealers have a higher markup on options.
- Consider waiting for a special-order car that has only the options you want. An overloaded model on the dealer's lot may be available immediately, but it will cost more.
- Be aware of dealer-installed options. Dealer-installed air conditioning is usually inferior in quality to factory-installed air conditioning. Options such as fabric protection, paint protection, and rust protection are available from independent sources at a fraction of the cost you will pay a dealer. Dealer markup for these options is enormous.
- Determine how long you intend to own the car and how many miles you expect to drive when considering an extended service warranty. Most basic warranties last approximately three years; however, read the fine print on what an extended warranty will provide after the existing warranty expires.

HOW CAN YOU GET THE BEST DEAL?

Buying from a Dealer

Do your homework if you plan to buy from an automobile dealer. Know exactly what model and options you want. Research the dealer cost for both the base price of the model and the options you want. Have a financing plan. Shop several dealers so that you are more likely to get a fair deal.

There are several advantages to buying from a dealer rather than ordering the car from the factory. First, there is very little time delay in getting the car you want. If it is not on their lot, most dealers can locate the car you want and execute a dealer trade within a few days. Second, you can see and thoroughly inspect the actual vehicle that you will be getting. Third, the dealer from whom you buy your automobile is likely to be more responsive to maintenance problems after the sale.

There are a couple of disadvantages to buying from a dealer, however. First, it is very possible that the available car that most closely meets your needs will have undesired, costly options. Second, you need to know which car you want and how much you are willing to pay for it before you start negotiating with a dealer whose goal is to sell his or her existing inventory and make a profit.

You can also factory order a new car from a dealer. Dealers would much rather sell you a car off their lot, because they get the profit immediately. An advantage of ordering your new car from a dealer is that you get and pay only for the options you want. A disadvantage is that you will have to wait from four to six weeks for delivery. Also, you cannot inspect the car before you sign a purchase contract.

Dealer Cost versus Retail Cost

Dealer cost (sometimes referred to as the invoice price) is the amount that a dealer pays the factory for an automobile plus gas, oil, advertising, and floor plan. Floor plan is the interest (probably about 1 percent per month) dealers pay banks on the money they use to buy vehicles displayed on their lots.

The difference between dealer cost and sticker price is dealer profit. You can determine dealer cost by reviewing a new copy of *Edmund's New Car Prices* at your library or by accessing it at one of the Internet sites listed in Appendix A. These references provide separate profit estimates for the base car and options. For example, the profit (as a percentage of price) on the base car might be 15 percent. The percentage of profit on the options might be 17.5 percent. On an average $15,000 car, the cost breakdown of the retail price might be as follows (ignoring floor plan, a cost that varies with time):

Dealer cost of base car	$10,646
Dealer profit on base car	$1,879
Dealer cost of options	$1,650
Dealer profit on options	$350
Gas, oil, advertising	$100
Freight	$375
Retail price	$15,000

Here the total dealer profit is $2,229. Let's see how you can estimate dealer cost from a sticker price of $15,000. Subtract the cost of gas, oil, advertising, and freight ($15,000 - $100 - $375 = $14,525). This gives you the retail price of the car including options. You can split this amount between the base price of the car and the total cost of the options. Here the sticker shows that the base price of the car was $12,525 and the total price of the options was $2,000. Profit on the base car is 15 percent. Thus, the dealer cost is 85 percent of retail, or $10,646 ($12,525 × 0.85 = $10,646). The profit on options is 17.5 percent. Thus, dealer cost is 82.5 percent on the options, or $1,650 ($2,000 × .0825 = $1,650). The retail price of the car plus options minus the dealer cost for the car plus options leaves a dealer profit of $2,229 ($14,525 – $10,646 – $1,650 = $2,229). Your goal when negotiating your new-car purchase is to reduce the amount of dealer profit as much as possible. The dealer's goal when he sells you a new car is to make as much profit as possible.

Remember, taxes and tags (license plates and registration) will add another $1,000 or so to the purchase price. This amount, with a down payment of about 10 percent, or $1,500, will result in an initial cash outlay of about $2,500 for a $15,000 car.

Dealing with a Dealer

If you decide to buy your car from a dealer, there are several things you must be concerned about and familiar with before you see the dealer. From the moment you set foot on the lot or in the showroom, you will undergo a battle of wits and several stages of negotiations with the dealer.

Negotiating with a dealer will be a matter of your personality type. There are any number of books and guides that will help you in developing your negotiating plan. Additionally, there are some things you can do to enhance your position before the negotiations begin. Timing, for example, is a significant indirect negotiating tool.

There are times when dealers are more favorable to making good deals than others. Dealers typically have monthly and quarterly sales targets. Frequently, dealers have bonuses tied to these targets and will be more likely to negotiate near the end of the period. Dealers are also more likely to make a good deal when business is slow. More customers shop for cars on weekends than during the week; therefore, midweek may be a better time to shop than on weekends. Also, some dealers have a bonus for the first sale made on a weekend, so Saturday morning may be a good time to deal as well. Weather also affects the number of customers. You are more likely to get a good deal when rain or snow keeps most shoppers away. Winter is simply not a time when most customers shop for cars. This makes it an ideal time for the bargain hunter. Automobile dealers are more likely to offer deals during and after the Christmas season for several reasons. There are fewer automobile customers during the holiday season because people are spending money for other things and do not have the cash available for down payments. Dealerships are also trying to cut year-end inventory for tax purposes. Also, as previously mentioned, summer may be a good time because dealers are trying to clear their inventory of last year's models to make room for the new models that arrive in the fall.

Location is also often a factor in getting the best deal for you. Automobile prices reflect the supply and demand in the area. Basic economics shows us that when demand is greater, prices are greater. Shop around—this can also be done on the Internet. A few hours' drive may be worth a couple thousand dollars in savings for you.

How do you know if you are getting a good deal from a dealer? Do your homework. You should use a pricing or buying service (discussed below) to determine the actual dealer cost of the car you want and to get a price quote. If a dealer cannot beat the buying service price, you may not be getting a good deal. You are getting a very good deal from a dealer if his price is near or below the pricing service quote.

Many car dealerships are honest businesses with an ethical sales force. You must watch for the ones that are not. The point of this section is to help you understand that you are dealing with experienced professionals who are adept at turning your money into dealer profit. Only human imagination limits the techniques automobile sales representatives use to sell cars. Some dealerships train their sales representatives to pass you off to another representative or the sales manager if they cannot sell you a car. You will usually negotiate your deal with a salesperson, and then he or she will try to get you into the closing room. There, the closer, whose specialty is writing sales contracts, will write up the deal. Sometimes the closer will intentionally manipulate the cost, trade-in, down payment, and financing numbers to confuse the customer. Customer confusion can equal dealer profit. Once the purchase order is written, the closer will try to add unnecessary, high-profit options, fabric protection, rust proofing, floor mats, dealer warranties, and even insurance. The closer must then present the purchase order to the sales manager for his approval and signature. Passing you off from person to person reduces your resistance to buying and creates confusion. Each person in the process tries to sell you additional options you do not want, change the terms of the deal, and get more money from you. Remember, these professionals have closed hundreds of sales transactions.

The following are some general guidelines that will be helpful if you decide to negotiate your new-car purchase with a dealer:

- Know what model automobile and what options you want, and have your financing prearranged, before you go to a dealer's lot with the intention of buying.
- Let the dealer know you are a serious buyer. You should be ready to buy a car if you get the deal you want. Say to him, "I will buy a car today if you have the car and deal I want."
- Keep the four major parts of the automobile purchase transaction separate. It is too confusing to discuss your trade-in, down payment, and financing while you are trying to negotiate the purchase price of a new car. Make each an

independent transaction: first, negotiate price, then trade-in, and finally down payment and financing. Tell the salesman, "We can discuss my trade-in and financing when we have agreed on the total sale price."

- If necessary, let the dealer know that you have done your homework. Tell him, "I know your cost for this car." When you confront a dealer with this information, he will often try to tell you that your information is outdated or incorrect. Do not allow him to convince you that you are wrong. Your cost estimate will be very close. Besides, you can always buy your new car from the buying service that provided you with the price quote.
- If you do not get the deal you want, tell the dealer that you think you can get a better deal by shopping around. Dealers hate to hear those words. Record the terms of the deal offered on the back of the dealer's business card.
- After you have negotiated a satisfactory deal with a dealer, do not allow him or another dealer representative to reopen negotiations.
- Make sure that the purchase contract or sales order lists exactly the car and options you want and that it stipulates that no dealer-installed equipment will be substituted for factory-installed options.
- If you order your car from the factory, make sure that the sales contract states in writing that the order is contingent on timely delivery within four to six weeks.
- Do not sign a purchase order or sales contract that has blank spaces. Write "N/A" in blank spaces before signing.
- Do not sign a sales contract or purchase agreement unless you have read every word. Question the dealer on any point that you do not fully understand. Remember, confusion on your part almost certainly means more dealer profit.
- Make sure that the sales manager or an officer of the dealership signs the purchase order or sales contract. Many dealerships will not honor a contract signed only by a sales representative.
- Domestic cars include dealer preparation charges in the basic list price. Dealer preparation charges for imported cars are separate from the list price. Make sure that the purchase order or sales contract is clear if there is a separate charge for dealer preparation. Watch out for extra dealer preparation charges and for unwanted dealer-installed options. Dealers sometimes charge customers for dealer preparations that they did not perform and attempt to add high-profit, dealer-installed options to purchase orders or sales contracts.
- Make sure your purchase order or sales contract records your deposit. The contract should have a stipulation that the deposit is refundable if the dealership does not meet the terms of the contract.
- If you have a trade-in, be sure that the purchase order or sales contract records its value.
- Any verbal promise from the sales representative must be explicitly written on the purchase order or sales contract if you expect the dealership to honor it.

Using an Automobile Pricing or Buying Service

If, like many Americans, you find the process of buying a new car difficult, expensive, and frustrating, a buying service will reduce the time and energy you spend searching for a car, and perhaps save you a considerable amount of money. Buying services allow you to order exactly the car you want equipped with only the options you want. You will pay the service a predetermined fee above dealer cost; with some models the fee is a fixed dollar amount, and with others it is a percentage above the dealer cost. In our example we will use a predetermined fee of 1.5 percent above dealer cost on the base car and options. The result is that you save over $2,000, as calculated below:

Dealer cost of base car	$10,646
Dealer cost of options	$1,650
Total wholesale cost	$12,296
1.5% of wholesale cost	$184
Gas, oil, advertising	$100
Freight	$375
Your cost	$12,955

If you don't mind negotiating with dealers, then you might investigate an auto pricing service. Most auto pricing services will provide you with detailed cost information on particular models, usually for less than $10 per model. Normally it takes two to four weeks to process your specific request. Also, they may offer to buy your car for you and to have it delivered to a local participating dealer. The USAA Auto Pricing/Buying Service provides both services, and regional services are available in many areas. Other services are available through the Internet, in which you can "surf" your way through various cars and options (see Appendix A for sites). Pricing services are worthwhile if only to estimate accurately the wholesale cost of an automobile to the dealer. This information will help you determine how much you should pay a dealer for a particular car.

Your cost estimate using a pricing service will not include a manufacturer's rebate to dealers called holdback. Holdback is an additional 3 to 4 percent profit built into the wholesale price (dealer cost) of domestic automobiles. Manufacturers rebate this percentage to dealers periodically based on total volume. Remember, dealer profit is a percentage above dealer cost. Holdback is a part of dealer cost. Holdback in our continuing example would range from $369 to $492 in additional profit to the dealer. This additional 3 to 4 percent profit gives dealers pricing flexibility that most automobile shoppers do not recognize even if they know the dealer's wholesale cost.

Buying a Used Car

Determine the kind of used car you want. Know your price range and decide where you want to buy your car. The primary advantage of owning a carefully selected used car is that it will be much cheaper to own and operate than a new car. You can save the significant cost of depreciation associated with new cars if you buy a one-, two-, or three-year-old car and avoid the expensive major repairs associated with older cars by keeping the two- or three-year-old car for only three or four years. This potentially large savings has an increased risk in that the car may break down at an inopportune time and require unexpected, expensive repairs.

When considering a used car, you should determine the repair history for similarly equipped cars of that model year. The *Consumer Reports Annual Buying Guide* provides this information for most models. *Consumer Reports* also lists whether the car is Automotive Service Excellence (ASE) certified, an indicator of its repair history. Information is also available on models that are prone to serious mechanical problems and require higher-than-average repair costs. *Motor Trend* magazine is also an excellent source of information (most libraries have back issues). You may also order a complete title history of any automobile for $20 from *carfax.com.* The few minutes you take to review a detailed, professional analysis of the automobile you plan to buy will be time well spent. Price guides such as the *Kelley's Blue Book* and the *NADA Official Used Car Guide* are also available in most libraries and on the Internet. Both provide you with average wholesale and retail value estimates. These guides will also provide you with information to make adjustments for high or low mileage and the options on the car. There is no substitute for a mechanical inspection by a trained mechanic to help you determine the value of a used car.

Good used cars are available at fair prices, but you must search carefully. Buying a used car from a private owner may allow you to buy a good car at less than retail. You will almost certainly pay near retail for a used car you buy from a new-car dealer, but you may get a limited warranty. Selling only quality used cars and providing warranties helps preserve their reputations. New-car dealers also have maintenance departments and probably have performed some minor repairs. You are likely to find the worst selection of used cars at a dealer that specializes only in used cars. This is where new-car dealers dispose of their worst used cars. Used-car dealers may not have very good maintenance facilities, probably will not provide a warranty, and probably will charge you a retail price.

Several generalizations may help you in considering the expenses of owning and operating a used car:

- Never buy a used car unless you get a mechanical inspection by a mechanic whom you pay. The mechanic's written list of mechanical deficiencies will ensure that you know what problems the car has. Armed with this information, you should be able to negotiate a reduced price for the used car roughly equal to required repairs. Buying a car with impending repairs is just like paying more for the car. You should have a mechanical inspection done only on cars you have inspected and want to buy. Mechanical inspections rarely cost more than $50, and the mechanical inspection will usually save you money in the long run.

- Several studies confirm that total costs of a three-year-old car are about two-thirds the costs of owning a comparable new car during its first year of operation.
- If you plan to own your car for only two or three years, a new car will be significantly more expensive to operate than a used car because of the rapid depreciation that occurs in the first two years of ownership.
- A used car ceases to be economical when major repairs become likely each year. This is likely to occur after the fifth or sixth year.

HOW LONG SHOULD YOU KEEP THE CAR?

You should keep your car until it is no longer economical to do so. The question is how to determine whether it is economical. You need to determine the cost per mile per month for operating your automobile, and you will need records of expenses and the number of miles you drive each month.

Also keep records of the maintenance performed (and the expense of such maintenance) on your automobile. You should maintain your car according to the manufacturer's scheduled maintenance recommendations. Calculate the monthly expense to maintain your automobile from your maintenance records. Your maintenance and repair records are essential in determining whether your car is still economical to operate.

When to trade in your vehicle is a personal decision. If you maintain accurate maintenance records and calculate the values shown in Table 8-6, you will know the cost of owning and operating your car and whether it is rising or falling. The decision to replace your vehicle should depend in part on a comparison between these costs and the costs that you estimate for a newer model. This comparison, together with your valuation of the convenience and added satisfaction of owning a newer car, should allow you to make an informed decision. If owning a newer vehicle is worth the added costs, then it is time to trade in your car.

One final point about maintaining your car: Good maintenance habits have other benefits and make economic sense. Fulfilling scheduled maintenance requirements will ensure that you fulfill the terms of your warranty. Changing fluids and filters frequently prevents costly maintenance problems and prolongs the life of your car. Your maintenance record will help you sell your car because it is of major interest to used-car buyers.

HOW CAN YOU GET THE MOST FOR YOUR OLD CAR?

For most people, disposing of a used car is an integral part of buying a new one. If you own an old car, you have essentially three choices concerning its disposition: You can trade it in on a new car to offset part of the down payment, you can sell it outright to a used-car dealer, or you can sell it to a private party.

Location can be particularly relevant when determining the trade-in or resale value of your car. To determine the basic trade-in value of your old car, you can visit the *Kelley's Blue Book* website and enter basic data that includes year, make, model, condition, and location by zip code. Again, based on local supply and demand, your car's trade-in value may vary by as much as $3,000. It is well worth your time to compare prices at a number of geographic locations within a day's drive.

The main advantage of trading in your used car is convenience. You drive to the dealership in your old car and drive away in a new car. The main disadvantage is that a trade-in confuses the negotiation process by making it more difficult to determine how much you are actually paying for your new car. Dealers can make up for a lower price on your new car by giving you substantially lower credit for your trade-in. The main disadvantage of this option is that you will rarely get more than minimum wholesale value.

Even if you don't sell your car to a used-car dealer, it is a good idea to get a price quote from one. This will give you an idea of the minimum trade-in value you should accept.

The advantage of selling your used car to a private party is that you will probably be able to sell it for a higher price that is somewhere between the car's wholesale and retail values. The main disadvantage is the inconvenience of dealing with the advertising and the actual sales transaction. You will probably get many calls from people who only want to look. If you decide to sell your used car yourself, you should develop some screening criteria to determine over the phone which buyers are serious. Another disadvantage is that you are unlikely to sell your car on exactly the same day as you pick up your new one. Therefore, you may have either no transportation or excess transportation for a period, and it may cause a financing problem if you plan to use the proceeds from the sale as a down payment on your new car.

Whatever method you use to dispose of your old car, there are several steps you should take to ensure that you receive top dollar:

- Thoroughly clean your used car from bumper to bumper. Steam-clean the engine and undercarriage, and scrub the wheels and tires. Shampoo the carpet and vacuum the trunk. Touch up chipped paint. Wash and wax all painted surfaces, polish the chrome, and clean the windows.
- Change the oil and bring all fluids up to the recommended level. Replace all burned-out bulbs. Check the air pressure in the tires, including the spare. Correctly mount the spare tire and jack in the trunk.
- Tighten every screw, nut, or bolt that you can find. Lubricate all moving parts such as hinges.
- Clean every piece of junk out of the glove compartment and trunk. Leave only the owner's manual in the glove compartment.
- Locate your title and check the procedures for transferring automobile ownership in your area.

Tips on Buying a Car

- Include all expenses (gas, insurance, and maintenance) when deciding what car you can afford.
- Stick to your budget.
- Check for financing from your bank before you shop, and see if a dealer can beat that deal.
- Use a buying service or an Internet site to learn the dealer's cost of the car before you shop.
- Keep your eye on the APR—it's your best indication of the true cost of a car loan.
- Do your homework for vehicle and option prices before you go to the showroom.
- Don't be pressured into buying something you do not want.
- Don't pay for options you don't need if they don't improve the resale value of the car.
- Keep the deals separate: first price, then trade-in, then down payment, then financing.
- Seriously consider buying a used car.
- Old cars that need frequent maintenance could be more expensive to own than a new car.
- Take care of your automobile to maximize its resale value.

If you decide to sell the car yourself, put a For Sale sign in the window. Make sure that the car is in a place where many potential buyers can see it. Put notices on bulletin boards and include tear-off tabs with your phone number. Use electronic bulletin boards if available. Advertise in your local free paper and in the classified section of your local newspaper. In your advertisement, clearly describe your car, especially its better features. Be sure to include your asking price and do all advertising simultaneously. State the times you prefer to receive calls, and be available when people want to inspect your car.

Once you've sold your old car, the whole process will begin again. Enjoy driving your new car knowing that you made a sound economic decision that will help bring you closer to your financial goals.

SUGGESTED REFERENCES

Check the Internet sites listed in Appendix A.

The Car Guide. Safety information published by the USAA Foundation.
Consumer Reports Annual Buying Guide. Used-car repair information.
Edmund's New Car Prices. Dealer profit information on new cars and options.

Kelley's Blue Book. Used-car wholesale and retail prices.
NADA Official Used Car Guide. Used-car wholesale and retail prices.

The following periodicals often provide information relevant to buying an automobile:

Car and Driver. Road tests and specific model information.
Consumer Reports. Especially the April issue.
Consumer Reports Online at *www.consumerreports.org;* for $3.95 a month, you will have online access to all reports, including buying and leasing tips, car safety, equipment, accessories and insurance.
Motor Trend. Specific model information and comparisons.

9

Automobile Insurance

In some circumstances, owning and operating a motor vehicle can be a risky adventure. In addition to the dangers of driving, the car can inflict injury on other individuals and/or damage property. As the owner or operator of a motor vehicle, you assume the risk and responsibility for compensating anyone injured or replacing damaged property when you are involved in an accident. Since most car owners cannot afford these potential payments, automobile insurance provides a necessary protection against these financial risks. Additionally, all states require automobile owners to carry some basic minimum insurance coverage.

This chapter provides general information about automobile insurance and guidelines to help you make educated insurance decisions. Money-saving hints, not at the expense of security, are provided. Finally, a checklist assists you with making this decision.

WHAT IS AUTOMOBILE INSURANCE?

The goal of an insurance policy is to protect you from the many risks associated with owning or operating a car. An insurance policy attempts to minimize each type of risk with a specific category of insurance coverage. Each type of insurance coverage has a specific cost, called a premium. The sum of these risk premiums is the total cost of your policy. As a policyholder, by adjusting the level (amount) of risk coverage and the related deductibles (amount you must pay prior to the insurance company paying for a loss), you can impact your total policy cost. As a general rule, the lower the risk coverage, the lower the premium; however, premiums do not increase in proportion to the increase in coverage. For example, increasing liability coverage from $10,000 to $25,000, a 150 percent increase, may increase your premium by only 10 percent. The premium-coverage trade-off is important since your primary concern should be to ensure that your assets are adequately protected against loss. Your second concern should be locating a policy that provides the necessary protection at the lowest cost.

AUTOMOBILE INSURANCE AS A MAJOR BUDGET CATEGORY

The cost of automobile insurance represents an annual expense (approximately) of $1,150 or about 5 percent of a newly commissioned second lieutenant's annual pay! Unfortunately, insurance costs are expected to increase at a faster rate than inflation in the future due partially to higher medical expenses and the growing popularity of lawsuits. Another factor influencing premium prices is the fact that as premiums increase, more people choose to "save" money by not fully insuring their automobiles. This creates a vicious circle in which all consumers lose.

Your Car Type Influences Your Insurance Premium

Since your automobile insurance premium is a major budget expenditure, this cost should be considered prior to purchasing a car. Different brands and car models have different claims histories. The claim history is the typical frequency that the model of car is involved in an accident and the cost required to settle all claims from that accident. Insurance companies use these claims histories and your personal information to calculate your premium. For example, a car with a poor claim history (typically involved in more accidents and repaired at a high cost) can produce a significantly higher cost of coverage than a car with a better claim history. Also, "safe" cars, equipped with dual air bags, anti-lock brakes, and active theft-deterrent systems, are sure bets for lower premiums compared to cars without these options. Additionally, these lower premiums can, over several years, offset the initial cost of purchasing these options on a new car. Likewise, when considering the purchase of a used car, a better claim history can, in the long run, make the more expensive model actually cheaper than a car with a poor claim history. Your insurance company can calculate your expected premium if you provide the relevant information (year, make, and model) on the cars that you are considering purchasing. Additionally, the many insurance company websites will provide the same information.

To review the claim history of a car, you can contact USAA and receive a copy of *The Car Guide.* Additional sources are *Consumer Reports, Consumer Reports Buying Guide,* and *Motor Trend* magazine, all of which provide this information.

SELECTING AN INSURANCE COMPANY

You should select your insurance company with the same diligence used to select your car. Policy prices, coverage, and service differ significantly among companies, so comparison shopping is a necessity in order to make an informed decision. Additionally, letting your insurance agent know that you are actively looking at policies from different companies may provide you an advantage in the policy price negotiation process.

As you shop around, avoid little-known and potentially "shady" companies with extremely low premiums. Remember you are entrusting these companies to protect your assets in the event of an accident! The company you select should have a proven track record in the insurance business. Longevity is typically an indicator of sound company management policies. Remember that you want the company to be there when you file a claim, not just there to collect your premium! Additionally, since military personnel move often, you probably want an insurance company that will provide coverage as you move from state to state and internationally. Though many Americans prefer dealing with the personal service of a local agent, military families may prefer the convenience of a toll-free number or Internet access that provides contact to an insurance professional from virtually anywhere, twenty-four hours a day.

HOW INSURANCE COMPANIES EVALUATE YOUR POTENTIAL RISK

Insurance companies continually analyze the financial risks that you present to their company and the likelihood that you will have a claim the company will have to pay. Since these companies cannot know everything about each and every policyholder, they make simplifying demographic assumptions and "pool" those policyholders with similar characteristics together. Insurance premiums are then based on which "pool" you are assigned. The riskier the pool, the higher the premium. By understanding how these pools are filled, you can materially affect the cost of your insurance premiums.

So what are the common characteristics that determine your pool membership? Besides the type of car, some other factors are driving record, age, sex, marital status, frequency and length of commute, annual mileage, zip code, and academic performance, to name a few. Once you are in a certain pool, insurance companies will move you as your personal demographics change. For example, you might think of the cost of speeding as the fines associated with the tickets. However, since speeding tickets affect your driving record, you will, most likely, move to a riskier pool with higher premiums. The end result could cost you thousands of dollars. Whatever you do, be honest with your insurance agent when discussing these demographics that affect your pool. You can get into serious trouble if you provide false information just to save a few dollars.

Additionally, forward planning and active pool management can help you reduce insurance costs. For example, when your marital status changes from single to married, the spouse with the better driving record should be the primary driver for the car that is more expensive to insure.

THE INSURANCE POLICY: EXPLANATIONS AND RECOMMENDATIONS

The typical automobile insurance policy consists of five basic types of coverage: liability, medical payments, collision, comprehensive, and uninsured motorist. There are also other optional coverages. The following is an outline of the types of coverages as well as some guidelines to consider. You must balance these guidelines with your personal financial situation and attitude toward assuming risk.

Liability Coverage

Liability coverage pays for injuries and property damage that you (or someone using your car) cause as a result of driving negligently. Liability coverage, mandatory in nearly all states, is the most expensive type of coverage and the most necessary. Individuals injured in an automobile accident often seek compensation for personal injury through the courts. You risk losing current and future assets if you fail to carry adequate liability insurance. Therefore, liability coverage is the last place you want to skimp. There are two types of liability coverage: bodily injury and property damage.

Bodily Injury Coverage. Bodily injury (BI) coverage pays for medical expenses and associated litigation fees for losses resulting from injury or death in an accident in which you were at fault. Losses can result from medical bills, lost wages, and pain and suffering. Court awards for pain and suffering can be enough to ruin you financially if you are underinsured. You can expect to be sued in court if you cause an accident that results in personal injury or death.

There are two types of bodily injury coverage: single-limit and split-limit (or multiple-limit). Single-limit BI coverage pays a maximum single amount per accident, regardless of the number of individuals injured. For example, if you carry a policy with $300,000 single-limit bodily injury coverage, one injured person could claim up to $300,000 from your insurance company, with the remainder coming out of your pocket. The second type of BI coverage, split-limit, is more common. It pays a maximum amount to each person injured in an accident, subject to a maximum limit per accident. For example, $100,000/$300,000 split-limit coverage means that the insurance company will pay up to $100,000 to each person injured, but no more than $300,000 per accident. If a single individual suffers damages of $150,000, the insurance policy would cover only $100,000 of the damages, and you would have to cover the remainder. If you injure six people in an accident, the company would be liable for up to $300,000 worth of damages.

Most states mandate minimum limits for liability coverage. The typical amount is $25,000/$50,000, a meager sum in our litigious society. A number of states have no-fault laws, meaning that an injured party receives compensation from his or her own insurance company, regardless of who is at fault. The theory behind no-fault is that the need for litigation after an accident decreases, so insurance premiums should decrease.

Bodily Injury Guidelines

1. Carry no less than $100,000/$300,000 (split-limit) or $300,000 (single-limit) coverage.
2. Buy as much bodily injury liability coverage as you can afford. Increasing liability coverage does not raise your premium proportionately. Even if you increase coverage from $50,000 to $300,000 (a 500 percent increase), your premium might increase by only 25 percent.
3. Follow guidelines 1 and 2 even if you live in a no-fault state.

4. If you own a home and/or assets worth more than $300,000, consider an umbrella policy that will provide even more protection (see chapter 12).

5. Obtain insurance that covers any car you legally drive, even if it is a rented or borrowed vehicle.

Property Damage Coverage. The second type of liability coverage is property damage (PD). PD pays for the necessary repairs when someone else's property (usually their vehicle) is damaged. PD also covers other types of property. The average state minimums are around $10,000—not even enough to cover the cost of a typical new car.

Property Damage Guidelines

1. Carry at least $50,000 property damage coverage. State minimums may be less, but consider the financial liability you could incur if you wreck someone's new Mercedes.

2. Obtain insurance that covers any car you legally drive.

Medical Payments Coverage

Medical payments coverage pays the medical expenses of individuals injured in your car. This coverage is normally optional in states without no-fault laws and coverage amounts range from $1,000 to $100,000 per person.

Most people already have some type of medical and hospital insurance so some may choose to forgo this duplicate coverage. Military families have hospital benefits, but remember that all passengers may not be immediate family members. A small amount of additional coverage may make sense because medical payments coverage often includes a funeral benefit.

States with no-fault laws may require you to carry personal injury protection (PIP) coverage. This is a more comprehensive form of medical payments coverage that covers medical bills, lost wages, and some funeral expenses for injuries to you or any passenger, regardless of who is at fault. Some states require a minimum amount of PIP, usually around $10,000, but amounts vary by state.

Medical Payments Guidelines

1. Consider $10,000 in medical payments coverage, even if you have a good health insurance policy for yourself and your family. This will help cover any medical expenses for nonfamily members.

2. If your state requires PIP, purchase $10,000 coverage (or the state minimum, if it exceeds $10,000).

3. If your state requires PIP coverage and your state's no-fault rules allow you to coordinate benefits with your health insurance policy, do so. This coordination may realize sizeable premium savings and means that you would seek reimbursement from your health insurance company before applying to your auto insurer. Military families should ask for coordination of benefits because of their access to the military health-care system.

4. Obtain insurance that covers you if you are injured while using someone else's car.

Collision Coverage

Collision coverage pays for physical damage to your car regardless of who is at fault and accounts for approximately 30 percent of the total insurance premium on a new car. Collision coverage carries a deductible (an amount you must pay before the coverage becomes effective). By selecting the size of the deductible, ranging from $100 to $1,000, you can affect your premium since the higher the deductible, the lower the premium. For example, increasing your deductible from $100 to $500 or $1,000 could save you from 25 to 40 percent on your premium. Remember, though, that if you are involved in an accident, you will need this deductible to repair your car.

Comprehensive coverage is related to the "blue book" value of your car. The blue book value (provided by your insurance company, bank, or *www.kbb.com*) on a car is the maximum amount your insurance company will pay you if your car is totaled. For newer cars, comprehensive coverage is essential and is usually required if you borrowed money to purchase the car. For cars between four and six years, the decision to carry collision coverage depends on the financial risk that you are willing to assume in the event that your car is totaled. For cars with a low blue book value, collision coverage is usually a waste of money since the cost of coverage will not be realized if the car is totaled.

Collision Guidelines

1. Carry collision on cars with substantial blue book values, but choose the highest deductible you can afford.
2. Drop collision coverage altogether on older, lower-value cars if you can afford to replace them.
3. If you financed your vehicle, check with your financial institution before canceling collision insurance.

Comprehensive Coverage

Comprehensive coverage reimburses you for damage caused by mishaps other than a crash, including vandalism, theft, falling objects, floods, glass breakage, and collisions with animals. It carries a deductible that normally ranges from $50 to $1,000. Additionally, for a relatively small additional premium, you can typically receive full glass damage coverage with no deductible.

Comprehensive Guidelines

1. Choose the highest deductible you can afford.
2. Adapt your comprehensive coverage to your post location. In cities with higher crime rates, it is a good idea to maintain comprehensive coverage.
3. Cancel coverage on cars with low resale value.
4. If you financed your vehicle, check with your financial institution prior to canceling your comprehensive insurance.

Uninsured Motorist Coverage

Uninsured motorist (UIM) coverage protects you and your passengers from damages caused by uninsured motorists and hit-and-run drivers. It is especially important in states without no-fault laws. UIM coverage reimburses you for bodily injury or death in accidents where the uninsured motorist is responsible. UIM covers payments for your medical expenses and losses due to permanent disability or death, loss of income, and any other damages entitled by state law. It does not reimburse you for property damages.

Minimum coverage offered by insurance companies normally coincides with a state's particular laws. Although UIM is a normal part of every insurance policy, you may generally elect to reject it. However, you must do so in writing. UIM premiums are on the rise because increasing numbers of drivers violate state laws and do not carry insurance. Therefore, the probability of having an accident with an uninsured motorist increases, which yields higher premiums.

There is a newer category of coverage called underinsured motorist (UNM) coverage. UNM coverage applies if you have an accident with another driver who is at fault but whose insurance coverage cannot provide sufficient compensation. UNM coverage pays when the other party's coverage stops. You can buy coverage limits similar to those available for liability. Different insurance companies treat UNM coverage differently. For some companies, UNM is an integral part of your policy. Other companies treat UNM as a separate coverage with a separate premium. State law determines what constitutes a UNM loss and under what conditions you will receive payment.

UIM/UNM Guidelines

1. Carry UIM in an amount comparable with your bodily injury liability coverage.
2. Carry UIM coverage unless you are in a state with outstanding no-fault laws or you have an excellent medical insurance policy for yourself and your family.
3. Check with your insurance company to determine if your UIM coverage includes UNM coverage; if not, ask for it.
4. Check to see if UNM coverage pays only if your policy exceeds the liability coverage of the underinsured motorist or if it pays for damages in excess (up to your limit) of the underinsured motorist's coverage.
5. Check with your insurance company each time you move to determine the requirements of your new state.

Optional Coverages

Insurance policies can have as many options as the car itself and just as you can save money by purchasing a car with fewer options you can do the same with your insurance policy! One way to save money is to avoid buying unnecessary options. There are many options, but we will discuss only the more prominent ones. If you have adequate personal property, health, and life insurance policies, you can reject any options related to these risk categories. If you need more life insurance, buy more life insurance; do not sign up for limited life insurance on your automobile insurance policy.

Rental Reimbursement Coverage. If you have an accident and your car requires repairs, rental reimbursement will offset the cost of temporary transportation until your car is repaired. This coverage pays a certain amount per day, for a specified number of days. Reimbursement is normally up to $30 a day and lasts for two weeks. If you own more than one car or if alternate transportation means are available (company car, local mass transit), rental reimbursement is not necessary.

Towing and Labor Coverage. The insurance company pays the cost of towing your car to a repair shop and pays for any immediate labor involved. If you are a member of an auto club that already provides this service, you should not carry this coverage. Also, read the fine print in order to understand the limits of the towing arrangement and exactly what labor costs are reimbursable.

SPECIAL INSURANCE SITUATIONS

Rental Car Coverage

Before renting an automobile, see if your insurance company provides coverage so that you can waive these additional rental car fees while still maintaining adequate insurance coverage. Calling your company is the best policy since your company may not cover renting classic automobiles or other expensive models. Additionally, make sure you have adequate coverage for the state where you are renting, since mandatory coverage amounts vary substantially from state to state and country to country. Be aware that if you damage a rental vehicle, the rental company can charge you for the rental revenue they lose while repairing the vehicle. Normally, if you damage a rental car, your credit card is charged immediately and you must file the claim with your insurance company to resolve the situation. Another source of rental car insurance coverage is your credit card. In many instances, especially if you have a preferred (gold or platinum card), your credit card company covers the collision damage on a rental car when you pay with this same card. If in doubt, purchase rental car coverage. Although it may seem expensive, the insurance could protect you from undue financial hardship. The peace of mind you buy may be well worth the money you spend.

Leased Automobile Coverage

Leasing an automobile is becoming a popular alternative to buying. Insurance coverage for your leased vehicle is similar to insurance for a vehicle you own, but there are a few significant differences. The first is that insurance requirements by the leasing company are often higher than the state minimums. Thus, if you lease a car, you may be required to carry more insurance than you would otherwise. You need to consider these added costs when evaluating a car leasing option, compared to purchasing the same car.

Another difference is that if your leased vehicle is stolen or totaled, most leasing companies consider this an early contract termination. You will generally owe the lessor more than your insurance company will pay, due to depreciation of the leased vehicle. The difference, or "gap," between what you owe and what your regular insurance company will pay needs to be covered by gap insurance or total loss protection. Some leases include gap insurance in the cost of the payments. Others do not and you will need to buy separate coverage or potentially face a large financial loss if something happens to your leased automobile.

AUTOMOBILE INSURANCE CHECKLIST

This checklist provides you with a list of most possible coverage categories as well as other areas of importance when shopping for insurance. Use this list to construct a spreadsheet for comparing insurance companies.

TABLE 9-1
AUTOMOBILE INSURANCE CHECKLIST

Description	Desired Level of Coverage	Company's Level of Coverage	Cost
Liability coverages			
Bodily injury protection	______	______	______
Property damage liability	______	______	______
Personal injury protection	______	______	______
Uninsured motorist	______	______	______
Underinsured motorist	______	______	______
Medical payments	______	______	______
Collision			
$100 deductible			______
$250 deductible			______
$500 deductible			______
$1,000 deductible			______
Comprehensive			
$100 deductible			______
$250 deductible			______
$500 deductible			______
$1,000 deductible			______
Special coverages			
Towing and labor			______
Rental reimbursement			______
Service record of the insurance company			
Claims:			
Average claim handling time		______	
Method to settle disagreements		______	
Number of estimates required		______	

Billing:
- Agent availability ________________
- Toll-free number (U.S.) ________________
- Toll-free number (international) ________________
- Internet presence ________________
- Internet level of service ________________

Accident forgiveness program ________________
- After how many years? ________________

Changing coverage ________________
Rate increases based on age? ________________
Cancellation standards ________________
Nonrenewal standards ________________
What moves you into higher-risk tiers? ________________
What brings you down from higher-risk tiers? ________________
Are rental cars also covered? ________________

Special discounts
- Annual mileage ________________
- Antitheft ________________
  - Active devices ________________
  - Passive devices ________________
  - Military post ________________
  - Etched windows ________________
  - Other ________________
- Antilock brakes ________________
- Air bag/dual air bag/air curtains ________________
- Automatic seat belts ________________
- Children at military academies ________________
- Children away at school ________________
- Children on active military duty ________________
- Certified driver education ________________
- Good driver ________________
- Good student ________________
- Multiyear ________________
- Multipolicy ________________
- Multicar ________________
- Nonsmoker ________________
- Professional (doctor, lawyer) ________________
- Senior driver ________________

Record with state agencies
- Department of Insurance ________________
- Department of Consumer Affairs ________________

Recommendations from family and friends ________________

____

Tips for Buying Automobile Insurance

- Make sure you are adequately covered against all reasonable risks.
- Carry the largest deductible you can afford to reduce your premiums.
- Ask for "coordination of benefits" to reduce your personal injury protection (PIP) premiums.
- Avoid duplicate coverage.
- Actively manage factors that can reduce your premiums: keep a good driving record and take a defensive driving class.
- Review your policy annually.
- Notify your insurance company immediately when your personal circumstances change.
- Shop around for the best coverage at a reasonable price.

AUTOMOBILE INSURANCE WEBSITES

The following websites will assist you in obtaining both information and premium quotes about your policy: *allstate.com, geico.com, nationwide.com, progressive.com, safeco.com, statefarm.com, usaa.com.* Note that some of the sites will provide quotes, but others will have a local insurance agent contact you to discuss coverage options and prices.

10

Meeting Medical Expenses

Unless you plan appropriately, your future financial well-being can depend on your health and the health of your family members. Most of us recognize that hospital and medical care costs can easily exceed hundreds of dollars a day. We understand that sophisticated medical equipment is costly and that the cost of intensive care and medical malpractice suits are passed on to patients. Although we know that it is possible for us to incur huge medical costs, many people do not take the time to plan how they would pay for these expenses. There are two ways to pay for these potentially large expenses. You can pay for them yourself "out of pocket," as they occur, which is generally not an option for most family budgets. Alternatively, you can pool the risk with others and buy a medical insurance policy. You should be aware that even with an insurance policy, you may have to pay deductibles, copayments, excess fees, and noncovered costs. Again, you can pay these costs out of pocket, which is the most common option, or you can buy yet another insurance policy called a supplemental insurance plan.

Since Americans spend approximately 5.4 percent of personal income on medical care[1] (and almost 20 percent of the federal budget is projected to be spent on Medicare and Medicaid alone),[2] medical insurance (the single largest health-care expense)[3] is one of the most important parts of military compensation. Today, a typical medical insurance policy for a family costs between $5,000 and $10,000 annually, depending on the type of coverage (and remember, if you buy it yourself, you have to use after-tax dollars). While you are on active duty, the military, like most other major employers, will provide you and your family a low-cost comprehensive medical and dental insurance policy called TRICARE.

---

[1]U.S. Department of Labor, *Consumer Expenditures in 1999,* Bureau of Labor and Statistics, May 2001, 2. Internet: *http://www.bls.gov.*

[2]Office of Management and Budget, "2. Where the Money Comes From—And Where It Goes," *A Citizen's Guide to the Federal Budget,* The White House. Internet: *http://www.whitehouse.gov/omb/budget/fy2002/guide02.html#Spending.*

[3]U.S. Department of Labor, *Consumer Expenditures in 1999.*

While the military provides some form of medical insurance to all active-duty personnel and their families at little or no cost, the same is not true for retirees and their families. Although we will discuss retired servicemembers' medical coverage later in the chapter, we want to make sure that you understand why this is important to you now—while you are on active duty. Paying for medical care after you are retired may seem like a distant thought, but you need to consider the future cost of medical care in your financial planning today so that you will be able to afford medical insurance when you leave active duty.

This chapter will discuss how servicemembers and their families can pay for medical care by discussing four important topics. First, we outline the medical benefits afforded by TRICARE. This includes explaining where TRICARE is offered and describing the three levels of coverage available, the costs associated with TRICARE, and the coverage for retired servicemembers and their families. Second, we discuss the military's dental program, TRICARE Dental Program (TDP), and the costs associated with it. Third, we describe how to pay for costs not covered by TRICARE with supplemental insurance and how you should evaluate supplemental insurance policies. Finally, we focus on a new area of concern in health-care management: long-term care. Included in this section is a description of long-term care and advice about whether military families need long-term care insurance.

In 1998, after several successful test programs, the military expanded its medical coverage program from CHAMPUS, the old military health insurance program, to TRICARE. With this change came more options for servicemembers and their family members—similar to the organization of a civilian health maintenance organization. However, because the TRICARE system can be rather complex and details could change, we do not intend to replicate the TRICARE regulations handbooks in this chapter. Instead, we will first discuss the benefits provided to servicemembers and their family members through TRICARE, and then we will look at ways of covering the risk of loss from medical expenses not covered by TRICARE. You should refer specific questions about TRICARE to the TRICARE Service Center in your region. Appendix A has the contact numbers for sources of additional information that is beyond the scope of this chapter.

MILITARY HEALTH BENEFITS—TRICARE

In 1992, the health-care financing debate revolved around the overall cost of the U.S. health-care system and how the government might intervene to constrain the cost. In the last several years, however, health-care inflation has leveled off, and most government proposals have been sidelined. The current financial debate centers around a single decision that you as the health-care consumer must make. That decision is cost versus choice. Simply stated, if you decide to retain the ability to choose the specific doctor you want to see, you will pay more to see that doctor. Should you decide to cede your ability to choose your doctor and join a managed care plan, the cost to you and your family for medical care will be less. This choice is definitely true in the military, but it is also generally true for those with civilian employers.

The TRICARE system is a defense-wide program combining the assets of the Army, Navy, and Air Force military treatment facilities (MTFs), supplemented by civilian health-care providers from the surrounding communities. In 2001, the Department of Defense (DOD) spent over several billion dollars on health care for eight million active-duty personnel, family members of active-duty members, and retirees and their family members.

The DOD, in an attempt to reduce medical costs and improve the quality of and access to care, is adopting the same philosophy as many large companies—providing health care through a health management organization (HMO) format. What this means to you is that if you decide to enroll your family in the military's managed care network, TRICARE Prime, the cost to you for your family's medical care will be greatly reduced. Should you decide to retain the option to choose a doctor for your family, TRICARE Standard, the cost of receiving medical treatment for your family will be greater.

Active-duty servicemembers have their health-care needs provided for them in the MTF managed care network. The mandate of military medicine is to preserve the fighting force; therefore, active-duty servicemembers have the first priority in the military health-care system. This care is provided free of charge at military treatment facilities.

Medical treatment provided to active-duty servicemembers in a civilian hospital will be paid for by the government only if it is an emergency. Nonemergency treatment at civilian facilities requires permission from the nearest military hospital. If you, as an active-duty servicemember, are not stationed near a military treatment facility, you must still receive permission from the nearest facility and your command before receiving any nonemergency treatment. Later in this chapter, we will discuss your financial responsibilities if you have to travel to a distant military treatment facility for care. If an active-duty servicemember is injured as a result of unauthorized or illegal behavior, the government may seek reimbursement from that member for all medical expenses. For instance, a soldier injured and treated while AWOL may receive a bill from the government for the treatment received.

WHAT IS TRICARE?

TRICARE is a regionally managed health-care program for active-duty servicemembers and their families, retired members, and retired members' families. To ensure that there are enough health-care providers for all of its beneficiaries, the military has created fifteen civilian health-care networks based on geographic regions to supplement the care provided by military treatment facilities. Additionally, all military hospitals have been realigned into these fifteen geographic regions, with each TRICARE region having a major medical center for major surgeries and several regional hospitals providing specific specialized medical care. This means that both servicemembers and their families may have to travel to receive certain medical treatment.

Figure 10-1
TRICARE Regions

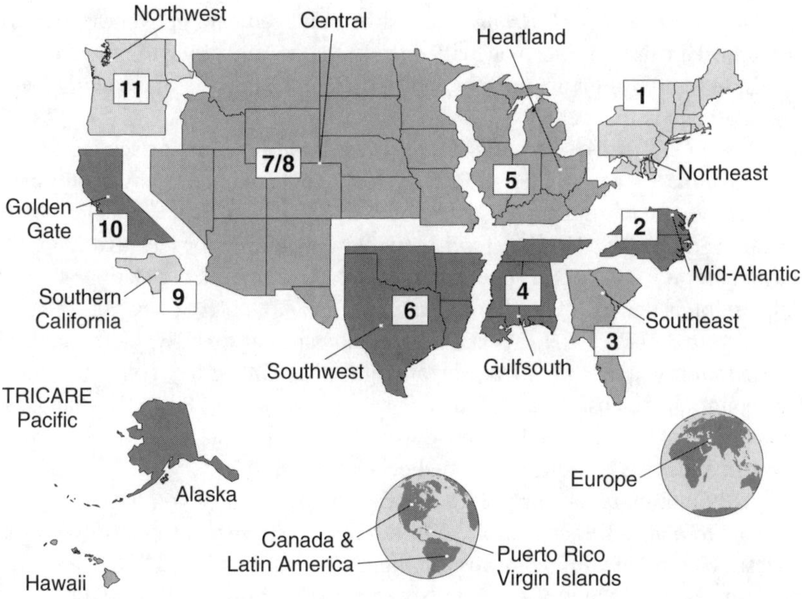

Source: *www.tricare.osd.mil*

TRICARE is not one large network. It is actually several separate networks that are independent of one another. You are authorized to enroll your family in the regional network where you are stationed. This is important, because if you decide to enroll your family in TRICARE Prime, the managed care option, you will receive a TRICARE Prime health-care card that your family must have to receive treatment. If a medical emergency occurs, they will use this card to seek care anywhere. If a family member needs nonemergency treatment and is outside his or her enrolled region, he or she will need to call the regional provider to receive permission before receiving treatment. Your family members are not authorized to receive nonemergency care in any of the other fourteen TRICARE Prime regions. For those whose family members live in different TRICARE regions (such as students away at college), you might be eligible for split enrollment in another region under TRICARE Prime, although the TRICARE Standard option may be a better choice, because it will allow you the flexibility to seek care anywhere at any time. Each of these options will be discussed in detail in the following section. Figure 10-1 shows each of the TRICARE regions. Phone numbers for each region are in Appendix A.

The TRICARE benefits package offers three options for all beneficiaries except active-duty servicemembers. Active-duty servicemembers are automatically enrolled in the TRICARE Prime option during in-processing, and other beneficiaries are considered to be in TRICARE Standard and Extra, unless voluntarily enrolled in TRICARE Prime.

- *Option 1: TRICARE Prime.* This is the managed care network option. If you enroll in this option, you will receive the majority of your care in the MTFs. In return for giving up your choice of doctors, the cost of receiving medical treatment is reduced.
- *Option 2: TRICARE Standard.* This is the traditional fee-for-service option and is similar to the old CHAMPUS system. You can choose any health-care provider you want, but the costs to you will be greater than with TRICARE Prime. Additionally, TRICARE will reimburse you only for fees that it deems reasonable. If TRICARE Prime is not available where you are stationed, your only option is to enroll your family members in TRICARE Standard.
- *Option 3: TRICARE Extra.* This option is similar to TRICARE Standard except that if you use providers who are on the TRICARE list, you will receive a discount on the costs you would have had to pay under TRICARE Standard. This option should be used by those who do not live near a TRICARE Prime network and wish to reduce their medical expenses.

Although there are three TRICARE options, initially you have only one decision to make. You can enroll your family in TRICARE Prime, which is the lowest-cost option with the fewest provider choices, or in the TRICARE Standard program, which will potentially expose you to greater financial risk but give you more flexibility in choosing your provider. If you choose the TRICARE Standard option, you can opt, on a case-by-case basis, to participate in the TRICARE Extra program, which can reduce your costs.

TRICARE Prime

TRICARE Prime is an HMO-like option, with enrollment fees and payments, but no deductibles. This option offers the lowest costs with the least choice. If you enroll your family in this option, most of the care will be provided by the MTFs, supplemented by the Preferred Provider Network (PPN) of the contracted regional service. Additionally, there is a point-of-service (POS) option that may be exercised by the enrollee at any time without referral from the assigned prime care manager (PCM). Although the POS option will probably provide faster service (remember, the military facility's priority is the active-duty servicemember), there are additional costs, as well as an applied deductible (there is no deductible at an MTF or a referred PPN visit). In return for giving up the choice of which doctor you can see, TRICARE Prime offers the following advantages: no enrollment fees for active-duty and family members; strict access standards, such as routine appointments offered within seven days; emphasis on prevention of disease and illness; additional preventive and primary-care services; a nurse advice program that is available seven days a week, twenty-four hours a day (in most regions); away-from-home coverage; and no paperwork.

Although TRICARE Prime offers many benefits, it does have some disadvantages. First, although it seems that there is no financial risk because of the copayments for POS treatment, a significant illness that requires many drugs and doctors' visits could cost copayment fees of $1,000 or more. Additionally, TRICARE Prime may not cover some treatments, which could be costly. Also, if you or your family members have another primary health insurance plan, TRICARE Prime will pay for care outside an MTF only after the civilian health insurance pays its allowances. Another problem is that TRICARE Prime is available only in communities with a significant military population (see paragraph for TRICARE Prime Remote below). If you do not live in one of these areas, TRICARE Prime is not available and you must enroll in the TRICARE Standard package. If you and your family do not live in the same region, you should consider enrolling in the TRICARE Standard option, although your family members may be able to split-enroll in TRICARE Prime in another region. Finally, if you travel away from your primary duty station often and need civilian care, TRICARE Prime will pay for it outside your normal area only if it is an emergency or urgent situation and the care was authorized in advance by the health-care finder. Thus, because you are locked into this plan for one year, you should consider the proximity of the military network, the waiting times associated with it, the copayment fees in the civilian network, and your personal preferences.

When you enroll your family in TRICARE Prime, you are assigned a PCM, who acts as the "gatekeeper" for your family's medical needs. The PCM is responsible for providing routine medical care, arranging for referrals, and coordinating your health-care needs. The PCM can include physicians who practice general or family medicine, internal medicine, pediatrics, and obstetrics/gynecology (OB/GYN). Nurse practitioners and physicians' assistants can also be PCMs. It is important to remember that if you choose a civilian primary care manager, you cannot use the military treatment facilities without a referral from the civilian PCM.

TRICARE Prime has an escape hatch for those who, for whatever reason, do not want to use the network-assigned doctor for a specific referral or illness. This escape mechanism is called the point-of-service option, and you can see any doctor you want if you exercise this option. The financial downside of exercising this option is tremendous. Even if you are an active-duty servicemember, you will incur a $300 deductible and a 50 percent copayment for all approved charges. This means that if TRICARE says the charge is excessive, you could incur costs up to the entire amount of the bill. (If you are considering a POS option because you feel a diagnosis or treatment may not be correct, remember that you may request that your PCM refer you out for a second opinion.)

Another program, TRICARE Prime Remote, is available only for servicemembers (not their family members) if they live and work more than fifty miles from an MTF. If possible, you will still be assigned a PCM, or if none are available, a TRICARE-authorized provider. Also, if you need specialty care, your

PCM must contact the regional health-care finder to see if a "fitness for duty determination" is necessary. You may obtain prescribed drugs through a civilian network or military pharmacy or through the National Mail Order Pharmacy. As with TRICARE Prime, there are no costs to the servicemember for authorized care.

An alternative to TRICARE Prime for all but active-duty servicemembers is the Uniformed Services Family Health Plan, which offers the same health benefits and cost structure as TRICARE Prime, but may be used by retirees and their family members who are over sixty-five.

TRICARE Standard

TRICARE Standard is a traditional fee-for-service option that is the same as the old CHAMPUS system (more choices, higher costs). Remember that this option is not available for active-duty servicemembers, regardless of their duty station. Under TRICARE Standard, you will be reimbursed only for a certain level of payments for certain procedures, and both deductibles and cost sharing are required. This means that you may wind up with a large uncovered medical bill. If your doctor accepts TRICARE payments, the doctor will file the claim and you will pay the difference; if the doctor does not accept TRICARE payments, you must pay the bill in full and file a claim yourself.

Along with paying only part of the cost of a medical procedure, TRICARE Standard can be slower in paying claims than either the doctor or patient may desire. This can create financial problems if you have to pay your doctor first and then await reimbursement. Additionally, a major hospital stay often involves many different doctors and test facilities, with each of these entities having different policies for dealing with TRICARE. It is your responsibility to coordinate the payment of your doctors, and if you are not careful, you could wind up with a larger-than-expected bill. Finally, to make sure that you will be reimbursed for any treatment you seek under TRICARE Standard, families whose zip codes are covered by a military treatment facility must first seek care from that facility before using TRICARE Standard. The mere fact that treatment is recommended does not mean that it is covered. Before one of your family members sees a civilian provider, he or she may first need to have a statement of nonavailability from the nearest military treatment facility. To minimize unexpected bills, you should make it a habit to contact your TRICARE benefits advisor before any family member receives treatment if he or she is enrolled in the TRICARE Standard option.

Since TRICARE Prime coverage is primarily restricted to the region you are enrolled in (unless you qualify for split enrollment under TRICARE Prime), the TRICARE Standard option is often the only choice for servicemembers with family members living in different regions or for families living outside the TRICARE Prime network. Whereas TRICARE Prime will not pay for treatment (except in an emergency) rendered outside its assigned network, TRICARE Standard provides partial reimbursement for all qualified and licensed providers if proper procedures are followed. As you can see, TRICARE Standard leaves you more exposed to potentially large and unexpected medical bills than does TRICARE Prime. To minimize the risk of having large uncovered bills when using TRICARE Standard, you should always consult your TRICARE benefits advisor and each doctor you see to ensure that all treatment is covered and that the fees are deemed reasonable by TRICARE.

TRICARE Extra

For those who choose the TRICARE Standard option, TRICARE Extra offers a discount (lower cost shares) to patients who use a provider that is part of the TRICARE network. You do not need to enroll into TRICARE Extra. TRICARE Standard patients who choose a doctor who is enrolled in the TRICARE Extra program will receive a 5 percent discount from the cost share that they would normally pay under the TRICARE Standard program (see Tables 10-1 through 10-3 in the next section) and will not need to file any paperwork. Additionally, TRICARE Extra providers agree in advance not to charge "excessive fees."

TRICARE Extra is not, however, a middle-of-the-road plan for the cost-conscious. TRICARE Extra will save you money compared with TRICARE Standard; nevertheless, you still have many of the same risks as with TRICARE Standard. You may also be required to get a nonavailability statement (NAS) for civilian inpatient care for areas surrounding MTFs. Remember, even in a remote region, your provider may be participating in the TRICARE Extra program. You can receive a list of participating physicians from your TRICARE service center. Additionally, if you want to use a specific provider, you can ask that doctor to join the TRICARE Extra program, and if he or she joins, you will be eligible for the savings under TRICARE Extra.

Who is eligible for enrollment in TRICARE?

The following groups are eligible for TRICARE medical coverage (however, note that in order to receive care at military medical facilities, all must be enrolled in DEERS, including newborns after 120 days):

1. Active-duty servicemembers.
2. Spouses and unmarried children (up to twenty-one years old) of active-duty servicemembers.
   - Children, twenty-one years and older, if handicapped prior to twenty-first birthday.
   - Children, up to twenty-three years old, if in school full-time (may not be eligible for TRICARE Prime if they live in a different region).
   - Divorced spouses are not covered except as in number 8, below.
   - Children (including stepchildren who are adopted by the sponsor) are covered even if the divorced spouse remarries (not eligible for TRICARE Prime if they live in a different region).
3. Servicemembers who separate before they are eligible for retirement and their eligible family members may receive TRICARE benefits for a period of

60 to 120 days after the separation date under the Continued Health Care Benefit Program.

4. Retirees (under sixty-five years old), their spouses, and their unmarried children.

- Children have the same restrictions as above.
- Retirees who are Medicare eligible are not covered at the current time. However, on 1 October 2001, retirees enrolled in Medicare Part B had their Part A eligibility restored if they lost it because of age.

5. Unremarried spouses and children of servicemembers who died. (Children have same restrictions as above.)

6. Spouses and children of reservists who are ordered to active duty for more than thirty consecutive days. (They are covered only during the reservists' tour. Children have the same restrictions as above.)

7. Spouses and unmarried children of reservists who are injured or aggravate an injury, illness, or disease during active-duty training and die as a result of the injury, illness, or disease.

8. Former spouses of active or retired servicemembers who served for at least twenty creditable years. There are other restrictions for this category. Contact your TRICARE Service Center for complete eligibility rules.

9. Dependent parents and parents-in-law do not qualify for TRICARE benefits. However, they may still use military medical facilities on a space-available basis.

10. Other categories of persons may be eligible for TRICARE benefits. Visit the TRICARE website or contact your TRICARE Service Center for the current information.

How do you enroll your family in TRICARE?

Enrolling in TRICARE is simple and can be done either through the TRICARE Service Center at the nearest military treatment facility or through the regional TRICARE Service Center. You need to reenroll in TRICARE whenever you move out of your current TRICARE region. Each region is a separate legal entity, and the rules in each region are slightly different. You must contact the nearest TRICARE Service Center once you arrive at your new duty station to reenroll.

Before you can enroll in TRICARE, all of your family members must be enrolled in the Defense Enrollment Eligibility Reporting System (DEERS), a computerized roster of people eligible to receive health benefits under the Uniformed Services Health Benefit Program. Active-duty servicemembers are automatically enrolled in DEERS and TRICARE Prime. Dependents and retired military personnel must be entered into the DEERS computer at the local military personnel center, not at the military treatment facility. Dependent children should be enrolled in DEERS following their birth or adoption. To resolve DEERS problems, contact either your local military personnel office or DEERS (see Appendix A).

What is the priority for care at the military treatment facility (MTF)?
The priority for care is set by law. It is as follows:

- Active-duty servicemembers.
- Active-duty family members enrolled in TRICARE Prime.
- Retirees, survivors, and their family members enrolled in TRICARE Prime.
- Active-duty family members not enrolled in TRICARE Prime.
- Retirees, survivors, and their family members not enrolled in TRICARE Prime.

Nonenrolled persons eligible for military care (e.g., dependent parents of active-duty servicemembers) may be seen at an MTF on a space-available basis.

What does each option cost?
For each TRICARE program, the military charges three different rates: E-4 and below, E-5 and above, and retirees. There is no cost for active-duty members who must receive all their medical treatment under the TRICARE Prime option. For everyone other than active-duty servicemembers, the cost of medical care is further subdivided between care at military treatment facilities and care at civilian facilities. For care at a military treatment facility, outpatient services are free and hospital charges are less than $20 per day. For care at a civilian treatment facility, the fees for 2001 are listed in Tables 10-1 through 10-3 (fees are subject to change).

Is there a limit to what you would have to pay out-of-pocket?
TRICARE, like most other major health insurance plans, has a limit, or catastrophic cap, on the amount of out-of-pocket expenses that an individual or family will incur. For TRICARE Prime, the cap for each year is $1,000 for an active-duty family and $3,000 for all others. For TRICARE Standard, the cap for each year is $1,000 for an active-duty family and $3,000 for all others. It is important to understand that the caps apply only to the amount of money required to meet your family's annual deductibles and cost shares based on TRICARE's allowable charges for covered treatment. You must pay any charges in excess of those that TRICARE determines to be allowable. Additionally, noncovered costs do not apply to the cap. This is especially important for those enrolled in TRICARE Standard. Although exceeding the cap is rare, the risk is present and should be a consideration when you determine whether you need supplemental insurance. Some servicemembers have had to pay medical bills in excess of $10,000.

What are the pharmaceutical benefits under TRICARE?
The pharmaceutical benefit has been and continues to be one of the most cost-effective medical benefits provided to you and your family by the military in terms of both time and money. An April 2001 change in TRICARE bases the cost share for drugs on where the drug is obtained and whether it is generic or name brand, not on your beneficiary category. As an active-duty servicemember,

you pay nothing for any medication you need. For all other beneficiaries, if the medication is available at the military treatment facility, there is no cost regardless of their TRICARE option. If the medication is not available at the military treatment facility or you are not located near one, then the cost structure in Table 10-4 applies.

TABLE 10-1
E-4 and Below Active Duty: Civilian Treatment Facility for Family Members

TRICARE Plan	Annual Enrollment Fee	Annual Deductible (Individual/Family)	Civilian Outpatient Visit	Civilian Inpatient Admission
Prime	None	None*	$0*	$0*
Extra	None	$50/$100	15%	$11.45/day
Standard	None	$50/$100	20%	$11.45/day

*If you decide to get care under the POS option, there is an annual deductible of $300 per individual or $600 per family. After the deductible is satisfied, your cost share for the POS care will be 50% of what TRICARE determines is a fair price for the service (not necessarily the actual cost of the service), and you may have to pay up to 15% above the TRICARE allowable charge if it is a nonnetwork provider. Finally, you will also likely have to pay the provider up front and seek reimbursement from TRICARE.

Source: TRICARE Management Activity, "TRICARE Cost/Co-Pay Schedule." Internet: *http://www.tricare.osd.mil/tricare/beneficiary/tricarecost.html.*

TABLE 10-2
E-5 and Above Active Duty: Civilian Treatment Facility for Family Members

TRICARE Plan	Annual Enrollment Fee	Annual Deductible (Individual/Family)	Civilian Outpatient Visit	Civilian Inpatient Admission
Prime	None	None*	$0*	$0*
Extra	None	$150/$300	15%	$11.45/day
Standard	None	$150/$300	20%	$11.45/day

*If you decide to get care under the POS option, there is an annual deductible of $300 per individual or $600 per family. After the deductible is satisfied, your cost share for the POS care will be 50% of what TRICARE determines is a fair price for the service (not necessarily the actual cost of the service), and you may have to pay up to 15% above the TRICARE allowable charge if it is a nonnetwork provider. Finally, you will also likely have to pay the provider up front and seek reimbursement from TRICARE.

Source: TRICARE Management Activity, "TRICARE Cost/Co-Pay Schedule." Internet: *http://www.tricare.osd.mil/tricare/beneficiary/tricarecost.html.*

TABLE 10-3
Retirees under Age 65:
Civilian Treatment Facility for Retired Members and Their Families

TRICARE Plan	Annual Enrollment Fee (Individual/ Family)*	Annual Deductible (Individual/ Family)	Outpatient Visit Civilian Provider Copays	Emergency Care Civilian Provider Copays	Inpatient Admission Cost Share
Prime	$230/$460	None	$12	$30	$11/day ($25 minimum)
Extra	None	$150/$300	20% of negotiated fee	20% of negotiated fee	Lesser of $250/day or 25% of billed charges; +20% professional fees
Standard	None	$150/$300	25% of allowable charges	25% of allowable charges	Lesser of $401/day or 25% of billed charges; +25% professional fees

*Under current DOD policies, the enrollment fee can be paid quarterly, subject to a $5 processing fee per installment.

Source: TRICARE Management Activity, "TRICARE Cost/Co-Pay Schedule." Internet: *http://www.tricare.osd.mil/tricare/beneficiary/tricarecost.html.*

TABLE 10-4
Pharmaceutical Cost Share:
Civilian Pharmacy for Family Members and Retired Service Members

Place of Service	Generic Drug	Name Brand
National Mail Order Pharmacy (up to 90-day supply)	$3	$9
TRICARE retail networks (up to a 30-day supply)	$3	$9
Nonnetwork pharmacies	$9 or 20% of total cost (whichever is greater); existing deductibles and POS penalty apply	

Source: TRICARE Management Activity, "New Pharmacy Co-Pay." Internet: *http://www.tricare.osd.mil/pharmacy/newpharmacy.html.*

How do I obtain emergency care through TRICARE?

Of course, you may seek emergency care at an MTF at any time. If you enrolled in TRICARE Prime and use a civilian facility, then you must notify your Managed Care Support Contractor (the TRICARE Service Center) within twenty-four hours of receiving the care. Any follow-up must then be scheduled through your PCM.

If you're not sure it is an emergency, you may call the Nurse Advice Line (available in most regions) to get guidance.

Once you choose a TRICARE option, may you change your mind?

Enrollment in TRICARE Prime is for a twelve-month period unless you move from the area or lose your eligibility for medical care (for example, through divorce). After the twelve-month period is over, you will automatically continue to be enrolled in TRICARE Prime, but on a month-to-month basis, or you may change your TRICARE option. If you are dissatisfied with your prime care manager at any time, you may change that individual by contacting your TRICARE Service Center.

How does TRICARE fit with the Program for Persons with Disabilities (PFPWD)?

Most families with exceptional family members, because of the costs associated with their care, will be encouraged to join TRICARE Prime. However, because some services are provided by other state and federal laws, coverage for some exceptional family members' needs cannot be covered by TRICARE Prime. Since every TRICARE region will be slightly different, you should contact the TRICARE Service Center in your region to be assigned a multispecialty case manager, who will help you choose which option is best for your family.

What happens when I leave the military?

Since 1994, servicemembers and their families have been able to purchase a health insurance plan called Continued Health Care Benefit Program (CHCBP). This insurance plan is meant to cover you and your family for only the short time between your leaving the military and getting a new job that provides you some type of coverage. The coverage and deductibles are similar to that of the TRICARE Standard option. When separating from the service, you must disenroll from TRICARE and then reenroll in CHCBP. Failure to do so could delay your coverage. You have up to sixty days after you lose your military health-care benefits to enroll in CHCBP, and you can buy coverage in ninety-day blocks for up to eighteen months. Family members may continue buying coverage for up to thirty-six months after the servicemember separates. The 2002 quarterly premiums were $933 for one person and $1,996 for a family (based upon Federal Employee Health Benefit Program rates). For more information, contact

Humana Military Health Services, Inc.
Attn: CHCBP
P.O. Box 740072
Louisville, KY 40201 or call
(800) 444-5445

How does TRICARE work for retired servicemembers under the age of sixty-five?

As a retiree under age sixty-five, you and your family members and survivors are eligible for TRICARE Prime, TRICARE Standard, and TRICARE Extra. For TRICARE Prime, retirees must submit an enrollment application and pay an enrollment fee of $230 for an individual and $460 for a family.

The enrollment fee paid by retired members and their families for TRICARE Prime is intended to provide better coverage and should reduce the risk of severe financial hardships. Again, you are trading off the choice of doctors for reduced costs and less financial risk. Unless you plan to retire near an active military base, TRICARE Prime probably will not be available to you. When planning for retirement, you should plan for the possibility of financial expenses for medical care.

What about retired members who are Medicare eligible?

Medical care under Medicare is divided into two parts. Part A (hospital insurance) provides basic protection against the costs of inpatient hospitalization and is automatic. Part B (medical insurance) coverage is voluntary and provides some protection against medical costs and other expenses not covered under Part A. Part A coverage is paid from Social Security funds and is provided without charge to anyone sixty-five or older. Part B is voluntary and is paid for by the individual, although it is heavily subsidized by the federal government.

TRICARE eligibility was restored on 1 October 2001 under a program called TRICARE for Life, but those eligible must already be enrolled in Part B. One of the medical benefits that Medicare-eligible retirees keep is use of the military pharmacies. As of 1 April 2001, this benefit was automatically restored under a program called TRICARE Senior Pharmacy for all those over sixty-five (as of 1 April 2001) who were already enrolled in Part B. Those who turned sixty-five on or after 1 April 2001 must voluntarily enroll in Part B to receive the pharmacy benefit.

Although retirees and their dependents are still eligible for medical care in military treatment facilities after age sixty-five on a space-available basis, there is no guarantee that this care will be available. Therefore, even with Part A coverage, you should enroll in Part B Medicare at age sixty-five. However, because there are many very large gaps in the Medicare coverage that can leave you with enormous medical bills, we also recommend that you buy private supplemental Medicare insurance and, when Part A comes available, that you do not cancel your Medicare supplement if you already have it. A number of military associations offer group policies at reasonable rates. Supplemental policies are discussed later in this chapter.

What happens if you or your family members have to travel to receive medical care?

As an active-duty servicemember, you will be placed on temporary duty (TDY) orders and be reimbursed for travel expenses involved with your travel to distant treatment facilities. If you are being treated as an outpatient, your unit will provide you with the travel orders and funds. If you are being treated as an inpatient, your travel orders and funds will come from the hospital that ordered you to travel. Either way, you need to make sure that you get your travel orders before you depart. Additionally, if you cannot drive, the military will provide transportation or place another servicemember on escort duty orders if needed. One of the financial problems associated with the servicemember being hospitalized at a distant facility is that the services will not pay for a family member to travel with you. This is an expense that you must incur if your family wishes to be near you during your treatment. One of the largest costs associated with family member travel is accommodations at the distant facility. To assist with this, Zachary and Elizabeth Fisher have established guesthouses that can assist in minimizing these costs (see below).

If a family member needs to be treated at a distant medical facility, you will not be reimbursed for the cost of his or her travel. However, you, as the active-duty servicemember, may be placed on escort duty orders to escort your family member for this treatment. Traveling as an escort is approved on a case-by-case basis and you must receive permission from the hospital and your unit to do it. Plan early and ask your personnel officer or commander as soon as you know that a family member must travel to a distant facility. Otherwise, you will incur this expense.

What are the Fisher Houses?

Zachary and Elizabeth Fisher ran a highly successful real estate construction business in New York City from the 1920s to the 1980s. After this long and successful career, the Fishers channeled their energies into numerous charitable efforts. One of those efforts is the Fisher House program. This program will eventually provide homes at several major military and Veterans Affairs medical centers to comfort and support the families and dependents of hospitalized military personnel. These houses provide well-kept accommodations and kitchens at low rates if you or your family members should need care at an adjacent military medical facility. To find out the availability and rates for each specific Fisher House, contact the base operator or hospital where the Fisher House is located.

The following are Fisher House locations:

California:	David Grant USAF Medical Center, Travis AFB
	Naval Medical Center, San Diego
Colorado:	Denver VA Medical Center
District of Columbia:	Walter Reed Army Medical Center I and II
Florida:	West Palm Beach VA Medical Center
Georgia:	D. D. Eisenhower Army Medical Center, Ft. Gordon
Hawaii:	Tripler Army Medical Center
Maryland:	Malcolm Grow Medical Center, Andrews AFB
	National Naval Medical Center I and II, Bethesda
Minnesota:	Minneapolis VA Medical Center
Mississippi:	Keesler USAF Medical Center
New York:	Stratton VA Medical Center, Albany
North Carolina:	Womack Army Medical Center, Ft. Bragg
Ohio:	USAF Medical Center I and II, Wright-Patterson AFB
Texas:	Brooke Army Medical Center I and II, Ft. Sam Houston
	Darnall Army Community Hospital, Ft. Hood
	Wilford Hall Medical Center I, II, and III, Lackland AFB
	William Beaumont Army Medical Center, El Paso
Virginia:	Naval Medical Center, Portsmouth I and II
Washington:	Madigan Army Medical Center, Ft. Lewis

What about being treated in a VA hospital?

The Veterans Affairs hospital system was originally built to take care of servicemembers who were no longer in the military but incurred a service-related disability. Over the years, its primary focus has become caring for veterans who are financially unable to care for themselves. The VA system is not for retirees, family members, or active-duty servicemembers. Having said that, you may find yourself being treated at a VA hospital. The reason for this is that TRICARE is contracting with VA hospitals for treatment and care. Do not confuse a referral to a VA facility by TRICARE as a right to use the VA hospital system. Part of TRICARE's contracted service includes emergency room treatment for any active-duty servicemember or his or her family.

Along with the VA hospital system, families of veterans with service-related disabilities (but not the veterans themselves) may be entitled to CHAMPVA. This program is not associated with CHAMPUS, and you should consult the nearest VA hospital or facility to determine your eligibility or contact CHAMPVA directly (see Appendix A). Veterans must contact the Department of Veterans Affairs for information related to their care.

Summary of Medical Benefits

The care provided through the military medical system is likely to vary significantly from place to place and from time to time. Your medical needs as an active-duty servicemember will receive prompt and professional care under almost all circumstances. The same may not, however, always be true for your family members while you remain on active duty, or for you and your family members when you retire.

From a financial perspective, unless you have a very strong tie to a certain doctor, you should consider selecting the TRICARE Prime option for your family. Although TRICARE Prime does not eliminate your financial risk, it can meet your family's medical needs at the lowest cost, and more importantly, it minimizes the risk of financial distress should an expensive emergency arise. If TRICARE Prime is unavailable, you should consider using TRICARE Extra certified providers whenever possible. Regardless of which TRICARE option you choose, you should consider buying additional insurance known as a CHAMPUS supplement (covered later in this chapter).

DENTAL CARE

As an active-duty servicemember, your dental coverage is provided by the military's Dental Corps free of charge. On 1 February 2001, the old TRICARE Family Member Dental Plan (FMDP) and the Selected Reserve Dental Program were combined to form the TRICARE Dental Program (TDP), which provides your family's dental coverage. With this change came improved service, including a shortened mandatory enrollment period and greater efficiency, because the contractor, United Corcordia, has access to DEERS to check eligibility. Although the TRICARE Dental Program is currently administered by United Concordia, the contract is negotiated every couple of years. This is important, because the information about what is covered, where it is covered, and how much you will have to pay can and will change.

Eligibility rules for family members are similar, but not exactly the same, as for TRICARE. Currently, the TDP covers most types of professional dental services in CONUS and OCONUS service areas. The plan has cost shares, maximums, limitations, and exclusions and is similar to most group dental plans. The typical coverage is given in Table 10-5.

Certain dental services are considered medical procedures and are covered under TRICARE–Medical, not TDP. Therefore, if your family requires dental care not listed below, check with your health benefits advisor to see if they are covered under TRICARE–Medical. Retired servicemembers and their families are not entitled to dental coverage. Retirees should contact Delta Dental of California at 888-838-8737 for information on the TRICARE Retiree Dental Plan.

What is the cost of the dental premium?

The cost of the TDP premium is shared between the servicemember and DOD. Your portion of the premium must be paid in advance through a payroll deduction. The monthly premiums for 2001–2002 are as follows:

TABLE 10-5
MONTHLY COSTS FOR THE TRICARE DENTAL PROGRAM

Component	Sponsor	Single Enrollee	Family Enrollment
Active Duty	N/A	$7.63	$19.08
Selected Reserve/IRR (Special Mobilization)	$7.63	19.08	47.69
Other IRR	19.08	19.08	47.69

Source: TRICARE Management Activity, "Fact Sheet 9: New TRICARE Dental Program," June 2001. Internet: *http://www.tricare.osd.mil/Factsheets/factsheet9.pdf.*

The following table is a partial list of cost shares for various dental services.

TABLE 10-6
DENTAL COST SHARES SUMMARY CHART (AS OF 2001)

Type of Service	Pay Grades E-1 to E-4 CONUS*	All Other Pay Grades CONUS	OCONUS**
Diagnostic/preventive	0%	0%	0%
Emergency care	0	0	0
Basic restorative	20	20	0
Sealants	20	20	0
Endodontics	30	40	0
Periodontics	30	40	0
Oral surgery	40	40	0
Prosthodontics/crowns	50	50	50
Orthodontics***	50	50	50
Other restorative	50	50	50

*Some services, including endodontic and periodontic services, are available at a reduced cost share for pay grades E-1 to E-4.
**Some exceptions for Selected Reserve and IRR persons.
***Orthodontic treatment has special conditions. Consult your local benefits counselor for details.

Source: United Concordia, *TRICARE Dental Program Benefit Booklet.* Internet: *http://www.ucci.com/tdp/TDPBenefitBooklet.pdf.*

The annual maximum benefit is $1,200 per family member, and the lifetime orthodontic maximum is $1,500 per family member. Enrollment is for a minimum of twelve months, with the sponsor having at least twelve months remaining in service. (Those enrolled in the old FMDP prior to 1 February 2001, however, are required to fulfill their original enrollment commitment of twenty-four months.) To enroll in TDP, family members must be enrolled in DEERS. United Concordia will automatically enroll your child at four years of age; however, you are encouraged to enroll your children by age one for better preventative dental care.

Can you find out in advance how much your dental bills will be?
If you are uncertain about whether TDP will cover a particular procedure, you can ask your dentist to submit a predetermination request. This request is a pretreatment, nonbinding written estimate of both the plan and patient costs. We highly recommend that you do this for any covered procedure, especially if it is complex and expensive (crowns, orthodontics, and so on). United Concordia will tell you how much the procedure will cost given the supplied information, and that predetermination will remain valid for six months.

Will it cost you more to use any dentist you want?
The short answer is yes. To minimize the cost to you, your family must use a United Concordia participating dentist. When you use a participating dentist, you will save time, paperwork, and money, because these dentists will complete the paperwork and charge you only your share of the bill. Your family may, if you desire, see any authorized licensed dentist. However, this will leave you financially liable for charges in excess of what TDP is willing to pay. When United Concordia says 100 percent coverage, that is only for their dentists, so if you use a dentist who is not on their list, United Concordia will reimburse you for only a fixed amount. Additionally, your dentist may require you to pay the bill in full and then file a claim for reimbursement.

What is your dental coverage overseas?
With the new TDP, the coverage for dental services is the same OCONUS as it is CONUS, with the exception of some services that are simply unavailable in certain countries. In any case, before you move overseas, make sure that every family member has had a checkup to resolve all known dental problems.

SUPPLEMENTAL HEALTH INSURANCE

Why would you need supplemental health insurance?
Obviously, it makes little sense to buy additional insurance for needs that will be met through programs to which your family is entitled. But there are gaps in the medical care provided by TRICARE, and supplemental insurance is

designed to provide coverage for these gaps. Since the cost of prolonged medical care for a dependent can substantially reduce your family's standard of living, it is wise to consider additional medical coverage, particularly if there is a family history of illness or disease that may require expensive care. In deciding whether to purchase supplemental insurance, you should consider the coverage provided by TRICARE, the cost of the supplemental insurance premium, the likelihood of future illness in your family, the type of care covered, your ability to pay both expected and unexpected medical expenses, and the age of your dependents. Remember, each TRICARE option exposes you to different risks. Financially, you have more exposure to large medical expenses under TRICARE Standard than TRICARE Prime. Therefore, the TRICARE option you choose will have a large impact on whether you need a supplemental policy. It is possible that due to family conditions even someone in TRICARE Prime may need a supplemental policy.

Supplemental TRICARE/CHAMPUS insurance pays only after TRICARE pays its portion. Coverage varies widely among supplemental insurance plans, as do annual premiums. The annual premiums for inpatient and outpatient care can range from $75 to $250 for an active-duty spouse and $20 to $90 for each child. These plans are provided through various commercial firms and typically have a period, normally six months or one year, for which the cost of care for a preexisting condition is not reimbursed. Rules on preexisting conditions vary depending upon your state and whether you had a previous insurance policy. You should ask each company specifically about its policy.

If we have TRICARE, why is it called a CHAMPUS supplement?

As you know, old names die hard. Since supplemental insurance policies are issued by private insurers, some of them have not yet changed their policy names to TRICARE. Therefore, you should assume that CHAMPUS supplements are aimed at those who have either TRICARE Standard or TRICARE Extra policies. Since TRICARE Prime is an HMO option, a supplemental insurance policy may not be needed. If, after reading this section, you feel that you might need supplemental insurance even though you have TRICARE Prime, contact one of the supplemental insurance companies. Some offer CHAMPUS supplemental insurance at a discount to those who participate in TRICARE Prime.

What if my spouse has health insurance?

For many active-duty servicemembers with a working spouse, health insurance may be provided for the spouse by the civilian employer. In this case, TRICARE is required by law to pay only after the private insurance plan pays its share. For your family members, this includes their stay in a military hospital. If you do not have additional civilian health-care insurance, you may want to consider a CHAMPUS supplemental policy.

How do you evaluate the different policies?

In evaluating the options offered in supplemental CHAMPUS insurance plans, you should first determine the specific coverage you need. As you compare policies, try to use the same criteria for each one, and do not be discouraged when you find that there are many different "packages" offered. The program that costs more may or may not offer additional coverage for your premium dollar.

As with any service or product you buy, read the terms carefully, and do not hesitate to ask questions about specific provisions that you do not understand. The long-term commitment you make to a health insurance program can easily add up to many thousands of dollars over your lifetime. It is worth your time to make the best decision you can when you buy such coverage, to review that coverage periodically, and to keep informed about new programs.

What happens when you turn sixty-five?

When you become Medicare eligible, you should properly enroll in Part A and Part B and consider buying a Medicare supplement insurance policy. By federal law, Medicare beneficiaries are guaranteed acceptance into any Medicare supplement for six months following the date they first become eligible for Medicare. If you do not sign up in the first six months, you risk being denied entry in the future. The decision process that you should use in evaluating these Medicare supplements is the same as in evaluating the TRICARE supplements.

What, besides the costs, should you consider?

- What are the plan's eligibility rules, and what are the grounds for termination of the plan?
- Is there a maximum limit on benefits (lifetime, annual, etc.)?
- Is there a preexisting condition clause? Is there a waiting period before the policy will pay for preexisting conditions? Most plans cover an illness that you've had treated within the last twelve months, but only after you've had the policy for twelve months and received no additional treatment. After twenty-four months, most plans will then cover the illness.
- Must you meet a deductible before the plan begins paying?
- If the plan has a deductible, is it in addition to the TRICARE deductible?
- Does the plan reimburse you for the TRICARE deductible, enrollment fees, or copayments?
- Does the plan pay excess, noncovered charges—charges above what TRICARE considers to be reasonable? Several plans pay unlimited excess charges after some initial limit, but most do not.
- Does the plan pay for services that aren't covered by TRICARE?
- Does the plan specifically not cover certain conditions?
- Must certain kinds of care be approved before getting the care?
- Is inpatient care covered? Outpatient care? Long-term care?
- What are the limits on hospital stays per year and on the number of outpatient visits? The average for the industry is sixty hospital days per year. There is

no standard on outpatient visits. Some plans limit the number to twenty visits per year; others set no limits.

- Does the plan limit continuous hospital care?
- Does the plan convert to a Medicare supplement? If so, must it be in force as a TRICARE supplement for any specified length of time before conversion?
- Will the plan cover you overseas? If you are overseas, you may not incur any disallowed charges under TRICARE Standard, because TRICARE Standard pays charges as billed overseas.
- Does the plan offer reduced premiums or premium adjustments when you participate in Department of Defense contracted managed health-care plans, such as TRICARE Prime or TRICARE Extra?
- Are the premium payments monthly? Quarterly? May you charge the premiums to a credit card?
- How often and under what conditions can the premiums change?
- Does the plan offer rates based on military status (active or retired) or on an age scale? What is the scale?
- What are the membership fees (annual, lifetime, etc.), if any, when you join the organization that sponsors the plan?
- Does the plan cover the servicemember when he/she retires?
- Does coverage continue for surviving spouses at no charge?
- What are the time limitations, if any, for claim filing? Most plans require that claims be filed between twelve and twenty-four months after the illness was treated.
- Are you a smoker? Does the plan have higher rates for smokers?
- If you're retired military and have a health-care plan through a civilian job (which pays before TRICARE), do you still need a TRICARE supplement if your employer's plan and the TRICARE health-care option you've chosen will pay most or all of your civilian medical bills?

As you consider the purchase of supplemental insurance, it is also helpful to consult your local TRICARE benefits advisor about the coverage that each TRICARE option does and does not provide. Additionally, if you are retired from the military and have a health-care plan under your current employer, you may not require further insurance.

Addresses and telephone numbers of organizations offering supplemental insurance are in Appendix A. Current terms and rates are available directly from these organizations and are also provided in many of the weekly service newspapers and other military publications.

LONG-TERM CARE

Long-term care is defined as the day-in and day-out professional care needed in the event of chronic illness or disability in which an individual cannot care for him or herself. Many types of care fall under this category, including, but not limited to, skilled nursing home facilities, custodial care facilities, adult day care, and visiting nurses.

It is estimated that 25 percent of those over age eighty-five will reside in a nursing home and 40 to 80 percent of those older than sixty-five will require a stay in a nursing home. Although the statistics show that most people who require long-term care are older, there is a small chance that you or a family member may require this care at a younger age. Since the average cost of a year in a long-term care facility can average $40,000 to $60,000 or more, the potential for a financial disaster exists.

If you are on active duty, do you need to worry?
The short answer to this question is maybe. When making decisions about long-term care, you should consider two situations: that you might need long-term care and that a family member might need long-term care. Let's first examine the case in which you need long-term care. Should you become permanently disabled, the military service will retire you, and you will receive a pension and medical benefits that are normally received by a retired servicemember. Under the old CHAMPUS program and the new TRICARE Standard program, a 20 percent copayment could be financially devastating if you have very large medical bills. TRICARE Prime may alleviate this problem if you live in the proper area. You would then have to decide where to live based upon where the TRICARE Prime network is functioning. The good news is that the chances of your becoming disabled and requiring long-term medical care are remote, and you probably will not face this difficult and expensive situation.

The second case to consider is if a family member needs long-term care. Under this scenario, we are assuming that you remain on active duty. If this is the case, you would then be eligible for the Exceptional Family Member Program (EFMP). If possible, the military will attempt to station you in an area where the appropriate medical care is available. Sometimes this may not be possible, but if you do have a family member who may qualify for this program, you should contact your personnel officer immediately for specific details.

Should you buy a long-term-care insurance policy?
The short answer to this complicated question is probably not. Although many insurance companies are beginning to sell these policies, there are several reasons why you may not want to buy this type of insurance at this time. First, the chances of your needing the policy before age sixty-five are slim. In general, you should not buy insurance for events that probably will not occur. Second, there is the risk that the insurance company will cancel your policy or go bankrupt when you need it the most. Third, if you were to take the money you would have paid the insurance company, often close to $1,500 a year, and invest it each year instead, you'd probably be able to afford a two-year stay in a nursing home, which is the length of an average stay. Finally, the government, through Medicaid, the health insurance program for poor people, will pay your long-term medical bills if you are insolvent and cannot pay them yourselves. Additionally, many wealthy people, once they are old and know that they will

Tips on Making the Most from Your Medical Benefits

- Ensure that your family is properly enrolled in DEERS.
- Select TRICARE Prime to minimize your out-of-pocket costs.
- If family members live in different TRICARE regions or if you are stationed in an area without a TRICARE Prime Network, see if you are eligible for split enrollment under TRICARE Prime in another region, or enroll in TRICARE Standard and try to use only TRICARE Extra approved providers. Also, consider buying a supplemental insurance policy.
- Always actively consult your TRICARE benefits advisor and each doctor you see to ensure that all recommended treatment is covered and that the fees are deemed reasonable by TRICARE.
- Always try to have your medication prescriptions filled at a military pharmacy.
- Enroll your family in the TRICARE Dental Program and use a participating dentist.
- Before going overseas or to any remote region, take full advantage of all treatment facilities available to you, and make sure all of your medical and dental care is up-to-date.
- Plan ahead and budget for expected medical problems such as children's orthodontics.
- Only purchase long-term-care insurance if you believe that someone in your family has a high probability of needing the care.

require long-term care, are able to transfer their money to their children and declare bankruptcy. In America, if you have no assets, the federal government will pay your long-term-care bills. Transferring money, however, may be illegal in certain cases, so you should consult your lawyer if you find yourself in this position.

The reason most long-term-care policies are so expensive is that there are not enough healthy people paying in to make the policies less expensive for those who need the care. For the insurance companies, these policies are a bad bet, because only those people who think they need care will buy the insurance. Therefore, premiums will probably remain high.

Because the chance is remote that you will require long-term care and the cost of the policies is extremely high, it is probably not in most military families' best interests to purchase long-term-care policies. Since the military has programs for active-duty members who become disabled and exceptional family members, most military families would be better off applying the $1,500 annual long-term-care premium toward their total financial savings program.

SUGGESTED REFERENCES

See the Internet sites, organization addresses, and phone numbers in Appendix A.

Gordon, Sol, ed. *1998 Uniformed Services Almanac.* Washington, DC: Uniformed Services Almanac, 1998.

Hunter, Ronald, and Debra Gordon, eds. *1998 Retired Military Almanac.* Washington, DC: Uniformed Services Almanac, 1998.

TRICARE Dental Program Benefit Booklet. United Concordia. Available online at *www.ucci.com.*

TRICARE Standard Handbook. TRICARE Support Office, Aurora, CO. Available online at *www.tricare.osd.mil.*

11

Housing

The American dream is often couched in the form of home ownership. Many members of the military purchase several homes over the course of their career, thus enjoying iterations of the American dream as they move from station to station. Whether you are planning on investing in a home, living on post in government housing, or simply renting, your decision on how to accommodate your housing needs is financially significant.

There are three basic options: military families can live in quarters provided by the government, rent housing on the local economy, or buy a house. The factors that influence this decision are not entirely financially motivated, but the choice is often constrained by finances.

This chapter discusses some of the housing choices faced by military families and suggests a way to analyze housing alternatives. Because determining where you live is ultimately a personal decision, our guidelines must be adapted to fit your particular situation. This chapter provides an outline of the primary considerations for most military families in selecting their housing. If you are considering real estate as part of your investment portfolio, you should also read chapter 18 concerning investing in real assets.

Regardless of whether you rent, buy, or live on post, the ability to search for housing options has become increasingly less costly with the advent of the Internet. Most posts have websites that contain links to local housing information, including real estate agents, rental housing, and the post housing agency. You should investigate the housing market on the Internet prior to traveling on permissive TDY for house hunting. This will give you a good feel for the market, allowing you to make the most of your time house hunting.

HOW SHOULD YOU DECIDE WHERE TO LIVE?

The first step is to determine whether there is any choice to make. Depending on the post to which you are being assigned, you may find one of two extremes: You may be required to live on post, or you may be forced to live off post because no government quarters are available. Check with the local housing office at your new duty station. They will have the most current information.

If you are not required to live in government quarters, then your family must make a decision. Start by making a "wish list" of desirable housing attributes. List your objectives in order of importance: low maintenance costs, closeness to community facilities, a good school system, low taxes, convenient public transportation, a quiet neighborhood, and so on. To make an informed housing decision, you must first understand your family's needs and preferences.

Next, get an idea of the alternatives available. Ask the housing office at your new duty station about the availability of both government and private housing. If you are going overseas, your options will probably be limited to government quarters or renting on the local economy. Likely CONUS sources of information include your sponsor, the local chamber of commerce, a local newspaper (particularly the Sunday edition), real estate agents, friends stationed at your new location, and Internet sites for the city, base, or post.

Now, determine your housing budget. You must consider your Basic Allowance for Housing (BAH) allowances, but don't stop there. Most American homeowners budget 30 to 35 percent of their after-tax household income toward their mortgage. BAH will often be significantly less than that amount, but servicemembers earn significant tax advantages when receiving BAH. BAH is not taxed as income since it is an allowance. This provides the opportunity to earn untaxed income and use it for a home, which provides significant tax advantages—a double tax benefit! The amount you decide is appropriate will depend on the amounts you must budget for transportation, entertainment, investment, maintenance, and other budget categories. Refer to chapter 4 for help with the budgeting process.

At this point you're ready to compare your housing budget with the available alternatives. First, consider the civilian versus government options. Comparing the local rental market to what is available on post is rather straightforward. The local housing office should have information on square footage of quarters, numbers of bedrooms and bathrooms, and appliances; this will allow for easy comparison with local rentals. Living in government quarters is essentially renting from the government for the price of BAH for rent and utilities. Usually the local rental market will give you greater variety from which to choose, but often at additional costs. In weighing your decision, make sure you properly evaluate costs of commuting (both time and gas) and costs of utilities, which together are minimal when living in government quarters. Driving the commute during rush hour times is a good way to estimate the additional cost in time it will take you to get to work. Then factor in the cost of fuel and wear and tear on your vehicle. Consider nonfinancial aspects of the choice as well. Each option affects your ability to choose neighbors, your sense of security, the flexibility of departure dates due to military necessity, responsiveness of maintenance workers, and other considerations.

Comparing the rental versus purchase decision is a bit more complicated but starts with the same considerations of desired housing attributes and nonfinancial factors. These aspects are covered in detail later in this chapter.

Following this general approach, you can accommodate your housing needs. However, you must have detailed knowledge of each of your options to make an accurate assessment. The sections that follow provide an outline of the data you need to gather, the places to look for it, and how to incorporate this information into your decision process. Because the civilian housing versus government quarters option has already been fully discussed, we will devote the remainder of the chapter to the rent versus buy decision for off-post housing.

SHOULD YOU RENT?

Some people think money spent on rent is "lost money"—you pay the rent and at the end of the contracted period you have nothing. This view is incorrect. Rent is payment for the purchase of housing services. These services may also be acquired through the purchase of a house, which implicitly combines the acquisition of housing services with an investment decision. For a more sophisticated analysis of the three basic choices, see this book's website *(http://www.dean.usma.edu/socs/econ/persfin/default.htm),* where you can link to an Excel spreadsheet, which analyzes on-post, off-post rent, and off-post purchase options. The spreadsheet uses net present value analysis to determine which option works best in a particular scenario, given your assumptions. The spreadsheet also shows sensitivity analysis to certain assumptions. You can download this spreadsheet and use it as a guide to model your own individual circumstances if you understand the time value of money and how to use Microsoft Excel. Time value of money concepts are covered in Appendix D.

The decision to rent should be made after a careful review of total costs and family goals. Owning your home almost always costs more each month than renting an equivalent dwelling. Many families decide to buy in the expectation that they will make money when they sell the home, in effect earning a return on the extra spending. However, you should be aware that homeowners do not always make money when they sell, due to the risk inherent in real estate investments. Further, you may decide to rent so that you can use your savings toward other financial obligations.

Generally, renting is more advantageous than buying if any of the following are true:

1. You do not have the cash available for the down payment and the closing costs required when you buy.
2. You don't want to incur a large mortgage debt.
3. You want lighter responsibilities regarding housing and do not wish to concern yourself and your family with the worries caused by taxes, utilities, maintenance, insurance, and the need to resell.
4. You prefer to spend a larger portion of your income on other priorities such as cars, travel, or entertainment.
5. You anticipate being at your new station for only a few years, or you don't believe local housing prices will rise during the period you anticipate owning the house.

6. You desire the amenities (swimming pool, tennis courts) readily available in some rental units.

7. You are not familiar with the area or do not think it is an attractive place to own property.

Checklist for Renters

At the end of this chapter, we present a checklist for buyers. Much of the investigation a buyer should perform is also applicable to a renter, particularly the topics listed under Neighborhood. In addition, renters should be sure that they and their landlords agree in writing on the following details:

1. Who pays for utilities (water, gas, oil, electricity, cable, garbage collection)?
2. Who pays for repairs?
3. Is the rent fixed or can it be suddenly increased after you have moved in?
4. Do you have the right to sublet?
5. To what extent are you liable for damages to the dwelling or surrounding property?
6. Is a deposit required, what does it cover, how and when will you get it back, and do you accrue interest on it?
7. Who pays for taxes and the insurance covering damage to the dwelling? What are the limits?
8. Are children, pets, pianos, waterbeds, or child-care providers allowed?
9. May you alter the dwelling? If so, do the improvements (added cabinets, toolshed, wallpaper) become the landlord's property? Will the landlord reimburse you for repairs and improvements?
10. Does the lease give the landlord unrestricted access to the property at any time?
11. Can the landlord put the property on continual public exhibition to prospective renters or buyers? (You should try to limit this to thirty days before you vacate.)
12. What is the role of the realtor, if applicable, and who pays the realtor's fees?
13. Are there any special fees, such as a health board fee when you vacate if you've owned a pet, a cleaning fee, a general maintenance fee, a renter's fee, a security guard fee, a community assessment fee, a delivery fee, or a sidewalk fee?
14. What are the parking, guest, and storage restrictions? Are there fees attached to these restrictions?
15. Who actually owns the dwelling, and what is that person's address and telephone number? Who is his or her legal representative? (This question shows that you have an interest in the proper management of the dwelling and should help to minimize potential "shady" actions by the landlord.)
16. What type of renter restrictions—age, marital status, income, race, and occupation—are there? Because of the antidiscrimination laws, this question may have to be asked in a number of different ways to get a true picture.

17. Are there any restrictions on appliances? Do you have to use existing appliances such as washer, dryer, and refrigerator, or may you bring in your own? How do any future purchases or repairs of appliances by your landlord affect your rent?
18. Is there an additional cost for storage facilities?
19. Are there any restrictions in the use of utilities?
20. How much notice must be given before moving, and what financial penalties must you pay if you leave early?
21. Finally, is a military clause included in your contract releasing you from your lease in the event of transfer or other reason? A servicemember should never sign a lease unless it includes a military clause (see the Sample Military Clause below).

Sample Military Clause

In the event the Tenant or spouse is or hereafter becomes a member of the United States Armed Forces, the Tenant may terminate this lease on thirty days' written notice to the Landlord in any of the following events:

a. If the Tenant or spouse receives permanent-change-of-station orders to depart from the area where the premises are located.

b. If the Tenant or spouse is relieved from active duty.

c. If the Tenant or spouse has leased the property prior to arrival in the area and the orders are changed to a different area prior to occupancy of the property.

d. If the Tenant or spouse is assigned government quarters.

e. If the Tenant or spouse receives temporary-change-of-station (TCS) orders to depart from the area where the premises are located for more than ninety days.

Rents due will be prorated if departure occurs during the middle of a month.

Be sure all the rental details are in writing; do not rely on verbal promises. In addition, check with former tenants or others in the neighborhood about the landlord's reputation. Calling the local military housing office, chamber of commerce, Realtors Association, and Consumer Affairs Office may help you identify questionable landlords. Finally, before you sign the lease, take it to your legal assistance officer for review. This is a free yet valuable service.

In summary, if the cost of owning a house in your new location exceeds your monthly budget, renting may be your best alternative. Even if you do have the financial resources, if you anticipate that home prices will not increase enough to offset the closing costs associated with ownership (discussed in the next section) and provide a reasonable return on your down payment, renting may be for you.

SHOULD YOU BUY?

A home is the biggest single purchase most people make in a lifetime, so a great deal of thought and effort should precede any decision to buy. That being said, it should not be a decision that engenders fear in the first-time home buyer. Many military members purchase numerous homes over the course of their career. Some accumulate homes as investments as they travel from post to post. The information in this section will help you determine whether buying is the right decision for you and your family. This chapter also explains the buying process.

Realtors expect to sell a house to a buyer after showing them houses for an average of four days. Their motivation is to get as large a commission as possible in the shortest possible time. They will often encourage you to make compromises on your goals or expectations regarding price. For this reason it is critical for you and your family to determine beforehand how much house you can afford and what housing attributes you desire. It is helpful to prioritize your needs and wants in advance so that you can make prudent adjustments if necessary.

How Much House Can You Afford?

Early in the home-buying process, it is important to get a realistic sense of how much house you can afford. An acre of land, a two-car garage, and a Jacuzzi in the master bedroom sound wonderful, but can you really afford them? Table 11-1 provides a simple method for estimating how much you can afford to spend on a house based on the amount of money you wish to budget for monthly housing expenses.

First, figure your ability to make a down payment. Total your liquid assets and liabilities, and deduct your emergency cash fund. What remains is the amount of money you have available for a down payment and closing costs (discussed later in this chapter).

Next, examine the monthly home ownership expenses to see what you can afford in the way of a monthly mortgage payment. From your monthly budget (see chapter 4), find the amount you can afford or desire to spend on housing each month. From this amount, subtract the necessary expenses associated with home ownership. Property tax and utilities figures are available from your real estate agent. Your insurance company can provide insurance costs. You or a reputable repair contractor can estimate maintenance costs. What remains is the amount you can afford to pay in monthly mortgage payments (principal plus interest).

Now you're ready to calculate the most expensive house you can afford. Using the current interest rate available for a thirty-year, fixed-rate mortgage, read down that column in Table 11-2. Find the number closest to the amount

TABLE 11-1
WORKSHEET—HOW MUCH HOUSE CAN YOU AFFORD?

Liquid assets			
Cash	________		
Savings	________		
Stocks	________		
Bonds	________		
Mutual funds	________		
Life insurance cash value	________		
Other	________		
TOTAL ASSETS			________
Liabilities			
Credit card balances	________		
Loans	________		
Other debts	________		
TOTAL LIABILITIES		–	________
Emergency fund		–	________
Total available for down payment and closing costs		=	________
Monthly budget for housing			________
Monthly home ownership expenses			
Maintenance	________		
Insurance	________		
Property taxes	________		
Utilities	________		
Other	________		
TOTAL EXPENSES		–	________
Amount remaining for monthly mortgage payment (principal and interest)		=	________
Maximum mortgage loan amount (see Table 11-2)		=	________
Closing costs (estimate 5 to 8% of maximum mortgage)		–	________
Amount available for down payment + closing costs		+	________
HOUSE PRICE You Can Afford		=	________

you calculated for principal and interest. Read across that row to the leftmost column to find the largest mortgage you can afford to repay. For example, if you calculated $850 per month available for principal and interest in Table 11-1, and interest rates are approximately 8.5 percent, then you could afford to repay a mortgage of $110,000. This is the largest mortgage you can afford, not the most expensive house. Subtract 5 to 8 percent of the mortgage amount as an

TABLE 11-2: MONTHLY PRINCIPAL AND INTEREST PAYMENTS ON A 30-YEAR MORTGAGE

	INTEREST RATE														
Amount Mortgaged	6.0%	6.5%	7.0%	7.5%	8.0%	8.5%	9.0%	9.5%	10.0%	10.5%	11.0%	11.5%	12.0%	12.5%	13.0%
50,000	300	316	333	350	367	384	402	420	439	457	476	495	514	534	553
60,000	360	379	399	420	440	461	483	505	527	549	571	594	617	640	664
70,000	420	442	466	489	514	538	563	589	614	640	667	693	720	747	774
80,000	480	506	532	559	587	615	644	673	702	732	762	792	823	854	885
90,000	540	569	599	629	660	692	724	757	790	823	857	891	926	961	996
100,000	600	632	665	699	734	769	805	841	878	915	952	990	1,029	1,067	1,106
110,000	660	695	732	769	807	846	885	925	965	1,006	1,048	1,089	1,131	1,174	1,217
120,000	719	758	798	839	881	923	966	1,009	1,053	1,098	1,143	1,188	1,234	1,281	1,327
130,000	779	822	865	909	954	1,000	1,046	1,093	1,141	1,189	1,238	1,287	1,337	1,387	1,438
140,000	839	885	931	979	1,027	1,076	1,126	1,177	1,229	1,281	1,333	1,386	1,440	1,494	1,549
150,000	899	948	998	1,049	1,101	1,153	1,207	1,261	1,316	1,372	1,428	1,485	1,543	1,601	1,659
160,000	959	1,011	1,064	1,119	1,174	1,230	1,287	1,345	1,404	1,464	1,524	1,584	1,646	1,708	1,770
170,000	1,019	1,075	1,131	1,189	1,247	1,307	1,368	1,429	1,492	1,555	1,619	1,683	1,749	1,814	1,881
180,000	1,079	1,138	1,198	1,259	1,321	1,384	1,448	1,514	1,580	1,647	1,714	1,783	1,852	1,921	1,991
190,000	1,139	1,201	1,264	1,329	1,394	1,461	1,529	1,598	1,667	1,738	1,809	1,882	1,954	2,028	2,102
200,000	1,199	1,264	1,331	1,398	1,468	1,538	1,609	1,682	1,755	1,829	1,905	1,981	2,057	2,135	2,212
210,000	1,259	1,327	1,397	1,468	1,541	1,615	1,690	1,766	1,843	1,921	2,000	2,080	2,160	2,241	2,323
220,000	1,319	1,391	1,464	1,538	1,614	1,692	1,770	1,850	1,931	2,012	2,095	2,179	2,263	2,348	2,434
230,000	1,379	1,454	1,530	1,608	1,688	1,769	1,851	1,934	2,018	2,104	2,190	2,278	2,366	2,455	2,544
240,000	1,439	1,517	1,597	1,678	1,761	1,845	1,931	2,018	2,106	2,195	2,286	2,377	2,469	2,561	2,655

estimate of the closing costs, then add back in the amount available for a down payment and closing costs that you calculated above. The result is the maximum house price you can afford. Compare this figure with home prices in your area to see if you can satisfy your housing desires.

This method will give you a financially sound estimate of the home you can afford based on your actual budget. Banks, however, do not follow the same approach and may tell you that you can afford much more or less than you calculated. Generally banks will calculate approximately 28 percent of your pretax income as your maximum mortgage and 36 percent of your pretax income as maximum payments for all debts (including credit cards, car payments, and others).

The fact that your numbers and the bank's numbers may disagree does not mean you are wrong. Your figures represent your own financial situation and budget priorities. The bank's figures are based on historical probabilities of default. Trust your own figures and do not be tempted into signing a large mortgage simply because a bank offers it to you. However, if a bank offers you less than your estimate, you may want to shop around for other lenders, readjust your housing priorities, or reconsider the rental option.

Finding the Right Home to Buy

Now that you've determined the maximum house price you can afford, you can start your search for the right home. Use the buyer's checklist at the end of this chapter to establish your priorities. Your first decision is whether to look for a house on your own or use the services of a real estate broker. If you are very familiar with the local area, have a good idea of what you are looking for, have a long lead time, and are familiar with real estate laws and the house-buying procedure, you may do well to conduct the search on your own.

On the other hand, if you are not familiar with your new area and time is of the essence, you may want to provide a listing of your housing needs to real estate agents and let them compile a group of homes that meet your criteria. You may want to tell the agents that you want a house that costs about 90 percent of the maximum you can afford. Whatever price you tell them will most likely become the least expensive house they show you. After all, they are paid a percentage of the sale price, so the more expensive the house, the better it is for them, even if it may exceed what you want to spend.

Regardless of how much you can afford, the three cardinal rules of real estate are location, location, location! This means that the same exact home (similar features, same quality) built in one area will have a different value if built somewhere else. Thus, a three-bedroom, two-car garage home in a rural village will probably cost less than the same three-bedroom, two-car-garage home built on a bluff overlooking the ocean. You can easily see that the geographic region, as well as community amenities and other factors, can significantly impact the value of a home. Thus, you should consider travel costs into your housing decision. If you really want a nice house and don't mind commuting each day, then look farther away from the central business district of the community near post. When choosing this option, you should factor the increased cost of fuel and wear on your vehicle, as well as the extra time you forfeit each day from the longer commute. During normal economic times, when there is no backlog of loan applications and inspection appointments, you should plan to visit your new station sixty to ninety days before your anticipated relocation date. Servicemembers are generally authorized permissive TDY to conduct a house-hunting trip, and you should request it from your commander. Unfortunately, house-hunting expenses are no longer tax deductible, but the money you save by buying the right house and having peace of mind as you move will usually be worth the trip.

When you make your house-hunting trip, take a few items with you. A street map will help you find the local area, schools, fire departments, shopping, transportation, and how to get to your new job. Brochures from realtors will help you identify the types of homes you want to consider. Experienced house hunters keep track of homes using paper outlined in matrix fashion, with the features they want (garage, bedrooms, and so on) listed vertically and the houses listed horizontally. Keeping this information on one or two sheets of paper makes comparison easier when decision time arrives. A still or video camera is often helpful to capture key aspects of homes that meet your criteria for selection.

Before you leave home, measure any oversize furniture. With this information and a tape measure, you will be able to determine if it will fit in a prospective house. A flashlight is handy for looking into areas such as cellars, crawl spaces, and attics. Although you will probably want to employ the services of an inspector on the house you ultimately choose, in your early searching you can note obvious and critical flaws. To check the electrical system, carry a night-light and plug it into several outlets in different rooms in the house. If the light doesn't work, you can anticipate electrical problems.

When viewing a home, try to visit during bright daylight hours. During times of limited visibility or at the end of a tiring day, your imagination may turn the "fixer-up" special into your dream house. Always go back to view the house one more time before you make a final decision. Also, if the house is not vacant, ask to move furniture to see the condition of walls and floors, particularly if the furniture looks out of place.

The Role of the Real Estate Agent

A real estate agent can greatly assist in the process of finding the right home. Specifically in the house-hunting process, however, an agent can prove invaluable for a person unfamiliar with the new location. Let's assume that you have found an agent you trust based upon the recommendations of some friends (or military personnel) who own homes in the local area. You can ask the agent for house listings with the features you require. You can also ask for valuations based on comparable sales in the neighborhood you are considering. For example, you find a three-bedroom, two-car-garage home in a neighborhood with a school that has a solid reputation. The home is listing for $100,000. Your agent can provide you with price information on homes that have sold in that same neighborhood. You can then translate those values into dollars per square foot to get a rough estimate of whether the asking price is high or low on the house of your interest.

Other functions the agent may perform are to help draft up an offer. Let's say that you have narrowed down your list to two or three solid choices and would like to make an offer on one in the neighborhood you favor most. The agent can help draft an offer or negotiate verbally with the seller's agent or the seller him or herself. Offers should always be made contingent upon you accompanying a housing inspector through the house and not finding any major repair requirements. Otherwise, the contract can be null and void or open again for bargaining. An agent should advise you in regard to matters such as fair value, how to bid, and any stipulations you should make. If they do not, make sure you ask. For reasons we will go into in the following section, the agent may have a conflict of interest that could lead you to terminate any further house hunting with that particular agent—read on.

In the past, the process of listing a house on a Multiple Listing Service (MLS) made any real estate agent who showed the house a subagent of the listing company. This meant that the real estate agent always worked for the seller and never for the buyer. This system is currently evolving to one in which you will be able to choose to work with a buyer's agent (an agent who works for you and must represent your interests) or a seller's agent (an agent who represents the seller even though the agent is showing you a number of houses). Which type of agent you should choose will depend on your circumstances and local real estate laws. Whatever relationship you choose to establish, you should clearly understand whom "your" agent represents and what that implies.

A buyer's agent has the fiduciary responsibility to represent the buyer. This normally means that the agent must show all properties that may meet the buyer's needs, including properties being sold by owners and other properties not listed in the MLS. Moreover, the agent will be expected to offer advice on the value of property and on your negotiations with the seller and/or his agent. The sticking point in using a buyer's agent is the source of the agent's compensation. Compensation options include an hourly rate, a fixed or flat fee, a percentage of the sales price, or in the case of houses listed in the MLS, a portion of the commission fees paid by the seller to the listing agency. The use of any of the first three compensation options may increase your purchase costs for houses listed with a real estate agency, because the seller is obligated to pay a set commission to the listing agency. Also, be aware that the Department of Veterans Affairs will not permit you to include any sales fees you pay to a buyer's agent as part of the acquisition cost when determining the mortgage amount that it will insure.

If the real estate agent with whom you are working is a seller's agent, the agent works for the seller, not you. The seller is considered to be the "client," and the buyer is the "customer." The seller agrees to list property with a firm that serves as the seller's agent to market the property. In return for finding a buyer, the agent receives a commission from the seller. The services offered are of considerable benefit to both the seller and the buyer—just remember that the agent is working for the seller first. If you reveal privileged information to a seller's agent (for example, how much higher you are willing to bid on a home), the agent is required by law to pass this information along to the seller. Ignoring this warning could be a very costly mistake.

What attributes should you look for in a real estate agent of either type? First, the agent should be well acquainted with the local real estate market. The ability to understand your family's needs and know which properties in the area fit them is essential. Besides being able to provide an independent check on your estimate of what you can afford to buy, the real estate agent should be familiar with different types of mortgages available. Check the qualifications of your real estate agent. Not all agents are professional Realtors. The professionals normally are members of the National Association of Realtors and must meet certain qualifications and abide by a code of ethics.

Probably the best means of finding an agent is to ask for referrals from friends or associates in the area. A satisfied customer is usually the best reference. You want an agent who will take the time to learn your family's needs and show you as many properties as necessary to meet those needs. If you cannot find any word-of-mouth testimonials, contact the local Board of Realtors and ask for the names of former Realtors of the Year or, if you are seeking a buyer's agent, for the names of real estate firms that offer such services. Realtors of the Year make good candidates because they are individuals who have distinguished themselves professionally or have demonstrated support for the community through civic activity. You might also consider visiting an open house hosted by a real estate agency. This will give you an opportunity to meet several realtors and evaluate their ability to make you feel comfortable during this time-consuming and emotionally draining period.

Support services offered by real estate firms might include computerized mortgage search capabilities and access to the local MLS. The mortgage search support can make the administrative hassles of applying for your mortgage easier, but it does not guarantee the lowest mortgage rate available. Mortgages are like any other commodity—you should always comparison shop. The MLS is a computerized network with a complete listing of all homes offered for sale in the area through the agents who use the service. It does not include homes for sale by owners, or by sellers requesting an exclusive office listing, or homes offered by real estate firms that are not members of the MLS. Using the MLS, the broker can quickly identify listed houses that meet your family's need.

A better understanding of how real estate firms earn their commissions will give you additional insight into the home-buying process. The firm that handles the sale receives a commission of approximately 6 percent (the actual commission is negotiated) of the selling price of the house, if the firm both lists (secures the client and places the property on the market) and sells the property. If the sale is by an agent from another firm, the commission is usually split fifty-fifty between the two firms. This explains why an agent will probably initially show you properties listed by his or her own firm. If you note this trend and the houses are not compatible with your needs, let the agent know. If you suspect you are not getting a complete picture of all the homes available in your area, find another agent.

The commission system also raises issues of dual agency when using a buyer's agent. Even if you hire a buyer's agent, that agent must act as a seller's agent for any properties listed with the agent's firm. In these cases, the agent faces the dilemma of dual agency—the obligation to simultaneously serve the interests of both the buyer and the seller. When this situation arises, the agent is obligated to declare his or her dual agency. You then have the choice of allowing the agent to serve in this capacity or of finding a buyer's agent from another firm. As a general rule of thumb, you should probably request to look at houses that the agent's firm is not listing. This strategy eliminates the issues that arise from dual agency. Be tactful in how you do this, however. There is no need to state openly that you do not want to look at houses listed by the agent's firm. When choosing to go view homes with the agent, simply don't choose any listed by their real estate firm. The agent will get the message, albeit in a much more subtle way.

We must reiterate the importance of understanding the role the agent plays in the process of buying a home and how that role varies with the type of agent. A buyer's agent is your representative, and a seller's agent is the seller's. Never tell a seller's agent you will probably pay higher than your first offer or any subsequent offers. Sellers' agents are required by law, at the risk of losing their license, to pass such information on to the seller. Wait until the seller refuses your offer before you volunteer that you are willing to spend more, no matter how comfortable the seller's agent makes you feel. Also, the more you pay, the more money the agent earns in commission.

Which type of agent should you use? At this time, sellers' agents are more prevalent and, therefore, easier to find. Also, with a seller's agent you don't have to include agent fees when estimating closing costs—the seller's agent's fee is paid by the seller. However, a seller's agent will not be working for you. As a rule, the less experience you have in purchasing a house and the less familiar you are with an area, the greater the value of hiring a buyer's agent.

What Are the Closing Costs?

Besides a down payment, normally 5 to 20 percent of the purchase price, prospective home buyers will encounter other expenses. These expenses, commonly referred to as closing costs, range from a bank's loan application fee to an attorney's fee for information about the zoning of the property. A brief description of these costs and estimates of each based on a $100,000 house follow; more expensive homes will have higher closing costs. (*Note:* Certain costs can be negotiated. Always inquire whether negotiation is possible.)

Appraisal. To ensure that you are paying a fair price for property, lending institutions, the VA, and the FHA require an appraisal of the property. The appraisal is usually based on what comparable houses have sold for recently, the current cost to build the same type of house, or the capitalized value of the rental income that the house produces. (The capitalization rate is a multiple of the annual rent. If comparable houses rent for $10,000 per year and sell for $100,000, then their capitalization rate is 10. Using the capitalization rate is a quick way to get a rough estimate of the value of the house.) Even though you pay for the appraisal, the lender requiring it will probably give you a copy only if you ask for it. So ask for it. An appraisal usually costs $200 to $350.

Attorney's Fee (Lender's). Financial lenders will likely require you to pay for the services of the attorney who presides over the closing proceedings, looking out for the mortgage lender's interest. Fees will be based on the price of the house and usually range from $400 to $800.

Attorney's Fee (Yours). Along with the lender's attorney, you will probably need an attorney to handle sticky phases of the purchase, such as the purchase-and-sale agreement and closing. Your attorney will coordinate all required activities associated with your house purchase, including preparing and reviewing contracts, filing necessary documents with local government agencies, and negotiating on your behalf with the seller or seller's attorney. A typical fee range would be $300 to $600.

House Inspection. A good house inspection can help you avoid a "lemon" and may aid in negotiating a lower price or ensure that the seller makes repairs before you buy the house. The inspector will alert you to structural flaws in the property. Areas of concern for older homes include the condition of the roof, gutters and drain spouts, water pipes, furnaces, water heater, central climate control unit, storm windows, insulation, and electrical wiring. Additionally, in some regions of the United States we recommend specialized inspections for pest infestation (termites, carpenter ants, etc). Finding a reputable inspector is crucial, particularly if the property is old. Get recommendations from real estate agents (they want your business again when you sell, so they have a long-term interest) or friends. Some inspectors may be part of a professional organization. Contact the American Society of Home Inspectors for information on inspectors serving your area. Their phone numbers and Internet sites are listed in Appendix A. These inspectors are certified by examination, which helps establish their credibility. You can expect to pay between $100 and $300.

A good inspection is well worth the money. Make sure you are present, and take copious notes, since the inspector can teach you things about the home's infrastructure, such as the furnace, utility systems, gutters, and so on. This analysis can be the basis for your to-do list after purchase. Ask plenty of questions, and you'll get an inexpensive but effective education.

House (Homeowners') Insurance. If an outstanding mortgage will be held on your house, the lender will require that you provide proof of insurance, in the form of a receipt for the premium for the first year's coverage, at the closing. Most lenders have working relationships with particular insurance companies. Consider them, but do some comparison shopping. Since the property purchase will usually consist of land and a structure (house), you do not need to insure for the entire purchase price. If the house is destroyed by some peril, the land and usually the foundation of the house will still be intact. A general rule of thumb is to insure for 80 percent of the replacement value of your home.

Firms that specifically offer policies to servicemembers price their policies competitively and provide outstanding service. The cost of coverage varies but generally ranges from $400 to $700 per year. The next chapter covers homeowners' insurance in detail.

Loan Application Fee. A loan application fee or origination fee is a nonrefundable fee paid to the lending institution to cover the costs of processing the loan application. It discourages "casual shoppers" from applying for loans without being serious about the purchase. The typical range is $100 to $300, or often 1 percent of the loan amount.

Points. Mortgage lenders want to make loans that will be repaid on time. To help ensure that a borrower can afford to make the mortgage payments, lenders often adopt the rule of thumb that the mortgage payment must be less than 28 percent of gross income or that all debts must be less than 36 percent of gross income. To reduce the payments and allow more families to qualify as good risks, lenders will offer to charge a lower interest rate on the loan if the borrower pays an advance interest charge, called points, to make up the difference. A point is 1 percent of the face amount of the loan. For example, a two-point fee on a $150,000 loan results in a charge of $3,000 that is included in the closing costs.

Because the IRS recognizes points as an interest charge, all "reasonable and usual" points paid to secure a mortgage are fully deductible from income for tax purposes in the year you buy your house. However, points paid to refinance your house must be deducted over the life of the loan even though they are tax deductible. Points raise the effective interest rate of your mortgage above the quoted rate. You must analyze the after-tax cash flow to determine whether a loan with points is better than a loan without points.

Private Mortgage Insurance. Private mortgage insurance (PMI) is designed to protect the mortgage holder against possible default by the homeowner. It is generally required by all lenders when a buyer pays less than 20 percent of the house purchase price as a down payment and does not use a VA mortgage. Typical costs are $600 to $900 at closing plus $25 to $30 each month. PMI is not mortgage life insurance, which is a life insurance policy that pays the outstanding balance of the mortgage in the event of death. Before buying mortgage life insurance, check with your current life insurance carrier to see if your mortgage balance is already covered.

Survey. To make sure you are buying the land area you think you are buying, lenders usually require a current survey. A new survey is expensive and sometimes not needed. During negotiations with the seller, inquire about the date of the last survey and ask for a copy. You can have it updated for a fraction of the cost of a new one. The cost for a full survey will range from $200 to $400; for an update, the cost will be $100 to $200.

Title Search and Insurance. Title insurance is a contract with a company that agrees to provide compensation up to the face amount of the policy against losses stemming from defects or failure in the title that indicates the proper owner of the property. The company researches by going back to the original owner of the real property and compiles a history to date, making sure no hidden flaws are in the deeds. This is a single-premium insurance policy, paid at closing and generally in the $500 to $800 range. It is normally a good idea to buy an optional owner's policy, along with the required lender's policy. This is discussed further in the next chapter.

Miscellaneous. Other costs you may incur, depending on the location, include mortgage tax (varies by region and price), recording fees ($30 to $75), pest inspection ($100 to $200), water purity and pressure test if the property has a well and is not on city water ($75 to $100), radon and lead hazard testing ($25 to $100), and prepaid interest and property taxes for the period between closing and the end of the month.

Sources of Money for a Down Payment and Closing Costs

The median price of a new home built in the United States in 2000 exceeded $168,000. The closing costs identified in the previous section, combined with a 20 percent down payment, means you would need about $35,000 in liquid assets to move into a house. Fortunately, servicemembers are eligible to participate in government-backed VA and FHA loan programs. Even when the down payment is reduced to 5 percent, or $8,400, you still need over $10,000 to buy a $168,000 house. If you don't have the necessary funds readily available, you may want to investigate the following sources.

Your Individual Retirement Account. Under certain circumstances, it may be advisable to use funds previously deposited into an IRA to bridge the gap. Refer to IRS Publication 590 for the specific details. The basic requirements are that you must be a first-time home buyer (defined as not having a home within the last two years), the total distributions can not be more than $10,000 (your spouse can also take $10,000), and other specifications. (IRAs are discussed in chapters 7 and 14.)

Carefully analyze your housing choice before using this option, since you will never be able to replace the tax-free compounding funds you withdraw from your IRA. If, however, you have identified your dream house or if you anticipate the house will appreciate in value greater than the after-tax cost of early withdrawals from IRAs, it might not be a bad idea. In any case, this is an expensive source of funds, and you should give careful consideration before using it.

Generous Parents. If your parents are able to assist you financially, they may be another source of funds. Under current tax law, each parent can give both you and your spouse up to $10,000 each year without incurring a gift tax. This could be an excellent means to start distributing estate assets at a time when an heir really needs the assistance.

Increase Personal Exemptions. After you buy a home, your tax liability will probably decrease because of increased deductions for interest and real estate expenses. With this in mind, you should consider increasing the number of exemptions you claim for tax-withholding purposes. Instead of receiving a larger refund each April, thus giving the government an interest-free loan, you can receive a larger after-tax paycheck each month. This will increase your cash flow to meet higher housing expenses. See your local finance office for instructions on completing a new W-4 form.

Advance Pay. Another source of money for down payments is available to military members who undergo a permanent change of station (PCS). Each time a servicemember undergoes a PCS, a total of three months of advance pay is authorized (one month is authorized at the departing duty station and two months at the new duty station) to help offset moving expenses. If you anticipate buying a home, you may want to take advantage of this interest-free loan to augment your down payment fund. Repayment is normally made over a twelve-month period, but the repayment period can be extended to twenty-four months in some instances. Your finance office will assist you in filing the proper request. If this is an option you plan to consider, remember to prepare for the drop in monthly income while you are repaying the advance.

Equity Sharing. This is another means for parents, other family members, or friends to help someone purchase a home. By providing all or a portion of the down payment, the "investor" (person providing the money) can share in the tax advantages that accrue to homeowners as well as any future appreciation. The resulting benefits and costs of home ownership can be divided many ways. This can be a worry-free way to invest, since the investor will probably have more confidence in a co-owner who is a family member. Even so, it is wise to seek knowledgeable legal counsel to prepare documents outlining such an agreement.

Cash Value of Life Insurance Policy. Many whole life policies allow the policyholder to borrow the cash value built up in the policy. As we discuss in chapter 19, this may be a good source of cash if you already have whole life insurance. If you do not, however, we do not recommend that you get such a policy.

Negotiate with the Seller. Most sellers are eager to sell their homes and will consider all reasonable attempts by a buyer to make the deal go through. If you find the home of your dreams but are unable to immediately pull together all the necessary financial resources, you may consider asking the owner about renting the property with an option to buy in the future. The seller may set a higher selling price for the property or charge above-market rents. This would compensate him for the risk he is taking that you may not actually go through with the deal, in which case he would have to go through the process of marketing his home again.

HOW SHOULD YOU FINANCE YOUR PURCHASE?

If you have to borrow a portion of the purchase price of your house (as virtually all home buyers must), then you have to decide the size of your down payment, the type of mortgage loan to use, and the length of the repayment period. Each of these is a fairly complex decision by itself. In this section, we will provide a brief sketch of how to examine these choices, and we will also give some general recommendations.

You can perform some background research on the Internet to investigate what the prevailing rates are. This will give you valuable information to benchmark quotes that banks provide you, especially if you are trying to prequalify for a mortgage. In general, prequalifying for a mortgage is a good idea. There are several advantages to doing this. You can disclose to an agent that you have prequalified so they don't waste your time trying to push homes on you that are beyond your financial limits. Realize that this cuts both ways, however. The agent will probably not show you any homes significantly below the amount that you have qualified for on your mortgage. Secondly, you will have less time to wait before closing a deal since you have taken care of the financing aspect already.

There are many websites on the World Wide Web where a buyer can find mortgage information. Many banks, such as USAA, post the information necessary to qualify for financing on the web. Many websites specialize in online financing. Even if you don't feel comfortable arranging for financing online, you should perform the research so that you have the information about the mortgage market before going through a bank. We won't list any of the websites in this chapter since they are so numerous. Simply perform a search on any web browser for "mortgages" and you will be inundated with choices.

Many of the websites online also provide useful tools like mortgage calculators. Simply type in the amount you wish to finance and answer a few quick questions, and the calculator tells you what your monthly payments of principal and interest will be. Remember that your actual payment includes principal, interest, taxes, and insurance, so it will usually be 20 percent more per month, as a general rule of thumb. Check with an agent to determine what taxes and insurance generally cost in your area to get a good idea of your actual monthly payments.

Down Payment Size

For most military families, the size of the down payment is constrained by lender requirements and the amount of available assets. They don't really have a choice. However, if your assets exceed the required down payment, you must decide whether and by how much your down payment will exceed the minimum. When making this decision, you should realize that if you make a down payment above the minimum, you are choosing to invest in your house. You should, therefore, base this decision on whether such an investment provides a better after-tax return than the alternative investments available to you. The return implicitly earned by your down payment is the after-tax interest rate you would pay on the additional mortgage amount. Given this return, you must decide what portion of your investment portfolio to place in your house. Chapter 14 describes how to analyze your options when constructing your overall investment portfolio.

Types of Mortgages

The most common mortgages today are fixed-rate and variable-rate (also known as adjustable-rate) loans. Make sure you understand the basic features of each before selecting a loan. If it is practical, you might also want to establish a banking relationship with a potential mortgage lender so that in times of heavy demand for loans, you will have priority. This normally occurs when mortgage interest rates decline significantly, thus allowing more potential buyers to qualify for loans.

You should also understand that many lenders make a large portion of their profits from fees associated with making loans. Lenders usually bundle or package their loans and sell them to investors, earning a fee of about three-eighths of 1 percent of the outstanding balance, or $375 for a $100,000 loan. The Federal National Mortgage Association (FNMA), commonly referred to as Fannie Mae, and other investor organizations support the mortgage market by buying mortgages from local lenders and thereby replenishing their supply of available funds. This is common practice, and you should not be concerned if your lender intends to sell your mortgage.

Fixed-Rate Mortgage. A loan with a fixed interest rate requires the borrower to make a monthly payment that does not change over the period of the loan. This payment includes interest on the loan and a partial reduction of principal. As the loan is amortized over time, the interest portion of the monthly payment decreases and the amount applied to repaying the principal increases so that the entire loan is paid off at the end of the agreed-upon period. An escrow payment, which is a prorated portion of the annual taxes and insurance charges, may be included in the monthly payment, but then changes in taxes and insurance costs will alter monthly payments.

This type of mortgage is ideal for purchasers who have a stable income and want predictable housing costs. Since the lender is taking the risk of forgoing higher future interest rates, fixed-rate mortgages are always provided at higher interest rates than comparable adjustable-rate mortgages. If you plan on keeping your mortgage at least five years and you feel comfortable with the rate and the fixed monthly payment, this may be your best choice. As we discuss later, you have the option to refinance if rates decline.

Adjustable- or Variable-Rate Mortgage. Adjustable-rate mortgages (ARMs) differ from fixed-rate mortgages in that the interest rate charged on the outstanding balance of the loan can change at intervals determined at the beginning of the loan. Changes in adjustable-rate mortgage interest rates are generally tied to changes in some financial index. The ARM interest rate will include a premium over the index rate to compensate the lender for the default risk in the loan. A typical specification for an ARM interest rate might be "the index of Treasury securities, adjusted to a constant maturity of one year, plus two percentage points."

Because your payments are adjusted according to interest rate changes in the economy, the lender shifts interest rate risk to the borrower. Therefore, the initial interest rates on an ARM are lower than for comparable fixed-rate loans. Many purchasers who cannot qualify for a fixed-rate loan, with its higher monthly payments, can qualify for an adjustable-rate mortgage. However, be certain you can meet possibly higher payments if you are forced to own the house longer than planned and interest rates rise.

Military families can benefit from many other aspects of ARMs. As frequent movers, they can benefit from the low interest charges on ARMs in the early years. Some ARMs are convertible, which includes an option to replace the adjustable rate with a fixed rate after a specified time. In addition, most ARMs are assumable. This means that a buyer can take over the payments on an existing loan and thereby reduce the financing costs. Overall, these features of ARMs make them ideal for many military homeowners. However, buyers should be fully aware of the following characteristics of ARMs before deciding.

The ARM has three important aspects to understand: adjustment periods, adjustment indexes, and adjustment caps. The adjustment period is the length of time between adjustments to the interest rate charged. As the borrower, you will generally be able to choose adjustment periods ranging from six months to three years. Mortgages with the shortest adjustment period will have the lowest initial rate and the fewest points, since the short adjustment period makes them less risky to the lender.

Adjustment indexes are standard, commonly reported interest rates that determine your interest rate. Some common indexes are the constant maturity indexes of six-month, one-year, three-year, and five-year Treasury securities and the Federal Home Loan Bank Board Cost of Funds index. If you think rates will increase, use a long-term index (such as the Treasury index), since they adjust more slowly; if you think they will decrease, choose a shorter-term index (such as the Cost of Funds index). Make sure the index is computed by an independent source and is published regularly in papers such as the *Wall Street Journal.* The final interest rate you will pay is based on the index value plus a premium, which ranges from one to three percentage points. If the constant maturity index for one-year Treasury securities is 5 percent and the lender adds a 2 percent premium, your interest rate would adjust to 7 percent at the beginning of the new adjustment period.

The last aspect of the ARM to understand is the cap. Most loans have a cap on the amount the interest rate can increase each adjustment period (usually 2 percent) and over the life of the loan (usually 6 percent). So a one-year adjustable loan with an initial 7 percent rate could increase only to 9 percent at the end of the first adjustment period and to 13 percent over the life of the loan.

Be careful of options available for some ARMs that guarantee that your monthly payments will remain constant over the term of the loan regardless of the direction and amount of the change in the index. This option can lead to negative amortization whereby the amount you owe grows instead of declines. In this configuration, the ARM resembles a normal fixed-rate mortgage. However, if interest rates increase, you actually add to the amount you owe the lender. In effect, you are borrowing funds from the lender to keep your payments constant. This can happen if the interest due for one month exceeds the amount of the agreed-upon monthly payment. You end up stretching the length of the loan beyond the originally stated term. Also, if you sell your house, the increased loan balance can actually cause you to owe more money at closing.

Mortgage Costs. When you compare the costs of available loans, be sure to consider all the costs involved. Ask each prospective lender to provide you with a written statement of all the costs involved in the home purchase—both initial, one-time costs, and recurring, monthly costs. Be sure the costs are fully itemized, complete, and in writing. Under a national law called RESPA, the lender is required to provide a projected Uniform Settlement Sheet, which details all these charges and more. This information must be available to you at least twenty-four hours before closing. Ask for it, and make sure you review it and understand each of the entries.

What about Seller Financing?

Seller financing can be used as a second mortgage to close a deal or as a means to finance the entire transaction. Under proper conditions, this can be beneficial for both the seller and the buyer. The buyer saves on many of the closing costs and often borrows the money from the seller at a below-market interest rate. The seller's benefits are also substantial. First, sellers who provide financing often find it easier to sell their property for the price they want. Further, although the interest rate to the seller may be less than a bank would charge, it may be more than the seller could earn in a certificate of deposit or a money market account.

Although the seller-financed mortgage is not a very liquid asset for the seller, the risk is not too great as long as the value of the property does not decline. The seller-financer is protected because the house is collateral for the loan; if the buyer does not make payments, ownership reverts to the seller. In an installment sale, the proceeds from the sale are reportable for tax purposes in the year they are received. The capital gains exclusion of $250,000 ($500,000 for couples in most cases) applies, and you will have to declare only the interest paid as ordinary income subject to taxation. See IRS Publication 593 for the most current law.

What Mortgage Assistance Should You Get?

There are three major means of securing a mortgage, each normally referred to as a particular type of loan: the conventional loan, the Department of Veterans

Affairs (VA) guaranteed loan, and the Federal Housing Administration (FHA) insured loan. Before you buy a house, you should fully investigate the availability and net cost of each method. The best one to use depends on a number of factors, including prevailing interest rates, your long-range plans for buying homes in the future, the willingness of lenders and sellers to deal with government bureaucracies, and your potential risk as seen by the lender. Keep in mind that the following information is based on laws and regulations that are subject to change and, in some cases, also subject to local conditions.

Conventional Loan. A conventional loan is a financial agreement between you and a lender in which there is no outside agency insuring repayment of any portion of the loan. If you seek a conventional loan, you will offer two kinds of security: the mortgaged property and your own credit or investment worth. The great majority of single-family homes are financed with conventional loans. In this type of loan, a financial institution lends its own money and takes the entire risk of loss. As a result, conventional loans are usually limited to 95 percent of the appraised value. Consequently, the buyer must make at least a 5 percent down payment, in addition to closing costs. Also, the rate of interest on a conventional loan tends to be higher than an FHA-insured or VA-guaranteed loan because the lender is assuming most of the risk.

VA Loan. The Department of Veterans Affairs offers a home loan guarantee program that has many advantages for veterans, active-duty servicemembers, and reservists. The principal advantages are lower interest rates, negotiable points, and smaller down payments. Other advantages include longer-term maturity, limits on costs, required inspections, and no prepayment penalties. The loan guarantee is a valuable benefit available to most servicemembers. However, the authority of the Department of Veterans Affairs to guarantee adjustable-rate mortgages expired on 30 September 1995.

Eligibility for loan guarantees remains quite simple. Generally, active-duty military personnel must have had more than 180 days' active service and veterans must have had two years in the military to be eligible. (Veterans serving in World War II, Korea, or Vietnam must have only ninety days' service.) VA regional office personnel can assist with eligibility questions. (See Appendix A for Internet listings of all VA regional offices.) Active-duty servicemembers can use their benefit more than once, as long as they fully terminate their previous VA loan liability before reapplying. Veterans and eligible reservists may use their benefit only once after active-duty service. The VA will guarantee up to 50 percent of a home loan up to $45,000. For loans between $45,000 and $144,000, the minimum guarantee amount is $22,500, with a maximum guarantee of up to 40 percent of the loan up to $36,000, subject to the amount of entitlement a veteran has available. For loans of more than $144,000 made for the purchase or construction of a home or to buy a residential unit in a condominium or to refinance an existing VA-guaranteed loan for interest rate reduction, the maximum guarantee is 25 percent up to $50,750. "Manufactured" or prefabricated homes are limited to a $20,000 guarantee. The VA no longer establishes a maximum loan amount; lenders generally limit the maximum VA loan to $203,000 because most VA loans are sold in the secondary market. The VA will require an appraisal of the property to ensure compliance with this stipulation.

Whatever the price of your home, the VA guarantee is very valuable to you. Since the government is guaranteeing a substantial amount of your mortgage, the VA greatly reduces the risk of the loan to the lender. This reduction in risk should cause the lender to charge lower interest rates and points and to require a smaller down payment than for a conventional mortgage. Under VA rules, each of these items is negotiable between the lender and the seller. The VA will review the conditions of the mortgage agreement to safeguard the soldier or veteran but will not stipulate them. Therefore, it is your responsibility to get the best deal possible. Shop around.

Current VA regulations allow the veteran borrower to negotiate payment of points with the seller. Either party may pay the points or split between them. But the veteran still may not add the points to the loan amount. Therefore, you should include who pays this large out-of-pocket expense when you negotiate the sale agreement.

The VA charges a "funding fee" for its services based on the loan category and a percentage of the loan. The 2001 fee structure is shown in Table 11-3.

TABLE 11-3
VA FUNDING FEE STRUCTURE

Loan Category	% on Veterans Loan	% on Reservists Loan
Home loan with 5% or less down or refinance/home improvement	2.00	2.75
Home loan with 5% to 10% down	1.50	2.25
Home loan with 10% or more down	1.25	2.00

VA Pamphlet 26-71-1 contains relevant information about VA manufactured home loans.

If you believe that you are eligible for a VA-guaranteed loan, you should submit a VA Form 26-1880, "Request for Determination of Eligibility," with the required documents to the VA to obtain a VA Certificate of Eligibility. This certificate must be shown to the lender before a VA-guaranteed loan can be arranged, so you should obtain your certificate at once even if you are not actively looking for a house.

The steps in arranging a VA-guaranteed loan are as follows:

1. Find the property that meets your needs. Decide to buy only if you are sure the price is right, the house is right, and you are completely satisfied in all respects.

2. Apply to a lending institution (such as a bank, credit union, savings and loan, or mortgage company) that makes the type of loan you wish to obtain.

3. Present your plan to the lender with your VA Certificate of Eligibility. Lenders generally have the forms and other necessary papers for applying for a VA loan. If your lender turns you down, see another one. The fact that one lender is not interested in making this particular type of loan does not mean that all potential lenders will turn you down.

4. If the lender accepts your application, the VA, at the request of the lender, arranges for an appraisal of the property and determines if the property meets acceptable standards of good construction. The appraisal cannot indicate whether the purchase is wise or unwise or what the future resale value may be. In addition, because valuations vary, the VA-appraised value could differ from that made by another appraiser hired by you, the FHA, or the lender.

5. As the result of the appraisal, the VA will forward to the lender a Certificate of Reasonable Value. At this point, the lender will notify you that it has approved the loan if it has "automatic" approval authority from the VA. If it does not have approval authority, the lender will send the paperwork—loan application, credit report, employment verification, copy of the executed sales contract, and so on—to the VA for approval.

6. The lender closes the loan and sends a report of the closing to the VA.

Overall, the VA home loan guarantee is an excellent benefit that can assist you in your home purchase. Besides the financial benefits outlined above, the VA safeguards veterans from unscrupulous lenders, sellers, and builders through a variety of measures. It inspects and appraises all properties, monitors any unfair actions of lenders and suspends violators from VA participation, and requires a one-year warranty on new homes. The VA also limits the chargeable fees on mortgages, allows early prepayment without penalty, and encourages forbearance by lenders if a borrower experiences financial difficulties. Before you get a mortgage, contact the VA at the numbers listed in Appendix A. Get a copy of *Federal Benefits for Veterans and Dependents* and VA Pamphlets 26-4 and 26-5.

FHA Loan. An FHA-insured loan is a private loan underwritten by the Federal Housing Administration. Like the VA mortgage program, the FHA does not actually lend the money but insures the lending institution (bank, savings and loan, insurance company, or mortgage company) against default by the borrower. The reduction in risk passes through to the borrower in the form of lower rates. In addition, the FHA makes stipulations about certain aspects of down payments and closing costs to assist the borrower.

The FHA will insure mortgages up to certain maximum amounts, which vary from one county to another. The borrower's loan amount, including financed closing costs, may not exceed the loan ceiling specified for that county. (See Appendix A for the FHA Internet site with loan ceilings.)

The FHA limits closing costs that can be financed with the loan amount. These fees include a 1 percent origination fee; attorney, escrow, and closing fees; recording fees; test and certification fees; and credit report and appraisal fees. Additional fees may be included at the discretion of the local HUD office. The only significant cost that can be financed is the Mortgage Insurance Premium (MIP). This premium, 2.25 percent of the value of the loan, is the cost of the FHA loan to the borrower, but it can be lowered to 2 percent if the new homeowner attends counseling before closing. Required down payments are still comparatively low. FHA requires 3 percent of the value of the property for loans less than $50,000. For loans greater than $50,000, FHA requires a down payment of approximately 5 percent of the value of the property. The total amount due at closing is the sum of the down payment and those closing costs not financed with the loan.

FHA guidelines allow borrowers to buy multifamily dwellings and to use the FHA benefit to refinance or rehabilitate a home. For refinancing, the down payment increases to 15 percent of the home value plus closing costs.

Although the FHA tightened its mortgage program, it is still quite attractive. By insuring the lender, the FHA program allows the borrower to buy a home with much less cash up front than a conventional mortgage. You should compare the FHA and VA loan programs when researching mortgage options. Also, if you have used your VA loan eligibility, then the FHA program offers another source for obtaining a guaranteed mortgage.

Selecting the Length of Your Mortgage

There are two standard lengths for mortgages—fifteen and thirty years—from which you must choose. The best length for you will depend on a number of factors, so a simple formula is impossible. However, we will describe the issues and provide suggestions on how to consider them.

Because you use the lender's money for half the time, and because the lender is exposed to the risk of default and unanticipated inflation for fifteen fewer years, fifteen-year mortgages are usually available at lower interest rates than thirty-year mortgages. One can typically find them for 0.10 to 0.50 percentage points (sometimes referred to as 10 to 50 basis points) lower. In spite of the lower interest rates, however, monthly payments for fifteen-year mortgages are generally larger, because the entire loan must be repaid in half the time. The lower monthly premium associated with thirty-year mortgages, in fact, is the main advantage of the longer repayment period for young families on a tight budget. For some families, the payment associated with a thirty-year mortgage is all they can afford, so they have no need for further analysis.

For families that can afford the higher payments of a fifteen-year loan, choosing the shorter repayment period can be better, especially if you can get an interest rate that is 0.5 percent lower. A longer repayment period would be superior if you could reinvest the difference between the premiums for fifteen- and thirty-year mortgages during the first fifteen years and pay off the remaining balance on the thirty-year mortgage with something left over. Calculation of the necessary return on your investment of this difference requires a careful cash-flow analysis, including tax considerations, since home interest payments are tax deductible.

Another way to analyze it is that the higher payment associated with a fifteen-year loan is essentially a forced savings plan. If you have the discipline to save that much money and earn a return that is greater than your mortgage rate, then a thirty-year mortgage may be better and would provide you with the flexibility to invest in something other than your house. You would, of course, have to be in an asset that is much riskier than your house, such as a stock fund (see chapters 14 and 16), to equal the benefits of a fifteen-year loan.

In summary, a fifteen-year repayment period is generally financially superior to a thirty-year period. The main attraction of a thirty-year mortgage is its lower monthly payment, which allows you to buy a more expensive house. Since this feature usually dominates other considerations, the thirty-year mortgage is the common (and valid) choice. If your financial circumstances permit you to buy the house you desire and finance it with a fifteen-year mortgage, you should seriously consider doing so. If this is not possible, then the thirty-year mortgage is appropriate for you.

Should You Pay Off Your Mortgage Early?

Some homeowners wonder whether they should pay off their mortgage after an unexpected windfall, like an inheritance, makes it possible to do so. The basic issues in this decision are similar to determining the length of your mortgage—paying off your mortgage early is analogous to choosing a shorter-term loan, while not paying it early is like choosing a longer-term loan. There are some differences, though. Most important, the prevailing interest rates will have changed since you got your mortgage.

From a financial viewpoint, you want to determine where the inheritance will earn the greatest after-tax return. If interest rates have increased since you initially financed your house, you are borrowing money inexpensively through your mortgage, and you're more likely to be able to earn a higher return elsewhere. In such circumstances, you probably should invest elsewhere rather than retire your mortgage. Conversely, if interest rates have fallen, your mortgage is an expensive loan, and your alternative investments are less attractive. Now you might want to retire the mortgage.

Another factor you should consider is that equity in your house is not very liquid. There are only two ways to use this capital for other purposes: sell your house or take out a home-equity loan. Therefore, if you anticipate the need for another loan in the not-too-distant future, you might want to invest the inheritance and then use it instead of borrowing and having to pay interest and loan application fees.

Finally, there is a certain peace of mind that comes from owning your house completely. If that's important to you, you might want to retire the mortgage.

When Should You Refinance Your Mortgage?

Homeowners unfortunate enough to buy their homes when interest rates are high are not necessarily stuck with those high rates forever. Refinancing your mortgage is a valuable option. In practice, this means securing a new loan and repaying the old mortgage. This option may be attractive to homeowners with fixed-rate as well as variable-rate mortgages. Those with fixed-rate mortgages could lower their payments and pay less interest. Variable-rate loans are set based on adding a premium to an index of market interest rates. If market interest rates decline, it is likely that the index, and thus the variable interest rate, will decline as well. Under these circumstances, you may be wondering why a homeowner with a variable-rate mortgage would want to refinance. Some home buyers take variable-rate mortgages not because they prefer the uncertainty about their future monthly payments, but because the interest rate they were offered was more attractive than that available on fixed-rate loans. However, when interest rates decline and fixed-rate mortgages become available at more reasonable rates, some homeowners may want to have the peace of mind that a low fixed-rate mortgage offers. Also, just as the rise in variable-rate mortgage is capped for each adjustment period, the decline is also capped.

Despite the advantages of possible lower monthly payments with a refinanced loan, don't rush to do it without considering all the consequences. The initial out-of-pocket expenses can be quite substantial. Generally, you will be required to pay many of the same closing costs you faced when you initially bought your home: appraisal, title search, loan application fee, and points. Also, your current mortgage may specify prepayment penalties.

A rule of thumb is that if current interest rates are at least two percentage points below your present rate, it may pay to refinance. Depending on the particular circumstances, the actual minimum differential required to produce a net savings may be smaller or larger than 2 percent, but this rule is a useful indicator of when it pays to examine this option.

You should also consider the length of time you plan to own the house: Will you have time to recoup the expenses of new closing costs from lower monthly payments? To find out, do this simple calculation:

1. Estimate the total closing costs associated with securing a new loan (5 to 8 percent of the outstanding balance of the old mortgage).
2. Determine the monthly difference between your old and new loan payments.
3. Divide the monthly savings into the total cost of refinancing.

This gives you the number of months you would need to remain in your current home to break even. For example, if your estimated closing costs are \$5,000 and your monthly savings from a lower interest rate are \$100, you would need to remain in the house more than four years before you would realize a net savings (\$5,000 ÷ \$100 = 50 months, or 4.2 years). We've ignored interest on the \$5,000 here, so the calculated number is actually too low—you would have to maintain ownership with the new loan for more than five years to make it worthwhile.

If you're determined to refinance and you don't have adequate liquid assets to pay for the associated costs, you still may be able to refinance. If you have accrued enough equity in the property (either from your down payment plus monthly payments or from appreciating property value, or both), you can finance the associated refinancing charges. For example, assume your current mortgage is $75,000 and you face $5,000 in refinancing costs. If your home is worth at least $100,000, you would be able to borrow $80,000 ($75,000 to pay off the old mortgage and $5,000 to cover refinance charges). Although your monthly payment will be a little higher, you can still save money in the long run if the interest rate differential is sufficient.

Another consideration that will affect a decision to refinance is the tax implications of points paid to refinance. The taxpayer must spread the deductions for points over the life of the loan. For example, if you paid three points on a thirty-year loan for $90,000, your out-of-pocket cost for points would be $2,700 (0.03 × $90,000). Instead of deducting the entire $2,700 during the tax year you refinance, your annual deduction is $90 per year ($2,700 ÷ 30 years). (As we stated earlier, this ruling did not change your ability to deduct the entire amount in the first year when you initially buy your house.)

One final strategy to save money in this area is possible. Ask the holder of your existing mortgage to renegotiate the interest rate. The lender may not go as low as the current market rate, but he may be willing to split the difference. This kind of deal is beneficial for both: The lender keeps you as a customer at a higher rate than current market rates, and the borrower saves on closing costs. However, if your loan has been packaged and sold to investors, you are out of luck; loans that have been packaged for resale cannot be renegotiated.

TAX CONSIDERATIONS FOR HOMEOWNERS

To promote realization of the American dream of home ownership, the tax laws are structured so that nonhomeowners subsidize homeowners. Certain expenses associated with home ownership are tax deductible and thus reduce the amount of income taxes that homeowners pay. Servicemember homeowners with mortgages enjoy an unusual advantage: They receive tax-free quarters allowances to pay interest expenses, which are themselves tax deductible.

The primary tax advantage is that all the interest paid on a mortgage loan is deductible from your income when computing your federal income taxes. Other advantages include the following:

1. Deduction of all points paid to secure an initial mortgage.
2. Deduction of property taxes.
3. Deduction of mortgage prepayment penalties.
4. Relief from capital gains tax on sale of home (see below).

In the past, home sellers were able to defer all their profits from the sale of their home by purchasing a house that cost more than the home that they sold.

The Taxpayer Relief Act of 1997 allows most couples who file a joint return to keep up to $500,000 of their resale profit tax free and lets single filers keep up to $250,000 regardless of whether they buy another home. It abolished the old "rollover residency replacement rule," which allowed a seller to defer paying taxes on all the profits from a home by purchasing a new home of equal or greater value. To qualify you must have lived in the home for two of the last five years.

The tax advantages of home ownership are significant, and they should be thoroughly analyzed before you make your housing decision. (See the Rent versus Buy section, below.) For more detailed information on the tax impact of selling your home, see IRS Publication 523, *Selling Your Home.*

WHEN AND HOW SHOULD YOU SELL YOUR HOUSE?

If you are required to relocate after buying your home, you will be faced with the decision of whether to rent your home (and become a landlord) or sell it. For more information about leaving your equity in your home and renting, see chapter 18, which deals with real estate investments. If you decide to sell, you also have to decide what price to ask, whether to use a broker, and whether to use seller financing.

If you choose to rent your home out, remember the residency requirements for capital gains exclusion. If you rent the home out for more than three years and do not subsequently live in it again, any capital gain on the ultimate sale is taxable. This can be a very expensive financial mistake.

Be sure to keep track of all selling expenses, including commissions, advertising fees, legal fees, and loan charges paid by the seller, such as loan placement fees or points, because they can be subtracted from the amount of the sale and may lower your capital gains amount to below the exclusion amount of $250,000 ($500,000 for couples).

Should You Use an Agent?

Before hiring an agent, you must decide what type of listing agreement you want to enter. Your choices are as follows:

1. *Exclusive Right to Sell.* The listing broker receives a commission if an offer for the house is accepted at any time during the listing period, regardless of who is responsible for locating the buyer and arranging the sale. The problem here is the need to pick a good agent who will aggressively market your house. At a minimum, your house should appear in the Multiple Listing Service, so agents from other brokerages can serve as subagents for the broker with whom you listed and earn a commission by selling your house.
2. *Exclusive Agency Listing.* The agent you hire is the only agent who may earn a commission for selling your house during the listing period. You are free to sell the property yourself and save on the commission. The problem here is that your house may not be listed in the Multiple Listing Service and thus not get the widest possible exposure to potential buyers.

3. *Open Listing*. You give the agent the right to sell your house, but you retain the right to sign contracts with other agents or sell the property yourself without paying a commission. This arrangement gives your agent little incentive to spend money to aggressively market your house.

Of course, you could attempt to sell the home without the services of an agent. The ultimate concern is which choice will give you a larger net amount: selling the house yourself and avoiding the commission, or using the professional marketing expertise of a real estate agent. After reviewing the agent's duties outlined below, decide if you have the time and temperament to accomplish them yourself.

If you decide to use a broker, you can expect that person to do the following:

1. Suggest the most cost-effective ways to improve the property appearance.
2. Price your house at market value based on recent sales. (This is a market analysis, not an appraisal.)
3. Screen buyers.
4. Schedule appointments with qualified buyers.
5. Help arrange financing.
6. Facilitate contract and closing procedures.

Whichever option you choose, remember that the commission is negotiable. A higher commission may cause the agent to work harder, but it leaves you with less after the sale. Also, it might be a good idea to sign a short contract at first, perhaps for two or three months, and closely monitor how aggressively the agent markets your home with open houses, newspaper advertisements, and so on. An agent's skill and resources can result in quick, efficient, and profitable sales, but not all agents are created equal. Do not renew a contract with an agent who is not working hard for you. Be aware that an agent will not want to bend on any of these points, so you must be an able negotiator to get a listing contract that best serves you, and not the broker.

Should You Sell It Yourself?

If market conditions are good and you have the skill and time, you may decide to sell your house without the help of an agent. If you choose this option, you should take care to do the following:

1. *Screen potential buyers over the telephone*. Do not grant appointments without first ascertaining how serious they are about buying. You can waste a great deal of time showing your home to casual shoppers.

2. *Price your house realistically*. This is difficult. If the price is too high, you may discourage potential buyers and your property will stay on the market longer. On the other hand, if you underprice, it will probably sell quickly but you will be "leaving money on the table." To avoid this, keep track of the sale of comparable houses in your area, and hire an appraiser to value your home (if the appraisal supports your asking price, use it during negotiations to convince potential buyers they are getting a good deal). You might also request a periodic market analysis (which is free) from a real estate agent.

3. *Present your home in the best possible light.* Keep it immaculately clean, always tidy, surrounded by well-groomed and edged lawns and shrubs. Take the time to freshen faded paint, replace dying shrubs, and make all other cosmetic repairs. Well-presented homes generally sell first and often command the best prices.

What About Negotiating?

If you are selling your house, the buyer will probably assume your price is more negotiable because you are not paying an agent's commission. You might consider setting a price that has room for negotiation and then increasing it by 3 percent. If the price is fair, don't lower it before first receiving an offer from a buyer. If the buyer asks if you will take a lower price, repeat the asking price and suggest that the potential buyer make an offer. If you show your hand first, you will have less leverage as the negotiations continue.

When negotiating with a potential buyer, it may be a good idea not to have your spouse with you. Having an excuse to leave the negotiating table to consult with someone is a powerful negotiating tool. This may make the buyer feel he is more powerful than you—since you do not have the ability to make decisions—and he may let his guard down and be less careful about what he says. If you're not married, say you need to consult with a friend, financial advisor, or lawyer.

If you're remaining in the same area and planning to buy a new home, include a contingency clause in your contract that makes the sale of your current home contingent on finding a new home. You must weigh the trade-off here. You might discourage some potential buyers with this restriction; on the other hand, you could conceivably end up with no place to live. Another way around this problem is to make the purchase of the new house contingent on selling your current residence at satisfactory terms. This reduces the strength of your negotiating position, however, and could result in your accepting less for your home than you would have received under normal conditions.

RENT VERSUS BUY: A QUANTITATIVE ANALYSIS

Because all owners of real property are allowed itemized deductions for real estate taxes and interest expenses, and because they may sell their property for more than they paid for it, a direct comparison of rental costs and mortgage payments is not appropriate. The homeowner's tax advantages and potential capital gains provide tangible financial benefits that must be explicitly considered in a quantitative rent versus buy analysis. Let's look at an example.

Captain Stan Smith and his wife, Mary, a school counselor, have one child and a combined family income of $60,000. Like many military families, the Smiths cannot now itemize their tax deductions; they don't own a home and don't have enough other deductions to make itemizing worthwhile. After reviewing their tax records, however, they find that they had tax-deductible expenses of $4,000 in the previous year; if they bought a home, they would have sufficient deductions to itemize, and this $4,000 amount could become tax deductible as well.

TABLE 11-4
RENT VERSUS BUY: TAX EFFECTS

	Rental	Purchase
Taxable income	$60,000	$60,000
Interest on MMF*	580	
Standard deduction	(6,700)	
Itemized deductions		(4,000)
Interest expense deduction		(7,624)
Real estate taxes		(2,200)
Net taxable income	53,880	46,176
Taxable income reduction, purchase		7,704
× Marginal tax rate (1996)		× 28%
Tax savings due to purchase:		$2,157

*Interest forgone = 0.04 × $14,500 = $580

TABLE 11-5
RENT VERSUS BUY CASH-FLOW SUMMARY

Homeowner (costs) or benefits	
Interest[a]	($7,624)
Real estate taxes	(2,200)
Insurance differences[b]	(200)
Maintenance	(600)
Utilities[c]	?
Transportation cost difference[c]	?
Forgone interest	(580)
Tax savings	2,157
Pleasure of owning your own home	?
Worry about reselling home and property values	?
Net cost of home ownership	(9,047)
Rental cost avoided[d]	10,800
Net benefit (cost) of home ownership	1,753

[a]Note that the $680 principal payment portion (of total mortgage payments) is not included. The Smiths paid it, but at the same time their ownership in the home went up by the same amount.
[b]This is the approximate difference between renters' insurance and homeowners' insurance with a high deductible.
[c]Include these expenses if the rental provides utilities or if it is closer to work.
[d]For individuals making comparisons to living in government quarters, use BAH as rental cost.

The Smiths are considering buying a house for $100,000 in beautiful Harker Heights, Texas. They want to compare the financial effects of buying to renting a comparable house for $900 a month. If they buy, they plan to allot $10,000 for a down payment and $4,500 for closing costs from a money market mutual fund, now paying 4 percent interest. The first year's property taxes are estimated to be $2,200; the interest on an 8.5 percent thirty-year loan of $90,000 would be $7,624; and the amortization of principal would be $680 for the first year. The Smiths made the calculations shown in Table 11-4 for the effects of home ownership on their taxes.

The Smiths would save $2,157 in taxes annually by buying, as compared with renting. Then they incorporated that tax savings into an overall cash-flow summary shown in Table 11-5.

In this example, it is $1,753 a year cheaper for the Smiths to buy than to live in a rented home. We do not mean to suggest that this will always be the case. In fact, many homeowners suffer negative cash flow as compared with their rental alternative but choose to buy anyway because they simply prefer to have their own home or because they expect to turn a profit when they sell the property.

A complete analysis of the rent versus buy decision should include the expected capital gain (or loss) as well as the monthly cash flows. The most important of these is the ability for the appreciation in your home to cover closing costs (including realtor commissions) when you depart. If housing prices increase approximately 3 percent per year, then after three years your closing costs should be covered—usually 6 percent if you use a realtor and 3 percent closing costs upon departure. This consideration can have a great impact on your rent versus buy decision and can dwarf any monthly savings that you might accrue.

If you are interested in making a more complete financial analysis that includes the effect of a change in your house's resale value, refer to chapter 18, which discusses real estate as an investment. Our simple example in this chapter can easily be fit into the analysis we illustrate there. Be aware, though, that some of the tax benefits of being a landlord (such as deducting depreciation) are not available to homeowners who occupy their own property.

A CHECKLIST FOR HOME BUYERS

Characteristic of Property (proposed or existing construction)

Neighborhood. Carefully take into account each of the following:

- Convenience of transportation.
- Location of stores.
- Location of schools.
- Absence of excessive traffic noise.
- Absence of unpleasant sights and odors.
- Availability of play areas for children.

- Fire and police protection and garbage collection.
- Residential usage safeguarded by adequate zoning.
- Community taxes and assessments.
- Check for neighborhood ordinances, which preclude certain activities or modifications to existing property.

Lot. Consider each of the following to determine whether the lot is sufficiently large and properly improved:

- Size of front yard.
- Size of rear and side yards.
- Fencing.
- Walks providing access to front and service entrances.
- Drive providing easy access to garage.
- Lot draining satisfactorily.
- Lawn and landscaping satisfactory.
- Irrigation system (if any).
- Septic tank (if any) in good operating condition.
- Pest control—has the house been treated. If not, what is the cost?

Exterior Details.

- Porches.
- Decks have been protected and are serviceable.
- Adequate lighting. For security purposes, motion detector lights.
- Terraces.
- Garages. (Garage door opener?)
- Gutters.
- Storm sash.
- Weather stripping.
- Screens.
- Breezeway.

Interior Details. Does the house provide what your family needs?

- Acceptable cost of heating and utilities (check and double-check this).
- Rooms large enough to accommodate desired furniture.
- Dining space sufficiently large.
- At least one closet in each bedroom.
- At least one coat closet and one linen closet.
- Convenient access to bathroom.
- Sufficient and convenient storage space.
- Kitchen well arranged and equipped.
- Laundry space ample and well located.
- Windows provide adequate light and air.
- Sufficient number of electrical outlets.

- Sufficient number of phone jacks and/or broadband Internet capability.
- Security system—local service and cost estimates.

Condition of Existing Construction

Exterior Construction. Inspect to see that the following appear to be in acceptable condition:

- Wood porch floors and steps.
- Windows, doors, and screens.
- Gutters and wood cornice.
- Wood siding.
- Mortar joints.
- Roofing.
- Chimneys.
- Paint on exterior woodwork.
- General design and architecture.

Interior Construction. Check to see whether:

- Plaster is free of excessive cracks.
- Plaster is free of stains caused by leaking.
- Door locks are in operating condition.
- Windows move freely.
- Any faucets leak. No plumbing issues.
- Fireplace works properly.
- Basement is dry and will resist moisture penetration.
- Mechanical equipment and electrical wiring and switches are adequate and in operating condition.
- Type of heating equipment is suitable.
- There is adequate insulation in walls, floor, ceiling, or roof.
- Floors are level and without cracks.
- These appear to be in acceptable condition:
  - — Wood floor finish.
  - — Linoleum floors.
  - — Sink top.
  - — Kitchen range.
  - — Bathroom tile and papering.
  - — Exposed joists and beams.

To be sure the house is a good buy, get expert advice on the condition of existing construction, paying special attention to the following:

- The basement will stay dry after heavy rains.
- The foundations are sound.
- There has been no termite or other pest damage.
- The title is free, clear, and unencumbered.

Tips on Making the Most from Your Housing Decision

- Do as much research as possible beforehand. Housing can be your single most important financial decision. Information is your most important asset. A realtor will take an informed buyer/renter more seriously.
- Take careful notes and a camera when you visit homes. Use a checklist for each house to enable easy comparison later.
- Never reveal anything to a real estate agent who is working with you in a "seller's agent" capacity that you do not want the seller of the home to immediately find out.
- Get a qualified home inspection done, and accompany the inspector if possible. Highly recommended!
- Carefully explore and compare all financing alternatives—conventional, VA, and FHA—to determine which is most financially advantageous.
- Consider refinancing your mortgage if interest rates have fallen 2 percent or more.
- Recognize that the decision to rent or buy has significant financial implications, but it also significantly affects your lifestyle and attitude about your community.
- Always sleep on a decision and discuss it with your spouse/significant other to ensure that the entire family can live with your choice.

12

Protecting Your Wealth with Insurance

Saving and investing to achieve your financial goals isn't always easy. Neither is keeping what you've already got. Your assets can be lost by accidental damage or theft, or you could be held liable for large monetary damages in a civil lawsuit. Reducing the risk of potential loss with insurance can be expensive. You will need to balance the amount of risk you are willing to assume against the cost of eliminating it with insurance. The purpose of this chapter is to provide general information on homeowners', property, and liability insurance, and to present guidelines to help you determine the right amount and type of coverage to select. At the end of the chapter we provide a checklist to assist you in your decision.

WHAT INSURANCE DO HOMEOWNERS NEED?

If you own a home, you will want to insure both real property (the structure itself) and personal property (the contents) against loss. Home insurance policies cover both types. Homeowners' insurance is a must for every family that owns a home. Although 95 percent of all homeowners are covered by homeowners' insurance, according to David Klein, an insurance expert from the Hartford Insurance Group, only about 70 percent of the population is properly insured.

There are two important decisions you must make: what policy to choose and how much coverage to get. Before you can decide on either, however, you must understand what the various policies cover and what each type of coverage offers. You need to consider four factors when comparing coverage:

1. What property is covered?
2. What perils (types of loss or damage) are covered?
3. To what extent will you be reimbursed for losses?
4. How much does the insurance cost?

Types of Homeowners' Policies

A home and its contents are exposed to direct damage by a tremendous number of perils, such as fire, flood, theft, loss, lawsuits, and breakage or other damage. Insurance is a way to transfer the financial risk of these perils to the insurance company. Although you cannot insure against all types of risk (for example, you cannot insure against a fall in the price of your home), many risks are insurable. There are many different homeowners' policies available to cover the amount of risk that best suits your needs.

The term *homeowners' insurance* is to some extent a misnomer. The standard homeowners' policy can cover just about everything you own. It can provide protection against personal liability and property loss, and sometimes it even covers medical bills. There are six basic types of homeowners' insurance, which are usually designated with *HO numbers* based on the forms that insurance companies use.

Some companies have their own names, such as silver or gold policies or broad and special policies. When you are getting comparisons, ask if it is equivalent to an HO 00-02, HO 00-03, and so forth to ensure that you are comparing prices for the same type of policy.

HO 00-02 is a broad form policy that covers damage to the buildings and personal property from 16 named perils: fire or lightning, windstorm or hail, explosion, riots or civil disturbance, aircraft, vehicles, smoke, vandalism or malicious mischief, theft, falling objects, weight of sleet, ice, or snow, accidental discharge of water or steam from various household systems, freezing of plumbing or other system of household appliance, sudden damage from artificially generated electrical current, and volcanic eruption.

HO 00-03 is an all-risk policy that covers personal property identically to HO 00-02 but provides coverage on the dwelling against all perils except those events specifically excluded from the policy (usually flood, earthquake, war, and nuclear accident). Consequently, HO 00-03 is somewhat broader than HO 00-02 and may have higher premiums.

HO 00-04 is renters' insurance with coverage similar to the HO 00-02.

HO 00-06 is condominium insurance with coverage similar to HO 00-04, with additional coverage for common areas of ownership found in condominiums.

HO 00-08 is coverage for older houses and is similar to HO 00-02.

Each type offers two basic coverage or protection plans: property protection and liability protection. Additional coverage is often included. Property protection reimburses you for losses or damages to your house and/or its contents. The amount of protection required is usually figured by computing the replacement cost of your house. Coverage for personal property is usually set at 50 to 70 percent of the home's replacement cost. It also usually covers 10 percent of the home's cost for damage to an external structure (shed, boathouse) and 5 percent of the home's cost for damage to shrubs. There are, however, limits to specific types of personal property—for example, in many policies silverware is limited to $2,500, computers to $3,000, and jewelry to $1,000.

Personal liability protection protects you against lawsuits for injury or damage to others that may have been caused by you or a family member. It also protects against accidents involving others that happen in or around your home and, in some cases, while you and your family are away from home. The protection extends to legal fees, and you need not be at fault for the injury for the limited medical coverage to apply.

Additional protection can include coverage of expenses in the event your home is rendered uninhabitable, coverage for lost or stolen credit cards, coverage for items taken off your person in a robbery, coverage for new locks in your home should you lose your keys, and much more.

How Much Coverage Do You Need?

Now that you are familiar with the types of coverage, you must determine how much coverage you need in order to adequately protect your home, its contents, and your liability.

Covering Your Home. The most important factor in determining your coverage is the value of your home. You should base your decision on your home's replacement value—the cost of rebuilding the same structure in the same location. Replacement value and market value are two entirely different concepts. Market value is simply the price a buyer is willing to pay for your home. It includes the value of the land and many intangibles (location, quality of schools, and so on). Replacement value does not include land value and varies over time, depending on things such as wage rates and the cost of building materials.

You can determine the replacement value of your home by estimating the cost based on construction costs in your area (multiply the total square footage of your home by the local building costs per square foot), asking the insurance company to calculate the replacement cost, or hiring an independent appraiser.

You generally do not need to insure for 100 percent of the replacement value of your home because the probability of a total loss of your home is very low. For example, even a severe fire will not destroy your house's foundation. For this reason, your mortgage lender will usually only require that you obtain about 80 percent coverage. If a home with a replacement value of $150,000 is covered for $120,000 (80 percent), the insurance company will reimburse the homeowner for losses up to a total of $120,000. Although you may be able to insure for less than 80 percent of the replacement value, some insurance companies do not fully reimburse you for partial losses if your coverage is less than 80 percent of replacement value. Be sure to understand the nature of your coverage and how the insurance company will reimburse you as the size of your loss varies.

For example, let's assume that you had a fire in your garage that totally destroyed the garage and adjacent kitchen and that the cost of repair is $25,000. If you have 80 percent coverage (of your $150,000 house), the insurance company will reimburse you the full $25,000. However, if you had only 70 percent protection, the insurance company might divide your actual 70 percent coverage by the 80 percent "required" coverage to determine its level of reimbursement in the event of such a partial loss (e.g., 70 ÷ 80 = 87.5% of $25,000, or $21,875). Another thing to keep in mind is that the replacement value you determine for your home when you first take out your policy is only valid at that moment in time. Given the general tendency for construction costs to rise, the replacement value of your home increases over time. So, 80 percent today may be something less than 80 percent tomorrow. However, if your insurance company offers a replacement cost endorsement option, you can shift the responsibility for keeping the replacement cost coverage up to at least 80 percent from you to your insurance company (for a premium, of course). If you subscribe to this option, your insurance company will most likely require that you insure for 100 percent of the replacement value they determine. Although the replacement cost guarantee itself may not cost much more, the fact that you must insure for 100 percent of replacement value may increase costs by 10 percent of the base premium or much more.

Covering Unique Older Homes. The "replacement value rule" is not applicable to unique older homes (Victorian homes, stucco homes, and so on) for which replacement either is not feasible or is prohibitively expensive. Given the structural problems commonly associated with older homes (e.g., bad pipes, poor wiring), the risks that typical HO 00-02 policies insure against are the accidents most likely to occur in older homes. To insure at 80 percent or higher of replacement cost, however, may be too expensive using an HO 00-02 policy. A more affordable alternative is an HO 00-08 policy that limits coverage to some portion of the full market value of your home (discounting the land).

Covering Personal Property. The term *personal property* includes your furniture, clothes, sports equipment, and other personal items. Most policies reimburse content losses for personal property up to 50 percent of the amount of insurance on the home itself. Content insurance comes with a deductible, typically $100 to $250. Your premiums go down as your deductible goes up. The default value of the loss is determined on an "actual cash value" basis (actual cost minus depreciation). So, when filing a claim based on actual cash value, you will probably be reimbursed for the item in an amount that you would expect to be able to purchase a similar item at a garage sale, or perhaps a bit more. This is normally far below the replacement value. You can, however, customize your homeowners' policy to better suit your needs. One way is to purchase a replacement cost insurance rider to enable you to replace a loss with equipment of comparable value at current prices (no reduction for depreciation).

You must be aware of the limits of your coverage by type of item—both the dollar limit and the causes of loss that the insurance company recognizes as reimbursable. See the "Special Limits of Liability" section of the policy you are considering to get this information. For example, coverage on computers is often limited to $3,000, and on jewelry, furs, and silverware it may be limited to $1,000. This means that if your $10,000 ring is stolen, you will get only $1,000 from your homeowners' policy. In general most policies won't cover "mysterious losses." Therefore, make sure your policy includes "accidental disappearance," meaning you will have coverage if you simply lose the item.

If you need more coverage on uniquely valued items, you can take out extra insurance with a personal articles floater or rider. These are simply endorsements attached to your base policy specifying the amount of additional coverage you have purchased and the specific item for which it was purchased.

An alternative method for securing additional personal property coverage is to purchase it through personal property insurance. If you need more coverage than is offered by your basic homeowner's policy, compare the cost of obtaining the additional coverage through riders to your homeowner's policy with the cost of a separate personal property policy. In either case, it is prudent to make sure your high-value items are insured to their replacement value.

Twelve Ways to Save on Homeowners' Insurance

You can save money on your homeowners' insurance in a number of ways. Discounts from your insurance company are often available for a number of reasons, ranging from the age of your house and security features to proximity to a fire station and type of building material. These discounts will vary by state and by insurance company. Be sure to ask your insurer about them.

Here are twelve ways you can save money on your homeowners' policy according to the Insurance Information Institute (III):

1. *Shop around.* Using the homeowners' checklist provided at the end of the chapter, get quotes from different insurance companies. Also get recommendations from friends and family.

2. *Raise your deductible.* The deductible is the amount of money you have to pay toward a loss before your insurance kicks in. Typically deductibles start at $250. Increasing your deductible to $500 saves you up to 12 percent on your premium, $1,000 saves you up to 24 percent, and $2,500 saves you up to 30 percent.

3. *Improve security and safety.* Items such as dead-bolt locks, burglar alarms, and smoke detectors can usually bring discounts of 5 percent each, depending on your company. Other discounts may apply if you have a security system installed. Check with your insurer to see what they will support.

4. *Buy your home and auto policies from the same company.* You may be able to get discounts for having more than one policy with the same company.

5. *Think about insurance when you buy your home.* When you are shopping for a new home, take the cost of insuring that home into consideration. Loca-

tion, condition, building materials, and so forth should all be considered. Lower premiums for things like newer plumbing or heating are things to think about.

6. *Insure your home, not the land.* The land your home sits on is not at risk from fire, theft, wind, or other perils that may affect your house. Therefore, don't include the value of the land in your insurance needs calculations.

7. *Nonsmokers.* Smoking accidents are responsible for more than 23,000 residential fires a year. Some insurers may offer lower premiums for homes that have no smokers.

8. *Senior discounts.* If you are at least fifty-five years old and retired, you may qualify for up to a 10 percent discount. Insurance companies have found that because retired people are home more, they have more time for maintaining their homes and they spot problems quicker.

9. *Group coverage.* Often alumni and business associations work out group coverage deals with insurance companies that include discounts for group members.

10. *Stay with one insurer.* If you have been with one insurance company for a number of years, you may receive special consideration. This could include a reduction in premiums of up to 5 percent after three to five years, and some companies may discount as much as 10 percent after six years.

11. *Check your policy annually.* You want to make sure that your policy covers the value of your home and belongings. If you review your policy annually, you will be able to make necessary adjustments. If, for example, you have made a major purchase or home improvement in the past year, you will need to increase your coverage.

12. *Look for private insurance if you are in a government plan.* If you live in a high-risk area—especially one that is vulnerable to coastal storms, fires, or crime—and you have been buying your insurance through a government plan, look around for a private insurance company instead. There are steps you can take that will allow you to buy insurance at a lower rate in the private market.

WHAT OTHER HOMEOWNERS' INSURANCE DO I NEED?

Flood Insurance

Damage caused by floods is not covered by homeowners' policies. If you live in a community susceptible to flooding and your community participates in the National Flood Insurance Program, you can obtain flood insurance through the Federal Emergency Management Agency (FEMA). Flood insurance will cover your home for up to $250,000 in structural damage and up to $100,000 in content loss. Premiums vary with risk of flooding and are government subsidized. For details about the program, contact FEMA at the number or Internet site listed in Appendix A. We recommend that you carry flood insurance if you live in an area susceptible to flooding.

Earthquake Insurance

Basic homeowners' policies do not insure against damage caused by earthquakes. Therefore, we recommend that you consider adding earthquake insurance to your homeowners' policy if you live in an earthquake-prone area. In major disasters, the federal government has generally provided some level of assistance to the owners of damaged homes, usually in the form of subsidized loans. As a result, many experts debate the need for this insurance. You will have to balance cost of purchasing private insurance against your family's tolerance for risk and the degree to which you expect the government to respond rapidly and generously in the event of an emergency. You can get more information on earthquake coverage from the California Earthquake Authority (CEA). Contact information for the CEA is listed in Appendix A.

Title Insurance

There are two types of title insurance: One protects your lender, the other protects you. The lender requires you to pay for a policy to protect them at settlement. You are not protected against a defective title unless you purchase a separate policy for yourself. "What could be wrong with the title?" you ask. A lawyer or lender will tell you any number of horror stories. For example, a previous owner may have had thousands of dollars in unpaid traffic tickets, and the state may have put a lien against his or her property. If the lien against the property is not noted until after the property is transferred, you would be liable for the unpaid tickets. It is better for an insurance company to deal with these rare but costly surprises. Once you've paid the mandatory fee for the lender's title insurance, you'll find that the cost of an additional owner's policy (for yourself) may be less than the price of a case of beer. We strongly recommend that you purchase an owner's title insurance policy when buying real property.

Mortgage Life Insurance (or Credit Life Insurance)

This insurance pays off the remaining balance on your mortgage in the event of your death or the death of your spouse. The premium is added to your mortgage payment. This is normally a very expensive form of life insurance, usually three times and in some cases about ten times more expensive than term life insurance coverage for the mortgage or loan amount. We recommend that you have adequate life insurance and avoid mortgage life insurance. For more information, see chapter 19 on life insurance.

WHAT ABOUT INSURING OTHER TYPES OF PROPERTY?

Insuring Your Rental Property

Military families often purchase a home and rent it out once they make a PCS move. Since they still own the home, they are responsible for insuring it. It is very important to check with your insurance company to determine what your homeowners' policy coverage protects once you move and for how long that protection is in force. Also, verify whether or not it matters if your home is vacant.

You should normally replace your homeowners' policy with a fire policy, which provides coverage for the dwelling itself and damage to personal property in the event of the perils named in the policy. It does not cover theft of personal property and furnishings left in the dwelling. Make sure that your tenants understand that they are responsible for arranging for their own renters' insurance to cover their personal property. To protect against theft, you can obtain a separate policy that covers the contents, if any, that belong to you. The fire policy may be extended to provide personal liability protection on request. However, if you have a homeowners' policy for your current home or a personal liability policy is already in force, liability coverage can be extended from that policy to the rental property.

Renters' Insurance

Given the high number of moves servicemembers make during a career, they often rent houses or apartments rather than purchase them. It is important to know that as a renter you have no vested interest in the building itself, but you may wrongly assume that losses sustained from fire, flood, or theft are covered by the landlord's policy. In fact, renters are provided little or no protection from the landlord's policy. Renters' insurance (HO 00-04) can provide you contents, liability, and off-premises-theft coverage. Renters' insurance can also cover your responsibility to other people injured at your home or elsewhere by you, a family member, or your pet, and it pays legal defense costs if you are taken to court. Policies may also cover additional living expenses (those above your normal monthly rent) in the event your rental unit is rendered uninhabitable and you are forced to live in a hotel or other temporary lodging facility.

Co-op or Condo Insurance

If you buy a co-op or condo, you will need insurance to cover your personal property as well as insurance to cover the shared areas of the building and/or property. The HO 00-06 will generally provide the coverage you require.

Insurance in Government Quarters

If you live in government quarters, you are "covered" by government insurance. However, such coverage is normally limited to personal property damaged in or stolen from your quarters, and the coverage limits are sometimes ridiculously low. The insurance provided by the government is very limited, especially when it comes to personal liability protection. You would be wise to take out specific insurance policies for personal property and personal liability protection or purchase a renters' policy (HO 00-04) that covers both categories of risk. Such a policy can provide protection wherever your tour of duty takes you.

WHAT ABOUT LIABILITY PROTECTION AND UMBRELLA POLICIES?

Liability Protection

Most homeowners' policies offer $100,000 liability coverage as a minimum, and your automobile insurance policy will usually include liability coverage. Given our litigious society, the amount of coverage in these policies is usually inadequate. The need to protect your home and the physical things you own is readily apparent to you; however, protecting your future income is not so obvious. Because liability judgments can include some portion of all your future income to someone you injure, you could lose not only everything you own today, but also a substantial portion of your future earnings. It is, therefore, imperative that you maintain adequate liability coverage.

We recommend that you carry at least $300,000 worth of liability coverage. If the limits available under your homeowners' and automobile policies are not adequate, consider an umbrella policy for $1 million of coverage or more.

Umbrella Policies

Automobile and homeowners' policies provide only limited personal liability insurance. An umbrella policy picks up where your existing coverage leaves off and goes to whatever limit you select, normally the $1 million to $5 million range. Coverage extends well beyond damages assessed for physical injury. An umbrella policy covers judgments for injuries on your property, unintentional libel or slander, catastrophic automobile accidents that exceed your policy limit, sickness or disease, shock, defamation of character, mental anguish, wrongful entry, malicious prosecution, wrongful eviction, and more. Compensation for defense costs and court costs is also included.

Such extensive liability coverage may seem ludicrous at first, but judgments in the $500,000 range and higher are common. Lawsuits are not at all rare if you own a home and are even more common if you rent your property. One mistake can ruin your financial future. All of your assets, current and future, are in the hands of the court. If your dog seriously injures a child or the letter carrier slips on your porch, you could face a major lawsuit. Even if you are not found liable, the cost of defending yourself can be substantial.

You must assess your total liability potential and compare it to the coverage provided by your homeowners' and automobile policies. First determine your asset base—anything you own that is cash or could be converted to cash, including an assessment of your future earnings. Compare your asset base with your "exposure"—the amount of driving you do, the number and ages of others insured on your policy, any recreational vehicles you or your family operate, your status in the community, the judicial environment in which you live, and so on. Identify the liability limits on your basic insurance policies. If a probable lawsuit could "wipe you out," consider an umbrella policy. In most cases, you would be well served with the additional protection.

Although umbrella policies do protect against a broad set of risks, their coverage has limits. In general, there are categories of losses that carry a deductible and personal liability losses that are either uninsurable or normally covered under a different type of policy. Most exclusions not covered under basic policies (such as flood, earthquakes, or lack of maintenance) are also not covered by the umbrella policy.

The insurance company providing the umbrella policy will normally specify minimum limits on your primary insurance policies. Also, the company might require that all your primary policies be with them. The cost can be quite low—a $1 million policy may be offered for as little as $125 per year.

Dog Bite Liability

Since many families have dogs as pets, it is important to be aware that you are liable for any injuries your dog causes. According to the Centers for Disease Control and Prevention (CDC), there are approximately 4.7 million dog bites per year. These bites cost over $1 billion, with the property/casualty insurance industry paying roughly $310 million in 1999, about 20 percent of total homeowners' insurance liability payouts.

While homeowners' and renters' insurance policies typically cover dog bite liability, insurers may charge more for certain breeds of dogs. According to the CDC, the following purebreds have been responsible for the greatest number of dog bite-related fatalities over the twenty-year period from 1979 to 1998: pit bulls, rottweilers, German shepherds, huskies, malamutes, Doberman pinschers, chow chows, Great Danes, and Saint Bernards. If you own one of these types of dogs, it is recommended that you check with your insurance company to ensure you have enough liability coverage.

HOW DO I CHOOSE A COMPANY?

All homeowners' policies are not the same, nor do all typical policies cost about the same. As with all insurance, the first rule is to shop around. When you shop for insurance, make sure you are comparing apples with apples. Because there are so many options, this is not as easy as it sounds.

There are hundreds of companies that provide homeowners' and related insurance. Two that are very popular among servicemembers are USAA and Armed Forces Insurance, but many other firms can serve your needs. You may find that local agents of nationwide firms have lower rates because they have better knowledge of the local housing market. Always get more than one quotation. You can also get more detailed information from insurance commissioners in your state. Many have established Internet sites that inform homeowners about the general details of home insurance and specific conditions in their state. Insurer stability is also important. Make sure the company you buy from is financially stable so you know they will be around to pay your claim. See Appendix A for the telephone numbers and Internet sites of firms that rate

insurance company strength, cater to the military, and/or provide more information about homeowners' insurance.

HOMEOWNERS' CHECKLIST

This checklist is provided to assist you in your insurance decision. Use it to set up a worksheet for comparing insurance companies. We suggest you compare no fewer than three companies when making your decision. Make sure all quotes are for the same type of insurance.

Initial worksheet

1. Replacement value of home (not land): $ ________
2. Percentage of #1 you wish to insure (at least 80%): ________%
3. Dollar value of desired insurance (#2 × #1): $ ________
4. Estimated replacement value of contents: $ ________

Compare the following:

1. Cost of $ ________ (line 3 above) worth of insurance on home.
   a. With $250 deductible: ________
   b. With $500 deductible: ________
   c. With $1,000 deductible: ________
   (A fairly standard deductible is $250. As you increase your deductible, your premium goes down.)
2. Cost of a replacement cost endorsement on the house: ________
3. Content coverage:
   a. Is it available for comparable replacement value of contents? At what additional cost?
   b. Are the limits suitable to my needs?
   c. If not, are floater policies available by item type?
      (1) Types and limits of floater policies I will need.
      (2) Cost of each policy.
4. If too many content floaters are required, is separate personal property insurance available? Cost?
5. If a discount ("teaser") subscriber rate is offered, will the premium get renewed at the "normal" rate? If so, what are the normal rates?
6. Is the insurance company able to meet my other insurance needs? If so, do they offer multipolicy discounts?
7. What are the discounts available for:
   a. Smoke alarms?
   b. Dead bolts?
   c. Fire extinguishers?
   d. Burglar alarms?
   e. Age of home?
   f. Other?

Tips on Making the Most from Your Insurance

- Insure your house for no less than 80 percent of its replacement cost.
- Maintain a detailed room-by-room inventory of all major items contained in your home. Keep this record in a safe place away from your house.
- Review your inventory annually; however, add major items as soon as you purchase or receive them.
- Review your policy annually to ensure you are covered for at least 80 percent of current replacement cost.
- Reevaluate your policy whenever there is a major change in the value of your home or its contents.
- If your insurance company offers replacement cost endorsement, include it in your policy.
- Carry the largest deductible you think you could afford in the event of a loss.
- Carry renters' insurance if you are living in government quarters.

13

Providing for College Expenses

Providing for children's college education is one of the primary financial concerns of American families today, second only to the purchase of a house or saving for retirement. The benefits of a college education to your children are significant and will last a lifetime. However, college is a formidable expense, and parents are wise to start a college savings program at the earliest possible opportunity. Part of college planning should include a consideration of steps that will maximize the effect of financial incentives from both college financial aid programs and government tax laws. As in all investment decisions, parents have to make a wise trade-off between the return necessary to finance a college education and the risks necessary to get higher returns. A sound college savings program should therefore consider three crucial factors: the portfolio risk-return profile, the program's impact on the financial aid process, and the tax structure of the college portfolio. One of the most important lessons of this chapter is that the earlier you start with your plan to provide for college, the better off you and your children will be. Even two or three years of not contributing to your college savings plan can mean a difference of thousands of dollars for your children's education.

HOW MUCH DO I NEED TO SAVE FOR MY CHILDREN'S COLLEGE?

You should take several factors into account when deciding how much you need to save for college. First, college savings should be viewed in the context of your family's other financial goals, such as saving for a house or your own retirement. College is important, but it is a much less significant expense than providing for decades of your own retirement. Second, you should take your current and future financial situation into account. Can you afford to save now, or will you have more significant income in the future? Finally, though the cost of a four-year college education is high and getting higher, you don't have to pay for the whole thing yourself. How much will you really need to contribute after taking financial aid into account?

This last factor is the focus of this section. We begin by examining the total cost of a college education. Then, we discuss how financial aid can reduce this cost. The cost after financial aid is how much you'll have to save in future value terms.

What Does College Cost?

The bad news: College is expensive, and costs continue to rise at about twice the rate of inflation. The components of college cost include tuition and fees, books and supplies, room and board, transportation, and other personal expenses. For the 1999–2000 school year, the College Board calculated that the total annual cost for the typical private college was $22,533. For public college the figure is $10,458 with in-state tuition and $15,686 with out-of-state tuition. For the last few years, college costs have risen at 5 or 6 percent per year. If costs continue to increase at this rate, a typical four-year private college education will cost over $270,000 dollars in 2018. A typical public college with in-state tuition will cost over $125,000.

To figure the cost of colleges to which your child might apply, find the current annual cost at that college's web page, then use a college cost calculator such as *http://www.finaid.org/calculators/costprojector.phtml.* For example, a Harvard education cost $36,000 annually in 2000. Compounded at 5.5 percent, that same education will cost a total of $410,000 for four years starting in 2018. If you want to send your newborn to Harvard in eighteen years, have no college savings yet, and earn 8 percent on your savings, you will need to put away $850 per month to cover that cost *(http://www.finaid.org/calculators/savingsplan.phtml).* Multiply that number by how many children you have, and the figures can become terrifyingly large.

How Does Financial Aid Work, and Will It Cover Part of the College Cost?

The good news: Financial aid can reduce college expenses. Financial aid is any type of assistance with college costs that is based on need. This aid may be provided by the federal or state government or by the college itself. There are two main categories of financial aid: grants and loans. Grants carry no obligation to repay the grantor, while loans must be repaid. Some major grant and loan programs are briefly outlined below. More detailed information on these and other programs is available from the annual *Student Guide* published by the U.S. Department of Education at *http://www.ed.gov/prog_info/SFA/StudentGuide.*

1. *Pell Grants* are available almost exclusively to undergraduates and are awarded on a need basis. This form of grant is available for full-time and part-time students.

2. *Federal Supplemental Education Opportunity Grants (FSEOGs)* are funded by the federal government but are administered by individual schools. These grants are available only to undergraduates and are awarded on a need basis. Priority of award is given to Pell Grant recipients with the most pressing need for assistance. Both full-time and part-time students are eligible.

3. *Federal Perkins Loans* are funded by the federal government but are administered by individual schools. They are available to undergraduate and graduate students and are need based. There are limits on the size of the loan, and the 5 percent interest rate is not charged during the period in which the student is in school. Graduates must begin repayment of the loan nine months following graduation. The typical repayment time for a Perkins Loan is ten years.

4. *Stafford Loans* are available to both graduate and undergraduate students, regardless of financial need, but are available only to full-time students. If the student demonstrates a financial need, the government may subsidize the interest on the loan during the schooling period and up to six months following graduation. Limits apply to the size of the loan that may be awarded, both in one year and on a cumulative basis. The loans are made by private lenders, and the interest rate can change each year of your repayment, but may never exceed 8.25 percent. Loans to students not based on need will typically include a loan origination and insurance fee. The loan period is typically five to ten years.

5. *PLUS (Parent Loans to Undergraduate Students) Loans* are subsidized loans to parents. The PLUS program allows parents to borrow on behalf of their children, but it is only available for full-time students, and the total of loans and financial aid received cannot exceed the total cost of schooling. The loans are not need based. The rate on these loans is variable but cannot exceed 9 percent. Repayment must begin within sixty days of taking out the loan, but repayment may be deferred until schooling ends. Unlike other subsidized loan programs, interest is charged on PLUS loans during the deferral period. These loans are made by private lenders and may involve origination and insurance fees.

6. *Federal Subsidized Work Study* programs offer students the opportunity to gain work experience while earning a maximum amount identified by the government. The federal government subsidizes the program, which is administered by schools. In this program, the student finds a job with an approved employer, typically a nonprofit organization or a professor. The government then subsidizes the student's paycheck with the employer.

7. *State-funded financial aid.* Though there is significant variance from state to state, parents should not overlook this important source of funding. Many states offer grants and subsidized loans along with federal programs, and parents should be sure to fully explore this option.

Unfortunately, the trend of recent years has seen many student assistance dollars formerly awarded as grants replaced by loans. Sixty percent of the approximately $60 billion given in financial aid in 1998 was in the form of loans. This trend was mainly caused by reduced financial aid resources. Less money available in the aid coffers meant less could be given out. However, at the time of printing, the trend has reversed itself. Colleges with well-managed endowments were flush with funds in the late 1990s, and a growing portion of tuition and other expenses is now being covered by financial aid at most universities.

Bottom line: The high cost of college is subsidized by financial aid for most students. At some private institutions, financial aid pays two-thirds of the typical student's college bill.

How Much Financial Aid Can I Get?

This is the wrong question to ask. Financial aid, remember, is determined by need. Thus, the correct question is "How much financial aid do I need based on where my child goes to college?" Based on your family's financial situation and other variables, colleges will expect you to contribute a certain amount to your child's education. Imagine that your child gets accepted to three different colleges:

	College A	College B	College C
Total annual cost	$5,000	$15,000	$30,000
Family contribution	10,000	10,000	10,000
Total need	0	5,000	20,000

The amount of financial aid you might be offered is based on your total need. If your child is able to get into each of these three colleges, then you would receive no financial aid at College A, but $20,000 at College C. Notice that the costs of Colleges B and C are identical ($10,000) after financial aid is considered. Thus, though total college expenses are important to know, the relevant figure for you as you plan your college savings program is your Expected Family Contribution (EFC). That is your best estimate of what you will have to pay!

Instead of asking how much financial aid you'll be able to get, ask "What is my EFC?" The EFC is determined in one of two ways: the federal methodology or the institutional methodology. While the two methods use similar factors to determine eligibility, you should find out the exact rules used by the schools you are considering when your child is one year away from entering college.

You can calculate your Expected Family Contribution given your family's particular situation at a number of different Internet sites. Good examples are *http://cbweb9p.collegeboard.org/EFC/,* provided by the College Board, and FinAid's *http://www.finaid.org/calculators/.* Even if your children are younger, the calculator will give you some idea of how much you should expect to pay for college. Answer the calculator's questions as if your child was starting college next year. Describe what you think your financial situation will be like when your child will actually start college. This means you will have to estimate future income and savings and enter those numbers in the calculator. Don't forget to factor in the effects of inflation! After you complete the calculator, be sure to multiply the annual result by four years. The result is the amount you will be expected to pay for your child's college education in the future.

If you don't have the patience to work through an online Expected Family Contribution calculator, consider some of the key factors upon which these calculators are built and on which colleges base their aid decisions. Both methodologies consider the parents' after-tax income and readily available savings. Approximately one-third of parental income is added to the EFC per year and up to 5.5 percent of parental assets. Parental assets under these methods do not include such items as insurance policies, retirement savings, or home equity in most cases. Colleges also consider any after-tax income that the child generates as well as readily available savings that are titled in the child's name, such as trust accounts. Half of student income over $3,000 is added to the EFC and 35 percent of all assets per year. Schools also consider family size and how many children the family will have in college in a given year. Finally, schools consider demographic information, such as the family structure (single- or dual-parent home) or special expenses, such as a family's obligation to care for handicapped children. Bottom line: Current income is more important than savings in determining the EFC, and students are expected to furnish a much larger amount of their income and savings toward the cost of college than their parents.

While financial aid is an important consideration in meeting the funding challenge, parents should caution themselves against some common financial aid mistakes.

- *The Expected Family Contribution is not set in stone.* Don't assume that the EFC is all you'll be expected to pay. Often you will be asked to pay more or less depending on the school's financial condition or admissions policies. Many schools assume that your children will work during the school year and contribute to college expenses from their earnings.
- *Focusing too much on the financial aid rules.* As with any system, the rules governing financial aid may change. Parents should guard against trying to arrange their finances so to maximize financial aid at the cost of sound financial decisions. Financial aid eligibility is an important consideration, but not a central one. Furthermore, many colleges are more willing to accept full-paying students than students they will have to support with financial aid.
- *Focusing on the zero tuition option, while failing to shop for value.* Parents and students should remember that college is a once-in-a-lifetime value decision. The lower-cost college whose tuition drops to zero after financial aid is not necessarily a better value than the higher-cost college whose tuition is reduced to an affordable (though perhaps painful) level. Remember that the college purchase is above all a value shopping decision subject to the same rules as any other consumer purchase. Parents and students should shop around, compare, and select the school that offers the best value for the price, given the preferences and ability of the student.
- *Remember: No is not final.* Parents with college-age children likely have many friends who can tell tales of negotiating with schools for better aid packages than the initial estimates indicated. Parents and students should actively seek out opportunities to maximize their eligibility for financial aid.

How Do I Apply for Financial Aid?

When your child applies to colleges, pay close attention to the financial aid information provided with the admissions packet. Submit whatever forms and other documents required by each individual school, even if you don't think you would qualify because you have saved too much or your income is too high. You may be pleasantly surprised that you qualify for a variety of subsidized loan programs. Often, schools will require you to submit both the Free Application for Federal Student Aid (FAFSA) with the Department of Education and the PROFILE Application with the College Scholarship Service between 1 January and 1 February of the year your child plans to enter college. Both forms should be available from your child's high school counselor and the financial aid offices at the colleges to which your child is applying. Both may also be completed online. The FAFSA can be found at *http://www.fafsa.ed.gov/*, and the PROFILE Application is at *http://profileonline.cbreston.org/*.

HOW DO I BUILD A COLLEGE SAVINGS PLAN?

In the first section of this chapter, we discussed the cost of college attendance and how financial aid can reduce college expenses. The first step to developing a college savings plan is to estimate the cost of college for each of your children. Then, calculate your Expected Family Contribution toward that cost for each child. Your college savings goal should be whichever is less: your Expected Family Contribution or your estimate of the cost of college. If the cost of college is greater that the Expected Family Contribution, you can reasonably expect to receive financial aid to cover the difference, whether in the form of direct grants or subsidized loans. Now that you have a college savings goal in mind, you must decide how to invest those college savings dollars.

Does It Matter How Old My Children Are?

Yes! Here's why.

Chapter 14 looks at general investment strategies that apply to all types of short-, medium-, and long-term goals. This section explains a strategy you can use for the specific financial goal of providing for college expenses. Chapters 4 and 14 discuss the historical returns of various assets, and one observation is clear: Stocks represent the only asset that you can reasonably expect to provide the compounded rate of return necessary to accumulate a sufficient college fund—as long as you start while your children are young. If you start a college fund shortly after your child's birth, time will work in your favor. A time horizon of eighteen years allows parents to construct a stock-heavy portfolio and capture potentially higher rates of return.

However, not all parents will have started a college savings plan when their children are young. The college financing objective is a moving target of sorts. The time horizon until you must start paying for college shrinks year by year. As your child approaches college age, you will want to hold less risky assets in your college savings portfolio. None of us would wish to tell our Harvard-bound prodigy that the local community college will have to do because the stock market took a bad bounce. You will, of course, want to have a separate college fund for each of your children. The number of years until each child begins college determines how much risk you will want to assume in that child's portfolio, and thus its asset allocation. Your eighteen-year-old's college fund should look very different than your five-year-old's. How should you approach the composition of a college fund over your child's life? Picturing a child's life as a series of stages helps to frame a useful answer.

Stage 1: Newborn to Preteen. During this period, parents can use historically superior stock returns to their advantage. If you start your college portfolio during stage 1, consider investing all of your child's fund in stocks, diversifying between large, small, and foreign stocks to reduce overall risk. Mutual funds are a good way for you to achieve this diversification. A less risky portfolio, but one still offering sufficient returns, might consist of an 85-15 percent mix of stocks and bonds. By mixing in the lower-risk bonds, you reduce the overall risk of your college portfolio. (Chapter 14 discusses the components of a balanced portfolio; you should read it before you begin your college fund.) You should set up a program of automatic periodic investments. Not only does this force you to save by diverting money to college savings before you can spend it, but it also takes advantage of dollar cost averaging, reducing the average price you pay for each share in your portfolio.

Stage 2: The Teen Years. This is the time for parents to reduce their college portfolio's risk. This generally means moving funds out of stocks and into bonds, certificates of deposit, or other types of fixed-income securities. In particular, you might consider locking in the first year's tuition through the purchase of zero coupon bonds set to mature in the summer before your child's freshman year. For example, if you expect to pay $10,000 in tuition in five years for your thirteen-year-old, you might buy zero coupon bonds with a face value of $10,000. If you select bonds with an 8 percent return, those bonds would cost you $6,800. With zeros, you must pay taxes annually on imputed interest, but you will receive a $10,000 payment at maturity that exactly matches your tuition needs.

You might also consider changing the dividend and capital gains distribution options on their college fund accounts to one which reinvests these proceeds in an intermediate-term bond fund. The three- to five-year duration of such funds matches your now-shorter investment horizon, helping to minimize interest rate risk. So now, instead of being 100 percent invested in stocks, you might want to move to a mix that includes 50 to 60 percent stock-based investments and 40 to 50 percent bond-based instruments. (This mix refers only to those investments set aside for your child's college fund. The mix of the rest of your investment portfolio would depend on your other investment goals, as discussed in chapter 14).

Stage 3: The College Years. As the child enters college, parents should convert their college funds over time to more liquid assets, such as money market funds. Many money market funds are almost as liquid as cash; they will allow you to access your funds by writing a check that can be used to pay for your child's college expenses. A common strategy is to "lock in" your stock gains in a manner similar to that mentioned in stage 2 by buying zero coupon bonds timed to mature the summer before each of the child's years in school. Buy enough zero coupon bonds to cover all of your expected expenses for a full year of college. Then, when the bonds mature, leave the proceeds in a money market account from which you can pay your bills. Remember that during freshman summer your final tuition payment is still at least three years away. You may want to leave at least a portion of the college funds in a stock-based investment to boost your returns. Though some advisors recommend holding no stocks once your child enters college, another common asset allocation for the freshman summer is 25 percent in money market funds, 50 percent in zero coupon bonds or intermediate-term bond funds, and 25 percent in stocks. By the sophomore summer you might have a third of your now-smaller college fund in money market funds and the remainder in zero coupon bonds laddered so that half mature during the junior summer and half during the senior summer. By the senior summer, you should have all of your college fund in money market funds.

Will My College Savings Reduce My Eligibility for Financial Aid?

If you completed the Expected Family Contribution calculations discussed in the first part of this chapter, you realize that anything you manage to save for college will increase your Expected Family Contribution per year by 5.5 percent of your savings. In other words, every $100,000 you save for college will increase your Expected Family Contribution by almost $15,000 over four years. To compensate for this effect, you might rerun the EFC calculator, being sure to include your expected college savings. Doing this might cause you to increase your college savings goal. You should bear three additional points in mind.

First, parents should exercise care in the amount of assets they place in their child's name. Schools expect children to fully commit their assets toward the cost of college. Therefore, student-owned assets more rapidly lower eligibility for financial aid than will assets placed in the parent's name. On average, each dollar the child owns will reduce financial aid by 35 cents per year, while the same dollar in the parent's name will reduce the financial aid package by less than 6 cents.

Second, family savings in the form of Individual Retirement Accounts, employer-sponsored retirement savings plans (such as 401k accounts), and home equity are not part of the financial aid consideration. These sources can themselves be important vehicles against which families may borrow to finance college tuition. Consequently, families should place the priority on funding these savings vehicles above all others, as their limited impact on the financial aid calculation makes these already attractive savings vehicles even better.

Third, if a child has significant expenses before they apply to college (such as summer camps, orthodontic work, or a cross-country trip to visit colleges), parents should carefully consider how they fund those expenses. If the parents' choice is to take money from their own savings or from the child's trust account, they should spend the child's money to reduced the expected family contribution to college. This expense shifting is legal since the parent is the trustee of the account until the child is twenty-one and the expenditure is clearly for the benefit of the child.

How Can I Take Advantage of the Tax Laws to Accelerate My College Savings?

UGMA and UTMA Accounts. The Federal government has established two types of tax-favored trust accounts in which parents may accumulate funds designated for their child's college education. These accounts are commonly referred to as the Uniform Gifts to Minors Account (UGMA) and the Uniform Transfers to Minors Account (UTMA). Both of these vehicles represent a low-cost, tax-advantaged means of saving for a child's college education.

UGMAs and UTMAs offer the same tax treatment and differ only in the type of asset that can be in the account. UTMAs allow parents to deposit any assets for the benefit of minors; UGMAs may hold only cash or securities. Parents may establish these accounts through a bank or mutual fund, and they usually designate themselves as the trustee.

Both accounts tax a portion of the account's unearned income at a lower rate than the parents'. For accounts of children under fourteen during tax year 2000, the first $700 of interest and dividends (unearned income) generated by the assets in an UGMA or UTMA was tax-free, while the next $700 of unearned income was taxed at the child's marginal tax rate (usually 10 percent). All unearned income in excess of $1,400 was taxed at the parents' marginal tax rate. UGMAs and UTMAs belonging to children over fourteen are taxed at the child's marginal tax rate, with a $700 standard deduction. These thresholds are adjusted for inflation annually. See IRS Publication 929 for the most current limits.

The UGMA and UTMA provisions represent rather sizable tax savings for parents in higher tax brackets. For instance, a parent in the 27 percent tax bracket would pay a tax of $378 on $1,400 of dividends and interest generated in an ordinary account. Assuming the child was under fourteen and in the 10 percent tax bracket, the same $1,400 in dividends in a UGMA would be assessed a tax of $70—a savings of $308. While this may not sound like a large amount, if the $308 is invested each year and earns just 7 percent, after taxes it will provide an additional $10,471 in eighteen years. That will come in handy at tuition time!

Obviously, the tax advantages of UGMAs and UTMAs come early in the child's life, so parents wishing to receive the full benefits of the account must set them up early. Also, the greatest tax savings come for parents in higher tax brackets. Parents in lower tax brackets will receive less benefits from UGMAs and UTMAs. However, these accounts are important tools, especially for dual-career couples who might find themselves in higher tax brackets.

The major disadvantage of the UGMA and UTMA is that assets transferred to these accounts are an irrevocable gift that belongs to the child at age twenty-one. Even if that once-cuddly bundle of joy becomes an ungrateful lout, the money in the UGMA or UTMA is his or hers. It can only be spent for the benefit of the child before age twenty-one, and it becomes the child's property at age twenty-one. Parents having any doubts about their child's financial savvy should consider carefully the wisdom of establishing an UGMA or UTMA accounts. Also, parents might find themselves irrevocably giving assets to a child who might be able to secure financial aid or scholarships on their own. Parents could find that they have transferred assets to one of their children that they more urgently need for another child's college fund or to put in their retirement portfolio.

The second major drawback to an UGMA or UTMA is the potential impact on the child's ability to secure financial aid. As discussed above, 35 percent of the student's assets will be added to the Expected Family Contribution each year, reducing the amount of financial aid available. Consider again this example: Imagine you are in the 27 percent tax bracket and have placed $20,000 in your child's UGMA. If you earn 7 percent, or $1,400, on those funds each year, then you would save $308 annually in taxes, giving you an additional $10,471 for tuition after eighteen years. However, that $20,000 would be counted in the EFC calculations as your student's assets, reducing your eligibility for financial aid by 35 percent of $20,000, or $7,000 in the first year alone! If you run the UGMA down to zero over 4 years, you would reduce your cumulative eligibility for financial aid by about $17,500. So even in the 27 percent tax bracket, the loss of financial aid seems to outweigh the tax gains from an UGMA. Of course, those in the 27 percent tax bracket are not usually eligible for much financial aid anyway, unless they have several children that they plan to send to expensive private schools. The chart below briefly summarizes the advantages and disadvantages of the UGMA and UTMA arrangements.

Advantages	**Disadvantages**
Tax-advantaged accounts increase the effect of compound interest; they maximize the time value of money in your favor.	Tax-advantaged accounts come at the cost of parental control over funds.
	Tax-advantaged accounts might reduce the child's ability to secure financial aid or reduce the size of that aid.

Consequently, the UGMA or UTMA seems appropriate for only the wealthier college saver. If parents decide to use the UGMA or UTMA for its tax advantage, they should do so only to the point that it annually provides approximately the maximum tax-advantaged earnings (currently $1,400). Other investments should be retained in the parent's names so that they can be more easily controlled and so that they are less likely to impact college financial aid formulas.

U.S. Savings Bonds. Some parents use series EE savings bonds as a partial way to fund their children's college education. The good news is that interest earned when redeeming Series EE bonds bought after 1989 is tax exempt if higher-education costs in the redemption year exceed principal and interest received. U.S. savings bonds are a safe form of investment offering a predictable rate of return further enhanced by the tax-free provision. However, parents might find that the rate of return on these bonds is lower than that desired to build a sufficient college fund. (The details of purchase, redemption, and interest payments on bonds are discussed in chapter 15.)

It is important to note the restrictions on the use of these bonds to ensure that the interest is tax-free. The bonds must be registered in the name of someone at least twenty-four when the original purchase is made. This person is considered the owner of the bond. College costs must be for the bond owner or the owner's spouse or dependent. (*Note:* These bonds can be bought by anyone, but must be registered as explained above.) Tuition and fees, but not room and board, are eligible costs. Costs offset by scholarships and employer aid are not eligible either. Also, if married, the owner will have to file a joint tax return in the redemption year, and the tax benefit is available only to people who meet certain income restrictions in the year the bond is redeemed.

More important, you need to decide whether the safe, conservative investment in savings bonds will yield enough return to provide the income you will need to finance your children's college education. Military families may put some of their college fund into tax-advantaged savings bonds, but most families will have a sizable portion of their children's college fund in stocks or mutual funds that invest in stocks.

Education IRAs. Education IRAs allow you to save for tuition expenses in a nondeductible account, then withdraw your earnings tax-free. The limit on contributions to education IRAs starting in 2002 is $2,000 per year per child. This limit is reduced for joint tax filers with over $190,000 in adjusted gross income, and those filers with over $220,000 in income may not contribute at all—not an issue for most servicemembers. Education IRAs can be opened by anyone for your child, but combined contributions cannot exceed the $2,000 cap per year per child. Previously, you could not fund an education IRA and a 529 plan (see below) in the same year, but now you can. Beware that the money in your child's education IRA will be considered to be student assets in EFC calculations, which will reduce your eligibility for financial aid.

Roth IRAs. Roth IRAs allow you to save for retirement expenses in a nondeductible account, then withdraw your earnings tax-free. Contributions are capped at $3,000 in 2002, $4,000 in 2005, and $5,000 in 2008. These contributions may be withdrawn tax- and penalty-free to fund education expenses. Furthermore, such contributions are not considered in the EFC calculations, so they do not reduce your eligibility for financial aid. However, once retirement assets are withdrawn to fund education, they cannot be returned to the Roth IRA. This method of funding college expenses would only make sense if you had substantially met your retirement savings goals in another type of tax-advantaged retirement account, such as a 401k.

State-Sponsored Qualified Tuition Plans (529 Plans). In 2001, thirty-six states offered 529 plans (so called after section 529 of the Internal Revenue Code). These plans can be used to fund qualified education expenses at accredited colleges and universities nationwide, not just in the state that sponsors the plan. States cap either your total contributions to their 529 plans or the balances held in those accounts. As this is being written, contribution caps range from $90,630 in Utah's plan to $202,225 in New Mexico's plan, and balance caps range from $125,000 in Michigan's plan to $250,000 in Alaska's plan. States hire securities firms to manage their plans, and they offer a variety of investment options. Many state plans are exempt from state taxes for their residents, so it pays to investigate your own state's offering before shopping for plans in other states. Many plans automatically adjust your 529's asset mix as your child approaches college age, which may cost a bit more in fees but takes much of the worry out of college savings. Annual contributions to a 529 plan should be limited by consideration of the gift tax, which generally permits tax-free gifts of $10,000 per year. A unique feature of the 529 plan is that $50,000 may be given in one year, with the gift prorated over five years to avoid triggering the gift tax.

Thousands of companies now support 529 college savings plans by kicking back a portion of your purchases from them to your 529 account. This is done through a nonprofit organization, Upromise *(www.Upromise.com).* As more firms join this service, it may be worthwhile to fill out the free application in order to accelerate your 529 savings.

WHAT IF I CAN'T SAVE ENOUGH TO PAY FOR COLLEGE?

The goal of your college savings program is to pay for the expected costs of sending your children to college. You should maximize your return commensurate with risk while considering tax implications and any adverse impacts on the financial aid decision. In the end, even the most carefully planned savings program may not yield enough funds to cover your college costs. This is the case for most families who must then face the fact that they will have to bear a large share of college funding themselves. This final section will touch on some vehicles that families may use to help finance college costs.

Gifts

Grandparents and relatives are important sources of funding, especially in the early years of a child's life. Often, it is the grandparents who have the most to gain from the tax advantages of UGMA and UTMA provisions, as they may be in higher tax brackets during the early years of their grandchild's life. Recognize that gifts to the student will reduce the level of financial aid available much more than gifts to the parents.

Merit Scholarships

Parents should not overlook the scholarship opportunities that their child's inherent talents might bring them. Scholarships range from partial- to full-tuition awards for scholastic, athletic, or artistic merit. Often, schools will not include scholarship awards in their financial aid calculations.

Financing College with Current Income (Working)

In addition, parents should not overlook the option of financing a part of college tuition from family monthly income, as many parents will find themselves still working during their child's college years. Parents should also consider the option of having their children bear some expenses with student jobs while in college. Many universities will expect students to work when they calculate your Expected Family Contribution, including their forecast of your student's future wages in your EFC.

Financing College with Future Income (Borrowing)

Families may also finance full- or partial-tuition costs through loans against their family's net worth. Subsidized student loans such as those mentioned earlier are one important source of funding. Parents may also find that years of mortgage payments have built an important source of equity against which banks will provide loans at very favorable rates. The interest on these home equity loans will be tax deductible. Many employers will also allow employees to borrow against the assets of their 401k or employer-sponsored savings plans.

However, families should be careful not to sacrifice the benefits of tax-deferred accounts to fund college costs if other alternatives exist. In particular, parents should consider the liquidation of their IRA and tax-deferred retirement accounts as a last resort. Liquidation of these accounts in any pattern other than a substantially equal payment over five years can trigger tax penalties of 10 percent over normal income taxes and costly withholding (up to 20 percent of account assets). A better option for parents, particularly older ones, is to finance college tuition through loans and defer the final loan repayment until age 59 1/2, when they can begin drawing from IRA accounts and avoid early distribution penalties. Parents will also find that their retirement accounts hold significantly more assets, having been afforded the opportunity to allow longer tax-deferred growth.

The Military Alternative

Students should consider the merits of military service as a source of college funds. All military services offer Reserve Officer Training Corps (ROTC) scholarships, which may pay for one or more year's schooling. These scholarships are available at hundreds of colleges and provide money based on merit to pay for tuition, books, and fees. A monthly stipend, currently $350 for seniors, helps defray other costs. Service obligations vary in length, with longer service required for more generous scholarship awards. Service may be performed in either the active, reserve, or National Guard components.

Parents should also consider the merits of a military academy education, which is tuition-free to the student, but carries a five-year service obligation. To explore this option, contact the admissions offices at the various academies. See the Internet Resources section at the end of this chapter for more information.

Finally, some students might wish to consider enlisting in the armed services. Currently, a four-year enlistment carries with it the opportunity to earn up to $50,000 in college funds, as well as the opportunity to build very valuable job skills. Those completing training in critical specialties can presently earn an additional $20,000 cash bonus. In addition to earning money for college after your term of enlistment expires, you can also go to college while serving, and the services pay 75 percent of the tuition for approved course work. Furthermore, many states now offer free in-state tuition to those who enlist in their National Guard or reserve units.

The Army also runs a new education portal on the Internet called Army University Access Online *(www.eARMYu.com).* At no cost, the enlisted soldier can work toward a degree online from a network of over twenty participating universities. The soldier receives a technology package to support his or her studies as well, also free of charge. This package includes a laptop computer, printer, and Internet access. Look for similar offerings from the other services in the future.

INTERNET RESOURCES

http://www.cga.edu: The United States Coast Guard Academy

www.collegeboard.com: Follow the "Paying for College" link for financial aid facts and calculators. The expected family contribution calculator is located at *http://cbweb9p.collegeboard.org/EFC/.* This site is published by the College Board, authors of the SAT.

www.collegeispossible.org: America's colleges and universities have prepared this site to guide you to the books, websites, and other resources that admissions and financial aid professionals consider most helpful. This site is published by the Coalition of America's Colleges and Universities.

www.collegesavings.org: The National Association of State Treasurers publishes this web page covering state-sponsored college savings plans. It has links to your state's program.

Tips to Get the Most for College Financing

- Start early—this will make the biggest difference in your ability to successfully fund your child's education.
- Have a separate college savings fund for each of your children so that each has an appropriate asset allocation and risk level.
- Use stocks to grow a child's college portfolio rapidly, then shift to bonds or CDs as tuition payments near.
- Consider 529 college savings plans, which now grow tax-free.
- Use UGMAs and UTMAs to earn no more than the maximum tax-advantaged amount ($1,400).
- Savings in the child's name is used first and at a larger percentage than savings in the parents' names in financial aid formulas.
- Consider tax-exempt savings bonds, but carefully compare their risks and return to other types of tax-advantaged investments.
- Consider the many loans that are available for college.
- Take advantage of the many scholarship opportunities available.
- Remember, college is an investment for a lifetime. Do not unduly focus on the finances. Select a college that provides the best value.

www.ed.gov/thinkcollege/early: The U.S Department of Education publishes this web page. It describes many aspects of college planning, including saving, with good calculators and links to other sites.

http://www.fafsa.ed.gov/: This Department of Education site contains the Free Application for Federal Student Aid and other information on financial aid.

http://www.finaid.org/: A complete source for financial aid information, including the wide variety of veterans and military benefits available. FinAid was established in the fall of 1994 as a public service. This award-winning site has grown into the most comprehensive annotated collection of information about student financial aid on the web.

www.savingforcollege.com: Provides data on and rankings of state 529 plans.

www.smartmoney.com/college: In 2018, four years at a private university will cost $225,000, but don't panic: This website shows you how to "foot the bill."

http://www.usafa.af.mil: The United States Air Force Academy

http://www.usma.edu: The United States Military Academy

http://www.usmma.edu: The United States Merchant Marine Academy

http://www.usna.edu: The United States Naval Academy

PART IV

Building Your Nest Egg

14

Developing an Investment Strategy

Strategy is all about figuring out where you want to go (your desired strategic ends), identifying what resources (or means) you have at your disposal, and then determining how you will utilize your means in order to achieve your desired ends (i.e., the ways in which you will link your means to your ends.)

Desired financial ends should be a function of personal goals. What do you want to have and how much will it cost? Means are generally wealth on hand, income over time, and time available for investments and wealth to grow. Ways have to do with how you choose to manage and invest your means over time, in order to achieve your ends.

Some simple basics of sound investment strategy include the following:

- Establish a budget and live within it.
- Pay yourself first by setting aside a predetermined portion of your monthly income to achieve your long-term investment strategy.
- Pay off debt—unless you are confident your investments will yield a greater rate of return than the interest rates you are required to pay on your debts.
- Once short- and medium-range financial objectives are met, strive to invest the maximum amount allowed by law in your IRA and the new Thrift Savings Plan (analogous to a 401k plan).
- With each pay raise, increase your long-term investments by an amount that you are comfortable with.
- Seek the highest return possible on your long-term investments, commensurate with your risk tolerance (i.e., if you are very risk averse and cannot sleep at night due to excessive worrying about your investments, you should consider switching to safer, more secure investment vehicles).

With this brief introduction to investment strategy, we will now delve into the details.

WHAT IS WEALTH?

Quite simply, wealth is the ability to buy goods and services. Is there a difference between wealth and money? Absolutely! While you need money to buy goods and services, the quantity of goods and services that you can buy represents your wealth. It's possible to have a lot of money and very little wealth, such as during the hyperinflation of pre-World War II Germany, when it took a wheelbarrow full of money to buy a loaf of bread.

WHAT IS THE "SECRET" TO INCREASING YOUR WEALTH?

To increase your ability to buy more goods and services, you must increase your wealth. To do that, you have to earn or accumulate more money than you spend. This is part of the budgeting process discussed in chapter 4. The next step is to take those funds and invest them to help them grow at a rate that outpaces the negative effects of inflation and taxes.

Factors Influencing Wealth Growth

Essentially, there are only three factors that influence the ability of the funds you accumulate to have increased purchasing power: rate of return, inflation, and taxes. Only one of these factors contributes to wealth growth; the other two diminish your ability to buy more goods and services.

Rate of Return. Figure 14-1 plots the annual increase of $1 invested in 2000 over seventy years in each of five investments. As you can see, the historical return for small and large company stocks is significantly greater than that of government bonds and Treasury bills. You will also notice that while the return of small and large company stocks is high, so is the variation from year to year. This annual variation causes the plots of the small and large company stocks to be much more jagged than the relatively smooth graphs of bonds and Treasury bills. This graph does not adjust for inflation or taxes.

Figure 14-1
Growth of $1 from 1926 to 2000

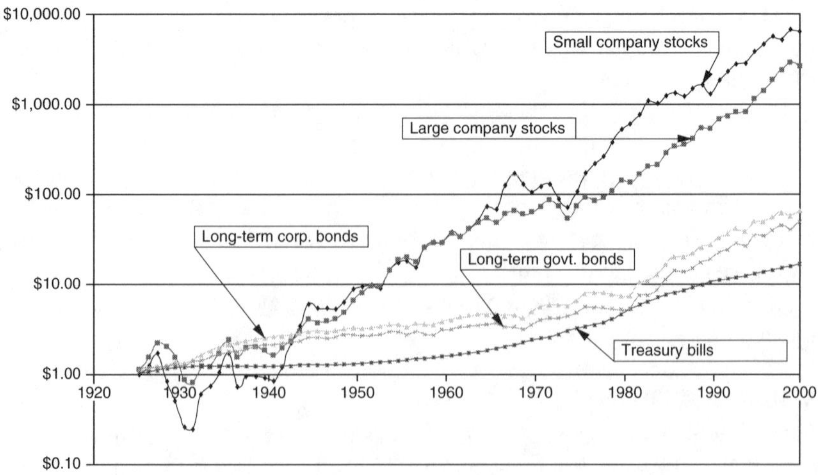

TABLE 14-1
ANNUAL RETURN, TAXES, AND INFLATION, 1926–2000

	Average Annual Return 1926–2000	Average Return after 27% Taxes	Average Return after Taxes and Inflation	Standard Deviation
Small company stocks	17.27%	12.61%	9.44%	33.44%
Large company stocks	12.67	9.25	6.08	20.32
Long-term corporate bonds	6.03	4.40	1.23	8.69
Long-term government bonds	5.71	4.17	1.00	9.42
T-bills	3.86	2.82	–0.35	3.18
Inflation	3.17	n/a	n/a	4.42

Source: Computations based on Ibbotsons Associates, 2001.

Taxes. Regardless of the asset you choose, taxes will reduce the amount that you earn. Table 14-1 reflects the average annual return represented by each asset. The first column shows the annual return. The second column is what's important to most investors: the return you will see after taxes (assuming a 27 percent marginal tax rate). Paying taxes on your returns reduces the overall return of the portfolio and takes away from the broad goal of increasing wealth. Though there are some investments that provide tax-favored treatment, such as retirement plans, IRAs, and variable annuities, most only permit deferring taxes until later. Certainly, the prudent investor takes advantage of these opportunities, but the deferral does not completely negate the impact of taxes; it just delays tax payments until later.

Inflation. The third column in Table 14-1 shows clearly why you would not want to invest all your money in conservative investments like Treasury bills and certificates of deposit (CDs). Note that a 100 percent Treasury bill portfolio would actually lose purchasing power! Why? The rate of return associated with Treasury bills is not enough to offset the negative impacts of taxes and inflation over time. This can have a significant impact on your ability to maintain and/or increase your wealth. If you retired at age fifty-five and put all of your money in Treasury bills or CDs, the purchasing power of your accumulated wealth would substantially decline during your retirement. That is true even before you withdraw any funds to meet living expenses! Since your ability and desire to earn a living will have diminished by the time you reach age seventy-five, you may want to consider an alternative to such a conservative approach.

Note also the minimal positive return on long-term government bonds. Returns associated with these investments barely maintain purchasing power for the investor after accounting for taxes and inflation. In contrast, the return for stocks not only outpaces inflation and taxes but permits an increase in wealth. Keep in mind, however, that these returns are historical averages. Year-to-year results can vary significantly, as shown by the standard deviation associated with each of the investments.

Risk. The rate of return of stocks and other asset classes with high returns cannot properly be evaluated without also discussing risk. As already shown, the way to make your portfolio grow most quickly would be to choose the investment that provides the highest return. Clearly, the return associated with stocks would enable the quickest growth. So why shouldn't everyone invest their entire portfolio in stocks?

Risk is the extent to which an asset's returns deviate from the expected rate of return. Stocks provide the greatest return, but stocks also provide the greatest risk, as reflected in their higher standard deviation. If not for the trade-off between risk and return, most investors would choose the investment that provides the highest rate of return.

Standard deviation, a mathematical measure of variability, serves as a convenient measure for risk. Figure 14-2 depicts the range of returns that are within one standard deviation of the average return for four investments.

You can see from Figure 14-2 that the greater return corresponds to greater fluctuations in return, as measured by the standard deviation. Clearly, the distribution of likely returns is smaller for lower-risk investments, such as Treasury bills. Based upon the data in Table 14-1, the range of expected returns for Treasury bills is from 0.68 to 7.15 percent (3.86 percent average annual return ± 4.42 percent standard deviation), whereas the range for large company stocks is –7.64 to 32.99 percent (12.67 percent ± 20.32 percent). It is possible for the returns to fall outside these ranges. In fact, a range of one standard deviation provides only a 68 percent level of confidence that a particular year's return will fall inside the range. To increase to a 95 percent level of assurance would require establishing a range using two standard deviations. For Treasury bills, such a range would be –2.51 to 10.23 percent, and for large company stocks, it would be from –27.96 to 53.30 percent.

Investment Time Horizon. How do you determine what combination of assets might be right for you? Part of the answer lies in understanding your time horizon to understand which risks are more relevant to you. Table 14-2 illustrates the impact of an investor's time horizon on which type of asset he or she should choose.

Note that either small or large company stocks had the best return in forty-nine of the seventy-five one-year holding periods. However, they had a negative return twenty-three times! If the time horizon for a particular goal is only a year away, the asset class that would provide the best opportunity for ensuring that the money required would be available if you already had the funds saved would clearly be Treasury bills, since there was only one instance in which they had a negative return in a one-year time horizon.

Moving a little further out on the investment time horizon, look at the five-year holding periods. Notice that small company stocks had nine five-year periods with a negative return and large company stocks had seven. That means that if you had randomly chosen five consecutive years since 1926 and invested in

Figure 14-2
Range of Expected Returns

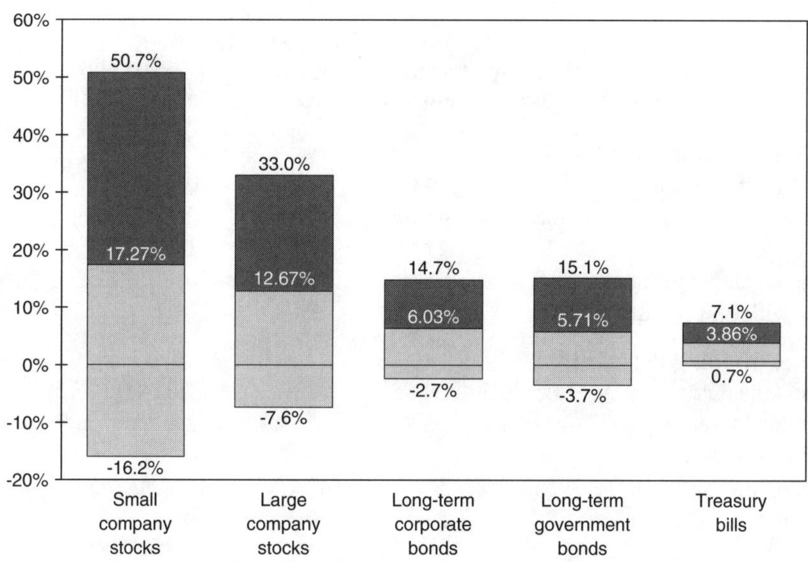

small company stocks, you would have lost money about 12 percent of the time. By contrast, government bonds were negative in only six periods—less than 9 percent of the time.

Now look at the twenty-year holding periods. Stocks not only had no periods with a negative return, but they also had the best return in each of the different twenty-year periods! Of those periods, small company stocks had the superior return fifty times and large company stocks six times. The important implication for developing an investment strategy is that the longer the investment time horizon, the more risk you can take in a portfolio to gain a better return. That is because over time, the good years have an opportunity to offset the bad years. On the other hand, the shorter the time horizons, the more important it is to invest in Treasury bills or bonds to reduce the impact of negative returns.

Considering the previous discussion, what should you conclude about risk? The greatest risk to a portfolio in the short term is the volatility of the stock and bond markets. Thus, you should place funds designated for short-term goals in an investment that provides the lower volatility—and, correspondingly, a lower return. On the other hand, the greatest risk to your portfolio over the long term is the negative impact of inflation and taxes. Thus, you should invest funds with longer-term objectives in assets that provide the greater return over time to outpace inflation and taxes. Though there is greater risk with such investments, over time the good years can offset the bad years, thereby creating a positive return and increasing wealth.

TABLE 14-2
COMPOUNDED ANNUAL RETURNS FOR VARIOUS TIME PERIODS

	Small Company Stocks	Large Company Stocks	Long-Term Corporate Bonds	Long-Term Government Bonds	T-Bills	Inflation
One-Year Holding Periods (75)						
Highest annual return	142.9%	54.0%	42.6%	40.4%	14.7%	18.2%
Lowest annual return	–58.0%	–43.3%	–8.1%	–9.2%	0.0%	–10.3%
Negative periods	23	21	17	21	1	10
Periods outpacing inflation	52	51	48	45	50	n/a
Periods with best return	32	17	0	14	12	n/a
Five-Year Holding Periods (71)						
Highest annual return	45.90%	28.55%	22.51%	21.62%	11.12%	10.06%
Lowest annual return	–27.54%	–12.47%	–2.22%	–2.14%	0.07%	–5.42%
Negative periods	9	7	3	6	0	7
Periods outpacing inflation	59	57	43	40	45	n/a
Periods with best return	37	23	0	9	2	n/a
Ten-Year Holding Periods (66)						
Highest annual return	30.38%	20.06%	16.32%	15.56%	9.17%	8.67%
Lowest annual return	–5.70%	–0.89%	0.99%	–0.07%	0.14%	–2.57%
Negative periods	2	2	0	1	0	6
Periods outpacing inflation	60	59	37	33	39	n/a
Periods with best return	37	22	0	3	4	n/a
Twenty-Year Holding Periods (56)						
Highest annual return	21.13%	17.87%	11.49%	11.99%	7.72%	6.36%
Lowest annual return	5.74%	3.11%	1.34%	0.69%	0.42%	0.07%
Negative periods	0	0	0	0	0	0
Periods outpacing inflation	56	56	32	22	36	n/a
Periods with best return	50	6	0	0	0	n/a

Source: Computations from Ibbotsons, 2001.

Diversification. Everyone has heard that they should not put all their eggs in one basket. Figure 14-3 shows why. Assume that you have a choice of two investments, depicted by curves A and B. Both have a positive return, and both fluctuate with the economy, stock market, technological progress, and other conditions. Over time, the upswings cancel the downswings and, on average, you will have a positive return. Unfortunately, no one can consistently predict when the swings will occur, and you may need the money from your investment just when it's in a trough instead of at a peak. To minimize that effect, you can buy equal amounts of both investment A and investment B so that the upswings of one can counter the downswings of the other. Line C represents this portfolio, in which half of your investment is placed in A and the other half in B. Portfolio C has less volatility than either A or B, without sacrificing any of the return. Because investments react differently to the same economic conditions, it is possible to put together a portfolio with reduced volatility. This is the advantage of diversification.

Now that you understand how rate of return, taxes, and inflation affect your investments and the importance of your willingness to accept risk, your time horizon, and the diversification of your portfolio, you can construct an investment strategy that will help you achieve your financial goals.

Figure 14-3
Benefits of Diversification

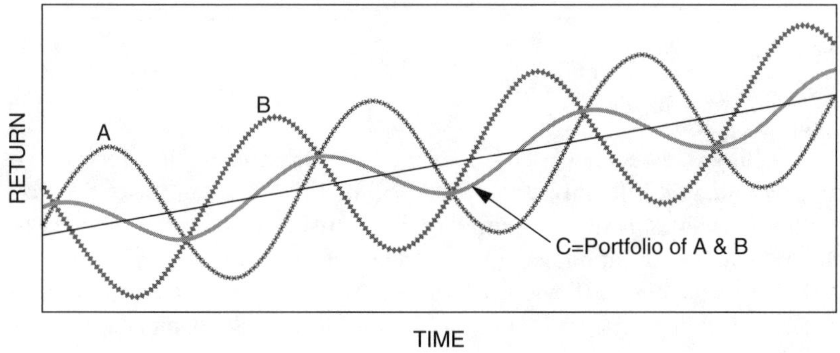

HOW DO YOU CREATE AN INVESTMENT STRATEGY?

Setting Financial Goals

In developing an investment strategy, start by asking where you want to end—what are your goals? Establishing goals and setting funds aside to accomplish them are the first steps on the road to financial freedom. By working through the financial planning and budgeting process described in chapter 4, it is possible to establish realistic, achievable goals. The time associated with each goal will be one of the factors that affects your investment strategy.

To help match specific investment vehicles to your goals, you should group your goals by time period: short-term (less than one year), medium-term (one through four years), and long-term (five years and beyond). To illustrate the development of an investment strategy, assume that you've completed the financial planning discussed in chapter 4 and have listed your goals in Table 14-3, based on the time when the money will be required for each goal.

TABLE 14-3
EXAMPLE OF FINANCIAL GOALS

Time Horizon	Goal	Date Desired (Years)	Cost*
Short-term (<1 year)	Emergency fund	Now	$3,000
	House down payment and closing costs	1	10,000
Medium-term (1–4 years)	New living room furniture	3	4,000
	10-year anniversary cruise	5	5,000
Long-term (> 5 years)	Children's college	10	80,000
	Daughter's wedding	15	15,000
	Retirement	30	600,000

*Measured in today's dollars.

Asset Allocation

Establishing an asset allocation is the process of determining the proportion of funds allotted to different asset classes within a portfolio. An asset class is a grouping of investments with similar characteristics or features. Figure 14-4 shows an asset allocation using three broad asset classes: stocks, bonds, and cash. While this figure shows a specific allocation to each of the asset classes, you should adjust these proportions to fit your own time horizon and risk preference.

How important is the asset allocation decision in relation to the returns of a portfolio? According to a study by Brinson, Hood, and Beebower,[1] 91.5 percent of the return associated with a portfolio can be explained by the asset allocation. Market timing and security selection explain only 1.8 percent and 4.6 percent of the returns associated with a portfolio, respectively.

Clearly, the most important decision is not which securities or funds to select, or when to get in or out of the market, but how to allocate holdings among asset classes. Most popular investment publications have countless articles on security and mutual fund selection and market timing strategies, yet very few on asset allocation (although fortunately, this is changing). As a result, many believe that investment selection and market timing are the most important aspects of their investment decisions. In truth, they are only minor issues. Even the *Wall Street Journal* trivializes the ability of portfolio managers to pick individual securities by pitting these managers' selections against a dartboard selection of stocks; more often than not, the dartboard wins!

[1]Gary B. Brinson, L. Ralph Hood, Gilbert B. Beebower, "Determinants of Portfolio Performance," *Financial Analysts Journal,* July–August 1986. Study updated by Brinson, Brian D. Singer, and Beebower in *Financial Analysts Journal,* May–June 1991.

Within the three broad asset classes depicted in Figure 14-4, there are other asset classes that can be used to divide your investment portfolio, as shown in Table 14-4. For additional information on specific financial instruments, see chapter 15.

Figure 14-4
Broad Asset Classes

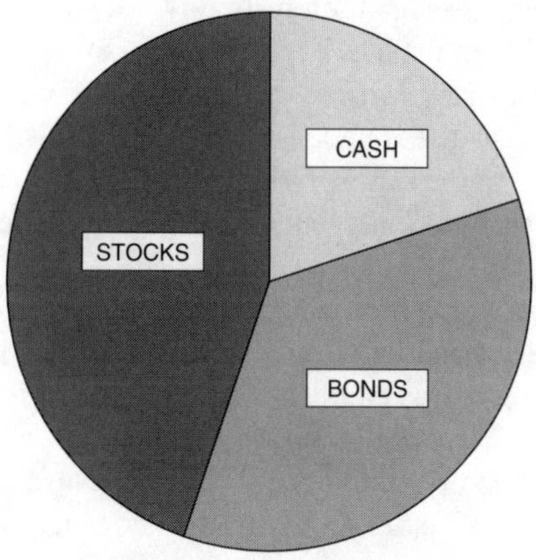

How do you decide the proportions of funds to allocate to different asset classes? To a large extent, this determination is based upon the timing of your financial goals.

TABLE 14-4
ASSET CLASSES

Cash	Bonds	Stocks	Other
Treasury bills	Treasury notes	Small company growth stocks	Balanced funds
Savings account	Treasury bonds	Small company value stocks	Real estate
Money market funds	Municipal bonds	Medium company stocks	Precious metals
Certificates of deposit	Mortgage-backed bonds	Large company growth stocks	Commodities
	Corporate bonds	Large company value stocks	
	High-yield corporate bonds	International stocks	
	International bonds	Emerging market stocks	

Because of when the funds might be needed, you would not want to take much risk with money you have saved to achieve short-term goals. After working for several years to save enough for a house down payment, it would be a shame to see those savings cut by 30 percent right when you need them because of an unexpected downturn in the stock or bond market. Since few people can predict such downturns correctly (and none can do it consistently), the safe thing to do is to put the money for short-term goals in an investment that will provide a high degree of principal safety. In this case, the extra return that might be earned by leaving it in the stock or bond market over the next year is not worth the risk that the market might take a dip at the very time you want the money. The asset classes listed under "Cash" in Table 14-4 would be suitable for the funds targeted toward short-term goals. In addition, these vehicles are the right place to invest your emergency fund, since you don't know when you might need it.

For medium-term goals (one- to four-year time horizon), it is prudent to take some risk to keep pace with the negative effects of taxes and inflation. Still, stock market downturns can be sharp and last for a number of years. It would be sad to think that a well-deserved second honeymoon cruise would be delayed or cost 18 percent more (on credit cards) because of a gamble for a few extra percent return. In this case, short-term bonds, longer-term CDs, and Treasury notes make sense as investment alternatives. Once a goal is only a year away, it then becomes a short-term goal, and you should move the funds into a cash equivalent investment.

For long-term goals (greater than five years), the greatest risk to increasing wealth and achieving the desired goal is failing to outpace inflation and taxes. Stocks offer the best chance to achieve that purpose. Considering the discussion of diversification above, you should divide your long-term funds among different investments to take advantage of the fact that different investments react differently to economic conditions.

A simple technique for the funds associated with long-term goals is to put one-quarter of the funds into large company stocks, one-quarter into small company stocks, one-quarter into international stocks, and divide the remaining one-quarter among the bond or other asset classes shown in Table 14-4. Using this portfolio as a baseline, you can adjust the proportions to accept more risk (by increasing the amount in small company and international stocks) or less risk (by increasing the amount in bond or large company stock investments).

As long-term goals become medium-term goals, the funds needed to meet the medium-term goals should be moved into an appropriate medium-term investment. For example, as a daughter enters ninth grade, it is time to shift enough funds out of the investment portfolio to fund the first year's college costs and put them into one of the medium-term investment vehicles. Similarly, when your daughter enters tenth grade, you should transfer the second year's college funds into a medium-term investment. A similar process continues each time a long-term goal becomes a medium-term goal.

You can now see the importance of starting out with a list of achievable goals. If you do not, you'll find that you will not have enough funds accumulated to meet your long-term goals, because you will have been continually pulling from the portfolio to satisfy unplanned short- and medium-term goals.

Investments

Once you've decided your asset allocation, it's time to select specific investments for each of the asset classes. As the Brinson study suggests, this decision is much less important than the asset allocation decision. In general, you can either choose the individual securities shown in Table 14-4 or invest in a mutual fund that invests in the same type of securities.

For most investors, mutual funds are the logical choice because of their professional management, low costs, and diversification. Chapter 16 describes mutual funds in detail.

Implementation

During the accumulation phase of your investment plan, you want to reduce the impact of taxes. If you are in the 27 percent tax bracket (or higher), consider a municipal money market fund for your short-term funds. The dividends of the municipal funds are federal income tax exempt, and in some cases you can obtain funds that are state tax exempt if your state has an income tax. For your medium-term funds, consider a municipal short-term bond fund for the same reason. For your long-term portfolio, consider placing investments that generate dividends or capital gains distributions into tax-favored plans such as an IRA or a 401k retirement plan. Since you don't need the income to meet your basic expenditures but are only planning to reinvest those profits, you should generally try to defer the taxes as long as possible.

One of the best ways to help implementation of your investment strategy work is to put as much of your investment program on "autopilot" as possible. You can use allotments, automatic checking account withdrawals, and mutual fund automatic investment plans to enforce the savings commitment you made when you developed your budget.

Monitoring and Rebalancing Your Portfolio

Because asset classes react differently to existing economic conditions, you should periodically check the values of each asset class to see if they are still in line with percentages you have chosen. In all likelihood, some investments will have done so well that their percentage of the long-term portfolio has grown. To achieve the desired asset allocation, you can either add new funds to other assets to bring them back up to the desired percentage or sell some of the investment that has done well to bring it back in line with the desired asset allocation. Keep in mind that if you sell a mutual fund that has done well, you will incur tax on the capital gain, so adding new funds is the more efficient option. If you choose to sell or buy mutual funds, inquire about the fund's annual or quarterly distribution date for capital gains and dividends. By buying at the "wrong" time, you can trigger an adverse tax event and end up buying a capital gains tax liability you did not earn. If the funds are in an IRA or 401k, you can move money between accounts without immediate tax implications, provided you never take possession of the funds.

Doing such rebalancing once or twice a year is adequate in most cases. Your portfolio rebalancing should be done at the same time as you review your goals and your need to move funds either from the long-term to the medium-term portfolio or from the medium-term to the short-term portfolio. Doing so will make for a much more efficient means of achieving the desired asset allocation. The goal would be to minimize the number of selling transactions to defer paying capital gains on the profits. Thus, newly accumulated funds (from your income or from having dividends and capital gains sent to a money market fund instead of automatically reinvested) can rebalance your portfolio without incurring additional taxes. Once you've made the necessary switches, you can forget about your plan until the next year. The peace of mind of knowing you have a workable plan will make you and your family confident that you will achieve your financial goals.

Adding Funds

New investment funds should be added to minimize tax impact and assist with portfolio balancing. The first place to consider is putting new funds into investments that would be the recipient of a big fund transfer at the next rebalancing, usually when one of your goals crosses time-frame boundaries, such as from long-term to medium-term or medium-term to short-term. Investing new funds in this way reduces the fund shifting required at the next rebalancing, thereby reducing taxes and transaction costs.

If this situation is not applicable, then look to add to your long-term portfolio by maximizing investments first into pension plans or IRAs, and then into your other long-term investments.

WORKING THROUGH THE PROCESS

John and Mary Smith are married and have one daughter, Amanda, who is fourteen. They want to develop an investment strategy that will enable them to achieve their goals. The Smiths have adequate funds for the emergency fund and the house down payment. They are still accumulating funds for their daughter's college and wedding, as well as for their retirement.

The Smiths have diligently budgeted and saved over the years, accumulating $75,000. They project that they can add $6,000 to their investments over the next year. Of their $75,000 in accumulated funds ($10,000 of which is in an IRA), they have targeted the money against certain goals, as shown in Table 14-6.

TABLE 14-5
SMITH FAMILY GOALS

Time Horizon	Goal	Date Desired (Years)	Funds Available
Short-term (<1 year)	Emergency fund	Now	$3,000
	House down payment and closing costs	1	12,000
Medium-term (1–4 years)	Daughter's college	4	40,000
Long-term (>5 years)	Daughter's wedding	10	15,000
	Retirement	30	600,000

TABLE 14-6
SMITH FAMILY GOALS MATCHED WITH AVAILABLE FUNDS

Time Horizon	Goal	Date Desired (Years)	Funds Available
Short-term (<1 year)	Emergency fund	Now	$3,000
	House down payment and closing costs	1	12,000
Medium-term (1–4 years)	Daughter's college	4	30,000
Long-term (>5 years)	Daughter's wedding	10	5,000
	Retirement	30	25,000

Matching Investments to Time Horizons

An appropriate investment for the emergency and the house funds, since they need to be available within a year, is a money market account. Since the Smiths are in the 27 percent tax bracket, a municipal money market account would be most appropriate. Along with earning a better rate of return than a savings account, many money market accounts permit check writing with minor restrictions.

Since Amanda is just starting her freshman year in high school, the Smiths need to put $10,000 (anticipated first-year college costs) into an investment that will provide them greater principal security than in their long-term portfolio but provide a better rate of return than a money market fund. A municipal short-term bond fund would be an appropriate investment for these funds. The remaining funds targeted for Amanda's college ($20,000) should remain in the long-term portfolio for now. As Amanda enters her sophomore year, another year's worth of costs will shift from being a long-term goal to a medium-term goal. The remaining $50,000 is targeted toward goals of five years or more, which will be considered for the long-term portfolio.

Designing an Asset Allocation for the Long-Term Portfolio

The Smiths consider themselves to be moderate risk takers, recognizing the need to take some risk to ensure that they are able to achieve their long-term goals. As such, they have decided to allocate their long-term funds as shown in Table 14-7.

TABLE 14-7
SMITH FAMILY LONG-TERM PORTFOLIO ASSET ALLOCATION

% of Long-Term Portfolio	Amount	Asset Class
25	$12,500	Large capitalization stocks
25	12,500	Small capitalization stocks
25	12,500	International stocks (both international and emerging markets)
10	5,000	Real estate
5	2,500	High-yield bonds
5	2,500	International bonds
5	2,500	Precious metals

The Smiths have chosen an allocation that reflects their moderate risk tolerance. After designating 25 percent each for large capitalization stocks, small capitalization stocks, and international stocks, they have divided the remaining 25 percent of their portfolio as shown. Since real estate, high-yield bonds, international bonds, and precious metals may not react to market conditions in the same way that the core stocks will, this diversification guards against downturns in the market.

Had the Smiths wanted to be very aggressive, they might have chosen to allocate their long-term portfolio as one-third each to large and small capitalization stocks and international stocks. A very conservative approach would have been to pare the 25 percent allocation to the core holdings back to 20 percent and then allocate 10 percent to real estate, 10 percent to Treasury bonds, 5 percent to mortgage-backed bonds, 5 percent to corporate bonds, 5 percent to international bonds, and 5 percent to precious metals.

TABLE 14-8
SMITH FAMILY LONG-TERM PORTFOLIO ASSET ALLOCATION WITH INVESTMENT SELECTION

% of Long-Term Portfolio	Amount	Asset Class	Investment*
25	$12,500	Large capitalization stocks	S&P 500 Index Fund
25	12,500	Small capitalization stocks	Russell 2000 Index Fund
25	12,500	International stocks (both international and emerging markets)	EAFE + Select EMF Index Fund
10	5,000	Real estate	Equity REIT Index Fund (IRA)
5	2,500	High-yield bonds	FIRB High Yield Bond Index (IRA)
5	2,500	International bonds	Solomon Brothers World Bond Index (IRA)
5	2,500	Precious metals	Precious Metals Fund

*Note: To avoid making specific fund recommendations, the investments listed here are indexes that represent the asset classes in the portfolio.

TABLE 14-9
SMITH FAMILY LONG-TERM PORTFOLIO AT END OF YEAR

Current Value	Current % of Long-Term Portfolio	Target % of Long-Term Portfolio	Investment
$18,750	33.0	25	S&P 500 Index Fund
13,000	22.9	25	Russell 2000 Index Fund
10,000	17.6	25	EAFE + Select EMF Index Fund
7,000	12.3	10	Equity REIT Fund
3,500	6.2	5	High-Yield Bond Fund
2,000	3.5	5	International Bond Fund
2,500	4.4	5	Precious Metals Fund
$56,750	100.0%	100.0%	Total

Now the task is to select investments for the asset classes. The Smiths believe in the relative efficiencies of the markets and do not feel that actively managed funds add significant value over time. As such, they have chosen index mutual funds where available for the asset classes chosen.

As a tax-efficiency measure, the Smiths decided to use the funds that would generate the most current income as their IRA funds to defer paying taxes on the dividends (and possibly capital gains distributions) that the selected funds would generate.

When completing the account applications, the Smiths chose to have dividends and capital gain distributions of their non-IRA funds automatically deposited to their money market fund to help rebalance their long-term portfolio. For their IRA funds, the Smiths chose the automatic reinvestment option.

Adding Funds

Once their initial asset allocation was in place, the Smiths needed to determine where they would put their monthly savings over the next year. By looking to see if any of the goals will cross time-frame boundaries (long- to medium-term or medium- to short-term), they recognize that once again they will need to move funds for a year of college expenses from the long-term portfolio to their municipal short-term bond fund (the medium-term goal investment). Wanting to minimize the effect of putting money into the long-term portfolio and then paying capital gains taxes (and possibly transactions costs) when they move it in less than a year, the Smiths chose to have the $500 per month that they invest monthly sent directly to the municipal short-term bond fund. The net effect at the end of the year will be the same as if they had put the $500 per month into the long-term portion of the portfolio, except that it will reduce the amount of money that will need to be shifted at the end of the year, thereby reducing potential costs.

Portfolio Rebalancing

At the end of the year, the Smiths sat down to look at their portfolio. They found that they had $17,550 in their money market account ($15,000 originally invested plus the dividends on the money market account as well as distributions from other funds) and $16,780 in their short-term bond fund ($10,000 original investment plus dividends on this fund plus $6,000 invested over the course of the year).

The Smiths knew that they needed $15,000 (emergency fund and their house down payment in their money market account). That left $2,550 to use for rebalancing. The Smiths also knew that they should have a total of $20,000 in their short-term bond fund to pay for Amanda's first two years of college. If they took the $2,550 excess in the money market fund and deposited it into the short-term bond fund, they would need to shift only $670 out of their long-term portfolio into the short-term bond fund. Shifting $670 will have a significantly smaller tax effect than shifting $10,000. That's the benefit of using the distributions to help with the rebalancing as well as planning ahead to where new funds should be applied.

Looking at the long-term portfolio balances at the end of the year, we can see that the S&P 500 Index Fund and the International Stock Fund are the only two that are more than 3 percent away from their target.

Since the S&P 500 Index Fund is 8 percent over its target, the Smiths will withdraw enough to bring the fund back to its 25 percent target percentage of the portfolio's current value of $56,750. That would mean taking $4,562 out of the S&P 500 Index Fund ($18,750 – $14,188 = $4,562). First, $670 of the money taken out can be put into the short-term bond fund. Of the remaining $3,892, the Smiths decide to hold enough out of the portfolio to pay the taxes on the gain ($1,232 = $4,562 × 0.27). They can then use the remaining funds ($2,660) to help bring the International Stock Fund up closer to its target percentage. Table 14-10 shows the long-term portfolio after rebalancing.

TABLE 14-10
SMITH FAMILY LONG-TERM PORTFOLIO (REBALANCED)

Current Value	Current % of Long-Term Portfolio	Target % of Long-Term Portfolio	Investment
$14,188	25.8	25	S&P 500 Index Fund
13,000	23.7	25	Russell 2000 Index Fund
12,660	23.1	25	EAFE + Select EMF Index Fund
7,000	12.8	10	Equity REIT Fund
3,500	6.4	5	High-Yield Bond Fund
2,000	3.6	5	International Bond Fund
2,500	4.6	5	Precious Metals Fund
$54,848	100.0%	100%	Total

Note that after the adjustment, the long-term portfolio is smaller, thereby changing the percentages shown before rebalancing. However, the current percentages are within the acceptable 3 percent range of their targets. (*Note:* It is not necessary to do exact rebalancing to get the funds exactly at their target percentage. Doing so needlessly incurs transaction costs and taxes. The 3 percent range around the target number is acceptable.)

Looking ahead to the next year, the Smiths check to see if any medium-term goals will become short-term or any long-term goals will become medium-term. Again, the only one that applies is moving Amanda's college funds for her junior year. As such, the Smiths will again target their $500 per month savings into the short-term bond fund to save from having to move more

Tips on Making the Most from Your Investment Strategy

- Establish goals with cost, time frame (short, medium, long), and amount from your budget.
- Deposit funds for short-term goals and emergency fund into an appropriate cash equivalent vehicle, such as a money market mutual fund.
- Deposit funds for medium-term goals into an appropriate medium-term investment vehicle, such as a short-term bond fund or certificate of deposit.
- Invest funds for long-term goals into a portfolio of several diversified long-term assets.
- Determine amount (in percent) for each asset class.
- Consider the effect of taxes:
  —Use tax-deferred or tax-free IRAs or pension plans for long-term investments.
  —Have dividends and capital gain distributions from non-IRA and nonpension plans sent to a money market fund to assist with rebalancing.
- Monitor and rebalance:
  —Adjust long-term asset allocation if any asset class is more than 3 percent from target.
  —Shift from long-term to medium-term or medium-term to short-term investments as your goal approaches.
  —Determine where next year's new investment funds should be sent to minimize tax impact.

funds than necessary at the end of the year. By continuing to manage their portfolio in this manner, they will achieve their financial goals, maximize returns, and minimize tax liabilities in the process. You can use the same approach as you develop your own investment strategy.

15

Investing in Financial Assets

Now that chapter 14 has explained how to develop an investment strategy and determine which broad asset classes are appropriate for your financial goals, the next four chapters will describe the assets within those classes so you can wisely invest to achieve your goals. This chapter will describe the common financial assets: bank accounts, savings bonds, Treasury bills, stocks, and other investment vehicles. Chapter 16 will describe the most common form of investment for military families: mutual funds. Chapter 17 will describe the various retirement savings options. Finally, chapter 18 will describe investments in real estate, which may be appropriate for some military personnel as part of a diversified portfolio.

When we think of investing, financial assets are normally what we have in mind—stocks, bonds, and certificates of deposit. In broad terms, there are two major categories of financial assets, and their features are quite different. The first major category includes all types of debt instruments for which the "investor" loans money to a financial intermediary, such as a bank, the government, or a corporation in return for a specified interest rate for a fixed period of time, at which point the principal (the amount loaned) is returned. We often call debt instruments "fixed-income assets" because the repayment schedule (which is income from the investor's perspective) is fixed. The second major category includes various equity instruments through which the investor buys a stake in the company's profits. In equity investments, no interest rate is specified in advance. The amount the investor earns (or loses) depends on how the company performs over time. As a general rule, financial assets with higher risk also have higher potential returns, while assets with lower risk have lower potential returns.

WHAT ARE THE VARIOUS DEBT INSTRUMENTS?

Checking Accounts

Banking laws permit many types of checking accounts to pay interest. You may not think of your checking account as a debt instrument, but in fact it's very much like one. You lend (deposit) your money to the bank, and they agree to pay you a specified amount of interest on it. Checking accounts are nearly perfectly liquid; that is, the money deposited into your account is very easy and inexpensive to exchange for other things. As you will see, with many other investments, as liquidity decreases, the return you should receive goes up to compensate you for this loss of the use of your money.

Many checking accounts pay interest, especially if you exceed a certain minimum balance. Credit unions offer share draft accounts, which are also interest-bearing checking accounts. Many military installations have credit unions, and you should investigate the services they offer. A share draft account can enable you to earn interest on part of your checking account money. (For details on how to select the best type of checking or share draft account, refer to chapter 5.) Many banks and other financial institutions also offer money market accounts. These accounts allow the investor to write some checks every month (with certain restrictions on minimum amount and number per month) and usually pay a higher rate of interest than a normal checking account. The drawbacks include the fact that they are not insured by the Federal Deposit Insurance Corporation (FDIC) and that since they are invested in short-term government and corporate debt, there is the slight chance that they can lose money if for instance there is a major market downturn.

Savings Accounts

Many financial institutions—commercial banks, credit unions, and savings and loan associations—offer various types of savings accounts. Regular passbook accounts usually pay interest at an advertised rate from the date of deposit to the date of withdrawal. Other savings accounts may pay higher interest, particularly money market savings accounts, with an interest rate that varies according to market conditions. When you select a savings account, consider the safety of the institution, convenience, interest rate, and other factors discussed in chapter 5.

Certificates of Deposit

Banks, savings and loans, and credit unions also offer certificates of deposit (CDs). The major distinction from a savings account is that a CD requires you to "lock up" your money for a certain time period and, therefore, is not suitable for emergency funds. Of course, you can always get your money before the CD matures if you really need it, but you will forfeit interest, depending on how your CD penalizes early withdrawals. A CD can be a useful means to accumulate money for medium-term goals. The benefits of CDs include stability of principal, a guaranteed rate of interest, a guaranteed amount at maturity, and a defined maturity date. Additionally, their value is not subject to market fluctuations, and they can be bought without sales charges or fees. Again, be sure to check very carefully the conditions attached to the CD and the compounding method before investing any money.

CDs have varying maturities, typically from a single week to several years, and they usually have a minimum deposit requirement, typically $500 to $1,000. Normally, you receive higher interest on your money by agreeing to leave it on deposit for longer periods of time. For example, in 2001 one-year CDs were available at interest rates as high as 5.00 percent, and five-year CDs could be found that paid 5.80 percent. This is not always the case. Long-term yields are occasionally lower than short-term rates.

One of the most important aspects of a CD you need to check is the early withdrawal penalty. Banks talk about "substantial penalties for early withdrawal," but, in practice, some banks levy much smaller penalties than others. A small early withdrawal penalty is valuable because it allows you to get your money out of a CD at low cost if you need it or if interest rates increase. This may allow you to earn the higher interest rate of a CD while still having ready access to your emergency funds and other short-term savings. In addition, it allows you to trade up at low cost to a higher-yielding CD if interest rates rise after you have bought a CD.

To see how this attractive feature of CDs works, suppose you put $5,000 in a four-year CD at 5 percent interest, compounded annually. At the end of four years, you would have $6,078. Now suppose that after one year rates on new CDs rise to 7 percent. At the end of that year, your CD deposit would be worth $5,250 ($5,000 × [1 + 0.05]). You'd like to withdraw your money from the 5 percent CD and put it into a new three-year 7 percent CD, but you know that the bank will impose a penalty. How much is the penalty? Many banks levy a penalty equal to three to six months' interest on the CD you're cashing in. At 5 percent interest, a three-month penalty on a $5,000 withdrawal is about $63. So you could get about $5,187 out of your 5 percent CD even after paying the penalty. If you put $5,187 into a new three-year CD at 7 percent, you would have $6,354 in three years. This is $276 more than the $6,078 you would have received if you'd kept the original CD. Other banks will reduce the interest on your CD to the passbook savings rate for the entire period you have owned the CD, along with an interest forfeiture. You have to read the fine print!

Shopping for the highest-rate CDs is quite easy—periodicals such as *Barron's* and *Money* rate the top-yielding CDs in every issue. In addition, Bank Rate Monitor (at the Internet site listed in Appendix A) tracks all bank and credit union interest rates throughout the country. Try to find CDs that combine high yields with lenient early withdrawal penalties. The best CDs offer an attractive means to save for future goals: They let you lock in high rates of interest when they are available and trade up to even better rates if they subsequently are offered. No other savings vehicle offers this feature. As we will see, bonds that are traded on secondary markets can be sold before maturity without any penalty, but their value in the market fluctuates with changes in interest rates. CDs can offer yields that approach government bond returns without the risk of losing some of your principal.

CDs can also get rather exotic, like the case of the brokered CD. Brokered CDs have been around for many years and recently have gained favor among many investors. The idea is that you get the security and certainty of a CD with higher rates of return. These CDs usually originate from small banks that do not have access to as wide a market as capable of supplying the amount of money they need. There can be problems if an investor does not read all the fine print on this investment (as with most investments). Once a broker sells the CD, it starts to act more as a bond than a regular CD. If you want to cash out, that is usually offered without a penalty on the interest you earned, but instead you risk that the broker will not be able to sell your portion of this much larger CD, which they split up, at the price you think you should receive.

U.S. Government Savings Bonds

Many small investors buy U.S. savings bonds for a variety of reasons. Savings bonds are easy to buy, are secured by the full faith and credit of the United States, earn market-based rates of return, provide a liquid long-term investment, can be used to finance college, offer tax advantages, and are good for America because they help finance the country's borrowing. Series EE savings bonds are sold at a 50 percent discount from their face value, and Series I savings bonds are sold at face value. They can be bought in denominations of $50, $75, $100, $200, $500, $1,000, $5,000, and $10,000. Individuals are allowed to buy $30,000 (face amount) of Series EE bonds each calendar year.

The face value itself really doesn't signify any particular maturity value, because the interest rate is variable. Effective 1 May 1997, Series EE bonds earn interest based on five-year Treasury security yields. The rate of interest for EE bonds will be 90 percent of the average yield of five-year Treasury securities for the preceding six months. In addition, EE bonds will increase in value every month instead of every six months. Further, a three-month interest penalty will apply to bonds cashed before five years. This will reward longer-term bond holders who then benefit from higher five-year rates over the full life of the bond.

For those individuals who purchased bonds before May 1997, the interest on bonds is determined differently. Specifically, people who hold bonds for at least five years get the higher of two interest rates: a guaranteed minimum 4 percent (6 percent on bonds bought before March 1993, and 7.5 percent on bonds bought before November 1986) or a market-based return adjusted every six months. The market-based rate for bonds issued before 1 May 1995 and held for at least five years is 85 percent of the average five-year Treasury security yield. Bonds issued between 1 May 1995 and 1 May 1997 earn interest at a specified savings bond rate. Bonds earn interest at a short-term rate during the first five years from date of issue; thereafter from years five to seventeen, interest is earned at the long-term rate. Because these rates are updated regularly, we suggest you refer to the U.S. Treasury Department home page for the most current data. The web address is listed in Appendix A.

Series I bonds are a relatively new invention of the Treasury. They offer the same advantages of other savings bonds coupled with the advantages of the new inflation indexed Treasury securities (see below). The interest on I bonds is determined in two parts. First every six months the Treasury sets a fixed base rate for any new bonds purchased in that window. This rate was between 3 and 3.6 percent from September 1998 to May 2001, and it will not change for as long as the bond is owned. Next, every six months, there is an added interest rate based on the inflation rate during that time. This rate is added onto the base rate to give the interest rate the bond will earn over the next six months. The advantage of this system is that as an investor you know that your investment is growing in real terms—in other words, you know that in the future you will be able to buy more with the money you invested since any inflation was factored into the interest you receive. The main drawback of this bond is that if the inflation rate is negative (in time of deflation, where the general price level is falling), then this amount is subtracted from the base rate. This sounds like a terrible deal, but periods of deflation are very rare, and even if there is one, the bond will never earn negative interest. If the deflation rate is greater than the base rate of interest on the bond, the bond will just not earn any interest.

The interest earned on savings bonds is exempt from state and local income taxes but not federal income tax. Because EE bonds do not actually pay periodic interest, all tax on the rising value of the bonds is due when they are redeemed. You may elect instead to pay tax on the accumulated interest from year to year if you desire. This is usually beneficial for bonds held by a child with few other taxable assets or by any child over fourteen. The interest earned on Series EE can be entirely tax-free, if the bonds are used for college education and several restrictions are met. See chapter 13 for a complete discussion of using savings bonds to meet college expenses.

An important thing to remember about your U.S. savings bonds is that if any are lost, stolen, mutilated, or destroyed, the U.S. Treasury will replace them free of charge. To report such a case, use application form PD-1048, which is available at most banks. It's still a good idea to record the bond numbers and put the list in a separate location; this makes the bonds much easier to trace. For additional information, refer to the savings bond section of the U.S. Treasury's Internet site (see Appendix A) or ask at your nearest financial institution.

Treasury Bills, Notes, and Bonds

These debt instruments differ from savings bonds because their return is not guaranteed (unless held until maturity) and they are negotiable, meaning they can be bought and sold by private investors, whereas savings bonds can be redeemed only by "reselling" them to the government. Major financial centers have active markets in bills, notes, and bonds, and savings invested in them are extremely liquid. There are, however, some drawbacks. They possess more price risk than simply having money in a bank account. Also, they cannot be bought without some kind of service charge or commission unless you arrange to buy newly issued obligations directly from one of the twelve Federal Reserve banks.

If buying a Treasury bill, note, or bond, it is most efficient and easiest to buy them directly from a Federal Reserve bank and forgo the service charges and commissions that a broker will charge. You can buy these bills, notes, and bonds from the nearest Federal Reserve bank by calling the bank to find out when the next issue will be available and then sending a letter of instruction with a cashier's check, or by simply logging onto the Treasury Direct website and downloading the forms necessary to open an account and set up electronic payment and deposit. You can also request an information kit on Treasury Direct by writing to Federal Reserve, P.O. Station, New York, NY 10045. Keep in mind that the Federal Reserve establishes a minimum purchase that varies between $1,000 and $10,000, depending on the instrument. Also, if you have a bank or broker buy government bonds for you, deduct their charges when you calculate your true yield.

Even though government bonds carry no risk of default, they have important elements of risk. The government will keep its promise stated in the bond to pay all principal and interest when due. The government does not, however, make any promises regarding the value of those dollars when you get them. If there is unanticipated inflation while you own government bonds (or other bonds or CDs), you will lose purchasing power even if you don't lose money. And, of course, there is price risk during the entire period you hold the bond. Bond prices change inversely with market interest rates, so the price at which you can sell your bond (and therefore the value of your investment) changes from day to day. Many investors have been disappointed after confusing default risk (against which government bonds protect you) with inflation risk and price risk (against which they cannot protect you).

Treasury bills are short-term obligations of the government that mature within one year. These are not normally suitable for small investors because the minimum denomination is $10,000. Treasury notes are intermediate-term obligations of the government that mature within one to ten years with interest paid semiannually. Notes are often quite attractive to small investors because their minimum denominations are small ($1,000 to $5,000). Treasury bonds are long-term obligations of the government that have maturities as long as thirty years. Again, the minimum denomination is $1,000.

For savers who take the time and interest to manage their savings funds actively, federal government obligations can frequently provide higher rates of return than savings accounts and CDs. The risk of default is negligible since they are backed by the full faith and credit of the United States. The government bond market is very active, making it easy to buy and sell bonds, and price and yield information is available daily in major newspapers. (Bond prices are quoted as a percentage of face value. If your $1,000 face value bond is quoted at 90, that means its market value—what you could sell it for—is $900.)

As with savings bonds, state and local governments do not tax interest earned on Treasury obligations. Remember that banks do not charge a broker's fee for CDs or savings accounts. Therefore, you should compare the return net of taxes and broker's fees when you choose among the various debt instruments.

Since January 1997, the Treasury Department has begun to offer a new Treasury security for long-term investors. The new security is called an inflation-indexed security. Inflation-indexed securities are bought and sold like normal Treasury securities, but their features are quite different. The interest rate remains fixed throughout the term of the security, but the principal amount of the security will be adjusted for inflation. The semiannual interest payments will be based on the inflation-adjusted principal at the time the interest is paid. The security will be adjusted to reflect changes in the Consumer Price Index for All Urban Consumers (CPI-U). This new security has several advantages: The principal keeps up with changes in inflation; it is guaranteed by the full faith and credit of the U.S. government; it is easy to purchase; you can sell your security on the secondary market; and inflation-indexed securities are exempt from state and local taxes.

U.S. Government Agency Securities

Many agencies established by Congress also issue bonds. Their securities are not guaranteed by the government, but it is unlikely that the government would allow them to default, because it supervises them and is often a part owner. Because of their slightly higher risk, these bonds pay a higher yield than those of the Treasury. The Federal National Mortgage Association (FNMA; the bonds are known as Fannie Maes), the Government National Mortgage Association (GNMA, or Ginnie Mae), the Tennessee Valley Authority (TVA), the Export-Import Bank, Federal Land Banks, and others issue such bonds. Interest earned on these obligations is taxable by federal and often by state and local governments. Be particularly careful when buying GNMAs. These bonds are backed by pooled mortgages and are the most popular of the agency securities. Brokers like to push GNMAs because of their high stated yields and monthly distributions. Because mortgage owners have the option to prepay their mortgages when rates fall, however, the return on some GNMAs may fall short of their advertised yields. This risk tends to be overstated due to the fact that most mortgages have repayment penalties that make it less appealing to the borrowers to pay back too soon.

Municipal Bonds

These bonds are the obligations of state and local governments, and their interest payments are often exempt from federal taxes and sometimes from state and local taxes, too. Partly because of their tax-exempt status, municipal bonds usually pay lower interest rates than taxable bonds, so they are not normally attractive to investors with low marginal tax rates. For a taxpayer in the 27 percent bracket, the tax-exempt yield on a 6 percent municipal would be the equivalent of an 8.22 percent taxable yield. (Calculate the tax-equivalent yield by dividing the tax-exempt yield by 1 minus your tax rate.) Investors in the highest marginal tax brackets gain the most from municipal bonds. These bonds are usually less attractive than other debt instruments for most military investors because they are less liquid than either government or corporate bonds and provide a lower return (unless you are in a higher tax bracket).

Corporate Bonds

Corporate bonds generally offer a higher return than savings accounts, CDs, and government bonds. They are not redeemable before maturity but may be resold in secondary financial markets, potentially at a profit or loss. There are two major classifications. Secured bonds are guaranteed by a mortgage on the company's assets, much like a mortgage on a home. Unsecured bonds, called debentures, are backed by the general credit of the company, similar to a signature or unsecured loan.

Both types of bonds promise to pay a specified sum at maturity and interest at a fixed rate regularly until then. The principal and interest are usually payable before the dividends on the borrowing company's stock. If the company goes bankrupt, bondholders have a claim on the company's assets ahead of the stockholders, but the company may still default on its debt. Besides default risk, corporate bondholders also face price risk caused by changes in interest rates and inflation risk if prices increase. Corporate bonds may be bought from a broker or indirectly through bond mutual funds (see the next chapter).

WHAT ARE EQUITY ASSETS, SUCH AS STOCKS?

One of the great American dreams is to get rich quick, and many people try to do that on Wall Street. Between 1982 and 2000, the Dow Jones Industrial Average went from below 800 to over 10,000. This represents a compounded annual return of over 13 percent—very good, but certainly not the get-rich scheme the media would have us believe. You would have also had to deal with the wild swings that affected the market as the Internet bubble burst in mid-2000. In fact, had you bought a five-year or longer certificate of deposit at your local bank in 1982, you also would have earned solid double-digit returns—at a fraction of the risk.

Investing in stocks need not be mysterious. As in all investments, there are risks and corresponding expected rewards. Anyone considering investing in the stock market must first do a bit of homework on those risks and rewards. The most likely way to lose money in stocks, as in any investment, is through ignorance. We hope to provide a starting point for that homework and to dispel a few myths along the way.

Historically, stocks have outperformed both short- and long-term bonds by a wide margin. Over the past sixty-five years, the average real return on stocks has been about 7 percent per year over inflation, and government long-term bonds have returned between 1 and 2 percent on average per year. Corporate long-term bonds have had only a slightly higher average real return. For the "safest" investments—U.S. Treasury bills—the real rate of return has been about zero. Apparently, rates of return on the safest, shortest-term bond investments are only adequate to compensate for inflation, but not large enough to provide an after-inflation rate of return.

It's important to understand that when we say stocks earn on average 7 percent above inflation, we do not mean to imply that stocks will have a return 7 percent above inflation every year. Quite the contrary; rates of return on stocks vary considerably from year to year. In some years stocks return much more than inflation; in other years they decrease in value considerably. That's why stocks are a risky means to save for short-term goals. In the past, the up years in the stock market have been sufficiently good to compensate for the down years and to provide a rate of return about 7 percent higher than inflation. Unfortunately, there is no riskless way to earn a rate of return substantially above the rate of inflation over the long term. Investors have to accept some risk to earn positive real returns.

The number of individuals investing in the stock market has increased greatly during the last five years as a result of low transaction costs offered by online brokers. Also on the rise were stories of friends, relatives, and acquaintances who have made large sums of money by picking "bargain" stocks. In April 2000, what many economists called the "net bubble" burst and the value of many tech and Internet stocks fell greatly. Many new investors had not fully considered the risks associated with investing in the stock market and as a result suffered severe financial loss.

For uninformed investors, investing in the stock market approaches the mystical. The odd vocabulary, the need to go through a broker, the sense that it is not an "even" playing field, well-publicized abuses—all seem to work against the individual investor. However, the average investor can—with careful homework, a tolerance for risk, and patience—earn greater returns in the stock market over time than in most other investment vehicles. This is not to say that small investors should invest directly in individual stocks. We recommend that most small investors start with mutual funds, a way to pool your investment with others. Mutual funds are covered at length in the next chapter.

What Is Stock?

A share of stock represents a part of the equity capital of a publicly held company. This means that a private company decided to allow the public to be part owners of the firm and sold shares of ownership through a stock offering. If a company has one million shares of outstanding stock, then owning one share means that you own one-millionth of that company.

So why would a company "sell out" to the public? Usually because the company has plans (and needs money) for growth and expansion, and its bankers feel that borrowing the money might create too heavy a debt burden. The company looks for "investors" to finance this growth and taps the public markets for these funds. Another reason for selling stock is that the founders of the company may want to realize some of their investment without selling the entire firm. William Gates, the founder of Microsoft (the computer software company), took his company "public" in the 1980s for this very reason.

A unique aspect of a publicly held company—a company in which the stock is traded on public markets—is that ownership and management of the company are separated. Management, as an agent for the stockholders, is responsible for maximizing the stockholders' share value through the firm's growth and profitability. Yet, one might ask, who is really serving the interests of the stockholders? Management decides everything from the direction of the company to the compensation of the top executives. How does the shareholder have any voice in the process? The board of directors acts as the voice of the shareholders and conducts meetings to ensure that the interests of the shareholders are being met. Shareholders usually have the right to elect board members.

Each shareholder is entitled to his or her proportionate share of all the earnings—that is, the profits—generated by the company. This is where the stock gets its true value. As a shareholder in that firm, you are entitled to a proportional share of this and all future years' earnings (after paying interest to the bondholders). However, these earnings may or may not be distributed to shareholders as dividends. Periodically, the board convenes to decide how much of the earnings will be paid to shareholders as dividends and how much will be retained by the company to finance future growth. This is a critical decision that reflects a careful balancing act between the present cash needs of the shareholders and the future potential of the company. For instance, had McDonald's paid out all its earnings in dividends in the early 1960s, its shareholders might well have sacrificed that company's enormous growth.

Different industries pay out varying percentages of their earnings as dividends. Electrical utilities, for instance, traditionally pay out most of their earnings, as they have relatively less need for expansion. Emerging growth firms, on the other hand, have many opportunities for expansion and thus tend to pay lower dividends or none at all.

One of the advantages of owning stock is the ease of trading it. After glancing at the newspaper, you can call a broker or connect to an electronic trading account on the Internet and instantly buy or sell most stocks listed on the organized exchanges. Note, however, that you are not buying stock from the company but from another owner of the shares who has decided to sell. When a company first brings its shares to the market, this is an initial public offering (IPO), or "new issue." Only when buying a new issue are you supplying capital directly to the company.

Immediately after the initial public offering, shares begin trading on the exchanges as investors call their brokers to buy or sell. Those shares are trading on the secondary market, the market among investors, as opposed to the primary market, that between the company and the initial purchasers of the shares. Although company management is not directly involved in trading the shares, it remains responsible to the shareholders and is quite concerned about the value of the shares in the secondary market.

Making Money in the Market

By now you should sense that the major factor in stock prices is the earnings potential, or profitability, of a company. The value of a company, and hence a share of its stock, is equivalent to today's assessment of the value of all future earnings paid out by that company. The secondary market is an auction market where prospective buyers of stock, represented by brokers, meet with the sellers of stock, represented by other brokers, to agree on the price.

If a company were to announce a major advancement, one that could double the earnings of the company in the future, a seller of stock would certainly expect a higher price than before the announcement. The buyer, on the other hand, would be willing to pay a higher price. Thus, we would expect to see the price of a share of stock climb immediately after a major announcement of this sort. Conversely, if a company announces bad news, we would expect the stock price to fall.

We will discuss the market as a whole later, but remember that the fundamental cause for stock price fluctuations is the changing projection of future earnings. In addition, all things being equal, falling interest rates cause stock prices to go up, and rising interest rates cause stock prices to fall.

There are two components of the returns from a share of stock: dividends and the price appreciation. We can express this equation as:

$$\text{Total Return in Percent} = \frac{\text{Dividends + Increase in Share Price}}{\text{Share Price}}$$

To be competitive in the market, therefore, a company must generate either high dividend returns or high share price appreciation. The board of directors decides dividends, based on earnings performance and need of funds for expansion; the market decides appreciation, based on expected future performance.

All long-term capital gains are taxed at the capital gains tax rate. However, it is still true that capital gains are not recognized as income until they are "realized"—that is, when stock is sold for more than its original purchase price. Hence, dividends are received and taxed annually as income, but long-term capital gains are taxed only when stock is actually sold. Net capital losses are subtracted from taxable income, but allowable losses are capped at $3,000 per year, with unused losses carried forward to subsequent years.

Investment Advice

If you were to ask most investors how they decide which stocks to buy, the responses would range from mystical to hysterical. In general, most investors rely on three sources: stockbrokers, the media, and friends. Unfortunately, none of them have any "secret insights" to advise you on which are the best companies. You should also cast a suspicious eye over stock recommendations in newspapers, unless you are the only person with a subscription. *USA Today*'s "Money" section covers stocks and virtually always recommends a "buy." At a rate of two per day, they could recommend the entire New York Stock Exchange within three years. The recommendations of friends and acquaintances should, obviously, be acted upon with care. Stockbrokers and other professionals in the business may be good sources of information but should not be considered infallible, nor do they possess special "inside information."

Stockbrokers are paid for generating trading activity, not for picking stocks, so don't be afraid to ask questions before setting up an account.

1. "How many other accounts do you handle?" Too many, and you may get lost in the shuffle, especially if you are one of the smaller accounts.
2. "How long have you been a stockbroker?" Often, new accounts are given to new stockbrokers. Try to meet an established stockbroker.
3. "May I speak to some of your other clients?" This is perhaps the best thing to do. It's the only way to get a reasonably reliable feel for this person's ability to give you good advice. If he won't refer you to any of his other clients, find a different broker.

Consider whether you should be using a broker at all. If you don't feel confident in your stock selections without advice from a broker, you may be better off investing in mutual funds (discussed in the next chapter).

Discount Brokers

The 1990s have seen significant movement from full-service brokers to full-service discount, to discount, and now to deep discount brokers. Consider using a discount or deep discount broker if you make your own investment decisions. Discount brokerage houses achieve substantial cost savings by hiring no analysts and dealing with customers through salaried employees rather than commission brokers. Thus, they cannot provide you with any guidance, but they do pass along most of their savings to you in substantially lower commissions when you trade. Discount brokerage firms provide the same service you get from conventional brokers with regard to trade execution and documentation, record keeping, and securities safekeeping. Table 15-1 lists several brokerage houses under each category:

TABLE 15-1
FULL-SERVICE TO DEEP DISCOUNT BROKERAGE HOUSES

Full-Service	Full-Service Discount	Discount	Deep Discount/Online
UBS Paine-Webber	Fidelity	TD Waterhouse	Brown & Co.
Merrill Lynch	Charles Schwab	Jack White	E-trade
Salomon Smith Barney	Quick and Reilly		

Before selecting any brokerage house, it's important to shop around. You need to decide the level of support and services you want, then find the firm that best meets your needs at the lowest cost. By contacting any of the above firms, you can receive information regarding all of their accounts and services offered. Because of the extreme competitiveness in the brokerage industry, coupled with advances in technology, the costs associated with trading stocks have been reduced substantially. Many of the deep discount firms can execute trades of one thousand shares or less for under $20.

The Uniformed Services Automobile Association (known to many as simply USAA) offers servicemembers a full range of services from online trading to providing detailed comprehensive financial planning services. USAA also offers several mutual funds, which we will discuss in chapter 16. Remember, you get what you pay for—personal consultation with an expert can cost you over $100 per hour, or if you prefer, you can rely on the research published on an online broker's website. Once again, the level of services that you will need should be your first consideration when choosing a brokerage firm.

Analyzing Stocks

If you are a serious investor who wants to invest directly in stocks, it's almost a requirement that you do some research yourself. Stock research comes in two forms: technical and fundamental analysis. Technical analysis is concerned less with the stock and its earnings and more with its trading history. Technical analysts, or technicians, claim to be able to spot trends and patterns in trading activity. They use arcane terms like "head-and-shoulder formations" and "resistance levels" and assert their ability to predict future price movements from historical patterns. There is certainly skepticism among teachers and practitioners of finance over whether there is any truth to their claims. In fact, one of the most respected voices on the subject of financial markets, Professor Burton Malkiel of Princeton, claims that prices on Wall Street are a "random walk," meaning that no information from the past can help predict future price changes. Yet the technicians persist and usually offer an opinion apart from the more earthbound analysts, the fundamentalists.

Fundamental analysis is the process of developing a business evaluation of a company, specifically its future earning ability. All available information about a company is incorporated into earnings projections. Once that information is gathered, the analyst then discounts those projections back to a fair present value of the stock. If the analyst's projections show that the stock is underpriced, it is rated as a buy; if the stock is overvalued, the recommendation is to sell.

One popular fundamental analysis process consists of four elements: economic analysis, industry analysis, company analysis, and pricing analysis. Each of the levels of analysis is a go/no-go screen; only companies that pass the screen are analyzed further. Once the screens are complete, the analyst has a list of stocks considered for purchase.

The first level, economic analysis, is a macroeconomic assessment of the entire economy. Because the stock market is a reflection of the U.S. economy, it will generally do well in strong economic expansions and poorly in recessions.

If the future macroeconomic outlook is for stable or falling inflation, lower future interest rates, and healthy economic growth, the climate for stock investments is positive. The best time to buy stocks is during recessions, just before other investors begin to anticipate renewed growth in the economy.

Further analysis focuses on the performance of specific industries within the current economic environment. Certain industries lead recoveries and business expansions, while others lag. If you anticipate a business recovery, industries such as electronics, metals, and automobile suppliers should be considered. In the latter phase of the recovery, industries such as automobile manufacturers, consumer goods, and recreational goods should be evaluated.

The purpose of the next level, company analysis, is not to identify the winners but to screen out the losers. In every industry, no matter how strong the economy is or how "right" that particular industry is, some companies are better and others are worse. Fundamental analysts use several tools here, such as company visits and ratio analysis (a technique by which key indicators of a company's financial health are compared with specific industry benchmarks). A detailed discussion of company analysis is beyond the scope of this book. If you want to learn more about financial analysis of individual companies, consult a good text in managerial finance.

The final level of analysis is a pricing analysis of the individual stock. It doesn't matter if IBM, for instance, passes all your screens and is the finest corporation in the world. If the stock price is too high, it's not a good buy. Pricing analysis estimates a reasonable price for a share of stock and compares it with the current market price. If the current market price is less than or equal to your "fair" price, it's worth buying. If it drastically exceeds your "fair" price, let it pass. Then, among all the stocks rated as "buys," select one or more that compete well against the others.

The problem with the approach described above is that it is difficult to execute. Individual investors are not trained to make these types of assessments. This work is very time-consuming to accomplish, and the payoffs to the research are minimal, unless you have an enormous investment portfolio. Perhaps even more important, most of this research is already incorporated into the current price of the stock. By the time an investor researches and reacts to positive information on a stock, a professional investor has already taken the price gains from that information. In the terminology of finance experts, markets have a tendency to be efficient. This means that the "fair" price for a stock at any given time is simply its current market price, which has already reacted to all available information. Even if markets are not efficient, professional money managers and traders are likely to snap up the bargains long before you notice them.

An Alternative Approach

Although the top-down approach described above is the most widely used and discussed stock-picking method for professionals, many consistently successful investors attack the problem from the opposite direction—a "bottom-up" approach. In *One Up on Wall Street,* successful former mutual fund manager

Peter Lynch states that any good management team with a decent product can do well in business. With the bottom-up approach, most of your analytical effort concentrates on specific individual companies in a search for good managers to trust with your money. A much smaller amount of time goes into industry analysis. The reasoning is that good people will make good money regardless of the nature of their business. Finally, many bottom-up practitioners take pride in doing virtually no macroeconomic analysis. Believing that broad cyclical moves in the economy are difficult if not impossible to predict, they feel more confident searching within the market for good relative values among individual stocks. Noticing good products and good managers before the Wall Street traders do is perhaps the only way that the individual investor can "compete" in an already overanalyzed market.

The purpose of fundamental analysis, it should be reiterated, is to give the investor a sense of what a particular share of stock is worth and how that stock compares with other investments. A careful analysis of a particular company can reveal insights and observations not seen by the casual investor. It allows the investor to be proactive in dealing with stockbrokers, rather than blindly accepting the broker's firm's analysis. It is an inexact science, but if performed carefully, the process will help you earn at least the fair returns of the market even if you are not lucky enough to surpass them. However, unless you commit to acquiring skills that are beyond this brief introduction, the best vehicle for making equity investments is probably mutual funds (see chapter 16).

DO SOME ASSETS COMBINE DEBT AND EQUITY INSTRUMENTS?

There are a wide variety of financial assets that combine a fixed return with equity. The rules concerning the fixed return and equity features are often complicated and vary with each asset. As a result, the investor should take great care when buying these assets. Two of the most popular types are convertible bonds and exchangeable bonds. A convertible bond is a corporate bond that can be converted at the option of the holder into common stock of the same corporation. An exchangeable bond is like a convertible bond except that the bond can be exchanged for common stock of a different corporation. In both cases, the conversion from a bond to a stock occurs at a predetermined price. The advantage of these types of assets is that they offer the safety and fixed income of a bond with some of the potential for large gains that you would enjoy as a stockholder. The market recognizes this advantage. As a result, these assets often sell at a premium over both their bond and conversion values. Before these assets are bought, a careful analysis is necessary to determine if their unique features are worth the additional premium.

What Are Options?

An option is also known as a derivative security, because the option's value is derived from the value of another security, such as a stock. Options can be purchased that are based on the value of many different assets such as stocks, commodities, gold, and even the future level of interest rates. At this point, it may seem like buying an option is like placing a bet; for the uninformed investor this may not be far from the truth. For example, when someone purchases a call option, they have bought the right to purchase an asset (for example, one hundred shares of stock) for a previously agreed upon price for a specified period of time. If the price of that stock rises above the agreed upon price, the holder of the option can redeem the option and receive the difference between the current asset price and the agreed upon price. Thus, a call option is like a bet that the price of an asset will rise above some agreed upon amount in a specific period of time.

A put option is similar to a call option; however, with a put option you are betting that the price of the asset will fall below some agreed upon amount in a specified period of time. You must buy the put option, and unless the price of the asset moves far enough in the right direction, you have nothing to show for your purchase. Once again, purchasing an option is like placing a bet, and the seller of the option is generally well informed about the value of the underlying asset.

HOW ABOUT PORK BELLIES AND OTHER COMMODITY SPECULATION?

One prominent member of a leading brokerage house concluded that more than 98 percent of small investors who enter the commodity markets "lose their shirts." He went on to marvel that there were always more people ready and eager to take the losers' places.

A major attraction of the commodity market is the chance to "make a killing" with a small stake by using margin. Margin allows a small investor (with perhaps around $1,000 to invest) to control a large commodity contract (tens of thousands of dollars). For example, $800 on an 8-percent-margin contract will allow you to control $10,000 worth of a commodity. Assume, for illustration, a speculation in a standard contract of 60,000 pounds of soybean oil. If the price goes up only 1 cent per pound, you make $600 on your margin deposit (ignoring brokerage expenses).

What risks do you run?

First, what if the price should drop? If there is a 1-cent drop, your margin is practically wiped out, plus you owe the broker fees and will have to replace your margin deposit.

Second, not all commodities are always actively traded. To control the wild gyrations in commodity prices somewhat, the exchanges impose limits on the price movements that can occur in a single trading day. Soybean oil prices, for example, can go up or down only 1 cent per day before trading ceases for the day.

Suppose you suddenly hear that a bumper crop of soybeans will be harvested and you call your broker to sell. Let us assume you're very lucky. Of 350 people who place hurried orders to sell, you are in the first 5 percent; in fact, you are number sixteen in a list containing all 350 sell orders. Except now the buyers also know that the price will fall and will not buy. As a result, only five buyers (who desperately need soybean oil) buy before the price drops the full 1 cent and trading stops. The next day only another five buy, the price drops 1 cent again, and trading stops. The third day is a repeat performance. Finally, on the fourth day, you (in the lucky top 4 or 5 percent) sell your contract. In the meantime, you have lost sleep and $600 per day plus fees and commissions. You can get "locked out" of the market like this and lose control over the extent of your losses.

At this point you may say, "Why sell at all? I'll just wait until the price goes up again." Unfortunately, all commodity contracts come due on a certain date. You must sell the contract before that date—unless you really want to have 60,000 pounds of soybean oil delivered to your local warehouse in your name in a tank car. If that should occur, you would of course have to pay the full $10,000 or the value of the commodity plus shipping and storing expenses! Even if you had a contract with a due date some time off and did not sell, you would still have to cover your $600 loss per day during the price drops.

All our discussion of commodity speculation so far has assumed that you are "buying long"—that is, you have obligated yourself to buy the commodity at the agreed price. This means you make money when the price goes up and lose when the price goes down. You could just as well "sell short," or obligate yourself to deliver the commodity for the agreed price. This way you win when the price drops and lose when it increases. You can bet either way on commodity price movements (and most active stocks too, for that matter), and you make money if you guess correctly. You lose if the price moves against you. Unlike stocks, though, commodities are a "zero-sum game." There's a short position held by an investor for every long position, so everyone's gains and losses offset in total.

Finally, you don't have to employ all the leverage available to you. You can choose to control fewer contracts than the maximum allowed with the money you put up. This would reduce your risk. It would also, of course, reduce your potential profit. For example, you might pay the full price in cash for a Canadian Maple Leaf gold bullion coin (around $400 in 1997). While this is a "commodity speculation," many people would see the purchase as a fairly conservative investment.

WHAT FINAL LESSONS SHOULD YOU KNOW?

Beware of Scams

Countless investors, eager for quick gains, are lured into fraudulent scams. The North American Securities Administration Association estimates that annual U.S. investment fraud totals $40 billion. You can avoid becoming a victim by recognizing a few telltale signs of a scam:

1. *Unsolicited telephone calls.* Beware of persistent salespeople on the phone promising quick profits. Just tell them you're not interested and politely but quickly hang up.

2. *High-pressure tactics*. Chief among these is that the salesperson will try to make you feel a sense of urgency: "We have only a few shares left in inventory at this low price and they're going fast," or "Better buy now before this news hits the street."

3. *Too good to be true*. This is the most reliable of all tip-offs. Every scam will be described as a deal offering huge profits at little risk. The only people who are giving away something for nothing are the poor souls who fall for these fish stories and invest their hard-earned dollars. Financial markets will "price" risk so that assets with higher average returns will also have higher risk. In other words, if something sounds too good to be true, it probably is.

If you are offered an investment that seems questionable, just say no!

Tax Avoidance for Small Investors

You need to be aware of the tax laws, because taxation can greatly affect your actual rate of return. Use tax-exempt and tax-deferred investments when they offer you a higher rate of return, but do not buy an investment simply because of its tax status. Do the arithmetic and make sure it's better for you than a fully taxable alternative.

The arithmetic involves comparing the after-tax rate of return on a fully taxable investment to the return on tax-exempt or tax-deferred investments. A simple method for obtaining the after-tax return is to multiply the taxable rate of return by 1 minus your tax rate. Don't forget about state income taxes. For example, if your federal tax bracket is 27 percent and your state tax bracket is 7 percent, for every dollar of extra income you earn, you pay 27 cents to the federal government and almost 7 cents to the state government. So if you can earn 8 percent on a fully taxable investment, you get to keep approximately 5.28 percent ($0.08 \times [1 - 0.27 - 0.07]$) after taxes. In this case, it would be wise to use a tax-exempt investment only if you could find one that paid more than 5.28 percent.

For investments that offer tax deferral until a later time, the comparison is a bit more complicated. Normally, when the tax law allows deferral of taxes, it will specify that all the returns will be fully taxable at some later time, usually after age fifty-nine. With tax deferral, the government "lends" you the current taxes for reinvestment without charging you interest. The practical effect of tax deferral is that you earn a higher compound rate of return, so your investment grows more rapidly. Thus, tax-deferred investments offer excellent ways to save for long-term goals. IRAs, annuity contracts, and cash-value policies sold by insurance companies have been among the most popular means to earn tax-deferred interest. Roth IRAs, a specific form of Individual Retirement Account, are tax-free provided that you comply with the law. Your contributions to the Roth IRA are nondeductible, but that is usually well worth it in exchange for tax-free compound growth and ultimate distribution to you. See IRS Publication 590 for additional information.

Tax deferral is certainly a valuable tax benefit. For example, if you earn 5 percent on a taxable savings account and you pay 27 percent of your earnings

Tips on Investing in Financial Assets

- Set financial goals based on your lifestyle and future consumption needs.
- Evaluate your risk tolerance and invest accordingly.
- Diversify your holdings using a variety of investment products.
- Shop around for reliable brokers, agents, or other professionals. Use their knowledge to your advantage, but beware of high fees.
- Inform yourself. Invest your time educating yourself before you invest your money.
- If you do not need investment advice, consider using a discount or deep discount broker.
- Keep records of your investment performance for tax purposes and to assess your progress toward your goals.
- Avoid commodities, except with risk capital you could lose (and unless you like to worry!).
- Beware of scams. If a deal sounds too good to be true, it probably is.
- Use available legal methods of tax avoidance and tax deferral to increase your after-tax return.
- Start early, start early, start early!

to the federal government (and you live in a state with no income tax), your after-tax rate of return is only 3.65 percent (0.05 × 0.73). A $10,000 investment earning an effective rate of interest of 3.65 percent would be worth $20,483 in twenty years. However, if you could defer the tax on the 5 percent earnings, your money would grow at 5 percent and you would have $26,532 after twenty years. Of course, in a tax-deferred investment, you will owe taxes on the accumulated interest ($16,532) when you receive it in twenty years. After paying 27 percent tax on your gain, you will still have $22,069 left, more than you would have with the fully taxable asset.

For additional details about the tax advantages and penalties involved with the most popular tax-deferred accounts for military families, IRAs, refer to chapter 7 on taxes.

16

Mutual Funds

Mutual funds provide a means of virtually hassle-free investing. With more than 10,000 different mutual funds, there is a vast spectrum of investment opportunities ranging from a country or industry sector to a diversified market portfolio.

WHAT IS A MUTUAL FUND?

Investment companies develop mutual funds by pooling money from different individual investors. Mutual fund companies sell shares in a particular fund to raise money to invest in different securities. When you buy shares, the fund uses the money, as well as the investments of other fund shareholders, to purchase stocks, bonds, and other financial instruments according to the fund's objectives. Some funds buy only one type of security—such as stocks of large blue-chip companies or stock from companies in one specific industry. Others have greater diversification. A typical fund portfolio may include anywhere from thirty to several hundred different investment instruments.

Professional money managers direct the mutual fund by continually buying and selling securities. Investors (mutual fund shareholders) gain profits or losses in proportion to the number of mutual fund shares they own. Shareholders can track the status of a mutual fund by checking the fund's price in the newspaper, by phone, via the Internet and through monthly, quarterly, or annual statements.

By law, mutual fund companies must provide a prospectus for every fund they offer. The prospectus is a valuable tool for analyzing the fund's objectives, learning about the management team, and receiving a summary of investments and fees. Typically, the prospectus will also include quarterly and annual reports and discuss recent performance trends. Most mutual funds require an initial investment of $500 to $2,500. Fund companies often waive this minimum if you enter into an automatic monthly investment plan of $100 or more per month. Once you have an account, you can usually make additional contributions whenever you like. The minimum additional investment is usually $50 to $100. These features are discussed in detail in this chapter.

WHAT ARE THE ADVANTAGES OF MUTUAL FUNDS?

The primary benefit of mutual funds for most investors is the diversification of risk. Mutual funds allow you to achieve a diversified portfolio by investing only a few hundred dollars. Since most mutual funds invest in more than thirty different stocks or bonds, even a small investor can have a diversified portfolio—particularly if the manager invests in a number of different asset classes.

Mutual funds permit small investors to have their money professionally managed. Professional managers have access to a wide range of information and can perform more extensive research than the small investor when selecting securities for a portfolio. Mutual funds are convenient to buy and sell. Many funds have telephone and online exchange and redemption options. Finally, mutual funds allow the investor to reinvest capital gains distributions and dividends in the fund, receive them directly, or transfer them to a money market fund. This flexibility enables investors to adjust their portfolios as necessary to maintain a desired asset allocation.

While the primary advantage of mutual funds is diversity, the large increase in the number and type of mutual funds allows investors to use them as a convenient method of investing in a specific sector or market. The large inflow of money, and the demand for more specialized investment opportunities, has led to the development of industry- and country-specific mutual funds. Because they target narrow sectors or niches, many of these funds no longer provide a great deal of diversification by themselves. Therefore, investors should include these types of funds only as part of a larger, diversified portfolio of different mutual funds.

WHAT IS A MUTUAL FUND FAMILY OF FUNDS?

Most mutual fund companies offer several different funds, typically called a family of funds. Some of the big name fund families include Fidelity, Janus, Vanguard, T. Rowe Price, and American Century. These family funds allow normal investors to move money back and forth among the different funds in the family at little or no cost. The different funds within the family usually offer a broad mix of mutual fund types to appeal to a full spectrum of investor objectives. Consolidated account statements also make personal financial planning a less daunting task for the beginning investor. Fund families give you the advantage of responding quickly to changes in market conditions, changes in your investment strategy, or the need to balance your portfolio by quickly transferring your money from one fund to another. Remember that profits and losses have tax implications. This is true even if you are redeeming shares to transfer from one fund to another within the same family of funds. Your mutual fund company will usually provide you with the information you must report to the IRS. Also, some families do charge a fee for transfers between different funds.

WHAT ARE THE DIFFERENT TYPES OF MUTUAL FUNDS?

Mutual funds are usually classified by their investment strategy. Table 16-1 lists the common fund categories and a general measure of their risk. These categories encompass typical investment objectives. Capital appreciation seeks an increase in the underlying price of the investment. Current income focuses on companies or investment opportunities that provide high dividend and interest payments.

What Are Open-End and Closed-End Mutual Funds?

All mutual funds can be further classified as either closed-end or open-end. Closed-end shares are sold on stock exchanges, just like normal stocks. They raise money for investing in securities all at once by issuing a fixed number of shares. Investors then buy and sell shares in the fund just like any stock in the stock market. An investor who buys or sells closed-end funds typically does so through a broker and must pay a brokerage commission just like someone who buys or sells stocks. The share price of a closed-end mutual fund depends not only on the current market value of the fund's assets, but also on the supply of and demand for the fund's shares on the market. Prices are quoted in relation to the Net Asset Value (NAV) of the fund. The NAV is simply the dollar value of one share of the fund's stock.

Most closed-end mutual funds trade at a market price below the NAV of the fund. This is called trading at a discount. If the fund becomes popular, then the fund's price on the market may exceed the NAV. You can find prices of closed-end funds in your newspaper's stock listings. As a general rule, favor closed-end funds that trade at a discount to their NAV, but don't expect that the discount will disappear soon. Realize that you risk a loss in your share price due not only to a decrease in the value of the fund's assets, but also to a possible decrease in demand for the fund's shares on the market.

The other major category of mutual funds is open-end funds. There are over 10,000 open-end mutual funds, compared to about 550 closed-end funds. In contrast to closed-end funds, the more you or other investors put in, the larger the fund grows. You can buy or sell shares in open-end funds from the mutual fund itself, through a financial advisor, or through a broker. Open-end fund shares do not trade on the stock market like closed-end funds. An open-end fund will sell as many shares as investors demand and must redeem (buy back) investors' shares whenever investors want to sell them. The share price of an open-end fund depends on the NAV of the securities in its portfolio and any load, if applicable. Thus, unlike closed-end funds, open-end funds' share prices are not directly affected by the supply and demand for their shares, but by the supply and demand for the securities in their portfolio. The remainder of this chapter will focus primarily on open-end mutual funds. They are more common and are generally favored by small investors over both closed-end funds and direct investment in individual stocks.

TABLE 16-1
MUTUAL FUND TYPES

Type of Fund	Primary Objective	Volatility/Risk
Aggressive growth	Capital appreciation	Very high
Growth	Capital appreciation	High
Growth and income	Capital appreciation and current income	Moderate to high
Balanced	Long-term capital appreciation and current income	Moderate
International stock[1]	Capital appreciation from foreign securities	Moderate to high
Sector	Invests in companies in a particular industry or commodity	Moderate to high
Income stock	Increasing dividend income, current income, and long-term capital appreciation	Moderate
Index	Invests in companies to replicate a specific index such as the S&P 500	Moderate
Income	Current income	Moderate
Bond[2]	Current income	Low to moderate
International bond[1]	Current income from foreign bonds	Moderate
Money market[3]	Current income	Low

[1] For international funds, you also need to consider the risk of currency exchange rate changes.
[2] Bond funds will typically specialize as corporate, government, or tax-exempt (municipal). Each has different risk structures and tax benefits.
[3] Money markets are generally not insured or guaranteed by the U.S. government, and there can be no assurance that the fund will be able to maintain a stable NAV of $1 per share.

What Is an Index Fund?

Since there are over 10,000 open-end mutual funds to select from, the task of selecting representative investments for each asset class may seem daunting! A simple technique that has gained popularity in recent years is the use of index or passive funds.

The object of an index fund is to replicate the return of a particular index such as the Standard & Poor's 500 (large capitalization stocks) or the Russell 2000 (small capitalization stocks). There are index funds for most asset classes. Index funds have low management and expense fees since they require less management. The fund manager is simply replicating an already determined portfolio. Also, since the index does not change often, low portfolio turnover results in better tax efficiency for the fund shareholders. Finally, index funds stay fully invested. In a sense, the investor "owns the market."

Index funds offer investors an inexpensive means to own a very diversified portfolio. We recommend beginning investors consider broad index funds, such as an S&P 500 fund, as a starting point for their portfolio. As one begins to accumulate wealth, these funds would serve as the core of a portfolio of mutual funds. The investor could subsequently diversify and build around this core by adding bond funds, industry funds, and country funds.

The biggest criticism of index funds is that they do not allow you to "beat the market" and achieve higher returns than the selected index. While this criticism is valid, so is the contrary—they do not perform substantially worse than the market. Index funds may be useful to the investor who does not wish to spend the time considering and analyzing the various criteria we discuss in the next section on selecting a mutual fund. They also help the investor avoid fund managers who stray from the stated objectives of a particular fund, thus making it difficult to maintain a desired asset allocation.

Investors who want to attempt to "beat the market" may opt for actively managed funds. In these funds, fund managers use research, analysis, and proprietary data to select securities that they believe will do better than a benchmark like the Standard & Poor's 500 or the Russell 2000. However, active funds provide no guarantee that you will achieve higher returns than passive funds and require you to devote more time in selecting an appropriate fund.

WHAT FEES DO MUTUAL FUND COMPANIES CHARGE?

Now that we have reviewed the advantages of mutual funds and types of funds available, this section will discuss the specifics that investors must know before they invest. First of all, fees will affect your return. Though mutual funds are the least expensive way to invest, you still pay three basic types of fees: loads, management fees, and 12b-1 fees. You will find these fees disclosed in the mutual fund's prospectus.

Load versus No-Load Funds

If you buy a mutual fund through a broker, then the fund is typically a load fund. A load is essentially a sales commission, and there are two types: front-end loads and back-end loads. With front-end loads, you pay a sales commission on your purchase and sometimes on any reinvestments. With a back-end load, you pay redemption fees when you sell your shares. By law, mutual funds can charge a sales commission of up to 8.5 percent of your investment. The typical range is 2 to 8.5 percent. Obviously, a large front-end load will significantly affect the amount of your investment actually used to purchase shares. For example, if you invest $1,000 in a mutual fund with an 8.5 percent front-end load, then only $915 goes into the fund, while $85 goes to the salesman who sold you the fund and possibly to the fund's underwriters. In reality, you are paying a commission of 9.3 percent ($85 ÷ $915 = 0.093); you pay $85 to get an actual investment of $915, not $1,000. This means you would have to get a return of 9.3 percent on your mutual fund before you break even on your initial investment of $1,000!

Back-end loads, often called redemption fees, charge a commission (usually 2 to 6 percent) to sell your fund shares. Funds commonly impose redemption fees to discourage short-term investing or market timing (switching in and out of a fund to make short-term profits). Redemption fees are not prominently advertised, so you need to read the fund's prospectus carefully to see if the fund has any. Some funds have declining redemption fees that start out high and then decline to a very low fee or no fee after you've held the shares for some time period. Five years is typical.

No-load funds, when purchased directly from the mutual fund company, do not charge commissions. However, investors will often be charged a fee if no-load funds are purchased through a broker or brokerage house.

Cautionary Note on Contractual Mutual Funds

The most expensive type of front-end load fund you can buy is a contractual mutual fund like Fidelity Destiny, Summit Investors, First Investors, and others. Insurance agents, commissioned financial planners, and other mutual fund peddlers prefer to sell you this kind of fund because the salesman's compensation is much more lucrative than with other load funds. Contractual mutual funds obligate you to invest a set number of dollars every month over a ten- to twenty-year time frame. This "contract" is not generally a legal obligation, and you can get out of it whenever you wish. A significant drawback to contractual plans is that they take the majority of your total (8.5 percent) commission for your expected investments over the full life of the plan and charge it "up front" in the first year. This means that up to 50 percent of your first year's investments go into the salesman's pocket, not into your account! Also, if you cancel your "contract," you may lose up to 40 percent of your initial investment because the up-front commissions are nonrefundable after your grace period (usually eighteen months) expires.

Annual Management Fees

These fees range from 0.25 to 1.5 percent of your investment. The fund pays these fees out of the fund's assets. Thus, the greater the fees, the less your net return. Most larger funds charge less than 1 percent of the principal.

12b-1 Fees

These fees cover marketing and advertising costs. About 50 percent of all funds charge this fee and it can significantly reduce your total return. 12b-1 fees are misleading since they appear quite small in comparison to typical front-end loads. Since fund companies charge them every year, their long-term effect on returns can be quite substantial compared to the one-time charge of a front-end load. For example, a 12b-1 load of 0.75 percent has the same effect as nearly a

4 percent front-end load if you were to hold the fund for five years. Over longer periods, even the smallest 12b-1 fees seriously degrade an investor's return.

Should You Ever Buy a Load Fund?

Considering the fact that loads buy you nothing and simply reduce your return, should you ever buy a load fund? Looking at all the available evidence, no study has shown that load funds consistently outperform no-load funds. Remember that the load fee does not pay for superior research or better management. It simply compensates the salesman for selling you the shares. Based on the evidence, you should only buy a load fund if you are willing to pay someone to pick a mutual fund for you. The simple example in Table 16-2 shows the difference a load can have on your return. You invest $100 each month for five years in each of three mutual funds: a no-load fund, an 8.5 percent load fund, and a typical fifteen-year contract fund. Assume the returns are 12 percent per year and management fees are zero for each fund. Your earnings in a no-load fund over the five-year time frame would exceed those of a load fund by about $700 and exceed those of the contract fund by about $1,200—a full year's worth of investment contributions. Although you will have to invest a little time to pick your own fund, no-load mutual funds provide a better return than load funds with similar characteristics.

TABLE 16-2
COMPARISON OF NET RETURNS IN LOAD AND NO-LOAD FUNDS (ASSUMING A STEADY 12% RATE OF RETURN)

Fund	Monthly Investment	Total Value of Investment Net of Load	After 5 Years
No-load	$100.00	$100.00	$8,167
8.5% load	100.00	91.50	7,473
Contractual	100.00	50.00 (1 year) 97.50 (2–5 years)	6,992

HOW DO YOU READ MUTUAL FUND PRICES?

Financial publications regularly review and rank mutual fund performances. You can also get a daily snapshot of your fund's performance by checking the mutual fund quotations section in most major newspapers or using an online service.

Some newspapers list the offer price and the NAV. The offer price is the price you would pay to purchase a share of the fund. The NAV is the price you would receive for redeeming a share of the fund. Funds determine the NAV by adding up the value of all of the fund's investment holdings and dividing by the number of shares. The difference between the offer price and the NAV is the load because commissions are included in the offer price but not in the NAV.

Other papers use a simplified format that doesn't include offer prices. The *Wall Street Journal* provides a detailed mutual fund quotation section. As shown in the excerpt below, it reports the mutual fund NAV, the change from the day prior, and the percentage return year to date (YTD). Superscripted letters highlight important parts of the quotation and are described below.

Name	NAV[C]	Net Chg.[D]	YTD % Ret.[E]
American Century Inv[A]			
Bond[B]	9.35	–0.02	+3.5
Real	14.83	+0.04	+5.1
Ultra	29.93	+0.12	–7.5
Pioneer Fund			
Grwth p[F]	16.29	+0.18	–5.3

[A]Funds are categorized by "family name" first. The first listing is from the American Century family of funds.
[B]Funds within the family appear in alphabetical order. Usually the name relates to the funds' objectives by category.
[C]NAV is the daily price of one of the shares.
[D]The net change is the change in NAV from the previous day's close.
[E]YTD percentage change assumes reinvestment of all distributions, after subtracting annual expenses. None of the figures include sales charges (loads).
[F]The *p* after the name indicates that the fund charges marketing and distribution costs or 12b-1 fees. An *r* after the fund's name would indicate that the fund charges a redemption fee or back-end load. A *t* would indicate that both r and p apply. An *x* would indicate the fund just went ex-dividend, which means it just distributed dividend earnings to its shareholders. An *e* would indicate ex-distribution, which means it just distributed capital gains earnings to shareholders.

HOW DO YOU SELECT A MUTUAL FUND?

Now that you are aware of the basics of a mutual fund, how do you select one? The following section uses the prospectus of a sample fund to cover the key steps you should consider in the selection process. Before you order a prospectus, you should 1) formulate your financial goals and financial objectives as discussed in chapter 4, and 2) select a fund category that matches your investment strategy as discussed in chapter 14.

Earlier chapters helped you formulate your financial goals and objectives. Now you need to match them to a fund category such as those outlined in Table 16-1. In general, the fund category you choose will depend on your own risk preference and time horizon. The longer your horizon, the less risky most funds become. You may also have to consider your tax situation and need for steady income.

As a basic guideline, you should invest savings for short-term goals (less than one year) in money market or low-risk bond mutual funds. For medium-term goals (one to five years), you should consider short-term government or corporate bond funds. To satisfy long-term goals, you should have a diversified mix of stock, balanced, international, and perhaps sector funds. Let's assume you have a long-range goal of saving for a new home ten to fifteen years in the future. You decide a growth and income fund provides the appropriate amount of risk for your situation.

Once you decide on the category of fund, how do you select a particular fund from within the category? The first step is to obtain and read a fund's prospectus. By law, funds must provide you a prospectus containing key information about the fund. In the past, prospectuses contained too much information and technical and legal jargon. In 1998 the Securities and Exchange Commission (SEC) adopted plain English disclosure rules to ensure that prospectuses are clear, concise, and understandable to investors. Investors can request a prospectus from a mutual fund company by telephone, in writing, or by submitting a request online at the company's website. Company websites frequently allow investors to download the prospectus immediately.

The second step in selecting a mutual fund is to assess the fund's performance relative to similar funds and market or industry benchmarks. There are many resources available for this type of research. On the World Wide Web, sites such as *Morningstar.com* provide insightful, professional, and objective analyses. There you can learn about a fund's returns, key holdings, risk level, management team, and more. In addition, these sites provide rankings relative to other funds in the same category. Other sources of information include financial magazines such as *Money* magazine and *Kiplinger's Personal Finance* magazine and financial newspapers such as the *Wall Street Journal.* The *Wall Street Journal* publishes *Mutual Funds Monthly Review,* which contains comprehensive data and performance tables. It also provides Lipper Fund Indexes daily in its "Money and Investing" section. This allows you to compare your fund's performance to selected indexes.

The purpose of reading the prospectus and researching mutual funds is to determine whether a particular fund is consistent with your investment objective, time horizon, and risk tolerance and to assess your individual fund's performance against benchmarks.

Below we will cover the key points you should look for in a prospectus by providing a hypothetical profile prospectus. A profile prospectus contains most of the essential information on the fund without the more-difficult-to-understand legal wording. A statement of additional information may be obtained from mutual fund companies when more details are required. Let's look at a sample growth and income fund: the ABC Growth and Income Fund. We provide some basic recommendations at the end of each part as benchmarks.

Sample Profile Prospectus: The ABC Growth and Income Fund

1. What Is the Fund's Investment Strategy? The hypothetical ABC Growth and Income Fund seeks a high total return by investing in stocks of domestic companies as well as some debt securities. The fund seeks to diversify by spreading its holdings among companies in different industries. The fund manager focuses on companies that pay dividends while offering strong earnings growth potential. The fund invests in debt securities rated at B or higher.

Recommendations: Ensure that the fund's strategy matches your financial goals and objectives.

Even within the same fund category, some funds have a higher risk than others. Spend some time here to note the significant risks. Also, look for the allocation of the fund's holdings.

2. What Are the Fund's Expenses? Shareholder transaction expenses you pay when you buy, hold, or sell shares of this fund:

Account maintenance fee (for accounts under $2,500)	$10
Maximum sales charges on purchases	None
Maximum sales charges on reinvested distributions	None
Maximum sales charges on redemptions	None
Exchange fees	None
Management	0.75%
12b-1 fee	0.25%
Other expenses	0.20%

Recommendations: We recommend you avoid load funds (those with sales charges). Earlier, we discussed some issues if you are considering a load fund. For stock funds, look for funds with a total expense ratio (management fee + 12b-1 fee + other expenses) of less than 1.5 percent. For a bond fund, look for a ratio less than 1 percent. Fees reduce your total return, so look for low expenses. However, you must compare fees to the total return.

3. How Has the Fund Performed? Table 16-3 shows the fund's past performance as well as a comparison to several different measures. Total returns are based on past performance and do not necessarily indicate future performance.

Recommendations: You need to spend time here. Compare the fund's returns to comparable funds and the overall market benchmarks. For bond funds, comparisons with government Treasury bonds are appropriate. We recommend you avoid funds that consistently perform below the average of comparable funds. Try to pick funds that have a track record of at least five to ten years. If you are a conservative investor, check out the performance during down markets ("bear" markets). Notice from our example that even sound mutual funds may occasionally experience negative returns. We will address this further in the section on when to sell mutual funds.

TABLE 16-3
BEST PERFORMANCE OF FUND

	1994	1995	1996	1997	1998	1999	2000
ABC Growth and Income Fund (% change)	-0.07	21.37	12.54	16.93	16.29	10.10	–2.66

	1-Year	3-Year	5-Year
ABC Growth and Income Fund	–10.9%	2.7%	8.5%
S&P 500 Index	–12.2	5.9	15.4
Lipper Growth and Income Fund Average	6.4	4.7	11.7

4. Who Is the Fund's Investment Manager? ABC Company is the fund's investment manager. Mr. Calvin A. Hobbes has managed the fund since January 1993. Mr. Hobbes joined ABC in 1985. He has an M.B.A. from the University of Texas and is a chartered financial analyst (CFA).

Recommendations: Ensure that the current fund manager was the person responsible for the success over the past few years that we measured in section 3. Ensure that the fund's management is achieving its objectives. Also evaluate the manager's investment style. Some styles do well at certain times but do poorly at others. We recommend funds that have continuity in managers.

5. How Do I Buy and Sell Shares? You can open an ABC Fund account by completing the enclosed application or calling the fund's 1-800 number by exchange or bank wire. The minimum initial investment is $2,500. Minimum additional investment is $250. The minimum is waived if you start a systematic investment plan of at least $100 per month. You can redeem shares by written request, telephone, wire transfer, or using our WWW service. Redemptions over $25,000 must be done in writing.

Recommendations: Many funds, particularly aggressive growth funds, have high initial investment requirements. Funds will often waive this amount if you start a systematic investment plan as shown above (see also the section on mutual fund investment strategies). For IRAs, the minimum is usually lower.

While funds require a written application to open an account, there are various options available for conducting subsequent transactions, such as investments, transfers, and redemptions. These options include telephone, wire, and Internet access. We recommend you deal with funds that allow a variety of services, such as phone and electronic options.

6. How and When are Distributions Made and Taxed? The ABC Fund distributes all of its net income and capital gains to shareholders each year in March, June, September, and December. We automatically reinvest distributions unless you elect another option. Distributions are taxable when paid, whether you take them in cash or you reinvest them. For tax purposes, income and short-term capital gains distributions are taxed as dividends, and long-term capital gains distributions are taxed as long-term capital gains.

Recommendations: We recommend that you automatically reinvest distributions unless you are paying them to a money market fund to assist in portfolio rebalancing, as discussed in chapter 14. The returns noted in most cases assume that funds are reinvested. You will receive a Form 1099 at the end of the year that will explain the amount you must report to the IRS as dividend or long-term capital gains. You do not have to pay taxes on distributions for mutual funds that you designated as an Individual Retirement Account (IRA) mutual fund. If you are in a fund that invests in bonds, some of the interest and dividends may be free of federal, state, or local taxes. Here is another place to verify that the fund's objectives match your own objectives. If your goal is current income, the fund should be making dividend or interest distributions.

7. What Services Are Available? ABC provides a wide variety of services, including twenty-four-hour telephone service, regular investment plans, free exchange among ABC family funds and online WWW service. ABC reserves the right to modify or withdraw the exchange privilege.

Recommendations: Many mutual funds and all large family funds now offer online information and services either with proprietary software or on the Internet. These range from very simple financial calculators to more sophisticated planners that allow you to develop a systematic investment plan to meet your financial objectives. They also provide an easy way to monitor your investments and transfer assets between different funds within a given family of funds. We recommend use of these services to help you develop and implement your financial plan.

8. Other considerations?

Recommendations: You may also want to consider the portfolio turnover ratio and review the diversification of the actual assets the mutual fund owns. Compare the portfolio turnover rate with other funds within the same category. If your fund has a significantly higher turnover rate, it will reduce your return because of higher brokerage costs. Also, most prospectuses list the largest holdings of the fund. Again, look here to see if the type of assets the fund purchases matches your investment objectives.

These are the basic areas you should consider. There is no precise formula to determine which fund is right for you or how you should weight each area. We recommend you feel comfortable that the fund matches your investment objective. Additionally, while past performance is no guarantee of future performance, look for funds that have a track record of beating the average for comparable funds. Avoid funds that consistently perform below the average in their fund category.

WHEN AND HOW SHOULD YOU INVEST?

There are many different investment strategies. Lump-sum investing and dollar cost averaging are the most common and the most frequently mentioned in financial news articles.

Lump-Sum Investing

Using the lump-sum approach, you simply invest all your money for the year at once. This strategy presumes that you already have a nest egg ready to invest. A variant of this strategy is to invest smaller portions of your lump sum over a few months (say one-third of the sum for three months) until the entire lump sum is invested. This variation allows you to enter the market more gradually and may assist you in sticking with your financial plan if the market goes down after your first investment.

Dollar Cost Averaging

What if you have not accumulated a sizable amount of money to invest yet or feel uncomfortable taking an investment plunge with all your money at one time? One simple way to reduce the risk of placing too much into a mutual fund when the price is at its high is dollar cost averaging. Dollar cost averaging simply involves investing a constant dollar amount at specific intervals, usually each month, into a mutual fund. Dollar cost averaging enables you to pay less per share than the actual average share price. The key to dollar cost averaging is that by purchasing the same dollar amount each period, you buy more when the market is low since shares cost less and buy less when the market is high since shares cost more. Consequently, you will earn a positive return even if you sell your shares at a price per share equal to the average price per share you paid. Table 16-4 illustrates the mechanics of dollar cost averaging using $100 per month for one year in three different market scenarios.

Most mutual funds make it simple and convenient to dollar cost average by offering systematic investment plans. The fund will take a constant amount out of your checking or savings account once every month. Many will also reduce or waive the minimum initial investment if you start a systematic investment plan. So if you don't have enough money to meet that minimum initial investment, check to see if you can avoid the minimum amount by initiating a systematic investment plan.

TABLE 16-4
DOLLAR COST AVERAGING

		Rising Market		Declining Market		Fluctuating Market	
	Amount Invested	Price Paid for Each Share	Number of Shares Bought	Price Paid for Each Share	Number of Shares Bought	Price Paid for Each Share	Number of Shares Bought
Jan	$100	$10.00	10.00	$10.00	10.00	$10.00	10.00
Feb	100	10.45	9.57	9.55	10.47	9.25	10.81
Mar	100	10.90	9.17	9.10	10.99	10.25	9.76
Apr	100	11.35	8.81	8.65	11.56	10.70	9.35
May	100	11.80	8.47	8.20	12.20	9.95	10.05
Jun	100	12.25	8.16	7.75	12.90	10.20	9.80
Jul	100	12.70	7.87	7.30	13.70	9.45	10.58
Aug	100	13.15	7.60	6.85	14.60	9.80	10.20
Sep	100	13.60	7.35	6.40	15.62	9.55	10.47
Oct	100	14.05	7.12	5.95	16.81	10.30	9.71
Nov	100	14.50	6.90	5.50	18.18	10.15	9.85
Dec	100	14.95	6.69	5.05	19.80	10.00	10.00
Total	$1,200		97.71		166.83		120.58
Average Share Cost[1]		$12.28		$7.19		$9.95	
Average Share Price[2]		$12.48		$7.53		$9.97	

[1] Average share cost = total dollars invested ÷ total shares purchased
[2] Average share price = sum of price paid per share column ÷ 12

Value Averaging

Another investment strategy is value averaging. With value averaging, you seek to increase the total value of your mutual fund by a set amount each month, as opposed to investing a set amount each month. For instance, assume your goal was to see the value of your fund account increase by $100 each month. If the current value of your fund account is $800 (200 shares × $4 a share), then you want it to rise to $900 in value next month. Suppose next month rolls around and the share price is still $4. You would need to purchase $100 worth of shares to bring the account value up to $900. What if instead the share price had risen to $5? Your account would then be worth $1,000 (200 shares × $5 a share). In that case, you would not have to invest anything that month to bring the value of the shares up to the target of $900. In fact, you could actually sell $100 worth of the fund. But since doing so may incur a tax liability, you might be better to just hold onto the excess value until next month when the value target increases to $1,000. If the share price had dropped to $3, your account would be worth $600 (200 shares × $3 a share) and you would have to invest $300 to reach your target of $900. The average cost per share with value averaging will be less than with dollar cost averaging. However, since this strategy involves other potential complications and requires more active management of your portfolio, readers interested in using this method should read the Edelson reference listed at the end of this chapter.

WHEN SHOULD YOU SELL YOUR MUTUAL FUND SHARES?

The basic answer is to sell your fund shares when you need the money for your financial goals. Another reason to sell your fund may be if the fund changes portfolio managers and the star manager leaves. However, you may want to follow the fund's performance over the next year to evaluate how the new manager does.

The performance of your fund may be another reason to sell. If the risk-adjusted return does not match your expectations or is consistently below returns of funds with similar objectives, then you may want to sell your shares and invest elsewhere. We recommend patience and discipline. Avoid the temptation to sell in disgust just because your fund or the market has a bad quarter or even a year. Even the best funds have periods of subpar performance. Always focus on the long-term record. Many inexperienced and undisciplined investors sell out at market bottoms, missing the ride back up to the top, and then buy back at the market peak when it's too late. We discourage this behavior.

Should an investor try to time the market by attempting to follow the economic cycle and adjusting which mutual funds to invest in accordingly? Probably not. Our economy is affected to a large extent by random, unpredictable events. Experts who spend their whole lives analyzing the economy have trouble accurately forecasting what will happen next or to what degree. Studies of investment newsletters that claim the ability to time the market show that few, no more than would be expected by random chance, are able to beat the return of a buy-and-hold strategy. The major results of attempting to time the market are more taxes, higher transaction costs, and lower average returns.

HOW DO YOU CALCULATE YOUR MUTUAL FUND RETURNS?

You've picked your mutual fund and held it for a while. Now you need to measure your return. Unless you invest a lump sum of money on 1 January or are interested in year-to-date returns, the figures published in the *Wall Street Journal* or financial newsmagazines will not be the same as your actual return. While these figures satisfy the needs of most investors, you may want to calculate the actual returns based on your individual investments and redemptions. Calculating your true annual return requires knowledge of the sources of return as well as the methods of calculating your return. You must keep track of the sources of your return. Most fund companies send annual summaries of your investment. We recommend you keep these statements as part of your financial record keeping.

What Are the Sources of Mutual Fund Return?

Mutual fund returns come from three sources: dividends, capital gains distributions, and changes in the share price of your fund. When a mutual fund earns dividends or interest on its securities, the fund passes those along to you, the shareholder, in the form of dividends. If a mutual fund sells some of its securities for more than it paid for them, it must pass that profit along to the shareholder in the form of capital gains distributions. Finally, if you sell your fund shares for more than you paid for them, you will earn a profit, or capital gain, on those shares. However, you could have a loss on the shares by selling them for less than you paid. Your total return on the mutual fund includes profits or losses from all three sources. Of course, if you paid a load, this will also reduce your return.

There are several ways to calculate your mutual fund return. The simplest method is only an approximation but is fairly accurate for short periods of time.

$$\text{percent return} = \frac{[(E - B) + D + C] \div n}{(E + B) \div 2}$$

where:
E = Ending price per share of the fund
B = Beginning price per share of the fund
D = Total dividends received per share
C = Total capital gains distributions per share
n = Number of years you owned the fund

For a more exact calculation of how you've done, you can use the Internal Rate of Return (IRR) feature of any computer spreadsheet software and most financial calculators. After you list monthly cash flows into or out of the fund, including its current value as a positive entry in the last period, the IRR function will calculate your exact percent return. You can then annualize the monthly rate of return using the methods shown in Appendix D.

Should You Worry about Taxes and Other Considerations?

Many investors have a hard time understanding the various distributions that mutual funds pay out and their tax implications. As stated above, mutual funds must pass along net investment earnings and realized capital gains (actual profits) to the investor. If the NAV of a fund is $6 per share, and then it makes a 70-cent dividend payment or distribution to the shareholder, the price, or NAV, of the mutual fund falls immediately by the amount of the distribution to $5.30 per share. The distribution is then taxable. These distributions create two common problems for investors.

Tips on Making the Most from Mutual Funds

- Read the mutual fund prospectus carefully. Ensure that the fund's objectives are consistent with your investment objectives.
- Avoid contractual plans for purchasing mutual funds.
- Don't let the returns for a mutual fund fool you. Always compare the return against the average of similar funds. Look for funds with a track record of beating the average.
- Take advantage of mutual fund features such as automatic investment plans and automatic reinvestment of dividends and capital gains distributions.
- Avoid buying shares of a fund just before a distribution since you incur the tax liability with no gain. Most funds make their largest distributions in December.
- Good record keeping is essential for both tax and investment planning. Keep at a minimum the quarterly and annual summary reports.
- Loads and fees reduce your overall return. Try to minimize them.
- Have an exit strategy. Avoid selling in panic.
- Sell when you need the money for your financial goals, if the fund's management is no longer consistent with your investment objectives, or if the fund performs consistently worse than funds with similar objectives.

First, you can incur a needless tax liability by purchasing shares of a fund just before it makes a large distribution. You would have to pay tax on the 70-cent per share distribution mentioned above, even though the value of the holdings has not changed. Check the distribution dates with the fund before you invest. It's best to wait until just after the distribution date to send in your money. (*Note:* This is a common problem if you invest in December since many mutual funds distribute in December.)

The second problem results from the reinvestment option that most investors choose: directly reinvesting distributions and dividends into more shares of the mutual fund. Many investors mistakenly pay tax twice on the reinvested shares by not adjusting the tax basis on those shares when they later sell them. In the scenario above, you have already had to pay tax on the reinvested shares bought with the 70-cent distribution and have reinvested those funds by buying new shares at $5.30 each. Your cost basis for this mutual fund should go up by the amount of the distribution. It's easy to forget this small point and pay taxes again on the same shares when they are sold.

This last problem brings up an important caution for investors in mutual fund shares—good record keeping is crucial! Many investors pay too much in taxes when they later sell mutual fund shares because they did not keep all the records of purchase that their fund sent them. You should keep records of purchases, reinvestments, dividends, capital gains distributions, and sales proceeds received for as long as you own any shares in that fund and then a few more years to satisfy the IRS. At a minimum, keep the annual summary statements as well as all tax documents.

Although there are no guarantees of profit, mutual funds offer the investor a convenient and low-cost method of achieving diversification. We recommend you consider mutual funds as part of your overall financial strategy.

SUGGESTED REFERENCE

Edleson, Michael E. *Value Averaging: The Safe and Easy Strategy for Higher Investment Returns.* Chicago: International Publishing, 1991.

17

Retirement Savings Options

RETIREMENT, TAXES, AND YOUR FINANCIAL PLAN

Our discussions so far have provided us with information on establishing our financial goals, budgeting, planning for taxes, and the options for the various types of investment classes.

The realization that we have to earn returns that allow our wealth to grow after factoring in inflation and accounting for taxes leads us to our next topic. If we can legally avoid paying taxes, or at least defer paying them, we will be able to increase our wealth faster and increase our likelihood of accomplishing our financial objectives.

Fortunately, the Congress has provided several means for investors to defer, and in some cases avoid completely, paying taxes on investments. Those include Individual Retirement Accounts; 401k and 403b plans; and for government employees, including military personnel, the Thrift Savings Plan.

We will discuss each of these options and provide you with information to maximize your wealth, minimize your taxes, and achieve your goals.

WHAT IS AN INDIVIDUAL RETIREMENT ACCOUNT?

An Individual Retirement Account is a personal savings plan that offers you tax advantages to set aside money for your retirement or, in some plans, for certain education expenses (see chapter 13).

For retirement purposes, there are two types of IRAs: traditional and Roth; (the educational IRA does not generate retirement income). The main differences center around whether or not your contributions are deductible and if the distributions are taxable when you start to withdraw the funds.

Three advantages of an IRA include the following:

1. You may be able to deduct your contributions in whole or in part, depending on the type of IRA and your circumstances.
2. Generally, amounts in your IRA, including earnings and gains, are not taxed until distributed or, in some cases, are not taxed at all if distributed according to the rules.

3. Amounts in an IRA are not counted into your family financial situation when colleges calculate your Expected Family Contribution (EFC) to determine your child's eligibility for financial aid (see chapter 13).

Traditional IRAs

Anyone can set up a traditional IRA provided that they have taxable earned income during the year and have not yet reached age 70 1/2, regardless of whether or not they are covered by another pension plan.

Current law allows annual contributions of up to $3,000 for 2002, increasing to $4,000 in 2006 and $5,000 (indexed in increments of $500) in 2009. Additionally, if you are over age fifty by the end of the year, you can take advantage of "catch-up" provisions and contribute an additional $500 for 2002 to 2005 and $1,000 for 2006 and later. However, if you earn less than the limit, your contribution can not exceed your earnings.

For adjusted gross incomes up to $63,000, a partial IRA deduction is available for joint filers, and singles can deduct if they have incomes under $43,000.

If your spouse is covered under a retirement plan but you are not, the phaseout for deductibility begins at $150,000 for tax year 2001, and at adjusted gross incomes of $160,000 and up, no contributions are deductible.

Advantages of traditional IRAs include tax-deferred growth of your investment and possible tax deductibility, depending on your income and filing status. These limits change regularly, so consult IRS Publication 590 for current limits.

Disadvantages of traditional IRAs include mandatory distributions starting 1 April in the year after you turn 70 1/2. You need to keep good records, possibly for a very long time, to correctly determine your taxes when you start withdrawing the money.

Roth IRAs

Roth IRAs were created in 1997 and named after the senator who championed the legislation, William V. Roth Jr. The main differences between Roth IRAs and traditional IRAs are that all your contributions are nondeductible and your withdrawals are not taxed when you begin to receive them.

The dollar limits for annual contributions are the same as for traditional IRAs, and the income phaseout begins at $150,000 for joint tax filers.

Advantages of Roth IRAs include the following:

- Tax-deferred growth of your investment.
- Tax-free withdrawals after age 59 1/2.
- Eligibility to withdraw up to $10,000 for a home purchase without penalty if you have held the investment for five or more years.
- No mandatory distribution date.
- No minimum required annual distribution.

The disadvantage of Roth IRAs is that the contributions are not tax deductible.

Figure 17-1
Roth IRA Growth

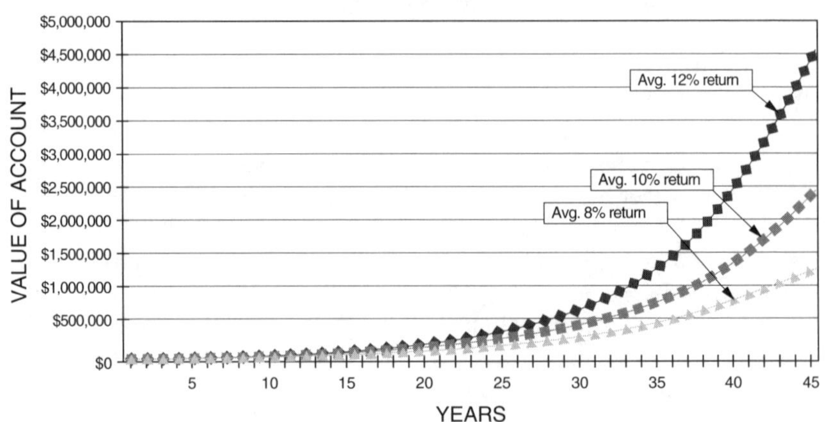

Comparison and Discussion

Given that all active-duty military personnel are covered by a pension plan, which makes all IRA contributions nondeductible, we recommend that any IRA you start be a Roth IRA. If you have an IRA and don't want to convert, you can just open a second IRA and make that a Roth.

For both types of IRAs, you can contribute the annual maximum for your spouse to a separate account, in addition to your contributions, raising your annual retirement savings to $6,000 for 2002 ($3,000 each for you and your spouse).

A Roth IRA is a powerful means of building wealth and helping to augment your retirement income. The tax-free compounding and withdrawals and reasonable restrictions make it a very attractive addition to your long-term financial plan.

To see how powerful this retirement option is, take the example of a twenty-two-year-old second lieutenant in 2002. She contributes the maximum allowed under current law for her entire twenty-year military career and does not contribute any more after military retirement. Further assume that the $5,000 annual contribution cap does not increase. Her contributions at the end of her military career total $92,000, but if invested in a stock mutual fund and growing tax-free, will have a future value at age sixty-five of $1,279,988 if she earns 8 percent on average (▲ in Figure 17-1), $2,465,855 at 10 percent (■ in Figure 17-1), and $4,741,237 at 12 percent (◆ in Figure 17-1).

THRIFT SAVINGS PLAN

The Thrift Savings Plan (TSP) is a retirement savings and investment plan that has been available to civilian employees of the federal government since 1987. The Congress passed legislation in 2000 allowing military personnel to contribute to the Thrift Savings Plan available to other government employees and directed the Department of Defense to implement that by 2001. That program is now operating.

The purpose of the TSP is to provide retirement income. It offers participants the same type of savings and tax benefits that many private corporations offer their employees under 401k plans. The TSP allows participants to save a portion of their pay in a special retirement account administered by the Federal Retirement Thrift Investment Board. The money that participants invest in the TSP comes from pretax dollars and reduces their current taxable income; investments and earnings are not taxed until they are withdrawn. Military personnel's contributions and earnings belong to them and are therefore portable when they retire or leave the service. Unlike a 401k, the government does not make matching contributions for military TSP participants.

Servicemembers have two "open seasons" per year to enroll. Open seasons are currently 15 May through 31 July and 15 November through 31 January. New members of the uniformed services have sixty days after joining the service to enroll in the TSP; thereafter, they may enroll during the semiannual open seasons.

Once you enroll, the TSP will invest your contributions in the G Fund until you submit a contribution allocation. You can invest any portion of your TSP account in the five TSP investment funds:

- Government Securities Investment (G) Fund.
- Fixed Income Index Investment (F) Fund.
- Common Stock Index Investment (C) Fund.
- Small Capitalization Stock Index Investment (S) Fund.
- International Stock Index Investment (I) Fund.

In 2002, you can contribute up to 7 percent of the basic pay you earn each month. You may also be able to contribute all or any whole percentage of any special or incentive pay (including reenlistment or other bonuses) you receive as long as you are contributing basic pay. However, the total amount you contribute each year cannot exceed the Internal Revenue Code's elective deferral limit for that year, $11,000 for 2002. Finally, the only means to contribute is through monthly deductions. Servicemembers can not make direct contributions.

Participation in the TSP does not limit your ability to contribute to an IRA. When you separate from the uniformed services, you may:

- Receive a single payment that can then be transferred to an Individual Retirement Account (IRA) or other eligible retirement plan (e.g., a 401k plan or a civilian TSP account if you continue to work for the government).
- Request a series of monthly payments based on a dollar amount, a number of months, or your life expectancy. All or a portion of certain monthly payments can be transferred to an IRA or other eligible retirement plan.
- Request a TSP annuity. You must have at least $3,500 in your account in order to purchase an annuity.

Tips to Make the Most of Your Tax-Favored Retirement Accounts

- Contribute the maximum amount to tax-free accounts (Roth IRAs).
- If your employer offers matching contributions for the TSP (nonuniformed military or civilian 401k), contribute at least enough to get the full matching amount.
- Do not borrow against your retirement account even if the plan allows for it. The true cost of this loan could be far higher than the interest you pay.
- Make sure your beneficiaries for your retirement accounts are kept current and are in line with your desires, especially if your life situation changes (divorce, death in family, etc.).

- Leave your money in the TSP. You may leave your money in the TSP, where it will continue to accrue earnings. You can not continue to make contributions after you leave the service, but you will be able to continue to make interfund transfers. You must begin withdrawing from your account no later than 1 April of the year following the year you turn age 70½ and are separated from service.

Advantages of the Thrift Savings Plan include the following:

- The value of the account is not counted in your family financial situation when colleges calculate your Expected Family Contribution (EFC) to determine your child's eligibility for financial aid (see chapter 13).
- Tax-deferred growth.
- The TSP is funded with pretax dollars, thereby reducing your current year's income tax liability.
- Portability: The funds and growth are yours when you retire or leave the service.

The disadvantages of the TSP are that there are no matching funds for uniformed military personnel and servicemembers can not make direct contributions to their account. Monthly deductions are the only method of contributing.

18

Investing in Real Assets

Chapter 14 explained how to develop an investment strategy and explained that an integral part of the process is the determination of which broad asset classes (stocks, bonds, cash, real assets) are appropriate for individual financial goals. Chapter 15 then described the common financial assets that come to mind when most people think of "investments." Chapter 16 described mutual funds as an important vehicle for individual investment in financial assets, and chapter 17 discussed retirement savings options. This chapter completes the picture by describing real assets and discussing the role of real assets in the typical investment portfolio.

WHAT ARE REAL ASSETS?

Much of this book discusses financial assets known as securities. Securities are ownership claims to firms' income such as stocks or bonds. In contrast to financial assets (pieces of paper such as legal documents, contracts, etc.), real assets are tangible goods. Real estate is the most widely held real asset, but there are other goods that also fit the definition, such as land, precious metals, oil and other physical commodities, precious gems and jewelry, antiques, stamps and other collectibles, and artwork.

SHOULD YOU INVEST IN REAL ASSETS?

With the exception of real estate (discussed next), investing in these sorts of assets is generally something that most investors should avoid. While many people have heard of someone who made a fortune with a coin collection, or know a friend that fixed up an antique car and sold it for a bundle, it is important to recognize that these individuals owe their spectacular returns to their specialized talent regarding that type of asset. In other words, the fortune made by the coin collector was the result of time and effort devoted to a hobby combined with an unusual ability to select coins, rather than an investment strategy that you or I could replicate.

The picture is quite different when you look at risk and return for the overall asset class. Complete, accurate data on historical returns and risk measurements is hard to come by, but data published periodically in the *Wall Street Journal* indicates long-run returns that range from mediocre (some classes of artwork have returns of 2 to 3 percent) to in-line with bonds and stocks. More importantly, none of the long-run returns significantly outpaced stocks. Some argue that an investor must hold real assets as an inflation hedge and point to the attractive returns on precious metals, artwork, and some of the collectibles enjoyed by investors in the inflationary periods of the late 1970s and early 1980s. Today, inflation-indexed bonds provide an inflation hedge that the ordinary investor should prefer to holding these assets, not to mention the fact that the Federal Reserve Board continually works to keep inflation in check.

The advantage of investing in real assets is the enjoyment that the owner can derive from ownership and participation in a favorite hobby or pastime. Disadvantages include the inability to quickly sell the asset, information disparity, and lack of current income. The bottom line is simple: Know thyself. If you are pursuing a hobby that you are devoted to and you know that you have a special talent for discovering hidden values, then enjoy! Otherwise, you would be well advised to steer clear of these types of real assets and focus on real estate for portfolio diversification.

WHAT ROLE SHOULD REAL ESTATE PLAY IN YOUR PORTFOLIO?

There is one type of real asset that is appropriate for most military investors: real estate. As mentioned in chapter 14, real estate can add diversification to a small investor's portfolio. Additionally, there are opportunities for military investors to acquire rental property in different geographic locations over the course of a military career, an option not available to many other people. Many military units have a senior noncommissioned officer or an officer who seems to have built up a portfolio of properties across the country. This sort of investing takes careful planning, however, and there are many difficulties associated with owning real estate outright, so think carefully about the issues involved. Fortunately, there is a fairly easy way to get the added diversification of real estate without the headaches. We will cover the role of real estate in your investment portfolio, then illustrate a method of diversifying your portfolio with real estate, and finally discuss some points to consider related to direct real estate ownership and management.

Real assets, including real estate, are risky. Financial asset risk can be managed through diversification—the notion that by combining many different securities into one portfolio, you eliminate much of the specific risk without sacrificing expected return. Diversification then leaves you with exposure to a fraction of market risk while still having the potential for significant returns over time. Because real estate is not highly correlated with stocks and bonds, it is especially valuable as a diversification tool. How can you achieve diversification with real estate assets?

One way to diversify a holding of real estate assets would be to buy a number of different types of properties (residential, commercial, hotel, industrial) in different locations around the country. The expected risk and return characteristics of this bundle of properties would clearly be superior to that of any single property. The idea of diversification in this context means that the specific risks of owning each property are reduced, as are the risks associated with owning property in a particular region (for example, a hurricane that destroys your house in Florida does not affect your duplex in Colorado at all). Again, the idea is that if things go poorly for one property or in one region, this will be offset by above-average performance in another region or specific property. Property-specific expected risk falls, and expected return is averaged among the various properties.

There is one limitation to this strategy: It would require a great deal of money. For example, acquiring a dozen or so single-family homes or duplexes that cost on average $100,000 each would require $400,000 down (plus a huge amount of mortgage debt). Banks will typically mortgage only 70 percent of the purchase price of nonowner-occupied homes. Certainly there must be a more realistic way for the small investor to gain diversified exposure to real estate assets.

When we discussed stocks and bonds, we ran into a similar problem: Small investors cannot efficiently build their portfolios with limited funds. Additionally, portfolio creation requires time and information, if only to make sure that investor risk preferences are mirrored in the portfolio. The solution to that problem was mutual funds, which allow the small investor to buy into one or more funds that already combine many securities into one diversified financial product. Fortunately, there is a similar solution in real estate with the Real Estate Investment Trust (REIT).

WHAT ARE REITS?

Real Estate Investment Trusts were created by Congress in 1960 to allow small individual investors access to diversified real estate portfolios. A REIT owns and operates income-producing real estate and sometimes finances real estate. A REIT is required by law to pay most (90 percent) of its taxable income to shareholders each year (a bondlike characteristic). A REIT is not a limited partnership as some people think, nor should it be considered exactly like a mutual fund. Because REITs own and operate their own properties, in form, they are more like operating businesses and should therefore be evaluated in a similar fashion to a common stock with a very high dividend. As of this writing, there are almost 200 REIT companies being traded, like stocks, on the major stock exchanges. There are many kinds of REITs. Some diversify across regions or types of properties (commercial buildings, residential apartments, or other types). Some specialize in certain regions or even types of properties, such as shopping centers and malls. Finally, there is also a selection of mutual funds that hold shares of different REITs.

REITs and mutual funds provide many of the same advantages to the small investor. Owning REIT shares provides the advantages of diversification, liquidity, and professional management. A REIT's legal structure provides the benefit of only one level of taxation. Possibly the most important benefit of buying into a REIT is that it diversifies away property-specific risk. In addition to this diversification within the real estate asset class, adding a REIT to your portfolio provides more complete diversification across all asset classes (stocks, bonds, cash, real estate). An Ibbotson Associates analysis, published in May 2001, found that REIT shares have a low correlation to stocks and bonds. This is the key to increased diversification. In other words, if stocks happen to be down in one period, then perhaps bonds or your REIT will hold their value. You might consider adding REIT exposure to your financial security portfolio totaling as much as 5 percent of the total value.

You should be careful about selecting a REIT, just as you would when investing in a mutual fund. Always read the prospectus and get opinions from journals or financial advisors. A good place to start looking for information on REITs is the National Association of Real Estate Investment Trusts (NAREIT). As of this writing, NAREIT maintains an informative website with information on historical risk and return, as well as good basic REIT information. What specific things should you be looking for when selecting a REIT? Be careful of a REIT with an unrealistically high dividend yield. If it looks too good to be true, it probably is, and the REIT will not be able to sustain the same dividend over the long term. Be skeptical of a REIT that is unwilling to provide any information on individual properties it owns. It may be trying to hide some "rotten apples." Finally, monitor the level of debt that a REIT uses. Most REITs use debt to finance property purchases, but excessive debt reduces flexibility, increases the chances of financial difficulty, and could mean the REIT will soon raise new equity, which will dilute your holdings.

As you determine how much real estate exposure you need in your portfolio, don't forget that if you own your home, you already have some (maybe a large part) of your investment portfolio in real estate. A REIT can allow you to synthetically create exposure to real estate without the hassle of ownership, but direct real estate ownership (through owning a home or otherwise) is an important subject for most people. Direct ownership of real estate is, therefore, the focus of the remainder of this chapter.

WHAT ABOUT DIRECT REAL ESTATE OWNERSHIP?

This section starts, appropriately, with a note of caution. For all but the wealthiest of us, direct ownership of real estate necessarily means taking on property-specific risk. Additionally, since there is usually a large amount of mortgage debt involved, an individual investor is literally heaping financial risk on top of asset risk. Don't forget that the attractive returns reported by some real estate investors are due, at least in part, to the financial leverage of debt (leverage increases risk also), hard work (time and effort sometimes termed sweat equity), and a talent for choosing properties, dealing with tenants, and fixing all things mechanical, structural, and electrical. What is the best and highest use of your time? You must make a determination beforehand that you will be able to handle the time pressures of a busy military career and the time-intensive management of your properties. That said, there are many advantages that come from owning your own home. Further, for the right person, owning and managing rental or income properties can be the source of significant financial rewards.

Full coverage of this topic is well beyond the scope of this book, and the person who is truly interested in rental income properties needs to consult one or more of the many books on the subject. What follows is a brief description of some of the basic, important points to consider when thinking of this type of venture.

Consider this fact: You have to live somewhere! Every time you pay rent, you could be paying a mortgage payment instead that is largely tax deductible and would build equity in a property that could be converted into a rental property when you move.

Buying a home can be an emotional experience. Many people are eager to own a nice single-family dwelling with a yard in a residential neighborhood. They agonize over every detail, down to the white picket fence and the names of the neighbors. This is a natural tendency, and depending on your preferences, you might be better off thinking of a house purchase in terms of finding the "home" that is best for you. If this describes you, you would be better off going back to chapter 11 and concentrating on the specific characteristics of home purchases. This space is devoted to discussing residential real estate as an investment.

First, what's wrong with single-family homes? Nothing, if you intend to live there a long time. A long time is hard to define, but it's probably longer than a normal military tour of two to three years. Although home prices generally hold or increase in real value, they, like any other asset, fluctuate in value from year to year. It is not uncommon to watch the price of real estate vary substantially, sometimes falling or rising for years at a time. If you intend to live in your home for a long time, you can ride out these fluctuations, eventually paying off your mortgage and living "rent-free" or selling your home for the equity and a substantial capital gain. Military personnel, though, move whenever they are told, which is not necessarily when the real estate market is right. When PCS orders arrive, you may have to sell the house at a loss. Remember, if you can't sell it for what you owe the bank plus brokerage fees, then you must come up with the cash difference at closing. This is exactly the sort of asset-specific risk that you want to minimize through diversification.

One alternative to selling a property is to rent it when you leave. This may be a good alternative, but remember, if home prices are down, rents will also likely be low; you may be committing yourself to years of negative cash flow. Another thing to consider: Rents for single-family homes are generally lower than most mortgages for recently purchased property. Additionally, you now hold the business risk of managing a business, along with real asset price-fluctuation risk.

If all this scares you a bit, that's good. The point is that borrowing a lot of money and buying a real asset such as a home can be very risky. But then again, with risk comes potential return. If you can find a way to handle this risk in the context of careful property selection and portfolio investing, then perhaps you should read on. The next section looks at what property selection and rental management strategies are appropriate for the military home buyer who has a definite appetite for a little more risk than that which is involved in typical portfolio investing. This assumes a situation in which a military home buyer wishes to purchase a dwelling, live in it during a typical three-year tour, then rent it out for a number of years for income, and eventually sell it for the equity and capital gain.

What Kind of Real Estate Makes a Good Investment?

For an individual investor, the kinds of properties to look for are condominiums and town houses in organized associations and (for the more ambitious) standalone duplexes or fourplexes. We will talk about why these properties hold less business risk than single-family homes later. First, we will try to explain why the income-to-mortgage ratio of these homes is often equal to or greater than one (as discussed in chapter 11, the mortgage includes principal, mortgage interest, taxes, and insurance (PITI), as well as condominium fees).

To calculate the income-to-mortgage ratio, divide monthly rent (income) by the monthly mortgage needed to buy the home. Often you will find that you'll pay the same or even less to buy a condominium or town house than you would pay to rent (a ratio greater than 1.0)! There are several plausible economic reasons for people willing to pay rent that costs more than buying. Typical renters are not typical home buyers; if they were, they would probably buy a single-family home. They may want convenience, are probably transitory dwellers, and may be relatively young. Finally, they may not qualify for a mortgage because of credit or income insufficiency.

The other piece of this ratio is the mortgage payment. This is a result mainly of price and secondarily of the mortgage interest rate. Interest rates are determined in the macroeconomy, while real estate prices are determined by both macroeconomic factors and microeconomic factors such as consumer taste. Consumer taste for homes favors the more ideal freestanding single-family home (that is what most people would buy if they were going to buy a home). Thus, it would appear that condominiums and town houses are often priced at a lower multiple of potential rental income than single-family homes.

What Property Should You Select?

What you need to do is look at residential property from the income perspective: Ask yourself what you could get each month for a particular property if you rented it. You need to understand the rent side of the real estate market before you even get to know the buy side. Get a map of your city area and go house hunting for rental units (apartments, town houses, and condos) in each area of the city. Location is a key determinant of real estate value. By talking to renters, apartment managers, and colleagues, you will quickly ascertain what areas are more desirable than others and get a rough idea of rents for different types of rental units based on overall size, number of bedrooms and bathrooms, amenities, and so on. Remember, you're looking for investment value. You're not going to live in this house forever; you just want to acquire a good asset to provide you and your family with future income and wealth. Once you have a pretty good idea of the rent side of the market, you are ready to proceed with the next step.

Analyzing the buy side of this equation is easier with the help of a real estate agent. A few words of caution from chapter 11 bear repeating here: First, most agents work for the seller (even when they have never met). If the agent is paid by the seller, he or she has both a legal fiduciary responsibility to the seller and an economic incentive to get you to buy at the highest price. Second, most real estate laws require that if you look at a specific property through a real estate agent, you cannot buy that property through a different agent. One way to obtain a reputable agent is to use a home-buying relocation service, as is offered by USAA. USAA will recommend a brokerage firm for you, and at closing, you will be paid $200 to $1,000 on the purchase of your home, depending on the price.

Sit down with your agent and explain what you want to do. Be honest—tell the agent that you are a serious potential buyer of a property you wish to turn into a rental unit when you move. Give the agent your price range and explain that you'll need to look at a lot of properties in different areas and that you're going to bargain for a good price that gives you investment potential. Include the fact that you are particularly interested in bank-owned or VA properties that have been foreclosed upon. The idea is to convince the agent that although you know you can change agents, you are a serious player and want to get to work in earnest. Although the agent is working for potential buyers, his or her help in persuading the seller to accept your offer may come in handy.

Just as you quickly learned much about the rental market, you also will quickly learn much about the purchase market. The next step is to get serious about offers. List prices are always higher than what properties typically sell for. Select three or four available units, and have your agent go into the local real estate database and print off actual closing prices of similar units in that area for the past several years. At this point, you will have demonstrated to your agent how serious you are. This should help in giving you credibility when you negotiate the price with the seller.

Making the Offer

There are many books written about how to negotiate the price of real estate. You may wish to pursue a very aggressive strategy of multiple offers and counteroffers. Often, though, you will be constrained by the fact that you must find a place fairly quickly. Given your market research, your biggest asset is that you now know the market and won't be ripped off. As a starting point for making an offer, you can bid below the list price by about 10 percent (maybe more), even below the recent closing prices. The seller will likely reject this offer and make a counteroffer. This is normal. When you negotiate, you may do so directly or through the agent. Don't appear too eager to buy, and prepare offers for other properties to signal to the seller that you can go elsewhere.

If you counter the owner's counteroffer, you may wish at this point to meet the seller partway but ask for some helpful conditions. You may need to move in quickly, so perhaps the contract could include a provision to move in and rent until closing (very helpful if you can't close quickly and have to start working). You can also ask the seller to pay your points and buyer closing costs. Points (prepaid interest on your mortgage) are tax deductible by the buyer regardless of who pays. Additionally, this method allows the bank to essentially finance the closing costs and points in a perfectly legal manner. You can also ask the seller to pay you a repair allowance at closing (for example, perhaps $1,500 or so to pay for carpet, plaster, and painting repairs). Thus, by raising your offer, you are in fact financing costs that many home buyers must use cash to settle.

Financing the Purchase

This chapter posits that condominiums and town houses are potentially priced lower than freestanding homes in relation to their rental value. If this is true, why don't investors buy up these "underpriced" properties? The answer may lie in the fact that you have an advantage over real estate investors—you are going to live in your home. The fact is that if you live in your home, you are more likely to pay your mortgage payments than someone who is an absentee landlord investor. Remember, everybody has to live somewhere. Nonowner-occupied mortgages typically require a 30 percent down payment, while conventional occupied mortgages typically require only 10 percent or less down, and FHA mortgages require 5 percent or even less. There may even be state or local programs available to help first-time buyers. As a servicemember, you can qualify for a VA loan, which is easier to qualify for and requires nothing down!

Many buyers may wish to pay as large a down payment as possible. This is only natural—buying a home is making a large purchase financed by borrowed money, and people want to play it safe or feel good about owing less. Remember, though, that this real estate purchase is only part of a larger strategy of collecting a portfolio of assets over a lifetime. Since mortgage interest rates are usually fairly low and the interest you pay is tax deductible, it is often best to obtain a mortgage with little or no money down. Furthermore, you should package the offer to the seller to minimize the amount of total costs that you have to pay in cash. Wouldn't it be great to walk away from closing with cash? To ensure that you keep the overall risk level of your portfolio where you want it, put the cash that you were considering putting down on your home into CDs or T-bills. This will add safety while preserving liquidity in your portfolio.

Sweat Equity

Once you close on your property, you will likely live in it for several years. By taking the time to get to know your unit and fixing problems or potential problems along the way, you will have a lot of information on how to manage it. Keep records of maintenance and other things that you do to improve your home (your "sweat equity"). When you leave your home, you should strive to have it freshly painted, clean, and well maintained. Remember, renters are looking for convenience, and you want to attract renters who are picky anyway, as such renters are more likely to take better care of your home.

Rental Management

Since many servicemembers may never return to the area in which they bought a home, they are usually absentee landlords. You should definitely consider hiring a reputable property manager to advertise for and screen tenants, collect rent, provide accounting statements, and handle problems in the interior of the unit. This service should be competitively available in most cities for a fee of 10 percent or less of your gross rents, only if collected. Maintenance costs should be limited to the interior of your unit because the homeowners' association will take care of common area and exterior maintenance. Because this maintenance is handled on a large scale and on very similar units, the association management can achieve lower costs and ensure the highest quality. This is another big advantage of buying a condominium or town house over buying a freestanding home.

Other Considerations

Here are some final points to keep in mind. It is important to be sure that, on an ongoing basis, you will have enough cash inflow from a property to cover all possible cash outflows. It does you no good for a property to appreciate significantly over a twenty-year period if you couldn't hold on to it because of cash flow problems. The biggest mistake most new real estate investors make is underestimating the costs associated with real estate management. You will quickly get a good feel for market rental rates, and many of your costs (mortgage payments and insurance payments, for example) will also be easy to estimate. Don't forget that many costs (maintenance, management services, etc.) will be variable and harder to estimate. It is essential to set aside a maintenance reserve of maybe 5 to 10 percent of gross rents to cover these "unexpected" costs. Don't forget that your rental will never be occupied 100 percent of the time and set aside an allowance for this also. Make sure you are taking advantage of all of the possible tax benefits since tax benefits are one of the advantages that direct ownership can provide. Keep an eye on how much financial leverage (debt) you use. Using debt can increase your returns, but too much can ruin you. Finally, don't forget that the healthy real estate returns of the past were due, in part, to rapid price appreciation. If the future brings moderate levels of inflation, you can't expect higher selling prices to bail you out of a bad decision.

Tips on Investing in Real Assets

- Unless you have a unique talent that gives you an advantage, do not invest in most real assets (precious metals, art, collectibles, etc.) unless you are doing so as part of a hobby that you enjoy and you don't expect any financial return.
- Most individual investors should have some exposure to real estate in their investment portfolios for increased diversification.
- REITs are an effective way for small investors to include diversified real estate assets in their portfolios.
- If you own your home, you already have significant exposure to real estate.
- Direct ownership of income real estate can be appropriate for the person with the right talents and time to devote to property management.
- For investment property, look with the view of not only the best property to buy, but also the best property to rent.
- Condominiums and town houses often have higher income-to-mortgage ratios than freestanding homes and can be attractive investments.
- Use a qualified, competent firm to manage your property when you are away.
- If you pursue the direct ownership route, don't forget about the risks associated with high leverage or underestimating costs.
- Real estate is a good way to diversify your portfolio, but it should not be your only investment strategy, or even the primary part of it.

Direct ownership of rental income properties can be a good experience that provides many financial benefits to the right person with the right talents and a willingness to put in time and effort. When making the decision to invest or not invest, ask yourself if you have the right temperament for this type of endeavor. Obviously, every case will be different. Armed with this information, you will be well prepared to determine whether real estate investment may be worthwhile for you.

PART V

Planning for Retirement and Later

19

Life Insurance

Life insurance is another important component of your personal financial plan. Unfortunately, life insurance is often poorly understood, and mistakes by breadwinners with or without life insurance invariably cause great misfortune for their survivors. The goal of this chapter is to provide you with a firm understanding of how life insurance fits into your financial plan, how to determine how much life insurance you and your spouse require, and what type of policy best fits your situation. To ensure that you can find the life insurance protection you need at a cost your family can afford, you need to answer three key questions before you talk to an insurance agent:

1. Do you need life insurance at all?
2. If so, how much life insurance do you need?
3. What type of policy should you buy?

The primary function of life insurance is to provide protection for you or your survivors from the economic consequences of the death of a member of your household. Three factors complicate the buying process. First, most people hesitate to confront their own death or the death of a loved one. Second, some life insurance policies have both an insurance component and an investment component, which can make it difficult to remember that the primary goal of life insurance protection should be replacing family income in the event of a breadwinner's or a family service provider's death. Finally, there is the somewhat mysterious nature of the life insurance business. The use of statistics and actuarial (life projection) techniques tends to discourage even the most careful shopper. Adding to the confusion are the special terms developed by the life insurance industry to make the subject more appealing and the product more marketable. The terms *premium, permanent insurance,* and *term insurance* must be translated so that the typical buyer can understand the full range of options. Because of all this, many people are so confused that they decide to simply choose an agent rather than the best product. This can be a very expensive decision.

There is over $11 trillion of life insurance in force in the United States alone. It is big business. The life insurance industry is a business designed to produce a profit for the company and an income for the agent as well as to protect your family's economic security. Because insurance agents operate primarily on commissions, they have a natural incentive to sell those policies that produce high commissions. Reputable agents will attempt to match an insurance program to your needs, but you should be aware of the substantial commissions involved and the possibility for high-pressure sales techniques. By doing your homework before talking to an agent, you increase the likelihood of making the best decisions for your family.

WHAT IS THE PRINCIPLE BEHIND INSURANCE?

Insurance is based on a very simple concept: The cost of infrequent but catastrophic events can be spread among a large group with a small cost to each member. Individuals share the risk at a fraction of the cost of the catastrophic event. Life insurance is perhaps the best example of insurance that "pays off" for an event that happens most infrequently (once in a lifetime) but with truly catastrophic effects. It is not the insured that life insurance is designed to protect. Life insurance is for the future well-being of the survivors of the policyholder. The policyholder benefits only from the peace of mind that the insurance provides.

What life insurance actually provides is protection for your survivors from the economic consequences of your premature death. Insurance will not help with the emotional loss, although it should remove the fear of economic hardship. The amount of insurance does not demonstrate your love for your family, nor does it delay your departure from this world. Life insurance is not an investment, although some policies have an investment component. Too much insurance results in high premiums that reduce your monthly budget and therefore your ability to enjoy other good things in life. A clear understanding of what one is buying, and why, is critical to develop a life insurance plan that is best for you, not your insurance company.

WHAT DO ALL THOSE LIFE INSURANCE TERMS MEAN?

The life insurance industry uses specific language to describe its products. Understanding this language is the first step you must undertake before you are ready to answer the three key questions. The face amount, the policy period, the premium, and savings are part of any life insurance policy and can be varied to fit the individual needs of each policyholder.

Face Amount

The size of your insurance coverage is determined by the face amount of the policy. This is the amount paid to the beneficiary (a person you designate) in the event of your death. The larger the face amount, the higher the benefit to the beneficiary but the higher the cost of the policy.

Policy Period

You can buy a life insurance policy for any length of time: a year or as long as your entire life. The premium you pay is often related to the length of the policy period. Although some policies are for a specific period, a policy can be renewed unless it is explicitly nonrenewable. Reentry policies can be renewed, but renewal requires a new physical examination, and the premiums may be recalculated based on the examination results. Renewable policies guarantee renewal without conditions, and the premium will change only with your age, not the condition of your health. Because the insurance company does not have the right to end its obligation to insure you or to raise your premiums should your health deteriorate, the premiums will be somewhat higher for renewable policies.

In general, nonrenewable policies and policies with shorter renewal periods or that base future premiums on new physical exams mean lower annual premiums today. Companies charge lower premiums for these policies because they have a chance to learn more at each renewal point about the factors (health, in particular) that affect the probability of death, and they can refuse insurance or raise premiums for very poor risks. If you are in excellent health, the cheapest possible coverage in the short run will be a one-year nonrenewable term policy. If you want a renewable policy, you will have to pay more.

Premium

A premium is nothing more than a payment, like a car payment or a mortgage payment on a house. The premium must pay the insurance company for administering the policy and pay the agent's commission, and with certain types of policies, part of the payment goes to a form of "savings." Premiums can stay the same, increase, or decrease over the length of the policy, depending on your policy type.

Savings

Permanent and variable insurance policies (discussed in the next section) build up a cash value and can be used as a method of savings. There are several advantages to this type of savings: You can borrow from your account (you will be charged interest for borrowing); after a period of years, your insurance policy can be paid up and you will no longer need to make premium payments; or you can end the policy and remove your "savings" portion to spend or invest elsewhere. There are also disadvantages: You typically earn a lower rate of interest on these savings than on alternative financial investments, and because these policies are both insurance and savings, their premiums will be higher.

WHAT TYPES OF LIFE INSURANCE POLICIES ARE THERE?

There are three main types of life insurance: term, which lasts for a specific period, with no savings component; permanent, in which premiums are paid until your death but also build savings; and variable, which has a flexible structure designed to allow greater return on the savings portion of the policy. Within these major categories, there are many variations that will allow you to meet your life insurance needs. As a policyholder gets older and the chances of a "premature" death increase, there may be a problem with steadily rising premiums.

To avoid this problem, you may select level term insurance or permanent insurance. Whatever the fine points, the underlying principle of distributing the risk over a large group to make it bearable remains the goal of any type of insurance. As we discuss each of the specialized types of life insurance, think about how the different options fit your personal needs.

Term Insurance

Term insurance protects the policyholder for a specified time period—one year, five years, twenty years, or more. It is pure insurance: The policy pays off only if you die within the specified period. In this sense it only provides protection to your survivors from the economic effects of your death. It has no savings feature and thus no cash value, so you cannot borrow against the policy. Term insurance must be renewed when the term is completed. Normally, renewal requires a physical examination, although some companies may relax this requirement. Since none of your premium is going toward savings, term premiums are initially far lower than permanent policy premiums. Thus, a young person who has a need for a larger death benefit, perhaps in excess of $200,000, but whose income is low may be able to afford the needed coverage by using term insurance.

You should be aware that many agents might try to steer you away from term insurance (or temporary insurance, as the agents like to call it) toward permanent insurance. Many agents sell both permanent (insurance plus savings) and term (insurance alone) insurance policies. Premiums for term insurance are based on the expected number of deaths per year for a given age group—and this number can be determined quite accurately using standard data, which makes for good competition among companies as they bid for your business with premiums only slightly above this base cost.

By contrast, the savings component of the permanent insurance policies requires a larger premium, and since the premiums collected greatly exceed the expected payout for death benefits, the insurance company can make a good income investing the "excess premium" in bonds and stocks. As a result, few of the larger companies will push term insurance, and they adjust their commission incentives to make this very clear to their sales personnel. When agents do sell term insurance, it is often with the goal of converting the policy to permanent insurance as soon as the policyholder can be persuaded to do so. Fortunately, some good companies do specialize in term insurance, and a number cater especially to the military community.

There is an apparent disadvantage to term insurance: As you get older, the premiums increase. At age twenty, you might be able to get a $100,000 term policy for approximately $150 per year, but at age forty-five, that same policy could cost you over $300 per year. The increase in premiums would eventually make term more expensive than the premiums on permanent insurance (bought now) for the same face amount. However, as we will see later, the insurance portion of permanent insurance effectively has the same characteristics. Also, as you grow older, your insurance needs will likely peak and then lessen. Once children are through with school, your insurance needs should decrease. You may not even need any life insurance when you are older. If you do, however, several different types of term insurance are offered to partially alleviate this deficiency.

Level Term. The face value and the premium for level term insurance remain the same throughout the period of coverage. This type of insurance was designed to lower the high cost of term insurance in the later years of the policy. One method used to calculate the premiums averages the payments so that an equal payment is paid each month, in effect overpaying the first half of the policy period and underpaying the last half. Even if the term was forty-five years (perhaps until anticipated retirement), the premium would still be less than a permanent policy for the same amount of insurance, because there is no savings component to the policy.

Servicemembers Group Life Insurance (SGLI) is level term insurance. Currently, a servicemember may elect to take up to $250,000 of coverage for 85 cents per month per $10,000 of coverage, regardless of age. This is very inexpensive insurance for older officers and noncommissioned officers. In effect, the large numbers of young servicemembers make possible low premiums for the older servicemembers. For this reason, and because it is convertible after you leave the service, SGLI should be the basic building block of your family's insurance program.

Effective 1 November 2001, spouses and children are automatically covered under family coverage under SGLI. The benefits are automatic: $100,000 for spousal coverage and $10,000 for each child. The rates are established based on the spouse's age, while the children's coverage is free for the soldier. Soldiers may elect to reduce or decline the spousal coverage in $10,000 increments, but the children's coverage can not be declined or reduced. The coverage start date for recently married or new parents will be based on the soldier's DEERS data for date of marriage or birth date of the child. The spousal coverage can be converted to a commercial policy upon retirement or separation, but the children's coverage terminates.

Decreasing Term. Decreasing term insurance has a constant premium over the term of the coverage, but the face value of the policy declines to reflect the higher risk of death as age increases. As an example, a $10 monthly premium might buy a twenty-five-year-old male insurance protection of $100,000; a man in his fifties would get only $15,000 of term insurance for this premium. A decreasing term policy may make a lot of sense if your insurance needs decrease as you get older. For instance, if you had an obligation that was decreasing, such as a home mortgage, matching decreasing benefits would also make excellent sense. Mortgage insurance, a form of decreasing term, is a fairly common (but often expensive) way of dealing with this particular situation and is not recommended.

Renewable, Nonrenewable, and Reentry Term. These term policies have special features that allow you to renew them at the end of the policy period if you meet certain standards. Renewable term eliminates the physical examination requirement: A person who was injured in combat or contracted cancer would still be able to renew the term policy. In this respect, term insurance is not really "temporary" at all. This renewal feature will not be available past age seventy when term insurance is no longer available or becomes too expensive. As noted, you may not need insurance coverage in old age when your children are on their own and you have sufficient assets to provide a comfortable retirement. Most of the companies that cater to the military sell renewable term.

The second type, nonrenewable, means just that: The policy ends and the policyholder must buy new insurance, qualifying for it with a new physical exam. Reentry term is less expensive than renewable term insurance. You must, however, pass a physical after the end of the term to "reenter" the low-cost policy. The danger is that if you fail the physical examination, you cannot reenter and must pay a higher premium or find a different policy. Finding a new policy can be quite expensive (or even impossible) if you have failed a physical examination. As an example, let's see what happens with a thirty-five-year-old nonsmoking male who buys a $250,000 five-year reentry term policy. His annual premium starts out at $400 and gradually rises to $550 over the five-year term. At the reentry point, the now forty-year-old male takes a new physical exam. If he passes, his premium goes down to $500 and gradually rises from there; if he fails, his premium starts off at $750. At forty-five years of age, the numbers would be $600 (pass) and $1,100 (not pass).

In comparison, once you pass the initial physical examination for a renewable term policy, your premium is the same as that for all others of the same age, regardless of what subsequently happens to your health. Reentry term is best for only a very select group: people who need a substantial amount of insurance for a short period of time. For others, the cost of reentry goes up when they can least afford it. For individuals seeking insurance, the risk of reentry term probably outweighs the small savings.

Convertible Term. Many term policies offer a feature that allows you to convert the term policy to some form of permanent insurance without having to provide evidence of insurability, usually through a medical examination. While you will pay the higher premium associated with your age at conversion (some policies will allow a retroactive calculation to the original age of buying the policy), you have protected yourself from the loss of insurability. This is a very desirable feature, as it protects you and your survivors in the event your insurability changes for the worse at the time that your term policy expires.

Permanent Insurance

The words permanent, ordinary, and whole life insurance have the same meaning in the insurance industry. These policies combine pure (term) insurance with an automatic savings feature (called "cash value") that provides the companies with funds that they invest to produce most of their profits. Insurance salespeople are offered the largest commissions for selling permanent policies and therefore emphasize them in their sales presentations.

TABLE 19-1
TERM LIFE INSURANCE

Advantages	Disadvantages
• Initial premiums generally are lower than those for permanent insurance, allowing you to buy higher levels of coverage at a younger age when the need for protection often is greatest. • It's good for covering needs that will disappear in time, such as mortgages, children's education, or car loans.	• Premiums increase or coverage decreases as you grow older. • Coverage may terminate at the end of the term or become too expensive to continue. • The policy generally doesn't offer cash value or paid-up insurance.

Perhaps "ordinary insurance" really refers to the fact that this is the type of insurance that a company would prefer to sell. Permanent can be explained by the important cash value feature. As years go by, the interest earnings on the savings will accumulate, slowly at first, but then faster in later years, until there is enough in the account to cover the face value of the policy. This, in effect, gradually replaces the insurance provided by the company with your own savings. The company eventually accumulates enough of a cash value for the policyholder to simply hand it back to the survivors when the policyholder dies. Permanent insurance is really a combination of a decreasing term insurance policy bundled with an enforced savings feature. The company, in paying off the face value totally out of cash value, would no longer be providing any pure insurance. These accumulated savings represent a cash value that may be borrowed against (with an interest charge) after a number of years.

An advantage of permanent insurance is that you are insured for your whole life for a constant premium. No matter when you die, if your policy is still in force, the company will pay the face amount to your beneficiary. Although the payments are much higher than term insurance early in life, they are less later because of the accumulated savings portion of the premium. The majority of permanent or whole life policies fall into two categories: straight life and limited-payment life.

Straight Life. Straight life (also called whole or ordinary life) is the most common form of life insurance sold. It provides both protection and savings for the policyholder, who pays premiums throughout his or her life and builds up a cash value in the policy. It has the same premium throughout the life of the policy (which is where the term straight comes from); the premium charged to you at age twenty is the same premium charged at fifty. The premium amount is determined primarily by your age when you buy the policy; the older you are when you start, the higher the premium. Your physical condition can also play a role.

Whole life policies build a cash value that steadily grows each year you have the policy. Be careful concerning this savings feature. If you close out your account, especially in the first few years, you will not have much savings. For example, one company's most popular permanent policy returns an average interest rate of 0.2 percent on the accumulating savings if you cancel it at the ten-year point. Policy cancellations are not unusual. A Senate subcommittee gathered data on sixty of the leading U.S. insurance companies and found that 25 percent of permanent policy buyers discontinue their policies within the first year, 46 percent within ten years, and nearly 60 percent before twenty years.

Although the industry's "average" policy has provided a return of 2.8 percent at the ten-year point, the return does depend on the length of time you keep the policy. Most policies forfeit all cash value if the policy is in effect for less than two years, with the average break-even point at eight years, which is where your accumulated savings have earned a 0 percent return. At twenty years, the average interest earned on savings in whole life policies has been 4.4 percent. Interest does increase slightly after twenty years but stays near the 5 percent level up to fifty years. Generally, a savings account at your local bank will earn as much interest as, and in some cases even more than, the savings portion of a whole life policy. However, the whole life policy accumulates interest in a tax-deferred fashion; no taxes are paid on the gains in your account until the funds are actually withdrawn.

Another often-stated feature of whole life is the availability of loans against the cash value of the policy. In 1997, most companies charged 6 to 7.5 percent for policy loans. Although this is less expensive than most signature loans, you must realize that you are really borrowing from your own savings, which are left to accumulate at a lower rate. Policy loans may not have to be paid back; however, borrowing from your policy in this fashion will reduce the death benefits of the policy by the amount you withdraw. This feature can come in quite handy as a ready source for short-term loans.

Limited-Payment Life. A limited-payment insurance policy provides life insurance protection throughout the policyholder's life similar to whole life. Instead of the same payment throughout, you pay the same (higher) premium for a limited number of years (perhaps ten, twenty, or thirty). At that point, the policy is "paid up," meaning that no further premiums are required. In comparison, a whole life policy does not get paid up until you reach age one hundred. Insurance protection, in the sense that the beneficiaries get the face amount of the policy upon the policyholder's death, remains throughout the policyholder's life.

Of course, the earlier the policy is paid, the greater the premium must be, so in the short run, these are usually the most expensive of all life insurance policy premiums. For example, a thirty-five-year-old man who purchases a $10,000 twenty-year limited-payment policy might pay $340 per year versus $220 for a whole life policy. Since the payments are so large, the amount of insurance that can be bought with a budgeted amount each month is smaller. Thus, a young couple using limited-payment life may be underinsured, even though they are paying a lot for insurance. These policies are also the most profitable for insurance companies, since more money comes to them up front.

TABLE 19-2
PERMANENT LIFE INSURANCE

Advantages	Disadvantages
• As long as the premiums are paid, protection is guaranteed for life.	• Required premium levels may make it hard to buy enough protection.
• Premium costs can be fixed or flexible to meet personal financial needs.	• It may be more costly than term insurance if you don't keep it long enough.
• The policy accumulates a cash value against which you can borrow. (Loans must be paid back with interest or your beneficiaries will receive a reduced death benefit.) You can borrow against the policy's cash value to pay premiums or use the cash value to provide paid-up insurance.	• Interest returns on the savings portion may be below market returns.
• The policy's cash value can be surrendered, in total or in part, for cash or converted into an annuity. (An annuity is an insurance product that provides an income for a person's lifetime or a specific period.)	
• A provision or rider can be added to a policy that gives you the option to purchase additional insurance without taking a medical exam or having to furnish evidence of insurability.	

Variable Insurance

In the 1970s, high interest rates available on alternative savings vehicles made the low rates of return on the savings component in whole life and limited-payment life financially unattractive. Sales of these products declined, and the insurance industry developed a whole new range of products with higher rates of return and increased flexibility. Some of these plans allow the policyholder to move between term and permanent insurance for a small fee, so that the savings and insurance components of the policies can be adjusted to meet the customer's needs over a period of years. Other new policies simply improve the return on the savings component of the policy. The most common types of these new policies are adjustable life, universal life, and variable life. Most of these policies also come in a "single-premium" variety, with one massive up-front premium that would not appeal to most servicemembers.

Adjustable Life. Adjustable life insurance allows policyholders to adjust the terms of the policy as their needs change. Policies can start off as whole life and be converted to term insurance by lowering the premiums or increasing the face value of the policy. Or the policy can initially offer lower-cost term coverage with little or no cash value buildup. Then, when the policyholder is better able to pay, the policy can be changed to permanent insurance with higher premiums and the accumulation of cash value. Dividends can be used to pay premiums or to increase the face value of the policy. The major advantage of this type of policy is flexibility. The interest rate earned is not much better than that of standard whole life policies. The disadvantage of adjustable life is that the policy owner may not have bought either the best term policy or the best permanent policy, but a compromise between the two.

Universal Life. Universal life is a combination of term insurance with a tax-deferred savings account that is tied to some market interest rate. In many respects, universal life acts like an adjustable life policy in that the face value and premiums can be easily adjusted to meet changing needs. The major difference is that the interest rate paid on cash values in universal life is closer to market rates than in whole life policies, so the investment portion grows faster. Universal life usually invests the savings portion of the premium in short- or medium-term bond investments that in the past have offered superior rates of return compared with whole life returns. The return, however, is not guaranteed; what you earn depends on the actual performance of the insurance company's investment portfolios.

It is probably true that the rate of return on a universal life policy's savings component will be higher than the return on a similar whole life policy, simply because the company attempts to tie the return to the performance of its investments. However, it is not clear that the actual return you will earn on a universal policy will be much higher when all the additional fees and restrictions are considered. Beware of sales claims that advertise a rate of return paid on the cash value after all fees and costs have been deducted from your premium payment. The relevant rate of return should be calculated based on what you have paid in minus the amount necessary to pay for the pure insurance, an amount that may be approximated by the cost of a decreasing, renewable term policy.

It's important to shop for the best universal life policy, as different companies offer slightly different options. Some companies will pay only 3 percent interest on the first $1,000 in the savings portion of the account; other companies allow you to vary the amount of your insurance coverage without incurring additional fees; and still other companies charge high first-year fees. The return on universal life insurance policies is usually guaranteed for one year but then fluctuates up or down over the long term with market conditions. Many companies will guarantee a high rate for the first year, and then a nominal rate after that. Look for maximum flexibility, highest guaranteed minimum rates of return, and lowest fees.

Variable Life. Variable life policies are designed to allow the insured to earn higher rates of return by choosing to put the cash value component of the policy into higher-risk investments: common stocks, bonds, money market instruments, or government securities. There is no guaranteed cash surrender value, because the value depends on the return actually earned on the investments. Additionally, you will not know exactly what the face amount of your coverage is, although some minimum is normally guaranteed. If the investment portion of your policy does well, the cash surrender value and face amount of your policy will rise. If your investment does poorly, the face amount of your policy will decline. It is important to recognize that the death benefit your survivors will receive from a variable life policy depends in part on the performance of the investment strategy you have the insurance company follow for you.

For example, if you choose to have the company invest the savings component of your variable life premium in common stocks, the death benefit paid to your survivors will be higher or lower, depending on how stock prices change. It is true that in the past long-term bonds and common stocks have paid higher average returns than more conservative investments, but it is also true that the variability of those returns has been much greater. Beware of counting on an assumed rate of return on your investment portfolio to deliver the insurance protection your family needs. The rates of return you may see in variable life sales literature are not guaranteed. Base the amount of insurance you buy on your family's needs, and be sure what you need is guaranteed to be paid if you die. The potential gains from higher investment returns in variable life policies should be viewed as a means to earn higher expected returns on the cash value by accepting greater investment risk.

ANSWERS TO THREE KEY QUESTIONS

Now that you have a basic understanding of life insurance, we can begin to answer the three critical questions.

Do You Need Life Insurance?

Since the primary purpose of life insurance is to protect your survivors from the adverse economic consequences of your premature death, if you have no survivors, you may not have a need for life insurance beyond the amount necessary to pay any outstanding debts and settle your estate. There are, however, other considerations that we will discuss shortly.

If you are married or have young children who are primarily dependent on you for their support, then you probably need some life insurance to protect your survivors. Even if you currently have no children, are not married, and have no outstanding debt, you must consider other factors in answering this critical question. If you are planning on getting married soon or have children on the horizon, you may still want to explore insurance options.

How Much Life Insurance Do You Need?

The total insurance outstanding in the United States is almost $120,000 per household. That is far too much insurance for most single servicemembers, and far too little for those who are married with children. Rules of thumb by themselves are dangerous, so you should make your own estimate of how much insurance your family needs. Don't forget to do the analysis separately for your spouse as well as yourself. In many families, the wife is grossly underinsured, even if the husband's insurance plan is well thought out.

The general idea in determining your insurance needs is to estimate your family's actual financial situation in the event you die. Life insurance is not a measure of devotion to loved ones or a monument to your self-importance. It is insurance in case of premature death, and it should be used to protect dependents against undue financial hardship. If you are not alive to provide for your family, your insurance coverage should be sufficient to enable them to live as you would want them to live. We recommend that you determine the expenses your survivors will incur in the years following your death and the income they will receive. By matching income with expenses, you can easily see any shortfalls (there may be none) that are best covered by life insurance. There are two methods you can use to calculate your insurance needs.

Method One: Net Present Value. Start by assuming that you die this year. Make a time line of your survivors' ages from today into the future. We recommend that you take the time line out at least as far as your youngest child turning age eighteen, but this method works for time horizons much longer than that. Once your time line is made, you can begin to place expenses and income at the appropriate points on a time line that reflects the year in which you expect the income or expense to occur. The following analysis should all be done in today's dollars.

You should plan for a basic monthly income for the family, plus additional needs such as education for the children, special medical care for predictable problems, and a reserve for emergencies. These needs usually arise during known periods. As you survive longer, some of the needs disappear; for example, if your children are grown and through college, there is no need to leave money for their education. Thus you will need to reevaluate your insurance needs periodically to make sure your survivors' situation hasn't changed. In any case, there is never a requirement to make your family wealthy upon your death; buy only the coverage for identifiable needs.

Estimate Expenses. You must first estimate family expenses. Some will be one-time expenses, such as for a funeral; others will be ongoing, such as food and shelter. The following are some of the expenses that life insurance should cover:

Expenses incidental to death: These include illness expenses, hospital bills, burial costs, and possibly moving expenses for your family. Many of these expenses will not affect military families, because their benefits provide for them. (Refer to chapters 3 and 20 through 23 for details.) An insurance industry rule of thumb to cover these expenses is to buy insurance equal to one year's take-home pay; however, $7,000 (measured in 2002 dollars) should be sufficient for most military families, because many expenses are covered by the military.

TABLE 19-3
DOD DEATH BENEFITS

Type	Amount
Body preparation and casket	$1,750
Interment private cemetery	2,000
Interment government cemetery	110

Monthly expenses: Simply estimate the monthly expenses you believe your survivors will face. If you don't know where to start in estimating these expenses, a good rule of thumb is two-thirds of your present monthly income for those years when children will be at home, and one-half after they have left.

One-time expenses: Be sure to include one-time expenses such as a college education for the children, paying off a home mortgage, or buying a new car. You may also want to pay off any outstanding credit card bills and personal loans.

Estimate Income. Fortunately, military servicemembers' survivors continue to receive income from service-related sources, as explained in chapters 3 and 22. This income includes Social Security survivor benefits, Dependency and Indemnity Compensation, and for the retirement eligible or retired member, Survivor Benefit Plan benefits (see chapter 23). Other sources of income include a death gratuity, Social Security children's education benefits, war orphans educational assistance, lump-sum death payment, and redeeming the accrued leave of the servicemember. Finally, the survivors have income potential. Children, for example, are often responsible for a certain portion of their higher education and will work summers and weekends to help achieve their educational goals.

Your estate will provide at least part of the established future needs. Your financial goal should be to accumulate enough assets to cover your family's financial requirements in the event of your death. To the extent you are successful in saving and investing, the protection provided by life insurance is less necessary. Remember that life insurance is needed only to provide an "instant estate" to meet the financial needs of survivors. You can easily estimate the amount of income your accumulated financial assets will provide by multiplying them by the interest rate (less the inflation rate) you think they will be earning. Your spouse's earning power should also be considered as a source of family income. Many spouses today are generating income that greatly reduces the requirement for insurance on your life. However, the earnings of a spouse probably should be covered with separate insurance on him or her. In some families, the required coverage may be dramatically reduced if no children are involved, and the spouse can go to school and learn a skill or profession.

Estimate Shortfalls or Windfalls. Once you've estimated your survivors' income and expenses for the years ahead, you need to find those time periods in which an "income gap" exists—where estimated expenses exceed estimated income. There may be years when estimated income is larger than estimated expenses. In those years, your survivors will be able to save to meet some of the future income gaps.

Net Present Value of Your Insurance Needs. The net present value of all the income gaps, both positive (where expenses exceed income) and negative (where income exceeds expenses), is the amount of insurance protection you need to prevent financial hardship for your survivors. If you do not know how to calculate the net present value, refer to Appendix D for present value and time value of money tables. The real problem with finding the net present value is deciding what discount rate to use. That requires some explanation. The net present value of the income gaps is the amount of money that, if you had it all today and invested it at a rate of interest equal to the discount rate, would grow to a sum large enough to cover all the income gaps you identify. Thus, if you assume the lump sum (that is, the proceeds from life insurance your family will receive if you die now) will accumulate interest at a high rate, you need less insurance. On the other hand, if you assume a low interest return on the insurance death benefit, you need to provide for a larger benefit.

Be realistic in assessing the rate of return your survivors will be able to earn. Perhaps more important, be sure your family understands that the insurance proceeds they receive if you die cannot be spent indiscriminately; they must be saved and invested to meet future needs. Since inflation is always a potential threat but was ignored in developing your income and expense numbers above, you should use a "real rate of interest"—the actual interest rate minus the projected rate of inflation (this concept was discussed in chapters 2 and 4). For example, if you expect the insurance proceeds to go into a money market account paying 7 percent interest and the annual inflation rate is 4 percent, then the purchasing power of the proceeds will earn a real interest rate of 3 percent. For your net present value calculations, you should then use 3 percent as the discount factor. In modern times, the real yields (interest rates) for very secure investments (such as bonds) historically have been approximately 1 to 3 percent. More sophisticated investors can, by accepting greater risk, earn real rates of return of 4 percent or more. In our illustrations, we have used an assumed real rate of return of 3 percent per year. When you have calculated the present value of all the income gaps, you have the amount of financial risk for your survivors that should be covered by insurance on your life.

Estimating the amount of life insurance you need is a time-consuming but important exercise. It can be done fairly easily using a computer-based spreadsheet program. Careful analysis is required if you are to get the amount of insurance you need but no more than that. To help you understand how the analysis is done, we present an example of an actual family situation.

Example of the Net Present Value Method. In this example, we determine the life insurance needs for the family of a twenty-six-year-old captain or Navy lieutenant (O-3) with five years of military service, a twenty-four-year-old spouse, and a two-year-old child. We assume the officer already has a $250,000 SGLI life insurance policy. In the analysis, we establish the economic consequences of the officer's death by finding the gaps in the family's needs for future income and answering the second question: How much insurance is required to fill the gaps? This process is used by many insurance agents to show clients how much more insurance they need. Agents often present a computerized analysis based on information you provide, but as this example shows, you can do the same thing yourself. And you are less likely to overestimate the true amount by a large margin, as a few unscrupulous insurance agents might do. If you do this exercise, you will better understand what the insurance agent is explaining to you.

The first step is to determine critical times when large expenses arrive and when major changes in survivor benefits occur. As discussed in chapter 22, for example, the amount survivors receive from Social Security depends on the number and ages of children. In our example, the important time phases are as follows:

- Phase 1 (years from today 0–14): Child is under sixteen; spouse and child collect Social Security.
- Phase 2 (years 15–16): Child reaches sixteen; spouse loses Social Security payments.
- Phase 3 (years 17–20): Child reaches eighteen and attends college.
- Phase 4 (years 21–41): Spouse is alone and under sixty-five; no Social Security coverage.
- Phase 5 (years 42–57): Time span covers period from age sixty-five to life expectancy of spouse (approximately 80.5, based on Table 19-4); spouse collects Social Security.

In phase 1, both the surviving spouse and child will be eligible for Dependency and Indemnity Compensation (DIC) and Social Security benefits. When phase 2 arrives, the spouse no longer is eligible for Social Security benefits because the child turns sixteen; however, the child's benefits continue until age eighteen. The child's earning potential also grows dramatically. Phase 3 represents a point where both income and expenses will change significantly. Once the child reaches age eighteen, Social Security benefits end, steady part-time income and major college expenses begin. In phase 4, the spouse will be receiving DIC, as in phases 1, 2, and 3, but will not be receiving Social Security. In phase 5, the spouse reaches age sixty-five and will again receive both DIC and Social Security benefits (reduced benefits could be taken at an earlier age). See chapters 3 and 22 for the details on eligibility for DIC and Social Security payments.

TABLE 19-4
LIFE EXPECTANCIES

Expected Remaining Life

Age	Male	Female
0	73.8	79.5
15	62.8	69.1
25	53.0	59.3
35	43.3	49.4
45	33.8	39.7
55	24.9	30.3
65	16.7	21.3
75	10.2	13.4
85	5.8	7.6

Example: A 25-year-old male has a life expectancy of 53.0 more years for a projected total life of 78.0 years. A 25-year-old female has a life expectancy of 59.3 more years for a total life of 84.3 years. The longer female life expectancy is the reason life insurance is less expensive for women.

Source: *Statistical Abstract of the United States,* 2001, online.

The second step is to estimate expenses the family will have in the phases outlined above. Consider three categories: expenses incidental to death; large one-time expenses; and monthly living expenses for each phase. Because the officer is on active duty, most of the expenses for a funeral and burial will be borne by the government, but we will assume the need for $7,000 to pay any expenses not covered. Large one-time expenses include repayment of debts, college funds, and other such needs. We will assume the family has debts of $18,000 that it would want to pay off in the event of the officer's death. To help with the child's college costs, the family wants to have $20,000 per year (in today's dollars) for the four years during phase 3. Finally, for provision of monthly living expenses, we allow for two-thirds of current income while the child is still under eighteen, and one-half of current income after the child leaves home in phase 3. Thus, for phases 1 and 2, we want to provide $3,106 per month ($37,272 per year), and for phases 3 to 5, $2,318 per month ($27,816 per year). These calculations include basic pay, BAH, and BAS, which total $4,637. Don't forget about housing expenses; government quarters will no longer be available to your family after you are gone.

The third step is to estimate income that will be available in each of the phases in the event the officer dies today and to inventory assets already accumulated that will be available to meet future needs. In our example, we will assume that the family has available assets of $15,000 ($5,000 in a money market fund as an emergency reserve and another $10,000 in a stock mutual fund set aside for the child's education). We decide not to count the $5,000 emergency reserve, as we want to leave it untouched for the family's use. We also need to know how much income DIC and Social Security will pay the officer's survivors in each phase. Using the information in chapters 3 and 22, we identify the sources of income that will be available in the event of the officer's death:

1. Lump-sum payments at officer's death.
   - VA death gratuity: $6,000.
   - Social Security death benefit: $255.
   - Fifteen days' accrued leave (assumed in this example): $1,744.
2. VA survivor benefits.
   - Phases 1 and 2: $911 DIC + $229 per child = $1,140 per month.
   - Phase 3: $911 DIC + $588 per student = $1,499 per month.
   - Phases 4 and 5: $911 DIC per month.
3. Social Security benefits. First we must calculate the primary insurance amount (PIA). For this officer, we estimate the PIA to be about $2,093. (See chapter 22 for PIA calculations, or contact your local Social Security office.) We estimate the Social Security benefits as follows:
   - Phase 1: $2,093 × 0.75 for spouse + $2,093 × 0.75 for child = $3,139 per month.
   - Phase 2: $2,093 × 0.75 for the child = $1,569 per month.
   - Phases 3 and 4: No Social Security benefits.
   - Phase 5: $2,093 for spouse.

You must remember to add in income sources such as work, which survivors are expected to undertake. In phases 3 and 4, spouse and children may be working.

The fourth step is to total all income and assets available in each year of the phases and do the same for the expenses. We will then look for gaps where the expenses exceed the income and assets available. It is these gaps that we need to fill with life insurance. Calculating the annual surplus or deficit in each phase, we find the following:

At death:				
Expenses:				
Incidental to death:	$6,000			
Pay off loans:	18,000			
Minus				
Income:				
Liquid assets:	10,000			
Lump-sum payments:	7,999			
Equals				
Deficit or (Surplus):	6,001			
Phase 1: Years 0 to 14				
Expenses:	3,106	per month	$37,272	per year
Minus				
Income:	4,278	per month	51,336	per year
Equals				
Phase 1 Deficit or (Surplus):			(14,064)	per year
Phase 2: Years 15 to 16				
Expenses:	3,106	per month	37,272	per year
Minus				
Income:	2,709	per month	32,508	per year
Equals				
Phase 2 Deficit or (Surplus):			(4,764)	per year
Phase 3: Years 17 to 20				
Expenses:	2,318	per month	27,816	per year
For college:			20,000	per year
Minus				
Income:	911	per month	10,932	per year
Equals				
Phase 3 Deficit or (Surplus):			36,884	per year
Phase 4: Years 21 to 41				
Expenses:	2,318	per month	27,816	per year
Minus				
Income:	911	per month	10,932	per year
Equals				
Phase 4 Deficit or (Surplus):			16,884	per year
Phase 5: Years 42 to 57				
Expenses:	2,318	per month	27,816	per year
Minus				
Income:	3,044	per month	36,048	per year
Equals				
Phase 5 Deficit or (Surplus):			(8,232)	per year

Now all we need to do is to bring the annual figures back to their present value at an appropriate real rate of interest and add them up. The resulting sum is the amount of insurance required to cover future needs in the event of the officer's death. To find the present values, we use the techniques and present value tables illustrated in Appendix D to convert annual amounts to equivalent lump sums and then convert those lump sums back to their present values. It may be helpful to organize the calculations on a worksheet like that shown in Table 19-5. To complete the worksheet, we record data as follows:

Line 1: Write down the number of years until each phase begins.

Line 2: Write down the number of years in each phase.

Line 3: Write down the factor from Table D-1 that gives the present value of $1 received or paid *N* years in the future, using an appropriate interest rate (we used 3 percent). For line 3, *N* is the number of years until the phase begins, found on line 1.

Line 4: Write down the factor from Table D-2 that gives the present value of an equal annual flow of payments that lasts for *N* years, using an appropriate interest rate. For line 4, *N* is the length of the phase from line 2.

Line 5: Multiply the present value factors in lines 3 and 4 together. This number represents the present value of $1 received annually for the number of years in each phase.

Line 6: Write down the deficit or surplus for each phase that you calculated above.

Line 7: Multiply the discount factor on line 5 by the number of dollars of annual surplus or deficit in each phase (line 6) to find the present value of the surplus or deficit.

Line 8: Add the present value of all deficits (subtracting the present value of all surpluses) in each phase in line 7. One optional enhancement that we include is not to count any surplus occurring during the final phase. This makes sense because the Social Security laws change so frequently that it would not be prudent to count on a surplus during your spouse's final years (taking the risk that later changes in the law would leave that spouse in poverty). Of course, you would always count a deficit in any period.

Line 9: Add the deficit (subtract the surplus) computed for the initial period.

Line 10: Subtract the amount of life insurance already provided; don't forget SGLI.

Line 11: The result is the amount of additional life insurance the family needs.

As stated previously, we assumed that the proceeds from the insurance policy would be invested to earn 3 percent after inflation and taxes. As we have shown in chapter 14, to earn even this much we will need to use a combination of bonds and stocks, because very safe investments like savings accounts historically have not provided a 3 percent rate of return after inflation and taxes. In Table 19-5, we have used data from the 3 percent column in Tables D-1 and D-2. You should check the tables against Table 19-5 to see how we found the present value factors used. In the case of the officer in our example, we find that his $250,000 SGLI policy provides adequate insurance coverage. However, to illustrate the steps that you would take to buy additional life insurance, we will continue our discussion as if additional insurance were required.

TABLE 19-5
LIFE INSURANCE WORKSHEET

Line	Description	Phase 1	Phase 2	Phase 3	Phase 4	Phase 5
1	Start year	0	14	16	20	41
2	Length of phase	14	2	4	21	16
3	PV factor from start of phase (Appendix D-1, 3%)	1.0	0.661	0.623	0.554	0.298
4	Annuity factor for length of phase (Appendix D-2, 3%)	11.296	1.913	3.717	15.415	12.561
5	Discount factor (line 3 × line 4)	11.296	1.265	2.316	8.539	3.743
6	Annual deficit or (surplus)	$(14,064)	$(4,764)	$36,884	$16,884	$(8,232)
7	PV of phase deficit or (surplus) (line 5 × line 6)	$(158,867)	$(6,026)	$85,423	$144,172	$30,812
8	Total of PVs for all phases' deficits	$95,514				
9	Add initial period deficit or (surplus)	$16,001				
10	Subtract existing life insurance/assets	$250,000				
11	Additional life insurance needed	$(138,485)				

Present value analysis of life insurance needs is based on the assumption that survivors will not spend the proceeds immediately but will draw upon them only to cover the deficits identified in the plan. It is very important that survivors understand how the insurance plan is designed to work.

Method Two: A Simple Rule of Thumb. If finding the net present value of the future income gaps is more than you are willing to attempt, a very simple rule of thumb may give you an acceptable estimate of your insurance needs. Here is the rule: Have life insurance coverage equal to four years' gross pay, plus an extra year for each child you want to help through college. You may want more if you have no other assets or have a lot of debt. You may want less coverage if your spouse has marketable skills or you have an extensive investment portfolio.

Other Ways to Determine Your Insurance Needs. If you want a more accurate measure of the insurance you need than the general rule of thumb but do not want to go through the trouble of the first method, you have two other alternatives. The Army and Air Force Mutual Aid Association (AAFMAA) completes the calculations described in method 1 for the phases in a family's life based on birthdays and other information. It updates those annually or whenever an AAFMAA member requests it. Alternatively, some insurance companies have "insurance calculators" online, which can provide a second opinion on the amount of insurance you need. These calculators understandably round up when determining insurance needed and may not include all benefits that your family would receive if you died on active duty, but they can provide a second opinion. See Appendix A for information on AAFMAA and useful Internet sites.

What Type of Policy Should You Buy?

Having established the amount of insurance you need, you now need to identify resources available to pay the life insurance premium. This is part of developing a monthly budget from your goals, as outlined in chapter 4. Although planning and budgeting require a great deal of self-discipline, they must be done by anyone trying to reach any level of financial independence.

If you are unable to afford the premiums for the amount of insurance you need, you have a variety of options. First, reduce your monthly outlays in other areas of your budget. A second option would be to buy less insurance than you had calculated; this will help your monthly cash flow but will not eliminate the need for insurance. Think of how important the financial well-being of your family is compared with reducing spending in some other area. A third and better option would be to choose an appropriate mix of lower-cost term with the more expensive permanent and variable life insurance policies. Refer to the discussion of term, permanent, and variable life insurance earlier in this chapter to decide what type is best for your needs. We believe that most families can afford the life insurance protection they need if they use the low-cost group term insurance policies that are offered to members of the military services.

Almost all active-duty members elect to take Servicemembers Group Life Insurance (SGLI). The maximum coverage currently is $250,000 in term insurance for $17 per month ($0.85 for each $10,000 of coverage). Check your Leave and Earnings Statement to see if you are paying for SGLI and are therefore covered. This low-cost term insurance should be turned down only after carefully reviewing your needs for insurance, and then only by those without any dependents. Be aware that SGLI can be converted to Veterans Group Life Insurance (VGLI) upon separation or retirement from active duty. VGLI is a renewable five-year term policy with a premium that is based upon your age when you leave the service.

Many of us have heard the rule "buy term and invest the difference." Before you rely on this, you must evaluate your own discipline to stick to the plan. If you buy term and do not invest the difference, your savings will not do better than the permanent insurance policy's cash value buildup.

Tips on Making the Most from Your Life Insurance

- Review your life insurance plan, particularly when your financial responsibilities undergo a significant change.
- Remember that the purpose of life insurance is to prevent economic loss from your untimely death.
- Term policies will generally provide military families with the most coverage for the smallest premium and are especially appropriate for young families.
- Consider SGLI as the foundation of your insurance plan and then purchase more if your analysis indicates a need.
- Estimate your total insurance needs by examining needs and various stages of your surviving spouse's life. Buy insurance to cover those gaps.
- Discuss the insurance plan with your spouse so that he or she understands which gaps the insurance proceeds are designed to fill.

For other term insurance, you must generally inquire about rates and collect data yourself. Since the profit margins are low with term insurance, many companies selling it do not have a sales force. You must decide the amount of insurance you need and then go out and get the best deal you can find. Group term policies at very attractive rates are frequently advertised in the *Army, Air Force,* and *Navy Times.*

If you are shopping for permanent insurance, this step requires merely a telephone call or two—assuming you have not already received offers from agents. Remember, agents work on commission and usually are eager to show their products. Your job is to tone down that enthusiasm and buy the right type and amount of insurance to fit your needs, not the agent's. This is not an easy thing to do. Keep in mind that over half the people who take out permanent policies cancel them within ten years. Know something about your options and your insurance needs before the agent makes the sales pitch. Remember also that the insurance companies with the least expensive policies will probably not have a sales force, so don't expect the best deals to come knocking at your door.

It's important that you select a financially secure company; insurance companies are subject to mismanagement, fraud, and poor economic conditions that can bankrupt weaker ones. You can find insurance company ratings in most libraries in *Best's Insurance Reports* and in magazines such as *Consumer Reports, Changing Times,* and *Money.* Each state also monitors the insurance companies licensed to sell policies within its jurisdiction. Insurance commissioners in your state should be able to advise you about complaints or company performance.

20

Military Retirement Benefits

Military retired pay has a long history that is often misunderstood. It is not a pension. Pensions are primarily the result of financial need. Military retired pay is not based on financial need but is regarded as delayed compensation for completing twenty or more years of active military service. The authority for nondisability retired pay, commonly known as "length-of-service" retired pay, is contained in Title 10, USC.

Because the profession of arms requires considerable energy and stamina, national policy makers have long provided a generous retirement plan for career soldiers, sailors, and airmen. Originally intended to provide for those who had spent their entire productive lives in service to their country, the military retirement plan now also serves a vital role in personnel policy. Because it is generous, it encourages early retirement, which helps ensure that servicemembers on active duty are youthful, energetic, and able to measure up to the physical demands of modern combat.

There are three ways to retire from the Armed Forces. The first and most common is retirement for length of service. You may retire after twenty years of active service, and in most cases, you must retire after thirty years of active service. The second way is retirement for age. Because comparatively few people are in this category, and because pay and benefit calculations are exactly the same as for length-of-service retirees, we will consider these retirees to be the same as length-of-service retirees. Finally, you can retire for disability if you suffer a physical or mental disability that is rated at 30 percent or higher.

This chapter, organized into four sections, will help you to understand your basic entitlements as a retired member of the Armed Forces. The first section covers retirement pay for length-of-service retirees; the second section covers retirement pay for disabled retirees; the third section considers the effect of working for the government after retirement; and the last section briefly covers other benefits for retired military members.

This chapter will not answer every possible question. You should refer additional inquiries to your Defense Finance and Accounting Service or your personnel office. For detailed information, refer to DOD Regulation 7000.14-R, "Military Pay Policy and Procedures for Retired Pay," or the references listed in Appendix A.

HOW MUCH IS "STANDARD" RETIREMENT PAY?

The retired pay you receive depends upon the length of service and the rank achieved before retirement. Congress has changed the retirement system in the past twenty years but has always "grandfathered" current servicemembers into the older system. Consequently, there are three ways to calculate your retired pay. The method you should use depends on the date you initially entered military service (DIEMS), which is reflected by the "DIEMS" entry in the remarks section of your Leave and Earnings Statement. The DIEMS date is not used for any other purpose (i.e., it is *not* used in the retired pay computation) than to determine the date a member first joined the service. DIEMS is not necessarily the date of entry on active duty or the pay base date. Members who first entered uniformed military service when they were enlisted, commissioned, appointed, or inducted into the service will have a DIEMS that matches their pay base date. Members who first entered uniformed or military service through the delayed entry program, a service academy, an advanced ROTC program, or either a reserve or federally recognized National Guard component will have a DIEMS that matches the date they entered those programs. In this case the DIEMS will be a date before their pay base date. For example, a member placed in the Delayed Entry Program a year before going to boot camp will have a DIEMS one year earlier than his or her pay base date. The same holds true for service academy graduates—their DIEMS is normally four years before their commissioning date. Officers who had an ROTC scholarship or who graduated from a service academy use the date of that scholarship instead of the pay date to determine which retirement system applies to them. The DIEMS that determine which retirement plan a member qualifies for are 8 September 1980 and 1 August 1986. Members who first "raised their right hand" and signed paperwork near the key dates of 7 September 1980 and 31 July 1986 should validate their DIEMS, especially if they were in the Delayed Entry Program. If you entered service before 8 September 1980, you are covered by System 1. If you entered service between 8 September 1980 and 31 July 1986, your retirement pay is calculated using System 2. If you entered service on or after 1 August 1986, then use System 3. The method for calculating your first retirement paycheck is described below. In all three systems for calculating length-of-service retirement pay, your retirement pay is subject to income tax. Regulations also specify that your retired pay must be paid by direct deposit (electronic transfer) on a monthly basis.

System 1: Entered Service prior to 8 September 1980

Under this system, your retirement pay is computed at 2.5 percent of your final month's base pay at retirement multiplied by the number of years you served, with an upper limit of 75 percent. For example, an O-5 who retires on the twentieth anniversary of her entry into service will receive 50 percent (0.025 × 20) of the monthly base pay of an O-5 "over twenty" from the pay table current at the time of retirement. An E-7 retiring after twenty-three years of service will receive 57.5 percent (0.025 × 23) of the monthly base pay of an E-7 "over twenty-two" (there is no seniority pay raise for twenty-three years). Those who serve more than thirty years will not receive more than 75 percent of their base pay. See Table 20-1 for a sample calculation.

There is one exception to this rule. Your retirement pay is subject to a time-in-grade "lock-in" provision. Enlisted servicemembers who accept promotion to a higher grade must serve two years in that grade before they are eligible to retire. Thus, an E-7 who accepts a promotion to E-8 at nineteen years of service is not eligible to retire until after he has completed twenty-one years of service. Officers (O-5 and above) have a three-year "lock-in" if they accept promotion, but there is an important difference. Officers can retire within that three-year period, but if they do, they retire at the next lower grade (unless they are granted a one-year waiver).

System 2: Entered Service between 8 September 1980 and 31 July 1986

If you entered service between 8 September 1980 and 31 July 1986 (that is, DIEMS of 800908–860731, including both end dates), calculate the percentage (of base pay) that you will receive exactly as before. In System 2, however, that percentage is applied to the average of the base pay over the highest (which is usually the last) thirty-six months (three years) of service instead of the base pay at retirement. The actual "high-three" calculation is computed using monthly pay, so there is little incentive for holding out until the day after you get a seniority raise and expecting it to count for an entire year.

For example, consider an O-5 who retired on his twentieth anniversary of service in June 2001 under System 2. Suppose he was promoted to that grade before seventeen years in service so that, even with the lock-in, he can retire at the grade of O-5. During his eighteenth year of service he is paid as an O-5 over sixteen, because the seniority raise does not come until he completes his eighteenth year. During the next two years of service, he is paid as an O-5 over eighteen. For retirement purposes, he receives a percentage of the average of these "high-three" base pays (see Table 20-1).

System 3: Entered Service on or after 1 August 1986

Soldiers with DIEMS dates on or after 1 August 86 are automatically covered under the "high-three" formula unless between their 14 1/2 and 15th years of active duty they elect the REDUX formula in return for a taxable $30,000 career status bonus (CSB) paid at the fifteen-year service mark. To qualify for the CSB/REDUX choice, you must be eligible for retention to twenty years and agree to stay for twenty years. The CSB/REDUX retired pay plan multiplier is less than that under the "high-three" if the soldier has less than thirty years of creditable service. Under CSB/REDUX, the retired pay multiplier is 2.0 percent per year for the first twenty years of creditable service and 3.5 percent for years twenty-one through thirty (not to exceed 75 percent) multiplied by the average of the member's highest thirty-six months of basic pay. For example, an E-7

TABLE 20-1
RETIREMENT PAY UNDER THE THREE RETIREMENT SYSTEMS

For an O-5 retiring in June 2001 at 20 years of service:

Base pay:			
	18th year	$4,845.00	(over 16, FY 99 pay table)
	19th year	5,368.20	(over 18, FY 00 pay table)
	20th year	5,637.00	(over 18, FY 01 pay table)
	Final	5,790.30	(over 20, FY 01 pay table)

	System 1	System 2[a]	System 3[a]
Years served	20	20	20
Percent of base pay	50%[b]	50%[b]	40%[e]
Base pay for retirement	$5,790.30[c]	$5,283.40[d] (high 3)	$5,283.40[d] (high 3)
Monthly retired pay	$2,895.15	$2,641.70	$2,113.36

For an E-7 retiring in June 2001 at 23 years of service:

Base pay:			
	21st year	$2,480.40	(over 20, FY 99 pay table)
	22nd year	2,599.50	(over 20, FY 00 pay table)
	23rd year	2,890.80	(over 22, FY 01 pay table)
	Final	2,890.80	(over 22, FY 01 pay table)

	System 1	System 2[a]	System 3[a]
Years served	23	23	23
Percent of base pay	57.5%[b]	57.5%[b]	50.5%[e]
Base pay for retirement	$2,890.80[c]	$2,656.90[d] (high 3)	$2,656.90[d] (high 3)
Monthly retired pay	$1,662.21	$1,527.71	$1,341.73

[a] Illustrative only. No one under System 2 or 3 is eligible for normal retirement in June 2001. System 3 assumes CSB/REDUX election at fifteen years' service.
[b] Years of service × 2.5%.
[c] Base pay in final month.
[d] Average of "high-three" base pays = (B1 + B2 + B3) ÷ 3.
[e] 40% + (years of service over 20) × 3.5%.

retiring at twenty-three years of service would earn 50.5 percent (0.02 × 20 + 0.035 × 3) of his "high-three" average base pay. The longer a member serves, the closer his or her CSB/REDUX retired pay multiplier would be to that of someone retiring with the same number of years of service under "high-three." At thirty years, the multiplier is the same under both plans (75 percent). When the member reaches age sixty-two, CSB/REDUX retired pay is recalculated to equal what it would have been had the member retired under "high-three" initially. That means that the retired E-7 will be returned to 57.5 percent (0.025 × 23) of his "high-three" average base pay when he turns sixty-two. See Table 20-1 for a sample calculation. The decision whether to take the CSB/REDUX option or not is complicated and dependent on several variables. A complete discussion and calculators are available at *http://pay2000.dtic.mil.*

Cost-of-Living Increases

Retirement pay is indexed to the consumer price index (CPI) to ensure that its purchasing power is not eroded by inflation. Under Systems 1 and 2, the benefits are fully indexed to the CPI. That means that if the CPI increases by 5 percent, the benefit should increase by 5 percent. Under System 3, the benefit is partially indexed at 1 percentage point less than the CPI increase. If the CPI increases by 5 percent, the retirement pay will increase by 4 percent. Indexation occurs on 1 December each year, so retirees get a cost-of-living pay raise in their December paycheck. CSB/REDUX members receive a one-time catch-up COLA at age sixty-two; the following year the COLA reverts back to COLA minus 1 percent.

Although currently the benefit is fully indexed under Systems 1 and 2, Congress has the authority to index the benefits by less than the full amount of the increase in the CPI. Congress has historically indexed the benefits under Systems 1 and 2 less than fully. In fact, in every year since 1984, Congress has increased current retirement pay by approximately 1 percent less than the increase in the CPI. If this trend continues, the purchasing power of your retirement pay will decrease by 1 percent per year. This type of CPI-minus-1 indexation is a common practice in pension plans. It does, however, have one very important implication: Every servicemember must have a personal savings plan to augment his or her retirement pay. Your financial plan and investment strategy, as discussed in chapters 14 through 18, should address this need.

WHAT ABOUT RETIREMENT PAY IF YOU ARE DISABLED?

Permanent Disability

When a servicemember becomes unfit to perform the duties of office because of a permanent physical or mental disability, he or she is eligible for disability retirement from the military. Medical authorities will rate the disability using a standard Department of Veterans Affairs rating schedule. Disabilities of 30 percent or greater qualify for retirement. A line-of-duty (LOD) investigation is also required. There are two methods of calculating your disability retirement pay—the length-of-service method and the percent-disability method—and you should select the one most favorable to you. Each has slightly different consequences for taxation. Your disability retired pay, using the length-of-service method, is determined according to the following formula: pay = monthly basic pay × years of service × 0.025. Using the percent-disability method, the retirement pay is given by the following formula: pay = monthly basic pay × percent disability.

TABLE 20-2
CALCULATING DISABILITY RETIREMENT PAY

		O-3 with 5 Years of Service and 40% Disability	E-8 with 26 Years of Service and 40% Disability
Length-of-service method			
Basic pay		$3,081.50[a]	$3,612.60[b]
× 2.5% (0.025)	×	2.5%	2.5%
× Years of service	×	5	26
= Retirement pay		$385.18	$2,348.19
Percent-disability method			
Basic pay		$3,081.50[a]	$3,612.60[b]
× Percent disability		40.0%	40.0%
= Retirement pay		$1,232.60	$1,445.04
Monthly retirement pay received		$1,232.60	$2,348.19
Plus severance pay[c]		$30,815.00 (10 months)	$86,702.40 (24 months)

[a] Average of "high-three" basic pays under Systems 2 and 3, because anyone with five years of service must have entered the service after 8 September 1980. Numbers are based on FY01 pay tables.
[b] Full basic pay at time of disability.
[c] Assuming a favorable LOD investigation.

Table 20-2 contains sample calculations. Note that the O-3 finds it in his interest to take the percent-disability pay, whereas the length-of-service calculation is preferable for the E-8. In general, the fewer years of service you have and the greater your disability, the more likely it is that you will choose the percent-disability method.

These formulas are affected by the date on which you entered service. If you entered before 8 September 1980, you use your full basic pay at the time of the disability in the calculation. If you entered on or after 8 September 1980, you use an average of your "high-three" monthly basic pay. The 1986 reforms did not affect disability retirement, however, so to determine disability retirement pay, everyone uses 2.5 percent, no matter when he or she entered service.

There are some exemptions in the personal income tax code that pertain to disability retirement pay. If your disability resulted from combat duty, then your disability pay is not subject to income tax. If the disability is not combat related and you use the percent-disability method to compute your pay, the pay is still not taxable. But if your disability is not combat related and you use the length-of-service method, then some portion of the retirement pay is taxable. For servicemembers who have been in the service for close to twenty years and who have low-rated disabilities, this taxation consideration might affect the method you should use. For more information, consult the Defense Finance and Accounting Service. Finally, all disability retirement pay is currently fully indexed to the CPI.

Temporary Disability

It is also possible to be retired for a temporary disability. If this happens, you calculate your retirement pay as you would for a permanent disability, but there is one difference: If you have a temporary disability, your disability retirement pay will be either one-half your basic pay at the time of the disability or the amount that you calculate for permanent disability, whichever is higher. You will also be given periodic medical examinations, at least once every eighteen months. If the disability disappears, you will be recalled from retirement at your former grade. If it does not disappear in five years, you will be permanently retired.

Severance Pay

Each disability retirement will be accompanied by a line-of-duty investigation. If the disability is not due to your intentional misconduct or willful neglect, and if it was not incurred while AWOL, then you are entitled to disability severance pay in the amount of two months' basic pay per year of service up to a maximum of twelve years. For example, the O-3 in Table 20-2 would receive ten (2 × 5) months' basic pay, and the E-8 would receive the maximum allowable twenty-four months' basic pay because he has more than twelve years of service.

WHAT ARE THE DUAL COMPENSATION LAWS, AND DO THEY APPLY TO ME?

Retired military personnel often take jobs with the federal government. These retirees can offer considerable experience developed during their military careers, and the government is always happy to benefit from that expertise. But due to the nature of the military retirement system, which permits early retirement compared with civilian employment, the government was in the past perceived to be, in effect, paying twice to obtain it.

The bottom line on these dual compensation laws was that retired military members were entitled to hold jobs with the federal government, but if their combined civil service and retirement salary exceeded a certain level, the retirement salary was reduced. The good news is the fiscal year 2000 Defense Authorization Act repealed these dual compensation laws. The repeal is retroactive to 1 October 1999. The repeal ends two former reductions in military retired pay that applied to some military retirees:

Tips on Making the Most of Your Retired Pay

- Understand what system you are under and the importance of timing your retirement.
- Consult a professional financial advisor regarding the feasibility of the CSB/REDUX option for your particular situation.
- If you entered the service after 8 September 1980, your retirement pay is based on your highest thirty-six months of paychecks.
- If you are promoted, you are "locked-in" for two years for enlisted and three years for officers to be eligible to retire at that grade.
- If you are disabled, calculate both the length-of-service and percent-disability payments, and choose the one that is more advantageous.

1. The pay cap that limited the combined total of federal civilian basic salary plus military retired pay to $110,700 (executive level V) for all federal employees who are retirees of a uniformed service.
2. The partial reduction in retired pay required of retired officers of a regular component of a uniformed service.

One other provision of this law should be mentioned here. Regardless of your rank, you must wait at least 180 days after you retire to take a job with the Department of Defense unless you have the written permission of the appropriate service secretary.

WHAT OTHER RETIREMENT BENEFITS ARE THERE?

Commissary and Exchange

Servicemembers, their family members, and unmarried surviving spouses are authorized to use the commissary and exchange on military installations when those facilities are considered adequate to support retirees without causing hardship to their active-duty customers. The local installation commander makes this determination, and the availability of this benefit varies by location.

Medical and Dental Care

You are eligible for the same medical and dental care you received while on active duty, but on a space-available basis. Your dependents and spouse may also be entitled to medical and dental care in an active-duty facility, again depending on the availability of resources. You are also eligible to participate in TRICARE, but at a significantly higher cost. (See chapter 10 concerning retiree medical benefits.)

FORMER SPOUSES

In 1983, Congress passed 10 USC 1408, the "Uniformed Services Former Spouses Protection Act." The act was amended by the "1991 DOD Authorization Act"—Public Law 101-510, 5 November 1990, Section 555. This law, as amended, allows a former spouse to be awarded up to 50 percent of the retiree's disposable retired pay. If you have a former spouse, check with your finance office on how this law could affect your retired pay.

The military retirement plan is generally quite generous and recognizes the sacrifices made by members of the Armed Forces. It is not, however, lavish. While the indexing provisions of the plan compare favorably with corresponding civilian pensions, Congress does not fully index retirement pay to keep up with inflation. These considerations make it clear that you may need to plan your finances now to be able to supplement your retirement income.

21

Estate Planning

Everyone has an estate. Although you may not believe your estate is large enough to warrant special planning, it is best that you do so. At a minimum you will help preserve your assets for your heirs, shield your loved ones from unnecessary legal hassles, and ensure a better quality of life for them. Countless vignettes illustrate the need for estate planning for all servicemembers. For example, prior to 2001, all too many Americans were unpleasantly surprised upon the death of a loved one to find that treasured family properties would have to be sold in order to pay the Federal Estate Tax. In another familiar situation, because of the lack of a will, a person may be prevented from receiving their share of an estate for years while the estate goes through the probate process. In the meantime, they were unable to assist their children in paying for college. Or, as if out of a movie, immediately surrounding an unexpected death, a family feuds over burial plots, location of treasured heirlooms, and which law firm is going to oversee the probate process. All of these events are tragic but occur frequently. The only ones who benefit from the lack of estate planning are estate attorneys.

After reading this chapter, you should be better prepared to avoid these unfortunate situations. This chapter discusses several basic but important estate planning topics: legal forms of ownership and powers of attorney, wills and other estate planning documents, trusts, the probate process, duties of an executor, income shifting, and estate planning resources. We will also discuss the nuances of the Federal Estate Tax and highlight the necessity of using expert assistance and various stages of the planning process. When finished, you should sleep soundly knowing that your loved ones will understand the steps required to maintain their standard of living in the event of your unexpected demise.

In addition to this chapter, servicemembers should be aware that they have several advantages in the estate planning arena. Commanders at all levels will assist you in arranging your legal affairs so that on deployments you will be able to concentrate on your duty with your unit knowing that your loved ones have the wills, powers of attorney, and other provisions that they need. Consequently, all military bases provide free legal assistance officers who will help you develop these key estate documents free of charge. This is especially important if you are one of the 6.5 percent of the Armed Forces who is either a single parent or dual military couple. Combine this legal assistance with a reading of this chapter and the chapters on budgeting, life insurance, mutual funds, and the Survivor Benefit Plan, and you can be fairly certain of your family's security and your peace of mind in the future.

WHAT EXACTLY IS MY ESTATE?

The first and perhaps most important step in estate planning is to take an inventory of everything you own. Legally, your estate is what you own, minus your debts. This includes all your property, tangible and intangible. Tangible assets include your home, cash, balances in checking and savings accounts, mutual funds, other financial assets, and your cars, boats, and furniture. Some intangibles include the death value of your life insurance policy, employee retirement plans, and IRAs. Table 21-1 summarizes what was taxable under the Federal Estate Tax (prior to 2001) and what was not. The next section will discuss some of the unfamiliar terms.

TABLE 21-1
TAXABLE AND NONTAXABLE ESTATE

Taxable Estate		Assets Avoiding Probate and Estate Taxes
Life insurance Annuities	Property estate Separate property	Irrevocable life insurance trusts
IRAs/pension plans	Tenants in common	Annual exclusion gifts
Community property with rights of survivorship	50% of community property	
Joint property		
Qualified joint property (with spouse)		
Transfer on death		

HOW IS YOUR PROPERTY CONTROLLED?

During your lifetime you will accumulate property as part of your estate. It can be either personal property (such as personal effects, household furnishings, automobiles, money, or stocks) or real property (land and associated buildings or fixtures). You may hold complete title to the property, in which case it belongs to you alone, or you may share ownership with another person or with a corporation (most likely the bank who lent you the money to acquire the property). There are three common variations of joint ownership:

1. *Joint tenancy with right of survivorship.* Each tenant (normally two) owns an undivided share in the property, and if one tenant dies, the title automatically passes to the surviving tenant(s).
2. *Tenancy in common.* Ownership is divided among the tenants, and each has the right to sell, assign, or convey his share in the property.
3. *Tenancy by the entirety.* A special form of joint tenancy; the tenants must be husband and wife.

Quite often a servicemember will hold property jointly with a spouse or children to reduce administrative problems and costs if one owner should die. Property held jointly passes apart from the will and thus avoids some of the expenses and problems associated with probate. By far, the most common form of joint ownership is joint tenancy with right of survivorship.

Real estate may be owned in joint tenancy with right of survivorship under proper deed. Joint title to personal property (such as a car), however, may make your spouse subject to personal property taxes on half or all of its value to the state where you are temporarily living because of your military duty.

Another common use of joint ownership is a joint bank account from which either party can draw funds. In a few states, funds in the account would not be available to the survivor until a tax release had been obtained. Be sure to inquire with the bank when you open an account or check with your legal assistance officer when you draft your will to ensure that you or your spouse will have access to funds if either one of you dies.

Some states have laws recognizing all property of married couples as "community" property. Laws of those states pose special problems for the servicemember's estate, for there are strict definitions for community property and community income. In certain instances, purchases by either spouse are considered community property if earned "community" funds were used in the purchase. Separate purchases made by either spouse while residing in other states might also be declared community property upon moving into one of the community property states. Special care must be taken in planning life insurance benefits and estate tax deductions to avoid paying excessive taxes in these states. In most instances a servicemember can exempt life insurance benefits in any state from estate taxes by transferring policy ownership to his or her spouse as a gift. Good legal advice is critical. The community property states are Arizona, California, Idaho, Louisiana, Nevada, New Mexico, Texas, and Washington.

WHAT ESTATE PLANNING DOCUMENTS DO YOU NEED?

Powers of Attorney

Because servicemembers are frequently absent or not immediately accessible when matters of personal business arise, it is advisable to designate an agent or "attorney" to act in the servicemember's name. Through a power of attorney, you give authority to act in your name and on your behalf to a family member or other person in whom you have complete trust and confidence.

Although requirements of a legally effective power of attorney vary among states, federal law now requires states to recognize powers of attorney prepared by military lawyers for servicemembers and their families. The power of attorney should be made under the advice of your legal assistance officer, who is familiar with the laws of the state where it will be used.

Most servicemembers would need a power of attorney in case of deployment or extended absence to allow someone to perform specific tasks in their place. For example:

- to ship and receive household goods or other property.
- to cash checks.
- to sell, buy, drive, insure, repair, ship, or receive a car.
- to request medical care for children (if they are not staying with your spouse).
- to accept or clear government quarters.

In most of these cases, your legal assistance officer will have a preprinted special power of attorney that complies with federal and state law. It is a special power of attorney because it is limited to the time and purpose that it can be used. Whenever possible, use a special power of attorney because it gives you a greater degree of control over the agent's activities. It is generally desirable to provide for a certain date of termination, usually two to three years. If you need to continue the power of attorney, you can complete a new power of attorney. Your agent (the person named in a power of attorney) need not be present for you to execute a new power of attorney. For example, if you are overseas, you could consult a legal assistance officer there to complete the power of attorney and then mail it back to your agent.

As an alternative to the special power of attorney, you can sign a general power of attorney, which gives your agent unlimited power to act in your name. You should seek the advice of your legal assistance officer to determine the type of power of attorney that is best for you. In any case, your agent will need the original signed document to act on your behalf and copies to provide when he or she uses it. You should retain one information copy. Your power of attorney is valid only as long as you are alive and competent. A power of attorney can also be made durable, that is, written to remain valid even if you become incapacitated or incompetent. Remember, however, that death always nullifies any power of attorney, even one made durable. Therefore, a power of attorney should not be confused with or substituted for a will!

Wills

You and your spouse should both have a will. If you die without a will ("intestate"), state law will determine the distribution of your property and the guardianship of your children. No matter how large or small your estate, not leaving a will results in some degree of hardship and inconvenience for your survivors. The untimely death of a loved one is emotionally devastating, and it should not be complicated by the administrative and legal hassles of administering an estate without a will.

By making a will, you can specify who will receive your property, when, in what amounts, how it should be safeguarded, and whom should handle the property. You can also settle the question of guardianship so that neither your spouse nor your children have to endure the rigors of settling such a matter in the courts.

This section highlights some points you should be sure to ask about when you see your legal assistance officer about drafting your will. Do not use a standardized form for a will except in an emergency; if you do use such a will, replace it promptly with one developed by legal counsel. If you are married, you and your spouse should discuss these matters and go to see the lawyer together, but you must make separate wills. The following are topics and questions that you should consider before seeing your legal assistance officer:

Personal representative. Your will specifies a person to act as your personal representative (sometimes called the executor of your will) to make decisions regarding your will. This is often your spouse or another trusted individual. You may also want to specify an alternate if the person you designate is unable to act as your personal representative. The person needs to be a mature decision maker because he or she will have many responsibilities. IRS Publication 559 outlines these duties, which include the following:

- Taking control of assets.
- Filing an inventory with the court.
- Liquidating selected assets and, if necessary, paying claims.
- Distributing estate according to terms of will.
- Making a final accounting to the court.

Domicile. Because of frequent changes in residence, it may be advisable to state your domicile in the will, although it will most likely be probated in your residence at time of death.

Military service. Your will should include the statement that you are now in (or have retired from, or served in) the active military or naval service of the United States, together with your grade and service (or Social Security) number.

Bequests. Your will specifies who is to receive your property and the manner in which it is divided upon your death. It covers both property that you own now and that which you acquire after you execute your will. You can also make specific bequests that fully describe particular property and then specify the person who should receive it.

Common disaster clause. You should also include in your will a common disaster clause that names beneficiaries (usually children) should both spouses die in the same accident. This avoids any possible litigation by relatives as to which spouse died first and which spouse, therefore, was the owner of the entire estate at his or her death.

Guardianship. Your will should specify the legal guardian (and possibly alternate guardians) for your minor children. Your will should be consistent with that of your spouse to preclude legal conflicts in the unfortunate event that both of you die in the same calamity.

Testamentary trust. A testamentary trust, discussed in the section below, helps protect the children's assets by putting them in a trust as specified in the will. This may substantially simplify matters for the children's guardian if both spouses die.

Events such as marriage, birth of children, divorce, death of a named beneficiary, or a change of personal representative affect the provisions of a will. As circumstances change, you can always change your will and revoke, either partially or entirely, your previous will. The most recent properly executed will governs the disposition of your estate when you die. Hence the term "last will and testament" implies that document replaces any previous wills. When a will is replaced, all copies of the previous will should be destroyed.

Only the original will should be signed. If you wish to keep a copy with you for reference or to give a copy to your personal representative or anyone else, it should be a "conformed" unsigned copy; that is, it should bear no signature, but your name as the maker and the names of witnesses should be printed or typed for information purposes.

Letters of Instruction

Along with a will, you should draw up a set of instructions for use by your personal representative and your survivors. This is an informational rather than a legal document that will help your personal representative and family to avoid confusion and major inconvenience in settling the estate. The best possible method for avoiding problems is to ensure that your spouse and children understand your plans and instructions now, before you die. This letter does not need to be notarized or prepared in any particular format and it can be updated at any time. A letter of last instructions should contain the following:

- The location of all valuable documents (including birth certificates, Social Security cards, certificates of marriage and divorce, naturalization and citizenship papers, papers establishing your right to government benefits, service records, insurance policies, and lists of savings accounts, bank accounts, stocks, bonds, deeds, and other evidence of ownership or debt).
- Instructions as to funeral and burial.
- Instructions concerning any business in which you may be involved.
- A statement of reasons for actions taken in your will, such as disinheritances.
- The location of your long-range planning charts, including instructions of how your assets can be used to satisfy the economic needs of the family.

Much of the information suggested here could be in your personal affairs record form, in the format outlined in Appendix E. A conformed copy of your will and associated letter of last instructions should be left with your personal representative. A fireproof box at home is probably a good place to keep these and other valuable documents. Alternatively, if your personal representative is not your spouse, you may want to ask that person to hold your will.

You should not keep your will in a safe-deposit box. Often, when a person dies, the safe-deposit box may be sealed by the bank and opened only by court order.

WHAT IS THE PROBATE PROCESS?

One of the main reasons you prepare a will is to avoid probate. Probate is a legal process that settles a person's affairs upon his or her death. It has two primary goals: 1) to make sure all debts are paid, and 2) to distribute property to the property recipients. All estates go through the probate process, regardless of whether or not the individual dies with a will and whether or not there is right of survivorship. However, it is a far easier process when there is a legal will and for couples where there is right of survivorship. Because the legal will is a set of instructions to a probate court judge for settling your estate, it allows you to avoid some of the more expensive aspects of probate and significantly shortens the process. The estate of an individual who dies without a will enters the probate court process. This means that the state's law of descent and distribution becomes the will. This can result in some very undesirable circumstances. If there is not a surviving spouse, guardianship of minor children will be decided by the court. State law will also decide the apportionment of your assets. In some states, adult children may receive up to two-thirds of the estate, forcing your spouse to sell the family home. As an added burden, in some states your spouse may be forced to report to the court annually to render a report of how he or she is safeguarding the children and your estate.

Probate does have some advantage. First, it prevents fraud in transferring a deceased person's property, and it protects inheritors by promptly resolving creditors' claims. But in truth, most property is transferred within a close circle of family and friends, and few estates face large creditors' claims. In many states, probate fees are what a court approves as "reasonable." In a few states, the fees are based on a percentage of the estate subject to probate. Either way, a probate attorney's fees for a "routine" estate with a gross value of $400,000 (these days, this may be little more than a home, some savings, and a car) can easily amount to $20,000 or more. In addition, there are court costs, appraiser's fees, and sometimes other expenses. However you look at it, the costs of not preparing a legal will are going to be high for your descendants in terms of finances, time, and effort.

WILL MY ESTATE BE SUBJECT TO THE ESTATE TAX IF I DIE?

In a spirited debate surrounding the repeal of the estate tax in the spring of 2001, some politicians argued that this tax hit only the top 1 percent of American families. The problem was that the top 1 percent was often not fabulously wealthy like Bill Gates, but rather was the "millionaire next door" described in the best-selling book of the same name. The heirs to individuals who had accumulated $675,000 or more in assets, including their homes, over their lifetime, stood to lose about 40 percent of their inheritance to the Federal Estate Tax. Often it was the typical grandmother, who left a suburban house valued at $250,000, a $100,000 whole life insurance policy, and $400,000 in savings and IRAs that she and her deceased husband had accumulated in the twenty years prior to retirement. She would consider herself middle of the middle class, and her situation would not be unusual for many servicemembers. Looking back to chapter 7 and IRA planning for a moment, we saw that the couple who each put their $2,000 in an IRA annually for the decade or so before and during the stock market rise of the 1990s might easily accumulate several hundred thousand dollars in assets by retirement age. In a sense, the estate tax prior to 2001 was penalizing the heirs to frugal and hardworking Americans who planned well for their retirement. The problem lay with a legislative-driven estate value cutoff that did not, like many political solutions, reflect changes in inflation and society. Americans are saving for a longer life using the IRA plans designed by Congress, often fearing that Social Security will not exist. In addition, more companies are providing 401k plans rather than the industrial age pension plan. No longer assured a guaranteed fixed pension income, average Americans are forced to forgo consumption in order to accumulate more retirement assets. Both of these societal changes increased the chances that the average American would be subject to the Federal Estate Tax, and hence, drove the need for change.

Unfortunately, the answer to the question above still remains as confusing as ever. The estate tax will be gradually reduced until 2010, both by cutting the tax rate and by increasing the exemption levels.

The grandmother in our example would not be subject to the estate tax in this scenario.

Then, in 2010, the estate tax will be completely repealed, but heirs will be subject to capital gains taxes on any of their inheritance that they sell. Capital assets, like property, stocks, and bonds, are currently assessed the capital gains tax only on value gained after the assets are inherited. But under the new system beginning in 2010, the tax would be based on the value gained since the original purchase. For example, today, if your father bought a stock for $10 and you inherited it when it was worth $100 and sold it at $150, you'd pay capital gains taxes on the $50 rise in value while you owned it. It wouldn't matter to the IRS how much your father had paid for it; all that would be important was how much it had gone up since you owned it. However, under the new system you would have to pay capital gains on the total $140 the stock had gained since your father had purchased it. Imagine the hardship for an estate executor trying to determine the value of stocks bought forty years before. This could become tedious quite quickly.

The estate tax will spring back to life in 2011 if Congress does not decide to address it before then. Consequently, it is very likely that the system created in 2001 will change again soon. As it stands now, not only are there still state estate taxes to consider, but also which year you die, the laws at that time, and the value of your estate. If you feel confused, you are in good company. Yet, this does not mean it is useless to conduct effective estate planning. Instead, the principles, documents, and diligence will be more important than ever. The answer to the question "Will my estate be subject to the Federal Estate Tax?" still begins with an inventory of your assets and ends with professional assistance in drawing up a will and other documents. In doing this, regardless of the year or estate tax in effect, you should continue to use some of the instruments discussed in the following pages to reduce your estate's tax bill. This discussion also highlights the point that with the introduction of Thrift Savings Plans, IRAs, and perhaps a second pension, long-serving soldiers may find themselves in a situation where they need to think about estate taxes.

WHAT IS A TRUST AND HOW MIGHT YOU USE IT TO AVOID ESTATE TAXES?

One of the most useful of all estate planning tools is the trust, and yet few people take advantage of it because it takes time to understand. Many people think of a trust as a complicated device involving a dour-looking trustee in a black frock coat (vaguely resembling a Dickens character), or a scheme used by the affluent to avoid taxes, or a financial straightjacket that deprives beneficiaries of the full enjoyment of property. It is none of these. A trust is simply a legal arrangement by which one's assets are held by a trustee. The trust department in a bank or an estate attorney's office easily enacts them. In fact, anyone who has a will most likely incorporated a testamentary trust into that document.

There are several dozen variations of trusts to serve different objectives. They are designed primarily to protect beneficiaries by providing more effective property management than an outright gift or bequest would provide. A trust can help you avoid the nasty probate process described above and reduce or otherwise provide for payments of estate taxes, should there be some in the year of your demise. This could be important, for you might prefer to liquidate cash assets rather than sell the family beach house to pay the estate tax. Without some sort of trust, a court would make this decision. In short, trusts ensure that your property serves a desired purpose after your death. The potential disadvantage is that it reduces the flexibility of the person who places assets into the trust. In some situations, even persons with only moderate estates can realize tax savings from setting up a trust, although taxes usually are a collateral factor.

Essentially, a trust is simply a three-party relationship that separates ownership of the same property into two parts: the legal and the equitable. The person who establishes the trust might be called the trustor, grantor, settler, maker, or donor (for consistency, we will use trustor). The person (or corporation) to whom the property is transferred and who has legal title to it is the trustee. Those who have equitable ownership are referred to as the beneficiaries. Beneficiaries are divided into two categories: income beneficiaries, who have the benefit of the property for a certain period, such as the income for life, and remaindermen, who receive the property when the income beneficiaries' interests end. An example would be for you (trustor) to put a sum of money in a trust for your children (beneficiaries) under the control of a bank's trust department (trustee). If you instead had interest income from the trust going to your spouse (income beneficiary), and then had the remaining trust proceeds going to your children upon your spouse's death, they would be the remaindermen.

What Types of Trusts Are There?

The two basic types of trusts used in estate planning are the living (or *inter vivos*) trust, which might be either revocable or irrevocable, and the testamentary trust (see Table 21-2). Another type we will discuss later is the unfunded life insurance trust. Each has its own attributes and offers a combination of advantages: separation of the burden from the benefit of property ownership; experienced management; strong legal safeguards; economy (a corporate trustee's fees usually are based on the value of the trust principal; from 0.25 to 1 percent a year is customary); protection for beneficiaries (especially important if the beneficiary is a minor or is financially inexperienced); assurance that the property will be used as the trustor desires; and continuity of assets and family income. Also, some trusts may offer significant savings in income and estate taxes.

TABLE 21-2
SUMMARY OF TRUSTS

Type	Attributes	Nontax Benefits	Income Tax	Estate Tax	Gift Tax
Irrevocable living	Trustor gives up property forever	Supervised control and investment	Taxed to beneficiary	Not taxable in trustor's estate	Taxable to trustor
Revocable living	Trustor can revoke	Same as above	Taxable to settler	Includable in trustor's estate	No liability
Testamentary	Created by will	Supervised control and investment	Taxed to beneficiary	Includable in estate of creator	No liability

Trust law is complex, so if you are wondering whether a trust is right for you, you should consult with a lawyer experienced in this specialized field and confer with a trust officer at your bank. There are also several good books on estate planning that cover trusts in detail. This section introduces you to trusts, highlighting some of the characteristics, possible uses, and principal consequences of the more common arrangements.

Revocable Living Trust. As its name implies, a living trust is created and operates during the trustor's life. When the trustor has the right to cancel or modify its terms, the agreement is called a revocable trust.

The primary objective of an arrangement of this nature is, of course, property management during the trustor's life or during the lives of a husband and wife. Another important advantage is that the property could be transferred to the trustor's survivors without the normal delays (from several months to several years) and costs (such as attorney's fees and executor's commissions) involved in the probate process. For instance, the agreement might provide that after both spouses die, the trustee will divide the remaining trust estate and distribute it to their children, either all at once or at stated ages. However, if the children already have adequate financial resources, it might direct that the trust continue, with the income to be paid to them during their lives, and with discretion in the trustee to use the principal for them if needed. When the children die, the principal could then go to grandchildren.

Because a revocable living trust does not involve a permanent surrender of control over property, trust income is taxable to the trustor (regardless of who the income beneficiary is) and is included in the estate for tax purposes. See Table 21-2 for a summary of trust characteristics.

Irrevocable Living Trusts. An irrevocable living trust is just what the name suggests: an arrangement under which the trustor gives up, either forever or for a stated period, any right to cancel or modify the agreement. It has most of the advantages of a revocable trust, including avoidance of probate, and it also permits some tax savings due to the income shifting. The income is not taxed to the trustor if he or she has relinquished all rights and control over it and transferred the future principal to a beneficiary. These savings could be substantial if you are in a high tax bracket and the beneficiaries are in a low bracket. Also, because the trustor has given up ownership of the property, its value would not be subject to death (estate) taxes.

Although a permanently irrevocable, nonreversionary agreement almost presupposes considerable wealth (and even then many people are reluctant to surrender permanent control over their property), there are a few situations in which such an arrangement might be useful. For example, a rich parent with a prodigal son might use an irrevocable trust to provide for his needs without indulging his excesses. An even more common use would be to provide a managed source of funds for a child's college education.

Testamentary Trusts. While a living trust can be quite useful in some situations, a testamentary trust, which is created by your will and does not operate until your death, deserves consideration by a broader range of people. Although no immediate income or estate tax savings are available, the other trust advantages should not be dismissed lightly. Any military family would probably benefit from establishing testamentary trusts in both spouses' wills. There are three reasons to consider establishing a testamentary trust:

Safety for Spouse. If a significant amount of property is left outright to a surviving spouse, lack of investment experience or the influence of well-meaning but financially inexpert friends could lead to the loss of much of its value or purchasing power. (Weep for all the widows and widowers who, before the inflationary spurt of the late 1970s, used much of what their spouses left them to buy fixed-income annuities.) For a small annual fee, these risks can be avoided and the survivor can be relieved of the burden of managing the property.

Protection for Children. A surviving spouse might remarry and later transfer title to the new spouse (and perhaps his or her children by a previous marriage), who might be enriched at the expense of the deceased's own children, who could end up with empty purses. The trust can easily be established to pay income to the spouse, and later provide the principal to surviving children.

Assistance for Guardians. A testamentary trust can be established from your estate for any children who may survive you and your spouse. This helps protect the guardian and the children's assets from cumbersome and expensive reporting requirements that most states have to keep guardians from raiding their minors' inheritance.

The trust is simply a paragraph in your will, putting your estate in trust for your child, appointing a trustee (who could be the guardian or someone else), establishing any restrictions on use of the assets, and providing for eventual distribution of the assets to your children, in whatever way you choose. This way, you decide how your assets are managed when you are gone, and not the state. To prevent the trust approach from being thwarted if you die first, your spouse's will should have similar provisions. This type of trust is a contingent testamentary trust, contingent on the circumstance in which both spouses die.

Although a testamentary trust is not for everyone, anyone who has much more than a moderate estate should consider it. However, if your estate consists mostly of nonprobate assets (such as jointly owned property or life insurance proceeds payable to a named beneficiary), so that relatively little would pass under the will, then you should consider some other way of achieving the same result (perhaps a life insurance trust, explained below).

While legal assistance officers will not generally be able to set up complicated trusts for you, almost all legal assistance officers will add a contingent or testamentary trust to your will if you desire. This is an important benefit that you should definitely consider.

A final reason to consider trusts is that there may be tax advantages for your family. One common technique is to divide the estate into two parts: one for the surviving spouse and the other in trust for the spouse's benefit while living, with whatever remains going to children or grandchildren after the spouse's death. Then, the trustee might be directed to distribute what is left to the children, either all at once or in whatever manner is specified. What such an arrangement does, essentially, is remove the principal of the trust from the spouse's estate for estate tax purposes, yet provides for the surviving spouse's needs as long as he or she lives.

Unfunded Life Insurance Trusts. A life insurance trust is merely a revocable trust that is funded with the proceeds of insurance on the trustor's life. Because the proceeds are not available until after death, the trust does not become effective until then, nor does it offer any immediate income or estate tax savings. Nevertheless, it meets the needs of some people because it provides professional management of life insurance proceeds.

If your estate consists of relatively little except a large amount of life insurance (a situation common in many young families), you could use the insurance to establish a trust for your spouse and children. After entering into a trust agreement, you direct the insurance companies to change the beneficiary to the trust. The trustee would hold the policies until your death, collect the proceeds, and then manage and distribute them according to the terms of the trust. The only expenses before your death are the attorney's fees for drafting the agreement (perhaps a few hundred dollars) and possibly a relatively small acceptance fee that some corporate trustees charge. You can change or revoke the trust at anytime before your death.

Life insurance could be used to fund a testamentary trust, of course, but the unfunded life insurance trust has several advantages. For one thing, if the proceeds were used for a testamentary trust, the insured's estate would have to be the beneficiary, which would subject the proceeds to administration, claims against the estate, and inheritance taxation in some states. The avoidance of probate, with its costs and extended delays, is itself a sufficient reason not to make an estate the beneficiary of life insurance. Also, a life insurance trust can serve as a convenient receptacle for other estate assets, which can be "poured over" into it by the testator's will.

The dismal shortcomings of periodic payment settlement options offered by insurance companies become immediately apparent if compared to a life insurance trust. The most important advantage of a trust is its flexibility: If an unforeseen emergency arises, the principal could be drawn on to meet it. Under an insurance annuity, on the other hand, the beneficiary would receive no more or less than the monthly stipend, regardless of the circumstances.

Perhaps more important, a trust should provide greater protection against inflation. The "prudent person" standard of most states requires trust investments to be geared both to producing reasonable income and to preserving capital—and preservation means not just maintaining the same number of dollars, but also increasing capital to offset inflation. There is no assurance, of course, that the trust principal will appreciate, nor is there any certain small return like that which an insurer guarantees. There is, however, the potential for gain, because, unless the trustor has directed otherwise, most corporate trustees usually invest the funds they manage in high-grade common stocks, bonds, and other securities.

Also, even if the trust principal does not appreciate, the income alone would probably exceed the payments guaranteed under a twenty-years-certain life insurance settlement option. What is more, when the trust beneficiary dies, the principal (less any amounts that might have been paid out of principal) would be available for the remaindermen. Conversely, with life insurance payments, on the death of the beneficiaries or at the end of the years-certain guarantee, nothing would remain for the children or others.

Contingent Unfunded Life Insurance Trusts. One variation of the typical unfunded life insurance trust is a contingent unfunded life insurance trust, in which the trustee is the contingent or secondary beneficiary. This arrangement might be used if you want your spouse to receive the insurance proceeds, but you want a trust for the children if your spouse dies.

Some of the advantages of a trust for minor children were mentioned earlier. First, a trust avoids the cost and inconvenience of appointing a guardian for their estates, the bonding expense, and the required periodic accounting by the guardian to the court. Second, the best guardian for your children may not have the financial expertise to manage the money that you have provided. Third, control of your children's assets is uncertain if the guardian dies during the guardianship period. Fourth, the guardian would have to be pay each child's share when the child reaches majority (eighteen in most states), even though the child's experience and financial ability might be questionable. Finally, a guardian's control of the children's estate is subject to the continued jurisdiction of the probate court, which might be undesirable, particularly if the children live in a state other than the one in which the will is probated.

Another limitation of naming young children as contingent beneficiaries of life insurance is that the proceeds would be divided equally among them. Better results are possible if the estate is used for the benefit of all the children, although their needs might be disparate. For example, assume that both parents die, survived by three minor children who, as contingent beneficiaries of life insurance, share $200,000 equally. If one child requires expensive medical care or special training, the costs would be borne by his or her share alone. After reaching majority, that child might have nothing left, but the other two might have sizable sums remaining. The parents can accomplish a more equitable division with a family trust that permits the trustee to "spray" or "sprinkle" the income and use the principal according to the individual needs of the beneficiaries, then distribute what remains when the children reach majority or when the trustor has directed.

What Details Should You Think about in Your Trust?

Administrative and Distributive Arrangements. Deciding what administrative and distributive provisions would be best depends, of course, on several factors, such as the size and nature of the trust estate, the desires of the trustor, and the needs of the beneficiaries. A trust is a personal and complex instrument that requires custom drafting by a knowledgeable lawyer. It is not something you can do for yourself by filling in spaces on a printed form. To provide your lawyer with a clear understanding of your desires, however, there are a few general matters you should think about, starting with whom you want to appoint as trustee. Legal assistance officers will probably be willing to talk to you and advise you about trusts, but will probably not draft trusts for you (other than testamentary trusts discussed above).

Selecting a Trustee. Similar to a personal representative, a trustee is a fiduciary, and so is held to the highest standards of loyalty. Unlike a personal representative whose duties are short-term, a trustee is required to manage the trust productively over a long time.

Selecting a trustee has an important bearing on the effectiveness of a trust. In the past, individuals (often relatives or family lawyers) were the usual choices. One advantage of an individual trustee is that he or she is more likely to know the beneficiaries' needs and to have a personal interest in their welfare. Also, if a qualified relative or friend serves without compensation, the trust avoids the expense of a corporate trustee (0.25 to 1 percent a year). Although these fees are reasonable, avoiding them means that more income is available for the beneficiaries. Often, however, the financial experience and abilities of individual trustees fall short of the competence needed. It also may not be fair to burden a friend or relative with such an onerous task without compensation.

Today, corporate trustees are more popular—over one-fifth of all banks have trust departments. They are not equally skilled, of course, but most are better equipped to perform investment duties than individuals. They provide continuity of management, and their long-term records are generally satisfactory. Although costs are too great to enable them to accept small individual trusts (perhaps less than $50,000 or $100,000, depending upon the particular institution), most states permit corporate trustees to combine small trusts into a common trust fund. Some banks have different funds for different objectives (such as high income or appreciation potential) that permit you to select among them.

Sometimes, both a corporate trustee and the surviving spouse are appointed as cotrustee. This does not reduce costs, for most trust departments charge a full fee anyway, and as a practical matter, such an arrangement tends to be inefficient. As an alternative, the surviving spouse could be given power to direct the trustee in certain matters, or he or she could be appointed in an advisory capacity.

Occasionally, circumstances suggest that an individual serve as trustee. For most long-term, family-type trust arrangements, however, there are advantages of using an established institution with a proven record of satisfactory performance. Ask friends in your community for recommendations and visit several bank trust departments before you choose one.

Be sure to discuss "investment powers" with your trustee, so that you both understand desired limits and goals for investment of trust principal. Also discuss "invasion powers," to set the extent to which the trustee can dip into trust principal in case income alone is inadequate for the beneficiaries' needs. In this area, as in others, a little forethought and planning can often eliminate serious problems later.

Providing for Guardian's Needs. Another provision that deserves consideration is whether part of the income can or should be used for the guardian's needs. If you have provided adequately for your family, your estate, supplemented by Social Security and other survivor benefits, is probably more than ample for your children alone. At the same time, their guardian might have limited income but large financial responsibilities, so that his or her own children are in a vastly different financial position than that of your children. Under these circumstances, the welfare of your children might be enhanced if the trustee is permitted to use some of the trust income to assist the guardian or the guardian's children, for they are the family that your children will then have.

Miscellaneous Other Provisions. There are many other matters that you should consider when planning a trust that are beyond the scope of this chapter. They include questions such as whether to include a "spendthrift" clause (to prevent a beneficiary from disposing of or encumbering his interest, and to protect the trust from creditors), how liberal the trustee's managerial powers should be, and at what ages distributions should be made to children (eighteen might not be best for a child, but is thirty-five too old?). You should discuss these and other concerns with your family, your lawyer, and the trustee.

HOW CAN YOU SHIFT INCOME TO OTHERS?

Many individuals would like to provide for children or elderly relatives and at the same time reduce the income tax liability associated with investing for this purpose or the ultimate estate taxes payable at death. Providing for dependents while reducing income tax liability involves the transfer of income-producing assets to the low-income taxpayer so that assets are accumulated at their lower tax bracket. Most of us, however, want to maintain control over our investments until some time in the future. Unfortunately, retaining control may not allow you to shift your income tax.

A comprehensive review of lawful means to minimize estate taxes is beyond the scope of this book, but every servicemember should understand some basic concepts. First, your taxable estate consists of the fair market value of all your possessions plus the face value of your life insurance policies. With a $250,000 SGLI policy, other life insurance for $250,000, and $150,000 in stocks, a home, and other possessions, you may already be at the point where government estate tax would have applied prior to June 2001. Considering our discussion of estate taxes earlier in this chapter, it is recommended that any servicemember with assets (including life insurance of $500,000 or more) needs to discuss estate planning carefully with his or her legal assistance office.

There are other ways to avoid future estate taxes besides trusts. This section discusses the characteristics, possible uses, and principal consequences of the more common arrangements. Probably the most familiar is joint tenancy or joint ownership (the "poor man's will") between a husband and wife. The following discussion summarizes some other methods of income shifting and/or avoiding probate; see also Table 21-3.

TABLE 21-3
INCOME SHIFTING SUMMARY

	Postpone Minor's Control	Reduce Income Taxes	Avoid Probate	Reduce Death Taxes
Outright gifts	No	Yes	Yes	Yes
Custodian gifts to minors	Yes, to majority	Yes[1]	Yes	Yes[2]
Joint ownership with right of survivorship	No	No	Yes	Yes
Survivor bonds and pay-on-death accounts (Totten trust)	Yes, until donor's death	No	Yes	No
Family annuities	No	Yes	Yes	Yes
Revocable trust	Yes, to age desired	No	Yes	No
Irrevocable trust	Yes, to age desired	Yes	Yes	Yes

[1] Unless used to satisfy legal obligations of parent.
[2] Unless donor or custodian dies before child's majority.

Outright Gifts

The most clear-cut way to reduce estate taxes and avoid probate is to dispose of property before death, and the simplest manner of doing so is to give it away. Consequently, if anyone has ample resources for present and future needs and could part with some assets while still alive, he or she should consider making outright gifts. IRS Publication 950, *Introduction to Estate and Gift Taxes,* outlines how you can go about doing this. These gifts not only shift income and avoid probate but also, in large estates, reduce estate taxes.

IRS Publication 950 describes many ways you can give gifts and avoid being taxed on the transfer of wealth from one generation to the next. For example, you can gift money to pay tuition or medical expenses for someone, and that person will not incur a tax. You can gift up to $11,000 to any person in a given year, and that person need not report that gift as income; hence, that person receives the gift tax-free. If someone decides to gift more than $11,000 to a single person in a given year (outside of medical or tuition expenses), then the generous donor will need to fill out IRS Form 709 and pay taxes on the excess gift amount (greater than $11,000), which may be adjusted for inflation.

To be effective, though, a present interest in the property must pass to the recipient. A "when I die it's yours" gift usually would not qualify. Also, if a gift is sufficiently large, a tax on the transfer might be incurred. However, the federal law grants everyone an annual, noncumulative exclusion of $11,000 per recipient ($22,000 if a husband and wife make a gift to a third person). If a couple had a daughter and son-in-law with three grandchildren, they could give that family $110,000 each year without affecting estate taxes ($11,000 to each person—dad, mom, and all three children—from both grandpa and grandma). To avoid taxes, a wealthy person should take advantage of the annual exclusion. If property left to someone other than the surviving spouse exceeds the exemption equivalent of the estate tax credit ($1 million for 2002), between one-third and one-half would be paid in taxes and never reach the beneficiaries.

Even parents who are not wealthy, for whom the savings might be more important, can stretch family dollars by making gifts of cash or securities to their minor children. The difficulty, though, is that outright gifts of titled or registered property can be complicated. To provide a gift, yet retain control of the funds until the child is twenty-one, parents should consider Uniform Gifts to Minors or Uniform Transfers to Minors Accounts. Since they are most often used for college funds, they are discussed in detail in chapter 13.

Joint Bank Accounts

Large numbers of husbands and wives, as well as many parents and children, maintain what are known as joint bank accounts. These are not true joint tenancies, because either owner, acting independently, may withdraw any or all funds on deposit. The usual registration takes the form of "Robert or Jane Doe, as joint tenants with the right of survivorship." There is no gift tax liability if the joint owners are married.

When one joint owner dies, the survivor owns the account, although a release from the state inheritance tax authorities normally would be required before it (or all of it above a specified amount) could be released to the survivor. What is more, for nonspousal accounts, the entire value is included for estate tax purposes in the estate of the first to die, except insofar as the survivor can establish that his or her property contributed to the acquisition. Hence, although a joint bank account (with, for example, a parent and child as co-owners) can be convenient, it generally would not, contrary to popular belief, result in any savings in federal or state death taxes in large estates.

Other Techniques

In the never-ending quest for ways to thwart the tax collector and keep a larger portion of property or income within a family, taxpayers have resorted to various other arrangements. Apart from the income-shifting techniques we have

Tips on Making the Most from Estate Planning

- Take advantage of the free legal assistance that is provided to military servicemembers.
- Have necessary powers of attorney available for your spouse to accomplish specific tasks for you when you are unavailable.
- Ensure that your will and your spouse's will are kept up to date. Avoid counting on legal software sold in retail stores.
- Keep an unsigned copy of your will for reference and a signed copy in a safe place—but not a safe deposit box, which may be sealed at the time of your death.
- Write a letter of last instruction for your family to assist them in the event of your death.
- Seek professional assistance from your legal assistance office or from lawyers that they may suggest for complicated trust or estate questions.
- Having your estate in order before deploying will help your family and yourself have peace of mind.

already considered, other methods of conserving assets within a family include loans and "private annuities," which offer unique advantages in some cases. For example, if reasonably wealthy elderly parents have responsible adult children, they might transfer property to them in exchange for their promise to pay them a monthly income for life. Such an arrangement, in which the children serve essentially like the issuer of a commercial annuity, saves commissions and other costs, avoids the expense and delay of probate, and enables the parents to leave more to their offspring. Another technique involves a gift and borrow-back of property, or hiring a child or spouse in an income-producing activity. If you think that some such arrangement is for you, ask your lawyer or tax advisor for suggestions.

DO YOU NEED PROFESSIONAL ASSISTANCE?

The answer to this question is YES! Still, one of the philosophical tenets of this book is that all servicemembers should understand as much as possible concerning the management of their financial affairs. The better your understanding, the more chance you have of maximizing the satisfaction from your economic resources. If you do not take the few minutes required to make sound economic decisions (determining your insurance needs, properly preparing a will and letter of last instruction, and so on), you and your family will suffer the consequences.

Along with learning to do things yourself, however, you also need expert assistance at times. Whether it is your banker or your legal advisor, you should go to that professional with a basic understanding of your problem and the kinds of solutions that might be used to solve it. Considering this advice, we do not recommend that you buy a "Make Your Own Will or Trust" kit and count on it to get you through tax and legal courts. Tax software packages are great tools, but one needs to be more cautious with legal software. They are not as foolproof yet. Still, the more knowledge you have, the easier it is for your advisor to explain the reasons for the advice he gives, the easier it is for you to evaluate that advice, and the surer you are that the decisions you make are good ones. Do not neglect to get help from professionals. It is their business to know and to provide you with the latest information required for you to make rational decisions about your estate.

It has been said that one who is his or her own lawyer has a fool for a client. This sentiment can be extended to anyone going it alone when it comes to estate planning. Start with an appointment with your legal assistance officer, and then follow through by completing a will and any other tools that you discover you need. Your legal assistance office may recommend lawyers in your area for you to use for complicated legal and financial matters. Sound financial and estate planning now will provide substantial benefits in the future.

22

Social Security and Veterans Benefits

An exhaustive treatment of Social Security benefits and veterans benefits is beyond the scope of this book, but this chapter provides an overview of their essential components and their impact on your personal financial plan. For more detailed information, contact your nearest Social Security Administration (SSA) or Department of Veterans Affairs office, or refer to the Internet sites listed in Appendix A.

WHAT IS SOCIAL SECURITY?

Social Security is actually a grouping of several programs designed to provide income insurance for American workers. The term Social Security is commonly used today to refer to only two of these programs: Old Age and Survivor's Insurance (OASI) and Disability Insurance (DI). There are several other major programs that come under the general heading of Social Security, including Medicare, Black Lung Benefits, and Supplemental Security Income. Also, the fifty states operate two other categories of "social security" programs: unemployment compensation and public assistance programs. This chapter is primarily concerned with Old Age and Survivor's Insurance and Disability Insurance.

According to the *Social Security Handbook,* Social Security is intended to provide for "the material needs of individuals and families; to protect aged and disabled persons against the expenses of illnesses that may otherwise use up their savings; to keep families together, and to give children the opportunity to grow up in health and security." Social Security benefits do not replace all the income lost when an insured worker retires, dies, or becomes disabled, but they help to maintain living standards. The average retired worker can expect to receive Social Security benefits replacing about 40 percent of preretirement income.

The first thing to understand about Social Security is how the system works. Social Security is not a savings plan. You do not pay your taxes into an account with your name on it, from which you draw payments after retirement. Instead, you pay taxes into general trust funds. The taxes you pay today are primarily paid out to today's retirees and disabled persons.

Social Security is a social contract. You agree to pay your taxes today for the benefit of today's elderly on the understanding that the government will provide for you in your retirement or disability by taxing tomorrow's workers. Thus, you should pay close attention to the political decisions concerning the future of Social Security. There is no guarantee that you will get back all that you pay in. If productivity continues to rise, then wages will rise and the tax base for Social Security will increase, ensuring that the system continues intact. If, however, productivity stagnates or if life expectancy increases, benefits may be curtailed in the future.

The amount of benefits you can expect has implications for the long-term savings plan that you establish as part of your budget (chapter 4) and your investment strategy (chapter 14). This is not meant to be alarmist—the Social Security system is currently solvent by most estimations. The key point is that you should have some type of savings plan to supplement Social Security in your retirement. By itself, even today's very generous system does not provide a truly comfortable lifestyle without other assets or income.

The Social Security Tax

Active-duty members of the uniformed services have been covered by Social Security on the same basis as civilian workers since 1957. Social Security is not optional—you must pay the Social Security tax, which is annotated "FICA" on your pay statements. For servicemembers, only basic pay is taxable for Social Security purposes, and taxes are withheld by law in the full amount from each active-duty monthly paycheck. If you or your spouse has additional income from self-employment, you must pay self-employment tax to the IRS. You must also file Schedule SE, "Computation of Social Security Self-Employment Tax," with your tax return if your net annual earnings from self-employment are greater than $400.

In 2001, you will pay a Social Security tax of 7.65 percent on your earnings. Of the 7.65 figure, 1.45 percent is applied to Medicare and 6.20 percent is applied to nonMedicare Social Security. This apportionment is important because the 1.45 percent Medicare tax applies to all income, while the non-Medicare rate is capped at an income of $80,400 (which is a tax of $ 4,984.40 for Social Security) per year. The $80,400 limit is automatically increased for inflation. Your employer matches every dollar you pay in taxes, so the total tax is 15.3 percent. In 2001, the government will pay over $410 billion in total Social Security benefits; retirement benefits account for slightly more than half of the total.

Eligibility for Social Security Benefits

Within the OASI and DI programs, there are three major types of benefits: retirement, survivor, and disability. Eligibility for each type of benefit depends on your insurance status, which, in turn, depends on your employment history. Because servicemembers pay Social Security taxes, they become insured workers. Working spouses (who must also pay Social Security taxes) become insured workers in their own right. Nonworking spouses are eligible for Social Security benefits based on the benefits of their working spouses.

Becoming Insured

The rules on how you get insured and how much money you are entitled to are a bit complex, but they are summarized here. In general, what matters is how long and how much you have paid into the Social Security system. Thus, the accuracy of your records at the SSA is crucial. You should request a statement of your earnings from the SSA every year or so. You can ask for a "Personal Earnings and Benefit Statement" (Form SSA-7004) from your local Social Security office, or contact the SSA at the phone number or Internet site listed in Appendix A. Within six weeks of your request, the SSA will send you a record of your earnings and an estimate of your projected benefits in today's dollars. Compare their numbers to your records (W-2 statements or LES) and write back to correct any errors immediately. The government is not obligated to correct mistakes in your earnings record that are more than three years old.

There are three types of Social Security insured status: fully insured, currently insured, and specially insured. The requirements always depend on the number of calendar quarters in which a worker has been paid some minimum amount of pay (currently $830). Once a worker has received at least that minimum amount of pay (and paid taxes on it), he or she is covered for that calendar quarter. A calendar quarter is any one of the following three-month time periods: January through March, April through June, July through September, and October through December. Except under unusual circumstances, a servicemember can expect to earn four full quarters of coverage for each calendar year of military service.

For retirement benefits, you are fully insured once you have credit for forty quarters. In other words, anyone who has completed ten years of active-duty service will be fully insured. For survivor and disability benefits, you are fully insured if you have at least one quarter of coverage for each calendar year after your twenty-first birthday and before the year you die or become disabled. You must have at least six quarters of coverage to be fully insured. Therefore, all servicemembers are fully insured for survivor or disability benefits after one and a half years of service.

Currently insured status is important as an alternative means of qualifying for survivor benefits. Individuals are currently insured if they have at least six quarters of coverage out of the thirteen quarters before death or disability.

Specially insured status is important for disability benefits. To be specially insured, an individual must have twenty quarters of coverage in the forty quarters preceding the disability. If you are disabled before age thirty-one, you must have coverage in half of the quarters since you turned twenty-one. A minimum of six quarters of coverage is required. Active-duty servicemembers are specially insured after eighteen continuous months of service.

Explanation of Benefits

This section explains the three types of benefits. The amount of the benefit is based on the primary insurance amount, or PIA. The next section shows briefly how to calculate the PIA. For further information, get your own estimate of your projected benefits from the SSA.

TABLE 22-1
CHART OF DELAYED RETIREMENT CREDIT RATES

Attain Age 65	Monthly Percentage	Yearly Percentage
Prior to 1982	1/2 of 1%	1%
1982–1989	1/4 of 1	3
1990–1991	7/24 of 1	.5
1992–1993	1/3 of 1	4
1994–1995	3/8 of 1	4.5
1996–1997	5/12 of 1	5
1998–1999	11/24 of 1	5.5
2000–2001	1/2 of 1	6
2002–2003	13/24 of 1	6.5
2004–2005	7/12 of 1	7
2006–2007	5/8 of 1	7.5
2008 or later	2/3 of 1	8

Retirement Benefits. To qualify for retirement benefits, you must be fully insured. There are three options for retirement under Social Security. Full retirement age is determined by the Social Security Administration based on the year of your birth. Workers who were born during or before 1937 (and will retire before 2002) can retire normally at age sixty-five, whereas those born after 1937 cannot retire with full benefits until a slightly later time. Most current servicemembers (born after 1959) cannot retire with full benefits until they are sixty-seven years old.

The following are the options:

- To retire at the full retirement age associated with your year of birth and receive full benefits. For most servicemembers, this will be age sixty-seven (those born in 1960 or later)
- To retire earlier than your normal retirement age and receive reduced benefits. This option starts at age sixty-two.
- To retire later than your normal retirement age but prior to age 70 and receive an increased monthly benefit as shown in Table 22-1.

Early retirement at age sixty-two is still possible under the rules outlined in Table 22-2, but because the normal retirement age is postponed, retiring exactly on your sixty-second birthday will mean that your monthly check will be an even smaller percentage of the PIA. For example, workers born after 1959 who retire at age sixty-two will receive only 70 percent of the PIA, as opposed to the 80 percent under the current system.

TABLE 22-2
FUTURE INCREASES IN RETIREMENT AGE

Year of Birth	Age 62	Normal Retirement Age (Years/Months)	Age 62 Benefit as Percent of Normal Benefit
1937 or earlier	1999 or earlier	65/0	80.0%
1938	2000	65/2	79.2
1939	2001	65/4	78.3
1940	2002	65/6	77.5
1941	2003	65/8	76.7
1942	2004	65/10	75.8
1943–1954	2005–2016	66/0	75.0
1955	2017	66/2	74.2
1956	2018	66/4	73.3
1957	2019	66/6	72.5
1958	2020	66/8	71.7
1959	2021	66/10	70.8
1960 or later	2022 or later	67/0	70.0

Survivor Benefits. An important goal of Social Security is providing for families when an insured worker dies, if family members are too young, old, or disabled to work. Benefits paid to the dependent family members of a deceased worker are called survivor benefits. There are many different categories of survivor benefits corresponding to the many circumstances that qualify someone to be a dependent family member of an insured worker. Table 22-3 presents information for four of the most frequently used categories of survivor benefits.

From the table, you can see that each child under age eighteen receives a monthly check for 75 percent of the insured worker's PIA. There is, however, a maximum family payment that reduces the amount paid to each child if there are many children. As of 2001 the maximum family benefit is 150 percent of the first $717 of the PIA, plus 272 percent of the next $317, plus 134 percent of the next $315, plus 175 percent of the PIA above $1,349. (These figures will change each year with inflation.) Notice also that nonworking spouses over age sixty who are not insured themselves are entitled to the benefits of the deceased spouse if that spouse was fully insured before dying. The benefit will range from 71.5 to 100 percent of the PIA of the deceased worker, depending on the age of the surviving spouse. Divorced surviving spouses are entitled to the benefits of a deceased worker if the marriage lasted at least ten years. Generally a surviving spouse over age sixty does not forfeit this entitlement by remarrying. There are several rules associated with remarrying, so we suggest you contact the SSA directly with your specific situation.

TABLE 22-3
SOCIAL SECURITY SURVIVOR BENEFITS

Benefit Insurance Status	Amount of Payment
Payment to each child under 18	75% of PIA
Payment to each child 18 or 19 and a full-time high school student	75% of PIA
Payment to a widow(er) caring for any children under 16	75% of PIA
Payment to a widow(er) over 60	100% of PIA

One final survivor benefit is the lump-sum death gratuity of $255. Surviving spouses living with an insured worker at the time of death are eligible; divorced spouses are not.

Disability Benefits. For the purposes of Social Security, disability means "the inability to engage in any substantial gainful activity by reason of any medically determinable physical or mental impairment which can be expected to result in death or which has lasted or can be expected to last for a continuous period of not less than twelve months." If a worker is fully or specially insured and has a serious disability, he or she will receive the full PIA. Disability of a servicemember involves not only the SSA but perhaps also the VA and the military disability compensation system. In this complex area, consult your legal assistance officer for all the entitlements.

Calculating the Primary Insurance Amount (PIA). The purpose of Social Security is to help maintain a reasonable portion of the standard of living that you achieved during your working lifetime. Therefore, the benefits you receive from Social Security will depend on the wages you earned (and the taxes you paid).

A secondary purpose of Social Security is to provide a minimum standard of living for all elderly persons. Therefore, workers who earned a lower level of wages will retain a larger percentage of those low wages in their benefits. For example, a lifetime minimum-wage worker will get a Social Security benefit of approximately 58 percent of his working wage, whereas a person who always earned the maximum covered earnings will receive a benefit of only about 24 percent of his working wage. The assumption is that the minimum-wage earner could not save enough to provide other income during retirement, while the well-paid worker could.

The primary insurance amount is based on your average indexed monthly earnings, or AIME. The idea behind the AIME is to adjust your actual earnings for inflation. The best way to find out what your benefits are is to ask the Social Security Administration to calculate your benefit for you. If you submit a *Request for Social Security Statement* (Form SSA-7004), the Social Security Administration will determine how much you will receive (in today's dollars) when you retire. As noted above, this will also verify that they have an accurate record of your earnings information.

The process that the Social Security Administration uses is as follows: First, they add all of your annual earnings since age twenty-one on which you paid Social Security taxes. Second, they multiply past earnings by index numbers to adjust them for inflation. Third, they eliminate the five lowest years (but you must have at least two years left to average together). Then they divide that figure by the number of months to arrive at the average indexed monthly earnings (AIME). You can roughly approximate their calculation by using your current monthly salary and then making a 10 to 40 percent reduction to compensate for the fact that you have had a real increase in salary during your military career.

Once you've figured out your AIME, determine your primary insured amount (PIA) by using the following formula. Most servicemembers will use the calculation from line two or three, based upon their average indexed monthly earnings.

If $\text{AIME} < \$561$, then $\text{PIA} = 0.9 \times \text{AIME}$.

If $\$561 < \text{AIME} < \$3{,}381$, then $\text{PIA} = \$540.90 + [0.32 \times (\text{AIME} - \$561)]$.

If $\text{AIME} > \$3{,}381$, then $\text{PIA} = \$1{,}407.30 + [0.15 \times (\text{AIME} - \$3{,}381)]$.

Index factors are accurate for 2001. Factors change each year; check with SSA office or Internet site for current factors.

This will give you a rough approximation of how much you will receive in Social Security benefits upon retirement or disability. The most reliable method is to send in Form SSA-7004.

Other Factors Affecting Your Benefits

Earnings Test for Retirement Benefits. If you are receiving Social Security benefits and have a large amount of earnings, then your benefits may be reduced. Workers who retire from the full-time workforce before reaching their full retirement age (sixty-seven for those servicemembers born in 1960 or later) will have their benefits reduced $1 for every $2 of income over $10,680 per year.

Workers who continue to work in the year they reach full retirement age will have their benefits reduced $1 for every $3 of income over $25,000 per year only for those months before they reach the full retirement age.

Once a worker reaches full retirement age, his or her Social Security benefit is no longer subject to the earnings test and is not reduced based on his or her income.

Taxation of Benefits. In addition to being offset in the manner described above, Social Security benefits may also be taxed as ordinary income for some retirees. For taxation purposes, total income is the sum of adjusted gross income, nontaxable interest from municipal bonds, and one-half of the benefit actually received (after the offset). Table 22-4 below lists the taxable income and tax rates based on your filing status:

TABLE 22-4
SOCIAL SECURITY TAX RATE

Tax Rate on Social Security	Single Filers	Joint (Married) Filers
0%	$0–$25,000	$0–$32,000
50	$25,000–$34,000	$32,000–$44,000
85	$34,000 and higher	$44,000 and higher

Cost-of-Living Adjustment (COLA). The COLA is probably the most valuable provision in Social Security. Once the benefit is determined, it is adjusted every year to protect its purchasing power from inflation. The COLA adjustment is determined by Congress each year.

WHAT ARE YOUR DEPARTMENT OF VETERANS AFFAIRS BENEFITS?

The Department of Veterans Affairs (VA) oversees many programs designed to help military veterans. For ease of explanation, we have grouped benefits into the following categories: disability and survivor benefits, educational benefits, medical benefits, financial benefits, and employment benefits. These benefits are subject to change by Congress, so check with the Department of Veterans Affairs at the address and Internet site listed in Appendix A for the latest details.

For the purposes of this discussion, a veteran is someone who has at least twenty-four months of active-duty experience and who either is still on active duty or has received an honorable or a general discharge from the service. Bad-conduct discharges and dishonorable discharges disqualify one from VA benefits. Discharges under other-than-honorable conditions qualify for some but not all benefits.

Disability and Survivor Benefits

Veterans disabled by injury or disease incurred in or aggravated by active service in line of duty are entitled to monthly payments if the disability is rated above 0 percent. (Veterans with a service-connected disability rated at 0 percent receive no compensation.) If the disabled veteran has dependents and if the disability is rated at 30 percent or higher, the benefit is increased. Except in cases of the most severe injuries, VA benefits are only supplemental income, and most veterans will want to find other employment.

The families of servicemembers who die while on active duty or from disease or injury incurred in the line of duty are entitled to Dependency and Indemnity Compensation (DIC). The dollar amount of the DIC benefit is $911 monthly for servicemembers' spouses. DIC pays an additional $229 per month in 2001 for each child under eighteen years of age. (These amounts are adjusted annually.)

The VA also provides a dependents education allowance. Your surviving spouse and children between the ages of eighteen and twenty-six (extended up to age thirty-one in certain cases) may be eligible for up to forty-five months of education benefits. Spouses must use the benefits within ten years of your death. Training may be in any approved vocational or business school, college, professional school, or establishment providing apprentice or on-the-job training. Monthly rates as of 2001 are $588 for full-time attendance and lesser amounts for part-time training.

When a servicemember dies on active duty, active-duty training, or inactive-duty training, the VA also pays a lump-sum death gratuity of $6,000 to the survivors. The VA will also pay up to $1,500 for burial if the death results from a service-connected disability. If the death is not service-connected, the VA will pay $300 for burial costs. Note that the VA will pay burial costs only if the veteran was receiving benefits from the VA at the time of his death or if the veteran dies in a VA hospital. If the death occurs while on active duty or after retirement from active duty, the deceased can be buried in a national cemetery. Finally, most veterans qualify for a burial flag to drape the coffin.

Education Benefits

The Montgomery GI Bill provides education benefits to active-duty and selected full-time National Guard soldiers who entered service on or after 30 June 1985. To participate, servicemembers must have contributed $100 for the first twelve months of service. Additionally, servicemembers must have a high school diploma or equivalent before starting training.

Benefits under the Montgomery GI Bill generally end ten years after the date of discharge or release from active duty. See your education office for details.

Tips on Making the Most from Social Security and Veterans Benefits

- Ensure that you file Schedule SE if someone in your family has a second job that earns more than $400 per year and does not have Social Security (FICA) tax deducted.
- Request your Social Security earnings status by filling a *Request for Social Security Statement* (Form SSA-7004) at least every three years. Correct any errors using your LES or W-2 forms.
- Social Security will provide only about 40 percent of your average wage before retirement (subject to a cap). Plan for other savings for retirement in your long-term goals.
- Be sure to apply for Social Security benefits. They are not automatically paid.
- Pay attention to your retirement or outprocessing briefings to know what veterans benefits you are eligible for.

Medical Benefits

Veterans who qualify for VA disability payments, former POWs, veterans who receive Medicaid, those exposed to Agent Orange, or those who suffer from Gulf War syndrome or from nuclear tests are eligible for hospital care through the VA. Other veterans are eligible for VA hospital care on a space-available basis. This care includes hospitalization, outpatient care (including prescriptions), alcohol and drug-abuse counseling, and readjustment counseling. Some veterans will have to make copayments for service and medication.

There is also a CHAMPVA program, which is essentially a health insurance program for dependents of disabled veterans and, in certain cases, for surviving dependents of deceased veterans. This program is independent of CHAMPUS and TRICARE. For details, contact the CHAMPVA Center at the address listed in Appendix A.

Outpatient dental care is available for some veterans, but eligibility is restricted to those who have service-connected dental disabilities or whose disability is rated at 100 percent.

In addition to these benefits, the VA also pays for nursing home care and in-home care in some cases.

Financial Benefits

The best-known VA benefit is probably the VA-backed home mortgage loan. The VA guarantees that a loan will be repaid, and that guarantee permits the lender to offer a lower interest rate. Because the VA loan does not require a down payment, veterans can qualify for a larger loan than they might otherwise. See chapter 11 for more information.

Employment Benefits

Disabled veterans may qualify for vocational rehabilitation training that prepares them for employment in a vocation of their choice. Also, veterans who served during a war period are given preference in job counseling, job information, and job placement services provided by the U.S. Employment Service.

Other Benefits

You may be entitled to other veterans benefits, one-time dental treatment on separation, employment assistance, and other benefits. Make sure that you are counseled thoroughly on these benefits before you leave the military. Also, don't forget to apply for unemployment compensation when you leave the service (if applicable).

SUGGESTED REFERENCES

See the Internet sites listed in Appendix A, which include the *Social Security Handbook.*

The most current edition of the *Uniformed Services Almanac* will give you much more detail about VA benefits than has been provided in this chapter, as will Budahn, P. J. *Veteran's Guide to Benefits,* 3rd ed. Mechanicsburg, PA: Stackpole Books, 2001.

One obvious source of information for Social Security and Department of Veterans Affairs programs is the local office of each administration; check your local telephone directory under "U.S. Government." They have pamphlets explaining each of their programs, which they will send you at no charge.

23

Retirement Survivor Benefits

By following the previous twenty-two chapters of this book, you have established a family budget; funded important purchases, including cars, homes, and college education; established and followed an investment strategy to achieve your goals; and finally, ensured that your survivors are protected by insurance. You understand what you will receive in retirement pay and from Social Security. There is one final important decision for you to make before you leave the military that affects what your survivors receive at the time of your death after you retire. That decision concerns participation in Survivor Benefit Plan (SBP). Because of the importance of that decision to your family's well-being, we devote this chapter to explaining the program to help you make the best decision for you and your family.

WHAT IS THE SURVIVOR BENEFIT PLAN?

The purpose of SBP is to provide the military retiree's spouse (or children, in certain situations) with an inflation-adjusted monthly income after the retiree dies. The critical point is that participating in SBP is a voluntary decision, but it is final. Every retiring soldier must decide whether to participate. The intent of this chapter is to help you make that decision based on a complete understanding of the program. The consequences of this decision are important and long lasting; this decision must not be taken lightly. Because of the profound consequences at retirement, full basic SBP for spouse and children will take effect automatically if you make no other valid election. The law states that spouses of servicemembers who do not elect SBP coverage or who elect coverage below that of retired base pay will be notified in writing of the implications of their choice. Sadly, some couples act impulsively and shortsightedly in this matter and later regret their decision.

It is important that you look at SBP as an integral part of your total estate planning. Decisions about participation should be based on family discussions with the advice of qualified personnel officers, insurance agents, bank trust officers, or others qualified in estate planning, such as the Army and Air Force Mutual Aid Association listed in Appendix A.

Coverage for Active-Duty Soldiers

What few soldiers realize is that SBP covers both the retired and retirement-eligible active-duty servicemember. As an active-duty member with sufficient time in service to retire, you are covered under SBP at no cost until you actually retire. If you die before retirement, your spouse receives 55 percent of the pay you would have been receiving had you been retired. If your retired pay would have been $2,100 per month, for example, the SBP annuity would be $1,155 per month until your spouse dies.

The fact that active-duty soldiers are covered only if they are eligible for retirement can present agonizing decisions for servicemembers if they are seriously injured on active duty. If a servicemember has a life-threatening injury, it is normally advantageous to expedite the processing to medically retire the solider and elect SBP coverage before he or she dies. Then the surviving family members will receive a portion of the retirement income for their lifetime, along with the servicemember's life insurance. If a servicemember who is not retirement eligible dies on active duty (without being medically retired), the family receives only the life insurance and Dependency and Indemnity Compensation (DIC) payments.

The annuity paid by SBP is reduced by any DIC payments, automatically paid by the Department of Veterans Affairs if death occurs on active duty. As of 2001, the amount of a surviving spouse's DIC payment was $911 per month, regardless of the retiree's rank or time in service. For a widow receiving $911 per month from DIC, only the SBP excess (in this case, $244) would be received, for a total payment of $1,155. If you die on active duty, your spouse will never receive less than the $911 per month DIC payment; however, the survivor benefits can be much greater than the DIC payment if your retirement pay and, consequently, SBP benefit are sufficiently large.

HOW MUCH DOES SBP COST AND WHAT DOES IT PROVIDE?

Basically, SBP continues to pay a portion of your retired pay to your surviving spouse after you die. That portion of your retirement pay, referred to as the monthly annuity, is always 55 percent of the base amount, an amount that you choose. The maximum base amount is your gross monthly retired pay; the minimum is $300. The examples in Table 23-1 illustrate how the amount of the annuity is determined.

Thus, you can ensure that your surviving spouse receives, for life, a monthly annuity check as low as $165 or as high as 55 percent of your retired gross pay. The cost of the program will depend on not only the amount of coverage you elect, but also whether you elect the coverage for spouse only, spouse and children, or children only. Let's now take a look at the costs.

TABLE 23-1
HOW ANNUITY IS DETERMINED

Gross Monthly Retired Pay	Base Amount That Retiree Elects	Spousal Annuity per Month
$2,100	$2,100	$1,155 ($2,100 × 0.55)
2,100	1,000	550 (1,000 × 0.55)
2,100	300	165 (300 × 0.55)

Spouse-Only Coverage

Computing the cost is just as easy as determining the base amount. Effective 1 March 1990, the cost is a flat 6.5 percent of the base amount. If you became a servicemember prior to 1 March 1990, you have the option of paying 2.5 percent for the first $509 of the base amount and 10 percent for the remainder. This will result in cheaper premiums for base amounts less than $1,091. An example is provided in Table 23-2.

TABLE 23-2
COMPUTING THE COST OF SBP

Gross Monthly Retired Pay	Base Amount That Retiree Elects	Spousal Annuity per Month	Cost per Month
$2,100	$2,100 × 0.55 =	$1,155	$136.50 ($2,100 x 0.065)
	2,100 × 0.35 = (after spouse turns 62)	735	(or $171.83*)
2,100	1,000 × 0.55 =	550	$65.00 ($1,000 × 0.065)
	1,000 × 0.35 = (after spouse turns 62)	350	(or $61.83*)
2,100	300 × 0.55 =	165	$19.50 ($300 × 0.065)
	300 × 0.35 =	105	(or $7.50*)

*Cost per month under the old pricing system (still available to retirees who had service time before March 1990) would be $171.83, $61.83, and $7.50, respectively, for the three options shown in this table.

The amount listed in the "cost per month" column will be deducted from your retirement check each month. As it is a deduction from income, it lowers your taxable income, which lowers your tax bill as well. Section 123 of the

Internal Revenue Code exempts the cost of SBP from federal income tax. However, only the cost is exempt; the annuity benefits to your spouse are considered taxable income. Furthermore, the SBP contribution, which is the amount deducted from retired pay to buy SBP insurance, is exempt from state income tax in all states but Mississippi. The annuity, when received by the survivors, is treated as taxable income by the federal government. The tax treatment of the annuity varies by state; contact your state tax division for specifics. (See Appendix A for state tax Internet sites.)

In the event of death, the SBP annuity (plus cost-of-living increases) will be paid to surviving spouses as long as they live. Should your spouse remarry before age fifty-five, however, the annuity would be suspended. If that marriage terminates, the annuity is again payable. Should your spouse remarry after fifty-five, the annuity continues uninterrupted. If your spouse dies before you do, deductions from your retired pay for SBP stop.

Spouse and Children Coverage

The additional cost for children is based on the ages of the youngest child, the servicemember, and his or her spouse and therefore varies tremendously. Your local personnel officer will be able to provide you with the factors for your specific situation. For example, let us consider a retiree who is forty-three, a spouse who is forty-one, and a youngest child who is ten. The cost factor for this particular situation is 0.00025. This factor must be added to the cost of the annuity for the spouse to determine the total cost.

TABLE 23-3
COST OF SPOUSE'S ANNUITY

Base Amount That Retiree Elects	Spousal Annuity per Month	Cost per Month	
$2,100 × 0.55 =	$1,155	$136.50	($2,100 × 0.065)
Plus children coverage		$0.53	($2,100 × 0.00025)
		$137.03	

The total SBP proceeds will be paid to your spouse, then, if the spouse dies or remarries, to the unmarried children. When there is more than one child, the proceeds are shared by all children. Payments terminate when the youngest child reaches age eighteen, or twenty-two if the child is in college. Deductions for coverage of children cease when the youngest child is no longer an eligible beneficiary. There is no age limit for eligible, incapacitated children, which includes unmarried children who are mentally or physically incapable of self-support because of a condition that existed before age eighteen (twenty-two if in school).

Children Only

Cost for the children-only coverage is based on your age and the age of the youngest child. However, the annuity payable is the same as for spouse-only or spouse and children coverage—always 55 percent of the base amount. For example, for a retiree who is forty-three and a youngest child who is ten, the cost factor is 0.0039.

TABLE 23-4
COST OF CHILDREN'S ANNUITY
Children only

Base Amount That Retiree Elects	Children's Annuity per Month	Cost per Month
$2,100	$1,155	$8.19 ($2,100 × 0.0039)

Here, too, deductions from pay cease when the youngest child is no longer an eligible beneficiary. In the event of your death, the annuity would be shared equally by all your eligible children. There are some additional combinations of coverage available in this program, including former-spouse coverage and retirees with no dependents.

Cost-of-Living Raises

Unlike ordinary insurance policies, SBP is fully protected by cost-of-living allowances (COLAs). Your retired pay is also protected with COLAs; thus, the cost of the SBP program increases each time your retired pay rises. However, the cost will increase only by the amount of the COLA, and your real (inflation-adjusted) pay remains the same.

So, although the COLA increases your retired pay and your monthly deduction, it also increases your spouse's benefits. Further, your spouse will continue to receive COLA increases after you die, even though you have stopped paying into the system. This is perhaps the greatest advantage of SBP—not only does the insurance benefit increase while you are buying it, but it keeps growing with inflation as long as your spouse receives benefits. This inflation protection is an extraordinarily valuable feature; you can't get inflation-indexed benefits like this with any ordinary commercial insurance product.

Social Security Entitlements

Many military people, secure in their own retirement and benefit programs, give scant attention to Social Security and what it can provide (see chapter 22). However, Social Security has a direct bearing on SBP benefits through what is known as the SBP offset. This essentially results in a two-tier SBP system. If you die before your spouse, the SBP annuity begins; however, once your spouse begins to receive your Social Security benefits, the SBP annuity will be reduced from 55 percent of the base amount elected to 35 percent.

The government, as your employer, contributes to the Social Security fund for active-duty personnel. In enacting the SBP law, Congress insisted that a spouse's annuity be reduced or offset by the value of the decedent's military-earned wage credits. Normally the reduction begins when the surviving spouse reaches age sixty-two, because that is when Social Security benefits can be paid. If you should die before your spouse is sixty-two, the SBP annuity will not be reduced before your spouse reaches that age unless there are dependent children in your household at the time of your death. Because a spouse with dependent children who are sixteen or younger also receives payments from Social Security, the SBP annuity may be reduced in such instances. Your spouse should contact the Social Security Administration, the Retired Officers Association, or the Army and Air Force Mutual Aid Association about current offset provisions if your survivors include dependent children.

SHOULD YOU TAKE SBP?

For any retiree, the question must certainly arise, "Is SBP a good deal?" We would reply, "Yes, but . . . " We carefully analyzed the program for the typical retiree with an average life expectancy and came to two conclusions:

- A similar system could not be bought at a lower cost "on the economy."
- It is an excellent program on its own merits.

But there are also important considerations that, for a few servicemembers, may make the selection of SBP unnecessary. Here we consider two ways of evaluating SBP: first an absolute analysis, then an analysis in relative terms.

SBP versus No Insurance

First we address the question "Am I better off with SBP or with nothing?" Clearly, for retirees who live longer than their spouses, SBP is a great expense with no benefit. On the other hand, if you die early and your spouse lives a long time after your death, the benefits received are very large in comparison to the costs.

In Table 23-5, we have illustrated the case of a male lieutenant colonel (O-5), age forty-two, with a forty-two-year-old spouse, retiring in 2001 after twenty years of service. His monthly retired pay is $2,895, and he chooses to use that as the full base amount for SBP.

To compare the costs and benefits of SBP, we can select an age at which the retiree might die. To illustrate, let's assume that he dies at age sixty-seven. Column C indicates the total deductions from the servicemember's retired pay up to that year (a total of $110,249). If his wife lives until her normal life expectancy (which is approximately eighty-four for a sixty-seven year-old woman; see Table 19-4), she would receive an after-tax benefit of $240,683, listed in column F.

TABLE 23-5
SBP COST AND COMPARISON

Age	Annual SBP Cost	Cumulative SBP Cost	Spouse's Age	After-Tax SBP Benefit	Value of After-Tax SBP Benefit	One-Year Term Life Premium	Cumulative Term Life Premiums	Savings (Costs) Compared with Term
A	B	C	D	E	F	G	H	I
42	1,637	1,674	42	16,241	374,163	465	476	(1,198)
43	1,686	3,474	43	16,728	377,392	545	1,055	(2,419)
44	1,737	5,407	44	17,230	380,303	630	1,747	(3,660)
45	1,789	7,481	45	17,747	382,871	716	2,558	(4,923)
46	1,843	9,704	46	18,279	385,063	802	3,494	(6,210)
47	1,898	12,084	47	18,828	386,850	893	4,565	(7,519)
48	1,955	14,630	48	19,393	388,198	987	5,781	(8,849)
49	2,013	17,351	49	19,974	389,067	1,085	7,152	(10,199)
50	2,074	20,258	50	20,574	389,449	1,195	8,698	(11,560)
51	2,136	23,360	51	21,191	389,303	1,304	10,425	(12,935)
52	2,200	26,668	52	21,826	388,582	1,423	12,353	(14,315)
53	2,266	30,193	53	23,481	387,235	1,553	14,500	(15,693)
54	2,334	33,948	54	23,156	385,210	1,687	16,882	(17,066)
55	2,404	37,944	55	23,850	382,453	1,838	19,526	(18,418)
56	2,476	42,195	56	24,566	378,905	1,995	23,450	(19,745)
57	2,551	46,715	57	25,303	374,510	2,152	25,667	(21,048)
58	2,627	51,517	58	26,062	369,197	2,328	29,210	(23,307)
59	2,706	56,618	59	26,844	362,898	2,520	33,110	(23,508)
60	2,787	62,033	60	27,649	355,542	2,732	37,403	(24,630)
61	2,871	67,779	61	28,479	347,185	2,982	42,147	(25,632)
62	2,957	73,874	62	18,666	337,625	3,271	47,401	(26,473)
63	3,046	80,335	63	19,236	337,903	3,705	53,337	(26,998)
64	3,137	87,182	64	19,803	337,788	4,207	60,055	(27,127)
65	3,231	94,436	65	20,397	337,263	4,763	67,646	(26,790)
66	3,328	102,118	66	21,009	336,317	5,334	76,165	(25,953)
67	3,428	110,249	67	21,640	334,955	5,897	85,646	(24,603)
68	3,531	118,855	68	23,289	333,192	6,423	96,093	(23,762)
69	3,637	127,958	69	23,957	331,034	6,944	107,547	(20,411)
70	3,746	137,586	70	23,646	328,496	7,520	120,109	(17,477)
71	3,858	147,765	71	24,355	325,580	8,190	133,925	(13,840)
72	0	154,460	72	25,086	323,253	8,918	149,111	(5,349)
73	0	161,459	73	25,839	318,458	9,748	165,834	4,375
74	0	168,776	74	26,614	314,102	10,684	184,272	15,496
75	0	176,423	75	27,412	309,120	11,716	204,600	28,177
76	0	184,417	76	28,235	303,487	12,879	237,039	42,623

Age	Annual SBP Cost	Cumulative SBP Cost	Spouse's Age	After-Tax SBP Benefit	Value of After-Tax SBP Benefit	One-Year Term Life Premium	Cumulative Term Life Premiums	Savings (Costs) Compared with Term
A	B	C	D	E	F	G	H	I
77	0	192,774	77	29,082	297,209	14,144	251,787	59,013
78	0	201,509	78	29,954	290,256	15,520	279,063	77,554
79	0	210,640	79	30,853	282,629	17,024	309,114	98,474
80	0	230,184	80	31,778	274,330	18,592	342,129	121,945
81	0	230,161	81	32,732	266,533	20,365	378,452	148,291
82	0	240,591	82	33,714	258,302	23,235	418,335	177,744
83	0	251,492	83	34,725	249,669	24,261	462,095	210,603
84	0	262,888	84	35,767	240,683	26,415	510,040	247,152
85	0	274,800	85	36,840	231,344	28,566	562,357	287,557
86	0	287,252	86	37,945	231,698	30,832	619,362	332,110
87	0	300,268	87	39,083	211,750	32,894	681,057	380,789
88	0	313,874	88	40,256	201,546	34,979	747,681	433,807
89	0	328,097	89	41,464	191,107	36,841	819,236	491,129
90	0	342,964	90	42,707	180,339	38,429	895,637	552,673
91	0	358,504	91	43,989	172,442	40,408	977,533	619,029
92	0	374,749	92	45,308	164,889	42,357	1,065,134	690,385
93	0	394,730	93	46,668	157,658	44,230	1,158,609	763,879
94	0	409,480	94	48,068	150,731	45,995	1,258,134	848,654
95	0	428,034	95	49,510	144,051	47,603	1,363,812	935,778

Assumes a 6.25% interest rate, 3.0% COLA, 27.5% tax rate before retiree's death, 15% tax rate after death.

Clearly, under these assumptions, SBP is an expected net benefit to the family of $130,614. As the table reflects, with a male servicemember and spouse of equal age, the expected benefits will normally outweigh the expected costs as long as the servicemember dies before reaching age eighty-three.

There are other circumstances, however, in which the costs outweigh the benefits. Clearly, if a retiree pays in for a number of years and the spouse dies first, there would be no SBP benefit and all SBP payments up to his wife's death would be a loss. If the spouse dies soon after the military retiree (before predicted life expectancy), he or she is not able to receive the SBP payments long enough to recoup the deductions from retired pay. Using Table 23-5, you can get an idea of the circumstances under which SBP "pays off" by delivering more benefits than it costs. In general, this occurs when the retiree dies several years before the surviving spouse.

Obviously, you cannot know for certain how long you will live and how long your spouse will live. The purpose of insurance—and SBP is a form of insurance—is to reduce the financial risk arising from undesirable events. In this case, the undesirable event is the premature death of the military retiree, and the financial risk is a spouse having insufficient income following the retiree's death.

Perhaps you have some reason to believe, based on family health history or your relative ages, for example, that you or your spouse will live a long or short time after retirement or that one is highly likely to die before the other. You can certainly use that information in making your decision about SBP, but you cannot completely eliminate the uncertainty. In any case, you may want to buy the insurance to protect your family. That raises the issue of the cost effectiveness of SBP as compared with privately available insurance, which is analyzed in the next section.

SBP versus Commercial Life Insurance

Perhaps you do not feel comfortable without the basic insurance protection that SBP or some other form of life insurance provides. A second way to evaluate SBP is to do a relative analysis—compare it with privately offered insurance.

Some retirees say, "I can do it myself. All I have to do is purchase a commercial term life insurance policy, and I'll be able to replicate SBP at a fraction of the cost." Columns G, H, and I in Table 23-5 compare the cost of SBP and the cost of commercial term life insurance in covering the income needs of surviving spouses.

Basically, the decision is between participating in SBP (and accepting the lower retired pay that goes with it) and turning down SBP in favor of taking full retired pay and using part of it to buy term insurance. SBP is cheaper than the term insurance option if the present value of the retired pay you give up is lower than the present value of the premiums required to buy the same protection with term life insurance.

In Table 23-5, the key figures are in columns C and H, where the cumulative costs of the SBP program and of term insurance are shown. The numbers in those two columns are compared in column I for each year's cost. The table shows that the cumulative cost of a one-year term insurance policy is cheaper in the short run. For example, the term option is cheaper by $1,055 in the year after retirement (retiree is age forty-three). In the long run, though, the increasing year-to-year cost of attempting to maintain insurance protection for the cost-of-living increases and the rising cost of buying term insurance as your age increases will make the cost of term insurance greater than the cost of SBP. By comparing the figures in the table, you can see that if you die ten years after retirement (age fifty-two), the present value of the amount by which the cumulative cost of SBP exceeds the cumulative cost of insurance for the period from your retirement until your death is $14,315. At age seventy-two, annual insurance costs are rapidly increasing, and the SBP option is more attractive. If you died at age eighty-two, the present value of your savings from electing SBP instead of buying term insurance would be $177,744.

If you are older than forty-two at retirement, term insurance will be more expensive than is shown here, and the analysis tilts more toward SBP. The opposite is true if you retire younger than forty-two. As we pointed out in our absolute analysis, if you have reason to believe that you will have a relatively short life expectancy, you might want to consider using term insurance rather than SBP to protect your family after your death. But if you're uninsurable or expensive to insure (due to medical problems or smoking), SBP may be your best deal.

The figures presented in Table 23-5 are available from military personnel retirement counselors. They are based on computer models from the DOD Actuary and are updated annually. Additionally, you can access various SBP calculators on the Department of Defense Retirement Services Office home page. These online calculators allow you to input your specific circumstances and make an informed decision before you have to make SBP decisions.

Some Additional Considerations

Our analysis shows that SBP is a reasonably cost-effective insurance plan for the typical retiree who lives a normal life expectancy. But there are some additional factors you should consider before you make your decision.

Do you need insurance at all? Remember that the only reason for participation in SBP is to provide for your survivors' needs if you should die before they do and your retired pay stops as a result. If you have substantial financial assets that meet your survivors' needs to provide them with a secure, adequate income or if they have valuable work skills, you may not need SBP or more term insurance to protect them. It makes little sense to buy insurance of any kind that you do not need.

SBP is inflation protected, and term insurance is not. A unique feature of SBP benefits is that they are regularly adjusted upward as the cost of living rises. With term insurance, the amount of coverage is fixed and cannot be adjusted for inflation. You have to raise the face amount of the policy to keep up with inflation, and you cannot do this without a medical exam, company approval, and a lot of extra cost and uncertainty.

Commercial insurance proceeds can be passed on to children. SBP cannot be paid to children who are older than twenty-two unless they are disabled. With term insurance, the face value of the policy is paid to your surviving spouse (or other beneficiary) at your death; the survivor then can decide what to do with that money—use it all for support or pass some of it along to your children. SBP benefits, by contrast, stop when your spouse dies or when your last child reaches twenty-two.

The SBP program is heavily subsidized by the government. This means that the average SBP participant is "buying" protection at a substantial discount from the "fair" price, and the government makes up the difference. This is certainly not the case for commercial insurance policies. Unless you have some special consideration that makes SBP unattractive to you and your family, it is not likely that you will find better protection for the price.

If you are thinking about not taking any SBP at all, strongly consider taking at least the minimum base amount at the 2.5 percent reduced cost rate, if that is an option for you. At $7.50 a month, this might be too good a deal for you to pass up.

Changes in Coverage

Except as permitted under the SBP open enrollment period, participation in SBP cannot be changed or modified once your application becomes effective with one exception. As an SBP participant, you have a one-year window to terminate SBP coverage between the second and third anniversary following the date you begin to receive retired pay. None of the premiums you paid will be refunded, and no annuity will be payable upon your death. Your covered spouse or former spouse must consent to the withdrawal. Termination is permanent, and participation may not be resumed under any circumstance; that is, future enrollment is barred. This termination option also includes reservists who begin receipt of retired pay on their sixtieth birthday.

As long as you have an eligible beneficiary for the annuity deductions from your retired pay continue until you have completed thirty years (360 payments) in the plan and reached age seventy. At that point you are considered "paid up" and no more premiums are owed, and an annuity is payable. Contact your personnel counselor for details on this feature, which is not effective for retirees until 1 October 2008.

Deductions from your retirement pay will be discontinued if your spouse dies before you do, you are granted a divorce, or your marriage is annulled. If the retiree remarries, he or she has the option not to provide coverage for the new spouse. The member's new spouse must be notified, and the option must be exercised within one year of remarrying.

Supplemental Survivor Benefit Plan (SSBP)

Effective 1 April 1992 (PL 101-189), eligible retirees of the uniformed services can enroll in Supplemental SBP (SSBP), which is a program that replaces some or all of the SBP annuity reduction when a surviving spouse or former spouse reaches the age of sixty-two. SSBP is only available to retirees who have elected SBP at the maximum level (base amount equal to full retired pay). This SSBP annuity is payable in increments of 5, 10, 15, or 20 percent. When increments are added to the "standard" SBP annuity (35 percent of base amount at age sixty-two or older), the total annuity to the surviving spouse or former spouse will equal 40, 45, 50, or 55 percent of monthly gross military retired pay.

SSBP premiums are added to SBP premiums (6.5 percent of the base amount elected) and depend on the retiree's age at the time he or she elects to add the supplemental annuity to his or her SBP. Once SSBP premiums are

Tips on Making the Most for Your Survivors

- The SBP decision is the most important financial choice you will make as you retire. Carefully study your options for SBP before you make this important, permanent decision.
- Consider your and your spouse's ages and health as you make your choice. In general, couples in which the military retiree's spouse is younger and healthier will benefit more from SBP.
- Remember that children's coverage is inexpensive but lasts only until they are twenty-two.
- Military retirement counselors will calculate SBP data for your particular circumstances.
- Consult a financial professional to get unbiased advice on SBP.

established, they will be treated in the same manner as SBP premiums. SSBP will be increased like SBP premiums and suspended whenever SBP premiums are suspended. SSBP rates can be obtained by consulting the references in Appendix A or your local military pay division.

If the retiree marries or remarries after retiring, he or she may elect, within one year of marriage or remarriage, to provide an SSBP annuity for his or her spouse as long as he or she is providing maximum SBP coverage (55 percent of monthly gross retired pay). The SBP coverage may be increased to its maximum before electing SSBP coverage. The retiree may not, however, reduce a maximum SBP annuity that he or she already had elected upon remarriage.

THE BOTTOM LINE

The decision to participate in or pass up SBP and SSBP is very important, especially because the choice is irreversible. You cannot decide later to join SBP, and you have only one opportunity to drop out of the program after retirement—between your second and third years of retirement—unless your spouse dies before you. Our advice is to analyze SBP as an insurance policy and buy it if you need the insurance protection that it provides. In almost all cases we recommend you purchase the benefit upon retirement and then reassess during your third year. If your retirement situation has changed, you have the opportunity to drop out of the program.

Considering the benefits of SBP and SSBP and their costs in comparison with other means of providing for your family after you die, we think SBP is a good program for many retirees because it provides excellent coverage for most retirees and, together with Social Security survivor payments, can guarantee a secure income that your spouse cannot outlive and that cannot be eroded by inflation. The peace of mind that those benefits offer to many retirees may be well worth the cost of the reduced retirement check.

Appendix A

Sources of Assistance

The World Wide Web has dramatically changed the sources of information that are available to any individual with a personal computer and Internet access. It enables us to continually update references and information as they change. Although most of the concepts and principles discussed in this book will generally be applicable for years, sources of assistance and references will change.

To provide you with the latest information and enhance the value of this book, the sources of assistance and other references will continually be updated on the Armed Forces Personal Finance home page. This Internet site will be accessible through the U.S. Military Academy Department of Social Sciences home page. Its Internet address is

http://www.dean.usma.edu/socs/econ/persfin/default.htm.

Bookmark this location and refer to it if any of the Internet sites, phone numbers, or addresses below have changed. The references below are arranged by order of chapter and topic.

Chapter 3: Military Pay and Allowances

Joint Federal Travel Regulation: *http://www.dtic.mil/perdiem/jftr.html*
Pay and allowances: *www.dfas.mil*
LES online: *www.dfas.mil/emss*

Chapters 5 and 6: Banking and Credit

For lists of credit card offers, contact:
Bankcard Holders of America, 524 Branch Drive, Salem, VA 24153, tel. (540) 389-5445
Ram Research CardTrak, Box 1700, Frederick, MD 21702, tel. (800) 344-7714 *http://www.ramresearch.com/home.html*

If you have problems with a credit report or want to obtain your credit report, contact:
Equifax: *http://www.equifax.com/consumer/consumer.html*
Experian: *http://www.experian.com/index.html*
Trans Union: *http://www.tuc.com/consumer/*

See also:
American Bankers Association: *http://www.aba.com/aba/persfin*
Includes mortgage, auto loan, and rent versus buy calculators.
Bank Rate Monitor: *http://bankrate.com*
Consumer Credit Counseling Service (CCCS):
http://www.powerhouse.com/cccs/
Credit Union National Association:
(800) 358-5710
http://www.cuna.org/
MasterCard: *http://www.mastercard.com*
National Foundation for Consumer Credit:
(800) 388-2227
Visa: *http://www.visa.com*

Chapter 7: Taxes
Internal Revenue Service: *http://www.irs.ustreas.gov/*
Tax Site Index: *http://www.uni.edu/schmidt/sites.html*
State Tax Internet Index: *http://www.uni.edu/schmidt/state.html*

Chapters 8 and 9: Automobiles and Auto Insurance
For car purchasing information:
Auto by telephone: *http://www.autobytel.com*
Will send you a quote.
Autosite: *http://www.autosite.com*
Lots of useful information.
Edmunds: *http://www.edmunds.com*
Invoice and MSRP data.
How to Beat the Dealer: *http://www.beatcar.com*
USAA: *http://www.usaa.com*
Useful book with tips.
Intellichoice: *http://www.intellichoice.com*
Invoice and MSRP data.
Kelley's Blue Book Online: *http://www.kbb.com*
New and used car quotes.
Microsoft's Carpoint: *http://carpoint.msn.com*
General information.
Vehicle zone: *http://www.vehiclezone.com*
Includes payment calculator.

For automobile insurance information:
Geico Insurance Company: *http://www.geico.com*
Maryland Insurance Administration: *http://www.gacc.com/mia/autoshop.html*
United Services Automobile Association: *http://www.usaa.com*

Chapter 10: Medical and Dental Care

For TRICARE Medical Information:

TRICARE: *http://www.tricare.osd.mil*

For TRICARE claims information:

Palmetto Government Benefits Administrators: *http://www.mytricare.com*

For TRICARE Prime Remote:

See the website for contact numbers by state:
http://www.tricare.osd.mil/remote/

TABLE A-1
TRICARE TELEPHONE NUMBERS

Region	Location	Telephone
1	Northeast	888-999-5195
2	Mid-Atlantic	800-931-9501
3	Southeast	800-444-5445
4	Gulfsouth	800-444-5445
5	Heartland	800-941-4501
6	Southwest	800-406-2832
7/8	Central	888-874-9378
9	Southern California	800-242-6788
10	Golden Gate	800-242-6788
11	Northwest	800-404-2042
12	TRICARE Pacific	
	Hawaii	800-242-6788
	Alaska	888-777-8343
15	Canada and Latin America	888-777-8343
15	Puerto Rico and Virgin Islands	888-777-8343
	Europe	888-777-8343

For DEERS:

Defense Manpower Data Center
Attn: DEERS Support Office
400 Gigling Road
Seaside, CA 93955-6771
(800) 334-4162 (California); (800) 527-5602 (Alaska and Hawaii);
(800) 538-9552 (all other states)
http://www.dmdc.osd.mil/swg/owa/DMDC.HOME

For National Mail Order Pharmacy:
(800) 903-4680
http://www.merck-medco.com

For Uniformed Services Family Health Plan:
(888) 258-7347
http://www.usfhp.org

For CHAMPVA:
VA Health Administration Center
CHAMPVA
P.O. Box 65023
Denver, CO 80206-9023
(800) 733-8387
http://www.va.gov/hac/champva/champva.html

For Continued Health Care Benefit Program:
Continued Health Care Benefit Program (CHCBP) Administrator
P.O. Box 1608
Rockville, MD 20849-6118
(800) 809-6119

For Dental Information:
United Concordia
TDP Customer Service
P.O. Box 69410
Harrisburg, PA 17106-9410
General information: (800) 866-8499; (800) 891-1854 (TDD)
Enrollment: (888) 622-2256
OCONUS, nonremote: (888) 418-0466 (toll-free)
OCONUS, remote: (717) 975-5017 (*not* toll-free)
http://www.ucci.com
Delta Dental Plan of California (TRICARE Retiree Dental Plan)
(888) 838-8737
http://www.ddpdelta.org

Websites
Fisher House Program: *http://www.fisherhouse.org/*
DOD Health Affairs: *http://www.ha.osd.mil/*
Department of Veterans Affairs: *http://www.va.gov*
U.S. Army Medical Command:
http://www.armymedicine.army.mil/armymed/default2.htm
Walter Reed Army Medical Center: *http://www.wramc.amedd.army.mil*

Organizations Providing CHAMPUS Supplemental Health Insurance

This information is current through the TRICARE web page at *http://www.tricare.osd.mil/supplementalinsurance/SupplementalInfo.htm.* Most organizations can be directly contacted about membership through their websites.

Air Force Association
1501 Lee Highway
Arlington, VA 22209-1198
(800) 727-3337
or (703) 247-5800

Air Force Sergeants Association
P.O. Box 10401
Des Moines, IA 50306-0401
(800) 882-5541

American Association of Uniformed Services
NEAT Management Group
P.O. Box 3686
Austin, TX 78764
(800) 222-0207

American Military Association
Ft. Snelling Station
P.O. Box 76
Minneapolis, MN 55440-0076
(800) 562-4076

American Military Retirees Association
AMRA Group Insurance Plan, Administrator
P.O. Box 2510
Rockville, MD 20852-0510
(800) 638-2610
or (301) 816-0045

American Military Society
P.O. Box 50282
Washington, DC 20091-0282
(800) 808-4514

AMVETS
4647 Forbes Boulevard
Lanham, MD 20706-4380
(301) 459-9161

Armed Forces Benefit Services, Inc.
AFBA Building
909 N. Washington Street
Alexandria, VA 22314-1556
Customer service:
(800) 403-7745
Claims: (800) 235-2322

Armed Services Mutual Benefits Association
ASMBA Group Insurance Administrator
P.O. Box 2510
Rockville, MD 20852-0510
(800) 638-2610
or (301) 816-0045

Army Aviation Association of America
Membership Services, Inc.
P.O. Box 4999
Reston, VA 20195-1465
(800) 421-1470

Association of Military Surgeons of the United States
AMSUS Group Insurance Administrator
P.O. Box 2510
Rockville, MD 20852
(800) 638-2610
or (301) 816-0045

Association of the U.S. Army
P.O. Box 10408
Des Moines, IA 50306-0408
(800) 882-5707

Enlisted Association of the National Guard of the United States
NGAUS
1 Massachusetts Avenue NW
Washington, DC 20001
(202) 789-0031

First Coast Fleet, Inc.
FCFI Group Insurance Administrators
3998 Confederate Point Road
Jacksonville, FL 32210
(800) 566-0420
or (904) 778-1565

Fleet Reserve Association
P.O. Box 10340
Des Moines, IA 50306-0340
(800) 424-1120

Government Employee Benefits Association
P.O. Box 241324
Montgomery, AL 36124-1324
(800) 240-2020
or (334) 272-4313

Harris Methodist Health Insurance Company
Texas Military Health Care
P.O. Box 90100
Arlington, TX 76004-9882
(800) 373-9779

Health Force
Membership Services, Inc.
P.O. Box 4999
Reston, VA 20195-1465
(800) 421-1470

Marine Corps Association
MCA Health Care Plan, Administrator
734 15th Street NW, Suite 600
Washington, DC 20005
(800) 368-5682
or (202) 393-6600

Marine Corps League
Membership Services, Inc.
P.O. Box 4999
Reston, VA 20195-1465
(800) 421-1470

Military Benefit Association
P.O. Box 221110
Chantilly, VA 20153-1110
(800) 336-0100

Military Health Benefits Association
P.O. Box 96987
Washington, DC 20090-6987
(800) 808-4514

Military Insurance Specialist, Inc.
208 Gunn Road
Montgomery, AL 36117
(800) 852-9162
or (205) 272-4313

Military Order of the Purple Heart
Membership Services, Inc.
P.O. Box 4999
Reston, VA 20195-1465
(800) 421-1470

Military Order of the World Wars
Membership Services, Inc.
P.O. Box 4999
Reston, VA 20195-1465
(800) 421-1470

National Armed Forces Association
NEAT Management Group
P.O. Box 3409
Austin, TX 78764
(800) 336-3219

National Association for Uniformed Services
Attn: Ingrid Miller
1101 Mercantile Lane
Suite 100
Springdale, MD 20774
(800) 808-4514

National Defense Transportation Association
Membership Services, Inc.
P.O. Box 4999
Reston, VA 20195-1465
(800) 421-1470

National Guard Association of the United States
NGAUS
1 Massachusetts Ave. NW
Washington, DC 20001
(202) 789-0031

National Officers Association
Membership Services, Inc.
P.O. Box 4999
Reston, VA 20195-1465
(800) 421-1470

Naval Enlisted Reserve Association
Seabury & Smith, Administrator, Group Insurance Program
1255 23rd Street NW,
Suite 300
Washington, DC 20037
(800) 424-9883
or (202) 457-6820

Naval Reserve Association
Seabury & Smith, Administrator, Group Insurance Program
1255 23rd Street NW, Suite 300
Washington, DC 20037
(800) 424-9883
or (202) 457-6820

Navy League
Monumental General Insurance Group
P.O. Box 17480
Baltimore, MD 21203-7480
(800) 752-9797
or (800) 883-5378

Reserve Officers Association
P.O. Box 10403
Des Moines, IA 50306-0403
(800) 247-7988

Retired Association for the Uniformed Services
RAUS Group Insurance, Administrator
P.O. Box 2510
Rockville, MD 20852-0510
(800) 638-2610
or (301) 816-0045

Society of Military Widows
Attn: Ingrid Miller
1101 Mercantile Lane, Suite 100
Springdale, MD 20774
(800) 808-4514

The Retired Enlisted Association
P.O. Box 50584
Washington, DC 20091-0584
(800) 808-4514

The Retired Officers Association
P.O. Box 9126
Des Moines, IA 50306
(800) 247-2192

The Uniformed Services Association
Membership Services, Inc.
P.O. Box 4999
Reston, VA 20195-1465
(800) 421-1470

Uniformed Services Benefit Association
3822 Summit
P.O. Box 418258
Kansas City, MO 64141-9258
(800) 821-7912

United Armed Forces Association
P.O. Box 2603
Waco, TX 76702-2603
(817) 753-0757

United Military and Government Employees Association
UM & GA Group Insurance Administrators
P.O. Box 2510
Rockville, MD 20852-0510
(800) 638-2610
or (301) 816-0045

United Services Association
USA Group Insurance Administrator
P.O. Box 2510
Rockville, MD 20852
(800) 636-2610
or (301) 816-0045

United Services Automobile Association
USAA Life Insurance Co.
9800 Fredericksburg Road
San Antonio, TX 78288
Health claims: (800) 531-9017
Health policy service:
(800) 531-6978
Health sales: (800) 531-6399

United Services Life Insurance Co.
4601 Fairfax Drive
P.O. Box 3700
Arlington, VA 22203
(800) 368-5680

U.S. Army Warrant Officers Association
Seabury & Smith, Administrator
Group Insurance Program
1255 23rd Street NW, Suite 300
Washington, DC 20037
(800) 424-9883
or (202) 457-6820

U.S. Coast Guard Chief Petty Officers Association/Coast Guard Enlisted Association
Seabury & Smith, Administrator
Group Insurance Program
1255 23rd Street NW, Suite 300
Washington, DC 20037
(800) 424-9883
or (202) 457-6820

U.S. Coast Guard Chief Warrant and Warrant Officers Association
Seabury & Smith, Administrator
Group Insurance Program
1255 23rd Street NW, Suite 300
Washington, DC 20037
(800) 424-9883
or (202) 457-6820

U.S. Naval Institute
HealthCOM
Association Group Administrators
1101 Mercantile Lane, Suite 100
Springdale, MD 20774
(800) 808-4515

Chapters 11 and 12: Housing and Home Insurance

Home purchase information:

American Society of Home Inspectors
(800) 743-2744
http://www1.mhv.net/~dfriedman/ashihome.htm

Consumer Mortgage Information: *http://www.human.com/proactive/index.html*

Federal Housing Administration: *http://www.hud.gov/fha/fhahome.html*

Homebuyer's Fair: *http://homefair.com/home*

Mortgage Mart: *http://www.mortgage-mart.com/*

Realtor Information Network: *http://www.realtor.com/*

Veterans Administration: *http://www.va.gov/vas/loan/index.htm*

Insurance:

Armed Forces Insurance:
(800) 495-8234
http://www.afi.org

Better Business Bureau Homeowners' Insurance:
http://www.bosbbb.org/lit/0072.htm

California Earthquake Authority:
(877) 797-4300
http://www.earthquakeauthority.com

Flood Insurance:
(800) 427-4661
http://www.fema.gov/nfip

Insurance Information Institute contains a listing of state insurance departments and commissioners under "where to buy insurance":
http://www.iii.org

Insurance rating companies:

A.M. Best Company, Inc:
(908) 439-2200
http://www.ambest.com

Fitch Ibca Inc:
(212) 687-1507
http://www.fitchibca.com

Moody's Investor Services:
(212) 553-0300
http://www.moodys.com

Standard and Poor's Insurance Ratings Services:
(212) 438-2000
http://www.standardandpoor.com

Weiss Research:
(800) 289-9222
http://www.weissratings.com

USAA Insurance:
(800) 316-4806
http://www.usaa.com

Chapter 13: Providing for College Expenses

In addition to websites for specific colleges:

College Board Online: *http://www.collegeboard.org/press/html*
Department of Education College Aid: *http://www.ed.gov/offices/OPE/*
Financial aid calculator: *http://www.collegeboard.org/html/calculator000.html*
State College Aid Agencies: *http://www.ed.gov/offices/OPE/agencies.html*
Time magazine: *http://www.time.com/tuition*
U.S. News & World Report: http://www.usnews.com/usnews/edu/
United States Air Force Academy: *http://www.usafa.af.mil*
United States Coast Guard Academy: *http://www.cga.edu*
United States Merchant Marine Academy: *http://www.usmma.edu*
United States Military Academy: *http://www.usma.edu*
United States Naval Academy: *http://www.usna.edu*

www.collegeboard.com:
Follow the "Paying for College" link for financial aid facts and calculators. The expected family contribution calculator is located at *http://cbweb9p.collegeboard.org/EFC/.* This site is published by the College Board, authors of the SAT.

www.collegeispossible.org:
"America's colleges and universities have prepared this site to guide you to the books, websites, and other resources that admissions and financial aid professionals consider most helpful." This site is published by the Coalition of America's Colleges and Universities.

www.collegesavings.org:
The National Association of State Treasurers publishes this web page covering state-sponsored college savings plans. It has links to your state's program.

www.ed.gov/thinkcollege/early:
The U.S Department of Education publishes this web page. It describes many aspects of college planning, including saving, with good calculators and links to other sites.

http://www.fafsa.ed.gov/:
This Department of Education site contains the Free Application for Federal Student Aid and other information on financial aid.

http://www.finaid.org/:
A complete source for financial aid information, including the wide variety of veterans and military benefits available. "FinAid was established in the fall of 1994 as a public service. This award-winning site has grown into the most comprehensive annotated collection of information about student financial aid on the web."

www.savingforcollege.com:
Provides data on and rankings of state 529 plans.
www.smartmoney.com/college:
"In 2018, four years at a private university will cost $225,000. But don't panic. We'll show you how to foot the bill."

Chapters 14–18: Investments

There are literally thousands of websites concerning investments. Here arc some that may be useful.

For general investment information or locating a financial advisor:
Institute of Certified Financial Planners: *http://www.icfp.org*
International Association for Financial Planning: *http://www.iafp.org*
National Association of Personal Financial Advisors: *http://www.napfa.org*

For general mutual fund and investment information:
Mutual Fund Basics: *http://www.brill.com/newbie.html*
Mutual Fund investor's center: *http://www.mfea.com/*
Mutual Fund magazine: *http://www.mfmag.com*
Mutual Funds Made Simple: *http://members.aol.com/plweiss1/mfunds.htm*
R. Douglas Pauley, M.B.A., CFP: *http://members.aol.com/DougPauley*
U.S. Treasury (bonds): *www.publicdebt.treas.gov*

For more information on specific mutual funds and mutual fund analysis:
Investorama general information: *http://www.investorama.com/funds.html*
Investorama analysis: *http://www.investorama.com/fundsite.shtml*
Morningstar: *http://www.morningstar.net/*
Networth: *http://networth.quicken.com/*
Edleson, Michael E. *Value Averaging: The Safe and Easy Strategy for Higher Investment Returns.* Chicago: International Publishing, 1991.
Gibson, Roger C. *Asset Allocation: Balancing Financial Risk, 2nd ed.* Chicago: Irwin Professional Publishing, 1996.

For specific brokerage firms and funds:
American Century: *http://www.americancentury.com*
Ceres: *http://www.ceres.com*
Charles Schwab: *http://www.schwab.com*
E-trade: *http://www.etrade.com*
Fidelity: *http://www.fidelity.com*
Jack White: *http://pawws.com/jwc*
Lombard: *http://www.lombard.com/dbd-home.html*
Merrill Lynch: *http://www.ml.com*
Paine-Webber: *http://www.painewebber.com*
Quick and Reilly: *http://www.quick-reilly.com*

Smith Barney: *http://www.smithbarney.com*
Vanguard: *http://www.vanguard.com*
Waterhouse: *http://www.waterhouse.com*

Chapters 19–23: Life Insurance, Retirement, Social Security, Veterans Affairs, and Survivor Benefit Plan

Armed Forces Benefit Association: *http://www.afba.com/afba/*
Army and Air Force Mutual Aid Association:
  (800) 336-4538
  http://www.aafmaa.com/home.asp
Army Retirement Services: *http://www.odcsper.army.mil*
Department of Veterans Affairs: *http://www.va.gov/*
Finance Center: *http://www.financenter.com/*
  Calculators and other information.
Request Social Security Earnings and Benefit Statement:
  http://s3abaca.ssa.gov/pro/batch-pebes/bp-7004home.shtml
Retirement Pay Regulation:
  http://www.dtic.mil/comptroller/fmr/07b/index.html
Right Quote: *http://www.rightquote.com/*
  Life insurance calculator.
Social Security Administration:
  (800) 772-1213
  http://www.ssa.gov/SSA_Home.html
Social Security retirement planner: *http://www.ssa.gov/retire/*
  Includes calculators.
Survivor Benefit Plan: *http://www.army.mil/retire-p/sbp/sbp.htm*
The latest edition of the *Uniformed Services Almanac.*
USAA: *www.usaa.com*

For sources of life insurance on the Internet:
Insurance News Network: *http://www.insure.com/*
Quotesmith: *http://quotesmith.com/*
Zurich Direct: *http://www.zurichdirect.com/*
Life Insurance Wiz: *http://www.lifeinsurancewiz.com/*
  Provides free online quotes for auto, health, homeowners', whole and term life insurance. Also provides a list of insurance resources and glossary terms.

Appendix B

Glossary of Financial Terms

abstract of title A history of the ownership of real property from some moment in the past down to the present, generally required in a real estate transaction.

accidental death clause A guarantee in the life insurance policy providing additional proceeds if the insured dies as a result of an accident. It is also called a double-indemnity clause.

accumulation plan An arrangement that enables an investor to purchase mutual fund shares regularly, usually with provisions for the reinvestment of income dividends and the acceptance of capital gains distributions in additional shares. Plans are of two types: voluntary and contractual.

actuary Primarily a person who applies to life insurance the principles that underlie all its computations, such as those of premiums, reserves, surrender values, apportionment of dividends, and the like. The word has now acquired a broader meaning and might be defined as "one versed in the mathematics, bookkeeping, law, and finance of life insurance."

add-on method A computational method where (1) the finance charge for an installment credit contract as a whole equals the add-on rate times the principal amount of credit at the start of the contract times the number of years in the credit contract; (2) the finance charge is added to the principal; and (3) the credit user receives the principal and pays back the principal plus the finance charge in monthly (or other periodic) installments.

adjustable rate mortgage (ARM) A mortgage loan for which interest rates are not fixed but vary with market interest rates.

adjusted-balance method of computing interest Interest is charged on the balance outstanding after it has been adjusted for payments and credits.

amenities The features of a property that are not a part of the space occupied and that create special attraction, such as recreation rooms, saunas, and pools, or "natural amenities," such as a view or ocean frontage.

amortization The process of retiring debt or writing off an asset. As regards a direct reduction of self-amortizing mortgage, amortization represents the principal repayment portion of an installment payment.

annual percentage rate (APR) The effective interest rate applicable to a loan. See the formula for APR in chapter 6, Table 6-1.

annual report The formal financial statement issued yearly by a corporation to its shareowners. The annual report shows assets, liabilities, earnings, how the company stood at the close of the business year, and how it fared in profit during the year.

annuity A stated sum of money, payable periodically at the end of fixed intervals.

annuity, certain An annuity payable throughout a fixed (certain) period of time, irrespective of the happening of any contingency, such as the death of annuitant.

annuity, contingent An annuity contingent upon the happening of an event that may or may not take place.

annuity, deferred An annuity modified by the condition that the first payment will not be due for a fixed number of years. Thus, an annuity deferred for twenty years is one on which the first payment is made at the end of twenty-one years, provided the annuitant is still alive.

annuity, life A fixed sum payable periodically so long as a given person's life continues.

annuity, survivorship An annuity payable throughout the lifetime of one person after the death of another person or persons.

annuity, variable A form of whole life insurance where the face value and cash value vary according to the investment success of the insurance company.

appraisal The estimation of market value of property.

assessed value The value assessed by the taxing authority for purpose of establishing real estate taxes. This value may not be directly related to market value.

assessment A charge against real estate made by a unit of government to cover a proportionate cost of an improvement such as a street or sewer.

asset allocation The distribution of funds among asset classes in a portfolio, for example: 10 percent cash equivalents, 20 percent bonds, 70 percent stocks.

asset class A group of investments with similar characteristics or features, for example: cash equivalents, which include savings accounts, checking accounts, money market funds, and Treasury bills.

assets The total monetary value of all property in a company's possession at a given time. Also, everything that a person owns, whether the items are paid for or not.

assumption clause A mortgage loan clause that allows the owner of a house to transfer the mortgage to a later buyer.

assumption of mortgage The taking of title to property by a grantee, wherein the grantee assumes liability for payment of an existing note or bond secured by a mortgage against a property and becomes personally liable for the payment of such mortgage debt.

ATM card Automatic Teller Machine card, issued by your bank, which allows you to withdraw cash from your account(s) and perform other simple banking transactions.

automatic paid-up insurance An amount of insurance, which, without further action by the insured and upon failure to pay a premium when due, is continued as paid-up insurance. (A lesser value than the original protection guaranteed by the policy.)

average-daily-balance method of computing interest Interest is charged on the average daily balance outstanding. The average balance is calculated by adding the balances outstanding each day and dividing by the number of days in the billing month. Payments made during the billing month reduce the average balance outstanding.

balanced mutual fund A mutual fund that invests in both stocks and bonds.

balance sheet A listing of what a person or business owns and owes at a certain point in a certain time period. It has three categories: assets, liabilities, and net worth.

bank credit cards Credit cards issued by banks. The most widely used ones are MasterCard and VISA.

bankruptcy A legal procedure that allows a person or an organization to give up certain assets in return for release from certain financial obligations.

bear A person who believes stock prices will go down; a "bear market" is a market of declining prices.

beneficiary The individual or organization that receives the proceeds of a life insurance policy when the insured dies. The primary beneficiary has the first right to proceeds, and contingent beneficiaries receive the proceeds if the primary beneficiary is no longer living.

bid and asked The bid is the highest price anyone has declared willing to pay for a security at a given time; the asked is the lowest price anyone will take at the same time. In mutual fund shares, bid price means the net asset value per share, less a nominal redemption charge in a few instances. The asked price means the net asset value per share plus any sales charge. It is often called the "offering price."

blue chip stocks Stock of highly stable and financially strong firms.

bond mutual fund A mutual fund that emphasizes safety and invests in high-grade bonds.

bonds A bond is essentially an IOU. The person who invests money in a bond is lending a company or government a sum of money for a specified time, with the understanding that the borrower will pay it back and pay interest for using it.

book value The book value of a firm is equal to its total assets minus total liabilities.

budgeting A system of record keeping involving detailed planning to account for all incomes and expenses.

bull A person who believes stock prices will rise; a "bull market" is one with rising prices.

business risk Risk associated with changes in the firm's sales.

buying on margin The investor borrows a portion of funds from the brokerage house to buy securities.

call loan A loan that may be terminated, or "called," at any time by the lender or borrower.

cancellation clause A unilateral clause in a lease or purchase and sale that terminates an agreement.

capital gain Income that results from the sale of an asset not in the usual course of business.

capital improvement Any structure erected as a permanent improvement to real estate, usually extending the useful life and increasing value of property. (The replacement of a roof would be considered a capital improvement.)

capital loss A loss from the sale of an asset not in the usual course of business.

cash surrender value The amount available in cash upon voluntary termination of a policy before it becomes payable by death or maturity.

closed-end investment company A mutual fund that invests in the shares of other companies. There are a fixed number of shares, and shares are available in the market only if original investors are willing to sell them.

closing The culmination of a real estate purchase and sale when the title passes and certain financial transactions occur.

closing costs Costs paid at closing, such as operating cost adjustments, legal and financial expenses, brokerage commissions, and transfer taxes.

closing date The date upon which the buyer takes over the property.

collateral Property, or evidence of it, deposited with a creditor to guarantee the payment of a loan.

commission With respect to insurance policies, usually means a percentage of the premium paid to an agent as remuneration for services; for stocks or real estate, a sum due a broker for services in that capacity.

common stock Evidence of an ownership interest in a corporation.

common stock mutual fund A mutual fund that invests in the common shares of properties.

community property Property owned in common or held together by husband and wife within the statutes of certain states.

conditional sales contract A sales contract in which title to the goods remains with the lender, while the buyer has physical possession of them. The title goes to the buyer when the loan is repaid. This type of contract is often used with items such as appliances and furniture.

condominium ownership A form of ownership wherein a multi-unit building is divided so that each owner has individual ownership of his unit and joint ownership in the common areas of the buildings and grounds. Condominiums are frequently used for residential housing and sometimes for office space. In addition to the initial purchase price, each owner in a condominium is liable on an annual basis for a predetermined portion of the expenses of maintaining the common areas.

contingency fund A fund that provides cash to be used if an emergency arises.

conventional mortgage A mortgage that is not insured by the FHA or guaranteed by the VA.

conversion A right to change from a term insurance policy to a whole life policy without a medical examination. This feature is also called a convertability option.

conversion price The price of common stock at which a convertible security can be converted.

convertible A bond, debenture, or preferred share that may be exchanged for other stock in a company.

cooperative ownership A method of indirectly owning a unit in a multi-unit property through a cooperation. A specially created legal corporation owns the building completely. Each shareholder of that corporation owns a predetermined number of shares that entitle him to a long-term lease on a specific apartment. After paying for the purchase of his or her shares, each shareholder is liable for an annual maintenance charge to support the basic services and debt financing in the multi-unit building.

corporate bonds Debt securities issued by corporations.

cost index An index developed by the insurance industry allowing you to compare different policy costs. A surrender cost index is used to determine the value of your policy if you decide to terminate coverage. A net payment cost index determines the value of your policy assuming you do not surrender the policy and take the cash value.

coupon interest Refers to the rate of interest on bonds implied by the annual dollar amount of interest paid and the bond's face value.

credit card A bank card (e.g., VISA, MasterCard) that allows purchases or cash advances on "open-account" credit up to your credit limit.

credit life insurance Term insurance designed to pay off the remaining balance on a loan in case of the borrower's death.

creditor A person, group, or company that extends credit; one to whom a borrower owes money.

credit union An institution whose depositors are also its owners. It lends money only to its owners.

cumulative preferred stocks Preferred stock that requires that any dividends missed be paid before dividends can be paid on common stock.

current yield For a bond, its annual interest divided by its current market price.

custodianship account for minors An account set up for a child in the form of gifts (the gifts cannot exceed $30,000) and managed by an adult other than the grantor.

debenture A bond not secured by liens against specific assets of the firm.

debit card Like a credit card, except purchases are deducted from your checking account—there is no "line of credit."

debt consolidation loan A loan that is taken out to repay debts outstanding. One loan payment is substituted for many debt payments.

declarations section of an insurance policy The section that contains the basic identifying details of the policy. It consists of the name of the policy owner, what is insured, the amount of insurance, the cost of the policy, and the time period covered by the insurance.

declination The rejection of an application for life insurance, usually for reasons of the health or occupation of the applicant.

decreasing term life insurance Insurance in which the amount of benefits declines over the life of the policy.

deductible clause A clause in an insurance policy that allows the insured to retain the loss equal to the deductible amount.

deed A legal document transferring title from owner to buyer, typically recorded with the clerk of the county in which the property is located.

deed restrictions Limitations placed on the use of the real property through deed covenants such as land coverage, setback requirements, architectural approval, or construction timing.

DEERS The Defense Enrollment Eligibility Reporting System, a computerized roster of people eligible to receive health benefits under the Uniformed Services Health Benefit Program.

demand deposit An account in a bank or other financial institution subject to withdrawal by check.

depreciation The decline in value of property due to normal wear and tear.

disability waver premium A guarantee that premiums will be paid on your policy should you become disabled.

discount broker A firm that processes securities transactions for relatively low commissions.

diversification Spreading one's investments among the companies in different industries. A company producing various lines of products is also considered diversified.

dividend In insurance, the part of the premium returned to you after the company pays its expenses. Dividends are paid only on participating term or whole life policies. For stocks, a dividend is usually paid quarterly, distributing some portion of earnings to shareholders.

dividend payout ratio Dividends per share of stock divided by earnings per share.

dividend yield Dividends per share of stock times 100 percent divided by the market value of a share.

dollar cost averaging (DCA) Buying a fixed dollar amount of securities at regular intervals. Under this system the investor buys by the dollars' worth rather than by the number of shares. DCA can be an effective way to limit risk while building assets in stock and mutual funds.

double indemnity An optional life insurance clause that provides payment of twice the face amount of the policy in death benefits if the insured is killed in an accident.

Dow Jones Industrial Average Daily index of stock prices of thirty large industrial corporations; a popular measure of the stock market's performance.

down payment The amount of money that the buyer puts up toward the purchase of a house, car, or other asset; does not include closing costs.

earnings per share Net income divided by shares of the stock outstanding.

effective rate, annual or monthly The finance charge as a percentage per unit of time of the average unpaid balance of the credit contract during its scheduled life. Also called actual rate or annual effective rate.

endorsement (insurance) A statement attached to an insurance policy, changing the terms of the policy.

endowment life insurance A life insurance policy that is fully paid up (endowed) after either a specified time period or when the insured attains a certain age.

Equal Credit Opportunity Act of 1975 Prohibits credit discrimination on the basis of sex or marital status.

equity The interest in or value of a property or estate that belongs to an owner, over and above the liens against it; asset value minus liabilities.

escalator clause A contract or lease clause providing for adjustment of payments in the event of certain specified contingencies such as an increase in real estate taxes or certain operating expenses.

escrow account Most mortgage lenders require that borrowers make monthly payments equal to one-twelfth of anticipated real estate taxes and insurance into this account. This assures the lender that there are funds from which the taxes and insurance can be paid.

estate All of a person's assets, including the appropriate portion of any jointly owned property.

estate planning The systematic accumulation, management, and transfer of a person's estate to achieve family goals.

estate taxes Taxes levied on the transfer of estates that are larger than a certain specified sum.

evidence of insurability Evidence of your health that helps the insurer decide if you are an acceptable risk.

exclusive agency An agreement of employment of a broker to the exclusion of all other brokers; if sale is made by any other broker during term of employment, the broker holding exclusive agency is entitled to commissions in addition to the commissions payable to the broker who effected the transaction.

executor A person or a corporate entity or any other type of organization named or designed in a will to carry out its provisions as to the disposition of the estate of a deceased person.

Federal Deposit Insurance Corporation (FDIC) A government agency that provides insurance for accounts held at banks; most banks carry FDIC insurance.

Federal Housing Authority (FHA) A government agency that provides mortgage loan insurance to financial institutions.

fiduciary A person who on behalf of or for the benefit of another individual transacts business or manages financial assets; such relationship implies great confidence and trust.

finance charge The dollar charge or charges for consumer credit.

finder's fee In real estate, a payment made for aid in obtaining a mortgage loan or for locating a property or tenant.

foreclosure The procedure through which property pledged as security for a debt is "repossessed" and sold to secure payment of the debt in event of default in payment or terms. The rights of debtors and creditors in foreclosure vary from state to state.

grace period Additional time allowed to perform an act or make a payment before a default occurs. In insurance, a period of time where if the premium is not paid, it is still in effect with or without penalty conditions. Generally in insurance the grace period is thirty-one days after the premium due date. Some credit cards have a twenty-five-day grace period to avoid finance charges.

growth stock Stock that is characterized by the prospect of its increase in earnings and in market value rather than by the cash dividends it earns for the stockholder.

guaranteed insurability clause A provision allowing policyholders to purchase additional insurance without having to pass a physical examination.

home loan A real estate loan for which the security is a residential property; in Federal Home Loan Bank Board statistics, a loan on a residential structure housing one to four families.

homeowners' warranty (HOW) program Builders in this program guarantee that their workmanship, materials, and construction are up to established standards.

"house poor" Buying more house than one can afford to buy.

income bond A corporate bond that pays interest only if corporate earnings reach a specified level.

income shifting The process of transferring income from a high-income taxpayer to a lower-income taxpayer or from a high-tax year to a low-tax year.

incontestability In insurance, a provision that the payment of the claim may not be disputed by the company for any cause whatsoever except for nonpayment of premium. A life insurance policy in force for at least two years cannot be contested.

insurance, paid-up Insurance on which there remain no further premiums to be paid.

interest In practice, a payment for the use of money.

interest rate The percentage of a sum of money charged for its use.

intestacy The condition resulting from a person's dying without leaving a valid will.

investor An individual whose principal concerns in the purchase of a security are regular dividend income, safety of the original investment, and, if possible, capital appreciation. See *speculator*.

joint account A checking or savings account in the name of two or more persons. There are two types of joint accounts. One type allows any owner to withdraw funds. Thc other type requires the permission of all owners before funds can be withdrawn.

joint and survivorship annuity An annuity that continues payment to a secondary beneficiary if the primary one dies; this annuity guarantees income for life to the surviving beneficiary.

joint ownership Two or more persons jointly own the property in question. There are three forms of joint ownership: (1) joint tenancy; (2) tenancy in common; (3) tenancy by the entirety.

joint tenancy A type of ownership wherein property is held by two or more persons together, with the distinct character of survivorship. In other words, during the life of both, they have equal rights to use the property and share in any benefits from it. Upon the death of either, the property automatically passes to the survivor(s).

junk bonds Bonds that investment advisors consider to be risky investments.

Keogh plan A retirement plan limited to self-employed individuals.

landlord One who rents property to another.

lapse The voidance of a policy, in whole or in part, by the nonpayment of a premium or installment on a premium date.

lease A contract, written or oral, between owner and tenant for the possession and use of land and/or improvements, and for rent or other income and other conditions of occupancy.

lease-option A lease written in conjunction with an option agreement, wherein the payments may be credited toward the purchase price if the option is exercised.

lessee The party contracting to use the property under a lease.

lessor The owner who contracts to allow property to be used under a lease.

lien A legal encumbrance upon a property interest created to ensure repayment of a debt or discharge of obligation.

limited payment whole life insurance Life insurance requiring premiums to be paid only for a specific time period but remaining in force after the payment period is over (e.g., twenty-pay life).

limited warranty A guarantee that is much more restrictive than a full warranty.

liquid assets Cash and other investments that can be converted into cash quickly, such as money in checking and savings accounts.

liquidity The cash position measured by the cash on hand and assets quickly convertible into cash.

listed stock The stock of a company traded on a securities exchange for which a listing application and a registration statement, giving detailed information about the company and its operations, have been filed with the Securities and Exchange Commission, unless otherwise exempted, and the exchange itself.

listing agreement A written employment contract between a property owner and a real estate broker whereby the agent is authorized to sell or lease certain property within specified terms and conditions.

load The portion of the offering price of shares of open-end investment (mutual fund) companies that covers sales commissions and all other costs of distribution. The load normally is incurred only on purchase. Some funds also charge a "back-end" load or "redemption charge" when the shares are sold, or an annual "12b-1" charge.

loading That addition to the net insurance premium that is necessary (1) to cover the policy's proportionate share in the expense of operating the company and (2) to provide a fund deemed sufficient to cover contingencies.

loan value The amount of money that can be borrowed from the insurance company, using the policy's cash value as collateral.

market value The highest price that a buyer, willing but not compelled to buy, would pay, and the lowest a seller, willing but not compelled to sell, would accept.

maturity The time at which a bond or insurance policy is due and payable. In insurance, the date at which the face value of an endowment policy is paid to the insured if still living.

mortality The statistical measure of the probability of death at each age group. The same age groups can have different rates depending on the amount of group risk. For example, a lower rate is charged a twenty-five-year-old nonsmoking male than a twenty-five-year-old male who uses tobacco.

mortality rate (death rate) The ratio of those who die at a stated age to the total number who are exposed to the risk of death at that age per year.

mortgage A legal document pledging a described property for the performance of promise to repay a loan under certain terms and conditions. The law provides procedures for foreclosure. The notations "first," "second," and so forth refer to the priority of the liens, with the lower number representing greater security for the mortgage holder. A direct-reduction mortgage involves a constant periodic payment that will eventually repay the entire loan, providing a specified return to the mortgagee.

mortgagee The party who lends money and takes a mortgage to secure the payment thereof.

mortgagor The person who borrows money and gives a mortgage on the person's property as security for the payment of the debt.

multiple listing An arrangement among Real Estate Board of Exchange members whereby each broker presents the broker's listings to the attention of the other members so that if a sale results, the commission is divided between the broker bringing the listing and the broker making the sale.

mutual wills Separate wills made by two or more persons (usually but not necessarily husband and wife) containing similar provisions in favor of each other or of the same beneficiary.

national charge cards Examples are American Express, Diners Club, and Carte Blanche. They are very similar to bank credit cards in use except that (1) while bank cards are sometimes free, national cards charge an annual fee; (2) national cards do not offer revolving credit as bank cards do; and (3) banks cards are accepted by substantially more businesses than are national cards.

negative cash flow Situation when cash inflows are less than cash outflows.

net asset value of a mutual fund The value of one share of a mutual fund. It is equal to the fund's total market value, less its liabilities, divided by the number of its shares outstanding.

net cost In insurance, the total gross premiums paid, less total dividends credited for a given period.

net surrendered cost The total gross premiums paid, less the total dividends credited for the given period and the surrender or cash value of the policy, plus the surrender charge (if any) for an insurance policy.

net worth What a person or business would own after paying off all liabilities. Assets minus liabilities equals net worth. The same as "equity."

no-fault insurance A form of automobile insurance where the insured collects from his own company regardless of who was at fault.

no-load mutual fund A mutual fund that does not charge a sales commission on the sale of its stock.

nominal interest rate The stated or advertised interest rate.

noncontributory pension plan A pension plan in which the employee does not make any contributions. Military retirement is an example.

nonforfeiture provisions Provisions whereby, after the payment of a given number of premiums, the contract may not be completely forfeited because of nonpayment of a subsequent premium but is held good for some value in cash, paid-up insurance, or extended term insurance. These values are usually stipulated in a table printed in the policy. One of the two latter options is usually effective automatically; any other option is generally available only upon surrender of the policy.

notary public A public officer who is authorized to take acknowledgments to certain classes of documents, such as deeds, contracts, or mortgages, and before whom affidavits may be sworn.

note A legal document in which the borrower promises to repay the loan under agreed-upon terms.

NOW account (negotiable order of withdrawal) Equivalent to checking accounts paying interest on the funds on deposit. Also, super-NOW account.

odd lot An amount of stock less than the established 100-share unit of trading: from one to ninety-nine shares for the great majority of issues.

offer An initial, brief written contract submitted by a potential buyer of real estate for approval by the seller, giving the price and limited other details.

open-end investment company A company, popularly known as a mutual fund, issuing redeemable shares, that is, shares that normally must be liquidated by the fund on demand of the shareholders. Such companies continuously offer new shares to investors.

open-end mortgage A mortgage under which the mortgaged property stands as security not only for the original loan but for the future advances the lender may be willing to make. Similar to a home-equity line of credit.

open listing A listing given to any number of brokers without liability to compensate any except the one who first secures a buyer ready, willing, and able to meet the terms of the listing, or secures the acceptance by the seller of a satisfactory offer; the sale of the property automatically terminates the listing.

option A legal agreement that permits the holder for a consideration to buy, sell, or otherwise obtain or dispose of a property interest within a specified time on specified terms described in the agreement.

over-the-counter A market for securities made up of securities dealers who may not be members of a securities exchange. Thousands of companies have insufficient shares outstanding, stockholders, or earnings to warrant listing on a stock exchange. Securities of these companies are traded in the over-the-counter market between dealers and customers. The over-the-counter market is the chief market for U.S. government bonds, municipal bonds, and bank and insurance stock. NASDAQ is an organized, computerized OTC market handling a large number of stocks.

"paid-up" limited payment whole life insurance Life insurance for which payments are made until the policy holder achieves a target age, after which the policy becomes "paid up."

participating preferred stock A preferred stock that shares with common stock in exceptionally large corporate earnings, thus getting a rate higher than the stated maximum rate.

personal property Property that is not attached to land, such as furniture, appliances, clothing, and other personal belongings.

points A loan fee charged by lenders. Each point equals 1 percent of the amount of the loan. Points are payable up front and add to the effective cost of a loan.

policy The life insurance contract between the life insurance company and the owner of the policy. The policy outlines the terms and conditions for both the company and the policyholder.

policy, installment A contract under which the sum insured is payable in a given number of equal annual installments.

policy, joint life A policy under which the company agrees to pay the amount of insurance at the death of the first of two or more designated persons.

policy, limited payment A policy that stipulates that only a limited number of premiums are to be paid.

policy loan A loan made to the policyholder by the insurance company based upon the cash value in a whole life or other permanent insurance policy.

policy, nonparticipating A policy that is not entitled to receive dividends. Such a policy is usually written at a lower rate of premium than a corresponding participating policy.

policy, participating A policy that participates (receives dividends) in the surplus as determined and apportioned by the company.

policy year The year beginning with the due date of an annual premium.

portfolio The aggregate investment holdings of an individual or institution. A portfolio may contain individual securities (stocks and bonds), mutual funds, collectibles, or other forms of investment wealth.

postdated check A check that has a date on it that is later than the date on which it was written.

power of attorney A written instrument duly signed and executed by an owner of property that authorizes an agent to act on behalf of the owner to the extent indicated in the instrument.

premium A stated sum charged by a company in return for insurance. It may be payable in a single sum or in a limited number of payments, or periodically throughout the duration of the policy.

premium, level A premium of a fixed and uniform amount, in lieu of a varying or increasing premium.

prepayment clause A clause in a consumer loan contract that provides for a refund to a debtor who chooses to repay an installment account early. Or a clause in a mortgage that gives a mortgagor the privilege of paying the mortgage indebtedness before it becomes due.

property Real property consists of land and, generally, whatever is erected or growing upon or affixed to it, including rights issuing out of, annexed to, and exercisable within or about the same. See *personal property*.

prospectus The official circular that describes the shares of a company and offers them for sale. It contains definitive details concerning the company issuing the shares, the determination of the price at which the shares are offered to the public, and so on, as required by the Securities and Exchange Commission's rules.

purchase and sales agreement A legal contract between buyer and seller of real estate that details the terms of the transaction.

rating The basis for an additional charge to the standard premium because the person to be insured is a greater than normal risk. A rating can result from anything from a dangerous occupation to poor health.

real estate investment trust (REIT) Similar to a closed-end investment company; specializes in buying real estate properties.

real estate syndicate A partnership formed for participation in a real estate venture. Partners may be limited or unlimited in their liability.

real property Land, buildings, and other kinds of property that legally are classified as real, as opposed to personal property.

Realtor A coined word that may be used only by an active member of a local real estate board affiliated with the National Association of Real Estate Boards.

redlining The refusal to lend money or issue insurance within a specific area for various reasons. This practice is illegal.

reduced paid-up insurance A form of insurance available as a nonforfeiture option. It provides for continuation of the original insurance plan, but for a reduced amount, and no further premiums.

reinstatement Restoring a lapsed policy by paying all unpaid premiums and charges by the policyholder.

renewable term insurance Term insurance that can be renewed at the end of the term, at the option of the policyholder and without evidence of insurability, for a limited number of successive terms. The rates increase at each renewal as the age of the insured increases.

rent The payment for use of someone else's property; the compensation paid for the use of real estate.

reserve (policy reserves) The amount that an insurance company allocates specifically for the fulfillment of its policy obligations. Reserves are so calculated that, together with future premiums and interest earnings, they will enable the company to pay all future claims.

retained earnings On an income statement, changes in retained earnings come from net income minus dividends paid for the year. On the balance sheet, this is cumulated from year to year.

retirement To give up one's work or business, especially because of age.

revenue bonds Municipal bonds backed by special sources of income.

reverse annuity mortgage Contract under which a homeowner can receive monthly income by borrowing against the equity in a home.

revocable trust A trust that is controlled by the grantor and can be revoked by him or her.

revolving credit A continuing credit arrangement between seller and buyer in which the buyer (1) agrees to make monthly payments equal to a stipulated percentage of the amount owed at the start of the month plus interest and (2) is permitted to make additional credit purchases as long as the total debt owed does not exceed an agreed-upon limit.

rider Any additional agreement to the insurance policy usually adding a benefit at an additional cost. A rider becomes part of the insurance policy.

rights or warrants When a company wants to raise more funds by issuing additional stock, it may give its stockholders the opportunity, ahead of others, to buy the new stock. The piece of paper evidencing this privilege is called a right or warrant. Because the additional stock is usually offered to stockholders below the market price, rights ordinarily have a market value of their own and are actively traded. Failure to exercise or sell rights may result in actual loss to the holder.

round lot A unit of trading or a multiple thereof. On the New York Stock Exchange, the unit of trading is generally 100 shares in stock and $100,000 par value in the case of bonds.

sale-leaseback A transaction in which the vendor simultaneously executes a lease and retains occupancy of the property concurrently sold.

sales charge The amount charged in connection with the distribution to the public of mutual fund shares. It is added to the net asset value per share in the determination of the offering price and is paid to the dealer and underwriter. Also called a "load."

sales contract A contract by which the buyer and seller agree to terms of sale.

savings Amount of income not spent.

savings account An interest-bearing liability of a bank, redeemable in money on demand or after due notice, not transferable by check.

savings and loan associations Financial institutions that have historically specialized in offering savings accounts and in providing mortgage funds.

savings banks Located in New England and eastern states, these banks provide services very similar to services provided by commercial banks.

secondary financing A loan secured by a mortgage or trust deed that is secured by a lien subordinate to that of another instrument.

secondary markets Buying and selling of securities that takes place between investors.

second mortgage A mortgage next in priority to a first mortgage.

secured installment loans Loans that are backed up by collateral; examples are loans for cars, home improvements, boats, furniture, appliances, and other durable goods.

securities Literally, things given, deposited, or pledged to assure the fulfillment of an obligation. In this narrow sense a mortgage is a security, but the term is now generally used in a broader sense to include stock as well as bonds, notes, and other evidences of indebtedness.

Securities Exchange Commission (SEC) A federal agency that oversees securities trading.

Securities Investor Protection Corporation (SIPC) A federal agency that insures investors' accounts at brokerage houses.

securities markets Places or networks where stocks, bonds, and other financial instruments are traded.

selling short Selling borrowed securities with the expectation of buying them back later at a lower price.

Series EE bond A nonnegotiable U.S. savings bond. Interest on these bonds is received only upon redemption.

Series HH bond A nonnegotiable U.S. savings bond that pays periodic interest, can be redeemed after six months, and has a maturity period of ten years.

service contract An agreement purchased by an appliance owner to keep the appliance in working order.

simple-interest method A computation method where the finance charge for a given month of an installment contract equals the monthly rate times the loan balance at the end of each month.

single-premium deferred annuity An insurance product with a large up-front payment to provide for retirement income and tax savings for high-bracket taxpayers.

speculator One willing to assume a relatively large risk in the hope of gain. His principal concern is to increase his capital rather than his dividend income. Safety of principal is a secondary factor. See *investor.*

Standard & Poor's 500 (S&P500) An index of 500 large stocks, a broad measure of the stock market's performance.

standard deviation As an investment term, standard deviation is used as a proxy for risk. It represents the possible divergence from the expected rate of return and can be used to establish a range of expected returns for an investment or portfolio.

stock dividend A dividend payable in stock rather than cash.

subletting A leasing by a tenant to another, who holds under the tenant.

suicide clause A provision in a life insurance contract that cancels the proceeds from a policy should the insured commit suicide within two years of taking out a life insurance policy. Illegal in some states.

surrender (cash) value The amount the insurer will pay the policyholder if the life insurance policy is canceled. Term insurance policies have no surrender value.

survey The process by which a parcel of land is measured and its area ascertained; also the blueprint showing the measurements, boundaries, and area.

tenancy in common The means of holding property by two or more persons, each of whom has an undivided interest. In event of the owner's death, the undivided interest passes to the owner's estate and heirs rather than to the surviving tenants in common.

tenancy by the entirety A tenancy created by husband and wife, who together hold the title to the whole, with right of survivorship upon the death of either spouse. It is essentially joint tenancy, but it is used only for husbands and wives and only in some jurisdictions.

tenant One who is given possession of real estate for a fixed period or at will.

term policy An insurance policy that provides that the amount of the policy shall be payable only in event of death within a specified term.

testamentary trust A trust that is created by placing an appropriately worded clause in the testator's will. The clause places the trust principal under the trustee's control on the testator's death.

testator A person who has made and left a valid will at death.

thrift savings plan a tax-deferred 401k-like investment vehicle that is available to military personnel.

time deposit account A savings account in which the account owner receives interest but cannot withdraw funds prior to maturity without a penalty.

time-share homes The buyer buys the use of the house for a short time period. The time varies from one week to six months.

title The right to ownership of a property.

title abstract A history of the ownership of the property.

title insurance A policy of insurance that indemnifies the holder for loss sustained by reason of defects in the title.

title search An examination of the public records to determine the ownership and encumbrances affecting real property.

traveler's checks Checks that are readily accepted as payment because the person must buy them in order to use them. They are safer to carry than cash as they can be replaced if stolen.

TRICARE A regionally managed health-care program for active-duty servicemembers, retired members, and their families. The military has created fourteen civilian health-care networks based upon geographical regions to supplement the care provided by military treatment facilities.

TRICARE Extra This option is similar to TRICARE Standard except that if you use providers who are TRICARE Extra approved, you receive a discount to the costs you would otherwise have to pay under TRICARE Standard. This option should be used by those who don't live in a TRICARE Prime network but wish to reduce their medical expenses.

TRICARE FMDP TRICARE Active-Duty Family Member Dental Plan (FMDP). This is the military's family member dental insurance plan and is administered by United Concordia.

TRICARE Prime This is the managed-care network option. Treatment is received in either the Military Treatment Facility Network or the Civilian Health Care Network. In return for giving up your choice of doctor, the cost of receiving medical treatment is reduced. Because of the costs of setting the networks up, this option is currently available only in regions that have large military populations.

TRICARE Standard This is the traditional fee-for-service option and is similar to the current CHAMPUS system. You can choose any health-care provider you want, but your costs will be greater than if you used TRICARE Prime. If TRICARE Prime is not available where you're stationed, you have to enroll in this option.

trust A fiduciary relationship in which one person (the trustee) is the holder of the legal title to property (the trust property) subject to an obligation to keep or use the property for the benefit of another person.

trustee A person who manages a trust.

trustor A person who establishes a trust.

underwrite The insurance company's decision on whether you qualify for life insurance based on reviews of your occupation, health, age, and so on. Also means the sale of original securities in the primary market.

usury Claiming a rate of interest in excess of that permitted by statute.

value averaging An accumulation method, like dollar-cost averaging, where you make periodic securities transactions to keep the value of your portfolio increasing at a preset target rate. See chapter 14.

variable annuity An annuity in which the dollar amount of benefits depends on the investment performance of the insurance company's fund managers.

variable rate mortgage A mortgage loan for which interest rates are not fixed. The rate applicable to the mortgage goes up or down as interest rates in general go up or down.

vesting The gaining of rights by a worker to the pension contributions made by an employer on the worker's behalf.

waiver-of-premium clause A provision committing the life insurance company to make premium payments for a policyholder who suffers an injury or illness causing a disability.

warranty The consumer's assurance that the product will work as it is supposed to. They are guarantees issued by manufacturers or suppliers of goods and services that explain their obligation and, generally, the user's or buyer's responsibilities also.

warranty deed The safest deed for the buyer, since it guarantees that title is free of any legal claims. There are two kinds of warranty deeds: general warranty deeds and special warranty deeds. A general warranty deed contains a promise by the grantor to "defend the property against every person or persons whomsoever"; in other words, it is a promise of protection against the whole world. A special warranty deed contains the more limited promise "to defend the property against every person or persons whomsoever lawfully claiming the same or any part thereof by, from, through, or under him." In other words, it is a promise to protect against the grantor, his heirs, or his assigns.

whole life insurance Life insurance that remains in force as long as the insured continues to pay the insurance premiums. The premiums remain level and fixed as long as the policy remains in force and the excess premiums collected in the early years of the policy's life accumulate interest as "cash value."

will A legally enforceable declaration of a person's wishes in writing regarding matters to be attended to after his death and inoperative until his death. A will usually relates to the testator's property, is revocable or amendable up to the time of his death, and is applicable to the situation that exists at the time of his death.

"window sticker" price Lists the manufacturer's suggested list price for a car and the itemized prices of the options.

yield The dividends or interest paid expressed as a percentage of the current price or, if you own the security, of the price you originally paid.

zero bracket amount An amount of income, based on filing status, below which a taxpayer does not have to pay taxes.

Appendix C

Military Pay Tables

TABLE C-1: MONTHLY BASIC PAY TABLE (EFFECTIVE 1 JANUARY 2002)

	YEARS OF SERVICE														
Pay Grade	<2	2	3	4	6	8	10	12	14	16	18	20	22	24	26
COMMISSIONED OFFICERS															
O-10	8,944.80	9,259.50	9,259.50	9,259.50	9,259.50	9,614.70	9,614.70	10,147.50	10,147.50	10,873.80	10,873.80	11,601.90	11,659.20	11,901.30	12,324.00
O-9	7,927.50	8,135.10	8,308.50	8,308.50	8,308.50	8,519.70	8,519.70	8,874.30	8,874.30	9,614.70	9,614.70	10,147.50	10,293.60	10,504.80	10,873.80
O-8	7,180.20	7,415.40	7,571.10	7,614.90	7,809.30	8,135.10	8,210.70	8,519.70	8,608.50	8,874.30	9,259.50	9,614.70	9,852.00	9,852.00	9,852.00
O-7	5,966.40	6,371.70	6,371.70	6,418.20	6,657.90	6,840.30	7,051.20	7,261.80	7,472.70	8,135.10	8,694.90	8,694.90	8,694.90	8,694.90	8,738.70
O-6	4,422.00	4,857.90	5,176.80	5,176.80	5,196.60	5,418.90	5,448.60	5,448.60	5,628.60	6,305.70	6,627.00	6,948.30	7,131.00	7,316.10	7,675.20
O-5	3,537.00	4,152.60	4,440.30	4,494.30	4,673.10	4,673.10	4,813.50	5,073.30	5,413.50	5,755.80	5,919.00	6,079.80	6,262.80	6,262.80	6,262.80
O-4	3,023.70	3,681.90	3,927.60	3,982.50	4,210.50	4,395.90	4,696.20	4,930.20	5,092.50	5,255.70	5,310.60	5,310.60	5,310.60	5,310.60	5,310.60
O-3	2,796.60	3,170.40	3,421.80	3,698.70	3,875.70	4,070.10	4,232.40	4,441.20	4,549.50	4,549.50	4,549.50	4,549.50	4,549.50	4,549.50	4,549.50
O-2	2,416.20	2,751.90	3,169.50	3,276.30	3,344.10	3,344.10	3,344.10	3,344.10	3,344.10	3,344.10	3,344.10	3,344.10	3,344.10	3,344.10	3,344.10
O-1	2,097.60	2,183.10	2,638.50	2,638.50	2,638.50	2,638.50	2,638.50	2,638.50	2,638.50	2,638.50	2,638.50	2,638.50	2,638.50	2,638.50	2,638.50
COMMISSIONED OFFICERS WITH OVER 4 YEARS' ACTIVE DUTY SERVICE AS AN ENLISTED MEMBER OR WARRANT OFFICER															
O-3E	0.00	0.00	0.00	3,698.70	3,875.70	4,070.10	4,232.40	4,441.20	4,617.00	4,717.50	4,855.20	4,855.20	4,855.20	4,855.20	4,855.20
O-2E	0.00	0.00	0.00	3,276.30	3,344.10	3,450.30	3,630.00	3,768.90	3,872.40	3,872.40	3,872.40	3,872.40	3,872.40	3,872.40	3,872.40
O-1E	0.00	0.00	0.00	2,638.50	2,818.20	2,922.30	3,028.50	3,133.20	3,276.30	3,276.30	3,276.30	3,276.30	3,276.30	3,276.30	3,276.30
WARRANT OFFICERS															
W-5	0.00	0.00	0.00	0.00	0.00	0.00	0.00	0.00	0.00	0.00	0.00	4,965.60	5,136.00	5,307.00	5,478.60
W-4	2,889.60	3,108.60	3,198.00	3,285.90	3,437.10	3,586.50	3,737.70	3,885.30	4,038.00	4,184.40	4,334.40	4,480.80	4,632.60	4,782.00	4,935.30
W-3	2,638.80	2,862.00	2,862.00	2,898.90	3,017.40	3,152.40	3,330.90	3,439.50	3,558.30	3,693.90	3,828.60	3,963.60	4,098.30	4,233.30	4,368.90
W-2	2,321.40	2,454.00	2,569.80	2,654.10	2,726.40	2,875.20	2,984.40	3,093.90	3,200.40	3,318.00	3,438.90	3,559.80	3,680.10	3,801.30	3,801.30
W-1	2,049.90	2,217.60	2,330.10	2,402.70	2,511.90	2,624.70	2,737.80	2,850.00	2,963.70	3,077.10	3,189.90	3,275.10	3,275.10	3,275.10	3,275.10
ENLISTED MEMBERS															
E-9	0.00	0.00	0.00	0.00	0.00	0.00	3,423.90	3,501.30	3,599.40	3,714.60	3,830.40	3,944.10	4,098.30	4,251.30	4,467.00
E-8	0.00	0.00	0.00	0.00	0.00	2,858.10	2,940.60	3,017.70	3,110.10	3,210.30	3,314.70	3,420.30	3,573.00	3,724.80	3,937.80
E-7	1,986.90	2,169.00	2,251.50	2,332.50	2,417.40	2,562.90	2,645.10	2,726.40	2,808.00	2,892.60	2,975.10	3,057.30	3,200.40	3,292.80	3,526.80
E-6	1,701.00	1,870.80	1,953.60	2,033.70	2,117.40	2,254.50	2,337.30	2,417.40	2,499.30	2,558.10	2,602.80	2,602.80	2,602.80	2,602.80	2,602.80
E-5	1,561.50	1,665.30	1,745.70	1,828.50	1,912.80	2,030.10	2,110.20	2,193.30	2,193.30	2,193.30	2,193.30	2,193.30	2,193.30	2,193.30	2,193.30
E-4	1,443.60	1,517.70	1,599.60	1,680.30	1,752.30	1,752.30	1,752.30	1,752.30	1,752.30	1,752.30	1,752.30	1,752.30	1,752.30	1,752.30	1,752.30
E-3	1,303.50	1,385.40	1,468.50	1,468.50	1,468.50	1,468.50	1,468.50	1,468.50	1,468.50	1,468.50	1,468.50	1,468.50	1,468.50	1,468.50	1,468.50
E-2	1,239.30	1,239.30	1,239.30	1,239.30	1,239.30	1,239.30	1,239.30	1,239.30	1,239.30	1,239.30	1,239.30	1,239.30	1,239.30	1,239.30	1,239.30
E-1 >4	1,105.50	1,105.50	1,105.50	1,105.50	1,105.50	1,105.50	1,105.50	1,105.50	1,105.50	1,105.50	1,105.50	1,105.50	1,105.50	1,105.50	1,105.50
E-1 <4	1,022.70														

Note: Basic pay for O7-O10 is limited to $11,141.70, Level III of the Executive Schedule

Note: Basic pay for O6 and below is limited to $9,800.10, Level V of the Executive Schedule

TABLE C-2: RESERVE DRILL PAY (FOUR DRILL PERIODS OR ONE WEEKEND) (EFFECTIVE 1 JANUARY 2002)

	YEARS OF SERVICE														
Grade	<2	2	3	4	6	8	10	12	14	16	18	20	22	24	26
COMMISSIONED OFFICERS															
O-10	0.00	0.00	0.00	0.00	0.00	0.00	0.00	0.00	0.00	0.00	0.00	1,546.92	1,554.56	1,586.84	1,643.20
O-9	0.00	0.00	0.00	0.00	0.00	0.00	0.00	0.00	0.00	0.00	0.00	1,353.00	1,372.48	1,400.64	1,449.84
O-8	957.36	988.72	1,009.48	1,015.32	1,041.24	1,084.68	1,094.76	1,135.96	1,147.80	1,183.24	1,234.60	1,281.96	1,313.60	1,313.60	1,313.60
O-7	795.52	849.56	849.56	855.76	887.72	912.04	940.16	968.24	996.36	1,084.68	1,159.32	1,159.32	1,159.32	1,159.32	1,165.16
O-6	589.60	647.72	690.24	690.24	692.88	722.52	726.48	726.48	750.48	840.76	883.60	926.44	950.80	975.48	1,023.36
O-5	471.60	553.68	592.04	599.24	623.08	623.08	641.80	676.44	721.80	767.44	789.20	810.64	835.04	835.04	835.04
O-4	403.16	490.92	523.68	531.00	561.40	586.12	626.16	657.36	679.00	700.76	708.08	708.08	708.08	708.08	708.08
O-3	372.88	422.72	456.24	493.16	516.76	542.68	564.32	592.16	606.60	606.60	606.60	606.60	606.60	606.60	606.60
O-2	322.16	366.92	422.60	436.84	445.88	445.88	445.88	445.88	445.88	445.88	445.88	445.88	445.88	445.88	445.88
O-1	279.68	291.08	351.80	351.80	351.80	351.80	351.80	351.80	351.80	351.80	351.80	351.80	351.80	351.80	351.80
COMMISSIONED OFFICERS WITH OVER 4 YEARS ACTIVE DUTY SERVICE AS AN ENLISTED MEMBER OR WARRANT OFFICER															
O-3E	0.00	0.00	0.00	493.16	516.76	542.68	564.32	592.16	615.60	629.00	647.36	647.36	647.36	647.36	647.36
O-2E	0.00	0.00	0.00	436.84	445.88	460.04	484.00	502.52	516.32	516.32	516.32	516.32	516.32	516.32	516.32
O-1E	0.00	0.00	0.00	351.80	375.76	389.64	403.80	417.76	436.84	436.84	436.84	436.84	436.84	436.84	436.84
WARRANT OFFICERS															
W-5	0.00	0.00	0.00	0.00	0.00	0.00	0.00	0.00	0.00	0.00	0.00	662.08	684.80	707.60	730.48
W-4	385.28	414.48	426.40	438.12	458.28	478.20	498.36	518.04	538.40	557.92	577.92	597.44	617.68	637.60	658.04
W-3	351.84	381.60	381.60	386.52	402.32	420.32	444.12	458.60	474.44	492.52	510.48	528.48	546.44	564.44	582.52
W-2	309.52	327.20	342.64	353.88	363.52	383.36	397.92	412.52	426.72	442.40	458.52	474.64	490.68	506.84	506.84
W-1	273.32	295.68	310.68	320.36	334.92	349.96	365.04	380.00	395.16	410.28	425.32	436.68	436.68	436.68	436.68
ENLISTED MEMBERS															
E-9	0.00	0.00	0.00	0.00	0.00	0.00	456.52	466.84	479.92	495.28	510.72	525.88	546.44	566.84	595.60
E-8	0.00	0.00	0.00	0.00	0.00	381.08	392.08	402.36	414.68	428.04	441.96	456.04	476.40	496.64	525.04
E-7	264.92	289.20	300.20	311.00	322.32	341.72	352.68	363.52	374.40	385.68	396.68	407.64	426.72	439.04	470.24
E-6	226.80	249.44	260.48	271.16	282.32	300.60	311.64	322.32	333.24	341.08	347.04	347.04	347.04	347.04	347.04
E-5	208.20	222.04	232.76	243.80	255.04	270.68	281.36	292.44	292.44	292.44	292.44	292.44	292.44	292.44	292.44
E-4	192.48	202.36	213.28	224.04	233.64	233.64	233.64	233.64	233.64	233.64	233.64	233.64	233.64	233.64	233.64
E-3	173.80	184.72	195.80	195.80	195.80	195.80	195.80	195.80	195.80	195.80	195.80	195.80	195.80	195.80	195.80
E-2	165.24	165.24	165.24	165.24	165.24	165.24	165.24	165.24	165.24	165.24	165.24	165.24	165.24	165.24	165.24
E-1 >4	147.40	147.40	147.40	147.40	147.40	147.40	147.40	147.40	147.40	147.40	147.40	147.40	147.40	147.40	147.40
E-1 <4	136.36														

TABLE C-3
MONTHLY BASIC ALLOWANCE FOR HOUSING (BAH)

Pay Grade	Single Full Rate	Partial Rate	Married Full Rate	BAH Type II Differential
O-10	979.80	50.70	1,205.70	238.80
O-9	979.80	50.70	1,205.70	238.80
O-8	979.80	50.70	1,205.70	238.80
O-7	979.80	50.70	1,205.70	238.80
O-6	898.80	39.60	1,085.40	197.70
O-5	865.50	33.00	1,046.40	191.10
O-4	801.90	26.70	922.20	126.90
O-3	642.90	22.20	762.90	126.60
O-2	510.00	17.70	651.30	149.70
O-1	429.60	13.20	582.60	162.00
O3E	694.20	22.20	819.90	133.20
O2E	589.80	17.70	739.80	159.00
O1E	507.60	13.20	683.70	186.30
W-5	814.80	25.20	890.40	79.50
W-4	723.60	25.20	816.30	97.80
W-3	608.40	20.70	748.20	147.60
W-2	539.70	15.90	687.90	156.00
W-1	452.40	13.80	594.90	150.60
E-9	594.30	18.60	783.30	199.50
E-8	545.70	15.30	722.40	186.60
E-7	465.90	12.00	670.50	216.30
E-6	421.80	9.90	619.80	208.80
E-5	389.10	8.70	557.40	177.60
E-4	338.40	8.10	484.20	153.90
E-3	332.10	7.80	450.90	125.70
E-2	269.70	7.20	429.60	168.90
E-1 > 4	240.60	6.90	429.60	199.50
E-1 < 4	240.60	6.90	429.60	199.50

TABLE C-4
SPECIAL AND INCENTIVE PAY (AS OF 1 JANUARY 2002)

Hostile fire or imminent danger pay	$150/ month
Incentive pay for hazardous duty (Flying duty as non-crew member, parachute jumping, demolition duty, handling toxic fuel, flight deck operations, experimental stress duty)	$150/month
High altitude-low opening (HALO) pay	$225/month
Foreign language proficiency pay (selected specialties)	$25-100/month
Enlisted Servicemembers	
Diving Pay	up to $340/month for master divers
Foreign Duty Pay, E-7 to E-9	$22.50/month
E-6	$20.00
E-5	$16.00
E-4	$13.00
E-3	$9.00
E-1 and E-2	$8.00
Officers	
Special pay for Navy nuclear-qualified officers:	
Nuclear Officer Accession Bonus	up to $4,000
Nuclear Continuation Pay (for 3-, 4-, or 5-year contracts)	up to $10,000
Special pay for diving duty	up to $240/month

TABLE C-5
AVIATION CAREER INCENTIVE PAY (AS OF 1 JANUARY 2002)

Years of Aviation Service as a Commissioned or Warrant Officer (Phase 1)	Monthly Pay
2 or less	$125
over 2	$156
over 3	$188
over 4	$206
over 6	$650
Total Years of Commissioned Service (Phase 2)	
over 14	$840
over 22	$585
over 23	$495
over 24	$385
over 25	$250
Hazardous Duty (Crew Member) Pay (nonAWAC)	
O7–O10	$150
O5 , O6	$250
O4	$225
O3	$175
O1, O2	$150
W4, W5	$250
W3	$175
W1, W2	$150
E7–E9	$240
E6	$215
E5	$190
E4	$165
E1–E3	$150

TABLE C-6: CAREER SEA DUTY PAY CHART (EFFECTIVE 1 JANUARY 2002)

COMMISSIONED OFFICERS

Grade	<1	1	2	3	4	5	6	7	8	9	10	11	12	13	14	15	16	17	18	19	20
O-6	100	100	100	315	320	320	335	360	370	395	405	420	435	435	455	455	475	475	500	500	535
O-5	100	100	100	315	315	315	315	320	345	350	365	370	370	370	400	400	420	420	440	440	475
O-4	100	100	100	260	265	280	285	300	310	310	315	315	335	335	380	380	395	395	405	405	420
O-3	100	100	100	210	225	260	265	275	285	300	315	315	335	335	365	365	380	380	395	395	405
O-2	100	100	100	210	225	260	265	275	285	300	315	335	335	335	350	350	365	365	380	380	395
O-1	100	100	100	210	225	260	265	275	285	300	315	335	335	335	350	350	365	365	380	380	395

WARRANT OFFICERS

Grade	<1	1	2	3	4	5	6	7	8	9	10	11	12	13	14	15	16	17	18	19	20
W-5	210	210	210	210	240	240	435	435	435	435	490	525	560	560	630	630	630	630	700	700	700
W-4	210	210	210	210	240	240	435	435	435	435	490	525	560	560	630	630	630	630	700	700	700
W-3	210	210	210	210	240	380	395	400	405	435	490	525	560	560	595	595	595	595	630	630	630
W-2	210	210	210	210	240	365	370	370	380	435	475	475	525	525	560	560	560	560	560	560	560
W-1	180	190	195	210	240	245	280	350	380	420	455	455	475	475	505	505	525	525	525	525	525

ENLISTED

Grade	<1	1	2	3	4	5	6	7	8	9	10	11	12	13	14	15	16	17	18
E-9	135	135	160	305	320	350	350	375	490	500	500	510	520	550	575	575	620	620	620
E-8	135	135	160	305	320	350	350	375	490	500	500	510	520	550	575	575	600	600	620
E-7	135	135	160	305	320	350	350	375	490	500	500	510	520	550	575	575	600	600	600
E-6	135	135	160	280	300	315	325	350	450	460	465	465	480	495	510	510	525	525	550
E-5	70	80	160	280	300	315	325	350	450	450	450	450	450	450	450	450	450	450	450
E-4	70	80	160	280	290	290	290	290	390	390	390	390	390	390	390	390	390	390	390
E-3	50	60	100	100	100	100	100	100	100	100	100	100	100	100	100	100	100	100	100
E-2	50	60	75	75	75	75	75	75	75	75	75	75	75	75	75	75	75	75	75
E-1	50	50	50	50	50	50	50	50	50	50	50	50	50	50	50	50	50	50	50

TABLE C-7
SUBMARINE PAY

	YEARS OF SERVICE													
	< 2	2	3	4	6	8	10	12	14	16	18	20	22	26
O8–O10	355	355	355	355	355	355	355	355	355	355	355	355	355	355
O7	355	355	355	355	355	355	355	355	355	540	535	535	410	355
O6	595	595	595	595	595	595	595	595	595	595	595	595	595	595
O5	595	595	595	595	595	595	595	595	595	595	595	595	595	595
O4	365	365	365	405	595	595	595	595	595	595	595	595	595	595
O3	355	355	355	390	595	595	595	595	595	595	595	595	595	595
O2	235	235	235	235	235	235	355	355	355	355	355	355	355	355
O1	175	175	175	175	175	175	355	355	355	355	355	355	355	355
W1–W5	235	310	310	355	355	355	355	355	355	355	355	355	355	355
E9	225	225	225	270	295	310	315	330	345	355	355	355	355	355
E8	225	225	225	250	270	295	310	315	330	330	345	345	345	345
E7	225	225	225	250	255	265	275	295	310	310	310	310	310	310
E6	155	170	175	215	230	245	255	265	265	265	265	265	265	265
E5	140	155	155	175	190	195	195	195	195	195	195	195	195	195
E4	80	95	100	170	175	175	175	175	175	175	175	175	175	175
E3	80	90	95	95	140	140	140	140	140	140	140	140	140	140
E2	75	90	90	90	90	90	90	90	90	90	90	90	90	90
E1	75	75	75	75	75	75	75	75	75	75	75	75	75	75

TABLE C-8: MEDICAL AND DENTAL SPECIAL PAY

MEDICAL OFFICERS

Creditable Service	Variable Special Pay	Additional Special Pay	Board Certified Pay	Incentive Special Pay
O-6 and Below				
Internship	$100.00	n/a	n/a	n/a
0–6 years	$416.66	$15,000	$208.33	up to $36,000
6–8 years	$1,000.00	$15,000	$208.33	up to $36,000
8–10 years	$958.33	$15,000	$208.33	up to $36,000
10–12 years	$916.67	$15,000	$291.66	up to $36,000
12–14 years	$833.33	$15,000	$333.33	up to $36,000
14–18 years	$750.00	$15,000	$416.66	up to $36,000
18–22 years	$666.67	$15,000	$500.00	up to $36,000
Over 22 years	$583.33	$15,000	$500.00	up to $36,000
O-7 and above				
Over 18 years	$7,000	$15,000	$6,000	up to $36,000

DENTAL OFFICERS

Creditable Service	Variable Special Pay	Additional Special Pay	Board Certified Pay	Incentive Special Pay
Annual Amounts				
Internship	$250.00	n/a	n/a	n/a
0–3 years	$583.33	$4,000	$208.33	up to $14,000
3-6 years	$583.33	$6,000	$208.33	up to $14,000
6-8 years	$583.33	$6,000	$208.33	up to $14,000
8-10 years	$1,000.00	$6,000	$208.33	up to $14,000
10-12 years	$1,000.00	$15,000	$291.66	up to $14,000
12-14 years	$833.33	$15,000	$333.33	up to $14,000
14-18 years	$750.00	$15,000	$416.66	up to $14,000
Over 18 years	$666.67	$15,000	$500.00	up to $14,000
O-7 and above				
Over 18 years	$1,000	$15,000	$6,000	n/a

DIPLOMATE/BOARD CERTIFIED PAY
(Non-Health Care Physicians, Veterinarians, and Psychologists)

Pay Grade	Under 3	3 & Over	6 & Over	8 & Over	10 & Over	12 & Over	14 & Over	18 & Over
All Grades	$166.66	$166.66	$166.66	$166.66	$208.33	$250.00	$333.33	$416.66

Appendix D

Time Value of Money and Present Value Tables

Virtually all servicemembers will at some time in their lives buy a home, take out a loan, invest in real estate, stocks, or bonds, decide on which type of life insurance to buy, or analyze a home improvement project. An understanding of the time value of money can greatly assist in making good decisions.

The most basic idea here is that we value less something for which we must wait. All of us would prefer to have a new sports car today rather than a year from now. We are impatient to consume and would probably pay more today for the sports car if we could have it right away than we would pay today for the right to receive the car a year from now.

An additional idea is that we have the opportunity to invest: Assets we have now can be deposited at interest so that later, say in a year, they will be worth more.

Consider the following example: A local bank decides to support local students by offering $1,000 to each student on graduation day, which is one year away. The prize is worth $1,000 one year from today. What is the prize worth today?

Suppose your teenage neighbor offers to sell you his prize today, one year from the time it will be worth $1,000. How much should you pay for the right to receive $1,000 one year from now?

If you could collect the $1,000 prize today, you would be willing to pay $1,000 to your neighbor, but since you must wait to collect the money, you will be reluctant to pay that much. On the other hand, your neighbor's prize is worth a lot more than nothing. You might reason as follows:

1. "I can earn 5 percent per year on money I have in my savings account." (Economists call that the opportunity to invest.) "I should not earn less than that by investing in my neighbor's prize."
2. "My neighbor's prize will be worth $1,000 next year. How much money invested in my savings account at 5 percent interest per year will give me $1,000 in a year?" Let *X* represent the amount in the account now. Then:

$$\$X(1.05) = \$1.000$$

$$X = \frac{\$1.000}{1.05} = \$952.38$$

3. "I could take $952.38 out of savings today, buy my neighbor's prize, hold it for a year, and be no worse off."

You offer your neighbor $952.38 for the prize. Your neighbor, impatient to consume, agrees to accept $952.38 for his prize today because he does not want to wait a year.

Notice two important points about this transaction:

1. You valued the prize at less than its $1,000 face value because you would have to wait to receive the $1,000.

2. Your neighbor was willing to accept less today than the face value of the prize because he could have the money immediately.

APPLICATION TO LOANS

These principles determine the basis upon which consumer loans are made. The borrower takes a sum of money from a lender today and agrees to pay back a larger sum later, perhaps in monthly installments. The lender agrees to loan the money today in exchange for a larger sum later. In the above example, you were the lender, and your neighbor (the borrower) agreed to give up $1,000 next year in exchange for $952.38 this year.

Let's look at a typical installment loan. You want to borrow $1,000 today from the bank and agree to repay that sum plus interest in three annual installments. Since you receive the $1,000 today, we call it the present value (PV) of the loan. Your three annual payments (PMT) will be made at the end of each of the three years the loan is outstanding and will, of course, add up to more than the PV. The rate of interest charged on the loan is (1+r).

$$PV = \frac{PMT}{1 + r} + \frac{PMT}{(1 + r)^2} + \frac{PMT}{(1 + r)^3}$$

For example, if the annual interest rate is 5 percent, then $1 + r = 1.05$, and

$$\$1,000 = \frac{PMT}{1.05} + \frac{PMT}{(1.05)^2} + \frac{PMT}{(1.05)^3}$$

$$PMT = 367.21$$

Notice that you will actually pay a total of $1,101.63 ($367.21 × 3) as you repay the $1,000 loan. This difference is the finance charge.

$$\$1,101.63 - \$1,000 = \$101.63 = \text{finance charge}$$

Most people are confused by the interest rate exponents in equations like those above. The exponents represent the number of periods (years in this example) between now and the time the payment (PMT) is made. Think back to the graduation prize example:

$$PV = \$952.38 = \frac{PMT}{(1+r)^1} = \frac{\$1,000}{(1.05)^1}$$

The exponent on the interest rate in that case was 1, because we had to wait one period to receive the payment of \$1,000. If we had to wait two years to receive the \$1,000 prize, we would pay less than \$952.38 for it today. In fact, we would pay only

$$\frac{\$1,000}{(1.05)^2} = \$907.03$$

because \$907.03 invested at 5 percent for two years gives us \$1,000 in two years.

$$(907.03) \times (1.05)^2 = \$1,000$$

Use of a Time Line

For more complex problems you may find it helpful to use a time line to portray graphically when payments will be made. For example, the time line for the loan example above is:

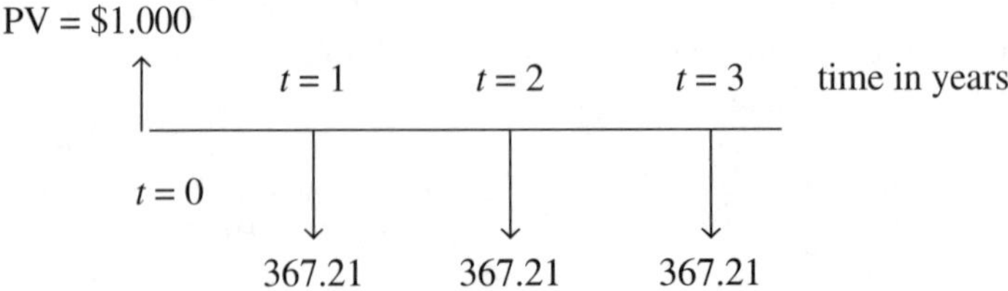

Amounts you receive are shown above the line; amounts you must pay are indicated below the line. The exponents correspond to the time period in which the payment is due.

VALUATION OF ASSETS

The concepts above can be extended to use in valuing productive assets such as factories, land, or investment opportunities in general. The time value of money is important because in many situations in our lives we invest funds today and receive returns in the future. For example, suppose you are buying a new car, an option on which is a five-speed overdrive transmission that will save you gas. You must pay for the option today and wait to receive the gas savings over a period of years. You calculate that the overdrive transmission will save you

$33 per year in gas. You plan to keep the car for five years, then sell it. Resale value will be $50 higher then if you have the five-speed. What is the value of the option?

$$PV = \frac{33}{1+r} + \frac{33}{(1+r)^2} + \frac{33}{(1+r)^3} + \frac{33}{(1+r)^4} + \frac{33}{(1+r)^5} + \frac{50}{(1+r)^5}$$

If the extra money you pay for the option would otherwise earn 5 percent per year, then 1 + r = 1.05. If you are borrowing the money for the car, use the loan rate of interest, say 1 + r = 1.12, or 12 percent per year.

PV = $182.05 if 1 + r = 1.05

PV = $147.33 if 1 + r = 1.12

PV indicates the value of the option today. You should not pay more than PV for the option because it is not worth it, at least not on the basis of gas savings and increased resale value.

APPLICATION TO ASSETS IN GENERAL

An asset is an "article of goods or property available for the payment of a person's obligations or debts." In general, an asset is anything that can be used as a store of value. You can use the methodology outlined above to determine the value of any asset. All you need to know is:

1. How much the asset will return to you in the future.
2. When those returns will be made.
3. The interest rate or "discount factor" that gives the opportunity cost to you of investing funds in a given asset rather than the next best alternative of equivalent risk.

Some additional considerations affect the practical use of the concepts above:

1. The interest rate you use must be the rate of interest per period. For example, if you are making or receiving monthly payments, 1 + r in your equations must be the monthly interest rate. If you know the annual effective interest rate, the gross monthly rate is the twelfth root of the gross annual rate:

$$(1 + r) = \text{annual rate} = (1 + i)^{12} \text{ where}$$
$$1 + i \text{ is the monthly interest rate}$$

$$\text{Thus: } i = (1 + \text{annual rate})^{12}$$

But since many stated interest rates (e.g., mortgages, car loans, credit cards) are simply the monthly rate times 12, you will not require the procedure above. You simply divide the stated annual rate by 12 to get the actual rate for monthly use.

2. At times, you know the PV and the PMT values and you want to find the rate of return, called the internal rate of return, on the asset or investment project.

Let's return to the example of the five-speed transmission; say it costs $200 extra. You could draw a time line to illustrate the payments and receipts (in this case receipts are gas savings and higher resale value).

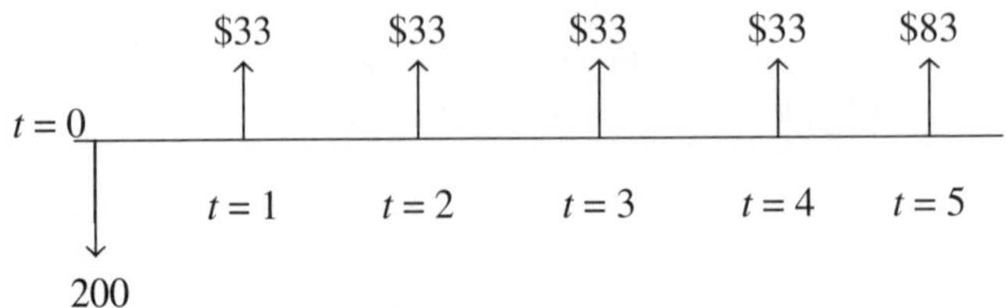

You must pay $200 now, so that is the PV. We equate PV with the stream of future earnings discounted by 1 + r, the unknown rate of return on "investing" in this gas-saving transmission.

$$\$200 = \frac{33}{1 + r} + \frac{33}{(1 + r)^2} + \frac{33}{(1 + r)^3} + \frac{33}{(1 + r)^4} + \frac{83}{(1 + r)^5}$$

The problem now is to find 1 + r that makes the equation balance. Using a hand calculator (a programmable one helps), you can solve this problem through trial and error by trying 1 + r values in computing the right-hand side of the equation. The value of 1 + r that makes the right-hand side equal $200 is the rate of return on your investment. In this case, 1 + r is 1.021, or 2.1 percent.

Obviously, the $200 five-speed is not a good buy if your money can earn a higher rate of return elsewhere. For example, if you can earn 5 percent on invested funds elsewhere, you would be foolish to invest them in the five-speed (if your objective was to save money). This is not surprising; remember we found previously that you should not pay more than $182.04 for the transmission if you can earn 5 percent on your assets elsewhere.

This analysis should help you avoid investing your scarce assets in projects that do not provide an adequate return. Inexpensive calculators can do the necessary calculations for you. For a small investment of your time and effort, you can easily make much better financial decisions using these techniques.

USING THE FINANCIAL TABLES

Financial tables are provided at the end of this Appendix to help you make some of the more common calculations referred to in the text. All calculations can be easily made using one of the modern financial calculators, and we recommend that servicemembers buy one and learn to use it. It is possible, however, to make close estimates of loan payments and other such amounts using the tables provided at the end of this section.

Table D-1, "Present Value of $1," shows today's value of money that will be received in the future (the number of years shown down the left-hand column) at various interest rates (as shown along the top of the table). For example, the present value of $1 to be received in ten years when the interest rate you can earn on your savings is 6 percent is shown in the table to $0.558, or about 56 cents. Table D-1 is useful for estimating the amount you need to set aside now in order to have a specified amount of money at some future time. Suppose you want to have $20,000 for a child's education in ten years and you can earn 6 percent on your savings for those ten years. According to Table D-1, $0.558 will grow to $1 in ten years at 6 percent interest. So if you want to have $20,000 in ten years, you must set aside.558 times $20,000 now, or about $11,160.

Table D-2, "Present Value of $1 Received Annually for *N* Years," shows today's value of savings at various interest rates (shown across the top of the table) for various periods (the number of years is shown along the left column). This table is useful for calculating the amount of savings you will have to accumulate in order to pay yourself a specified amount per year in retirement or to provide for your family in the event of your death. For example, suppose you can earn 6 percent on your savings and want to have your savings provide $6,000 per year for twenty years after you retire. Table D-2 enables you to determine the amount of savings that will be required when you retire. Looking at D-2 for a 6 percent interest rate and twenty years, we find 11.470. This means that the amount of money required to provide $1 per year for twenty years when the money is earning 6 percent is $11.47. Since you want to have $6,000 per year for twenty years, the amount of money you will need at retirement is 6,000 times 11.47, or $68,820. If you are currently ten years from retirement, you need to deposit 0.558 times that amount, or about $38,400, now so that it will grow to the required amount in ten years. (See the example for Table D-1).

TABLE D–1: PRESENT VALUE OF $1 RECEIVED IN *N* YEARS

Periods Until Payment	0.5%	1%	2%	3%	4%	5%	6%	7%	8%	9%	10%	11%	12%	13%	14%	15%	16%	17%	18%	19%	20%
1	0.995	0.990	0.980	0.971	0.962	0.952	0.943	0.935	0.926	0.917	0.909	0.901	0.893	0.885	0.877	0.870	0.862	0.855	0.847	0.840	0.833
2	0.990	0.980	0.961	0.943	0.925	0.907	0.890	0.873	0.857	0.842	0.826	0.812	0.797	0.783	0.769	0.756	0.743	0.731	0.718	0.706	0.694
3	0.985	0.971	0.942	0.915	0.889	0.864	0.840	0.816	0.794	0.772	0.751	0.731	0.712	0.693	0.675	0.658	0.641	0.624	0.609	0.593	0.579
4	0.980	0.961	0.924	0.888	0.855	0.823	0.792	0.763	0.735	0.708	0.683	0.659	0.636	0.613	0.592	0.572	0.552	0.534	0.516	0.499	0.482
5	0.975	0.951	0.906	0.863	0.822	0.784	0.747	0.713	0.681	0.650	0.621	0.593	0.567	0.543	0.519	0.497	0.476	0.456	0.437	0.419	0.402
6	0.971	0.942	0.888	0.837	0.790	0.746	0.705	0.666	0.630	0.596	0.564	0.535	0.507	0.480	0.456	0.432	0.410	0.390	0.370	0.352	0.335
7	0.966	0.933	0.871	0.813	0.760	0.711	0.665	0.623	0.583	0.547	0.513	0.482	0.452	0.425	0.400	0.376	0.354	0.333	0.314	0.296	0.279
8	0.961	0.923	0.853	0.789	0.731	0.677	0.627	0.582	0.540	0.502	0.467	0.434	0.404	0.376	0.351	0.327	0.305	0.285	0.266	0.249	0.233
9	0.956	0.914	0.837	0.766	0.703	0.645	0.592	0.544	0.500	0.460	0.424	0.391	0.361	0.333	0.308	0.284	0.263	0.243	0.225	0.209	0.194
10	0.951	0.905	0.820	0.744	0.676	0.614	0.558	0.508	0.463	0.422	0.386	0.352	0.322	0.295	0.270	0.247	0.227	0.208	0.191	0.176	0.162
11	0.947	0.896	0.804	0.722	0.650	0.585	0.527	0.475	0.429	0.388	0.350	0.317	0.287	0.261	0.237	0.215	0.195	0.178	0.162	0.148	0.135
12	0.942	0.887	0.788	0.701	0.625	0.557	0.497	0.444	0.397	0.356	0.319	0.286	0.257	0.231	0.208	0.187	0.168	0.152	0.137	0.124	0.112
13	0.937	0.879	0.773	0.681	0.601	0.530	0.469	0.415	0.368	0.326	0.290	0.258	0.229	0.204	0.182	0.163	0.145	0.130	0.116	0.104	0.093
14	0.933	0.870	0.758	0.661	0.577	0.505	0.442	0.388	0.340	0.299	0.263	0.232	0.205	0.181	0.160	0.141	0.125	0.111	0.099	0.088	0.078
15	0.928	0.861	0.743	0.642	0.555	0.481	0.417	0.362	0.315	0.275	0.239	0.209	0.183	0.160	0.140	0.123	0.108	0.095	0.084	0.074	0.065
16	0.923	0.853	0.728	0.623	0.534	0.458	0.394	0.339	0.292	0.252	0.218	0.188	0.163	0.141	0.123	0.107	0.093	0.081	0.071	0.062	0.054
17	0.919	0.844	0.714	0.605	0.513	0.436	0.371	0.317	0.270	0.231	0.198	0.170	0.146	0.125	0.108	0.093	0.080	0.069	0.060	0.052	0.045
18	0.914	0.836	0.700	0.587	0.494	0.416	0.350	0.296	0.250	0.212	0.180	0.153	0.130	0.111	0.095	0.081	0.069	0.059	0.051	0.044	0.038
19	0.910	0.828	0.686	0.570	0.475	0.396	0.331	0.277	0.232	0.194	0.164	0.138	0.116	0.098	0.083	0.070	0.060	0.051	0.043	0.037	0.031
20	0.905	0.820	0.673	0.554	0.456	0.377	0.312	0.258	0.215	0.178	0.149	0.124	0.104	0.087	0.073	0.061	0.051	0.043	0.037	0.031	0.026
21	0.901	0.811	0.660	0.538	0.439	0.359	0.294	0.242	0.199	0.164	0.135	0.112	0.093	0.077	0.064	0.053	0.044	0.037	0.031	0.026	0.022
22	0.896	0.803	0.647	0.522	0.422	0.342	0.278	0.226	0.184	0.150	0.123	0.101	0.083	0.068	0.056	0.046	0.038	0.032	0.026	0.022	0.018
23	0.892	0.795	0.634	0.507	0.406	0.326	0.262	0.211	0.170	0.138	0.112	0.091	0.074	0.060	0.049	0.040	0.033	0.027	0.022	0.018	0.015
24	0.887	0.788	0.622	0.492	0.390	0.310	0.247	0.197	0.158	0.126	0.102	0.082	0.066	0.053	0.043	0.035	0.028	0.023	0.019	0.015	0.013
25	0.883	0.780	0.610	0.478	0.375	0.295	0.233	0.184	0.146	0.116	0.092	0.074	0.059	0.047	0.038	0.030	0.024	0.020	0.016	0.013	0.010
26	0.878	0.772	0.598	0.464	0.361	0.281	0.220	0.172	0.135	0.106	0.084	0.066	0.053	0.042	0.033	0.026	0.021	0.017	0.014	0.011	0.009
27	0.874	0.764	0.586	0.450	0.347	0.268	0.207	0.161	0.125	0.098	0.076	0.060	0.047	0.037	0.029	0.023	0.018	0.014	0.011	0.009	0.007
28	0.870	0.757	0.574	0.437	0.333	0.255	0.196	0.150	0.116	0.090	0.069	0.054	0.042	0.033	0.026	0.020	0.016	0.012	0.010	0.008	0.006
29	0.865	0.749	0.563	0.424	0.321	0.243	0.185	0.141	0.107	0.082	0.063	0.048	0.037	0.029	0.022	0.017	0.014	0.011	0.008	0.006	0.005
30	0.861	0.742	0.552	0.412	0.308	0.231	0.174	0.131	0.099	0.075	0.057	0.044	0.033	0.026	0.020	0.015	0.012	0.009	0.007	0.005	0.004
40	0.819	0.672	0.453	0.307	0.208	0.142	0.097	0.067	0.046	0.032	0.022	0.015	0.011	0.008	0.005	0.004	0.003	0.002	0.001	0.001	0.001
50	0.779	0.608	0.372	0.228	0.141	0.087	0.054	0.034	0.021	0.013	0.009	0.005	0.003	0.002	0.001	0.001	0.001	0.000	0.000	0.000	0.000

Example: What amount invested today at 2% interest (after inflation) would cover a $10,000 education in 10 years?
Present value = (0.820 × $10,000) = $8,200

Note: By interpolation you can estimate value for "periods of payment" between 30 and 40 and between 40 and 50.

TABLE D–2: PRESENT VALUE OF $1 RECEIVED ANNUALLY FOR *N* YEARS

Years Payments Received	0.5%	1%	2%	3%	4%	5%	6%	7%	8%	9%	10%	11%	12%	13%	14%	15%	16%	17%	18%	19%	20%
1	0.995	0.990	0.980	0.971	0.962	0.952	0.943	0.935	0.926	0.917	0.909	0.901	0.893	0.885	0.877	0.870	0.862	0.855	0.847	0.840	0.833
2	1.985	1.970	1.942	1.913	1.886	1.859	1.833	1.808	1.783	1.759	1.736	1.713	1.690	1.668	1.647	1.626	1.605	1.585	1.566	1.547	1.528
3	2.970	2.941	2.884	2.829	2.775	2.723	2.673	2.624	2.577	2.531	2.487	2.444	2.402	2.361	2.322	2.283	2.246	2.210	2.174	2.140	2.106
4	3.950	3.902	3.808	3.717	3.630	3.546	3.465	3.387	3.312	3.240	3.170	3.102	3.037	2.974	2.914	2.855	2.798	2.743	2.690	2.639	2.589
5	4.926	4.853	4.713	4.580	4.452	4.329	4.212	4.100	3.993	3.890	3.791	3.696	3.605	3.517	3.433	3.352	3.274	3.199	3.127	3.058	2.991
6	5.896	5.795	5.601	5.417	5.242	5.076	4.917	4.767	4.623	4.486	4.355	4.231	4.111	3.998	3.889	3.784	3.685	3.589	3.498	3.410	3.326
7	6.862	6.728	6.472	6.230	6.002	5.786	5.582	5.389	5.206	5.033	4.868	4.712	4.564	4.423	4.288	4.160	4.039	3.922	3.812	3.706	3.605
8	7.823	7.652	7.325	7.020	6.733	6.463	6.210	5.971	5.747	5.535	5.335	5.146	4.968	4.799	4.639	4.487	4.344	4.207	4.078	3.954	3.837
9	8.779	8.566	8.162	7.786	7.435	7.108	6.802	6.515	6.247	5.995	5.759	5.537	5.328	5.132	4.946	4.772	4.607	4.451	4.303	4.163	4.031
10	9.730	9.471	8.983	8.530	8.111	7.722	7.360	7.024	6.710	6.418	6.145	5.889	5.650	5.426	5.216	5.019	4.833	4.659	4.494	4.339	4.192
11	10.677	10.368	9.787	9.253	8.760	8.306	7.887	7.499	7.139	6.805	6.495	6.207	5.938	5.687	5.453	5.234	5.029	4.836	4.656	4.486	4.327
12	11.619	11.255	10.575	9.954	9.385	8.863	8.384	7.943	7.536	7.161	6.814	6.492	6.194	5.918	5.660	5.421	5.197	4.988	4.793	4.611	4.439
13	12.556	12.134	11.348	10.635	9.986	9.394	8.853	8.358	7.904	7.487	7.103	6.750	6.424	6.122	5.842	5.583	5.342	5.118	4.910	4.715	4.533
14	13.489	13.004	12.106	11.296	10.563	9.899	9.295	8.745	8.244	7.786	7.367	6.982	6.628	6.302	6.002	5.724	5.458	5.229	5.008	4.802	4.611
15	14.417	13.865	12.849	11.936	11.118	10.380	9.712	9.108	8.559	8.061	7.606	7.191	6.811	6.462	6.142	5.847	5.575	5.324	5.092	4.876	4.675
16	15.340	14.718	13.578	12.561	11.652	10.838	10.106	9.447	8.851	8.313	7.824	7.379	6.974	6.604	6.265	5.954	5.668	5.405	5.162	4.938	4.730
17	16.259	15.562	14.292	13.166	12.166	11.274	10.477	9.763	9.122	8.544	8.022	7.549	7.120	6.729	6.373	6.047	5.749	5.475	5.222	4.990	4.775
18	17.173	16.398	14.992	13.754	12.659	11.690	10.828	10.059	9.372	8.756	8.201	7.702	7.250	6.840	6.467	6.128	5.818	5.534	5.273	5.033	4.812
19	18.082	17.226	15.678	14.324	13.134	12.085	11.158	10.336	9.604	8.950	8.365	7.839	7.366	6.938	6.550	6.198	5.877	5.584	5.316	5.070	4.843
20	18.987	18.046	16.351	14.877	13.590	12.462	11.470	10.594	9.818	9.129	8.514	7.963	7.469	7.025	6.623	6.259	5.929	5.628	5.353	5.101	4.870
21	19.888	18.857	17.011	15.415	14.029	12.821	11.764	10.836	10.017	9.292	8.649	8.075	7.562	7.102	6.687	6.312	5.973	5.665	5.384	5.127	4.891
22	20.784	19.660	17.658	15.937	14.451	13.163	12.042	11.061	10.201	9.442	8.772	8.176	7.645	7.170	6.743	6.359	6.011	5.696	5.410	5.149	4.909
23	21.676	20.456	18.292	16.444	14.857	13.489	12.303	11.272	10.371	9.580	8.883	8.266	7.718	7.230	6.792	6.399	6.044	5.723	5.432	5.167	4.925
24	22.563	21.243	18.914	16.936	15.247	13.799	12.550	11.469	10.529	9.707	8.985	8.348	7.784	7.283	6.835	6.434	6.073	5.746	5.451	5.182	4.937
25	23.446	22.023	19.523	17.413	15.622	14.094	12.783	11.654	10.675	9.823	9.077	8.422	7.843	7.330	6.873	6.464	6.097	5.766	5.467	5.195	4.948
26	24.324	22.795	20.121	17.877	15.983	14.375	13.003	11.826	10.810	9.929	9.161	8.488	7.896	7.372	6.906	6.491	6.118	5.783	5.480	5.206	4.956
27	25.198	23.560	20.707	18.327	16.330	14.643	13.211	11.987	10.935	10.027	9.237	8.548	7.943	7.409	6.935	6.514	6.136	5.798	5.492	5.215	4.964
28	26.068	24.316	21.281	18.764	16.663	14.898	13.406	12.137	11.051	10.116	9.307	8.602	7.984	7.441	6.961	6.534	6.152	5.810	5.502	5.223	4.970
29	26.933	25.066	21.844	19.188	16.984	15.141	13.591	12.278	11.158	10.198	9.370	8.650	8.022	7.470	6.983	6.551	6.166	5.820	5.510	5.229	4.975
30	27.794	25.808	22.396	19.600	17.292	15.372	13.765	12.409	11.258	10.274	9.427	8.694	8.055	7.496	7.003	6.566	6.177	5.829	5.517	5.235	4.979
40	36.172	32.835	27.355	23.115	19.793	17.159	15.046	13.332	11.925	10.757	9.779	8.951	8.244	7.634	7.105	6.642	6.233	5.871	5.548	5.258	4.997
50	44.143	39.196	31.424	25.730	21.482	18.256	15.762	13.801	12.233	10.962	9.915	9.042	8.304	7.675	7.133	6.661	6.246	5.880	5.554	5.262	4.999

Example: How much would you have to invest today at 8% to draw out $6,000 at the end of each year for 20 years?

Present value = (9.818 × $6,000) = $58,908

Appendix E

Sample Personal Affairs Record

PERSONAL AFFAIRS RECORD OF

____

(Name) (Grade) (Social Security No.) (Component)

I. Personal Data

Religious preference ______________________

Birthdate ____________ Place of birth ______________

Permanent legal address ______________________

Local (or emergency) address ______________________

Telephone no. ______________________

Father's name and address ______________________

Father's date and place of birth ______________________

Mother's name and address______________________

Mother's date and place of birth______________________

Names, addresses, and ages of brothers and sisters

____

____

____

____

Date and place of marriage ______________________

Location of marriage certificate ______________________

Name of spouse ________ Social Security No.______________

Spouse's permanent legal address ______________________

Spouse's birthdate ______________________

Spouse's place of birth ______________________

Children's names, date and place of birth

____

____

____

____

Birth certificates located as follows:
Myself ____________________ Spouse ______________________
Children ____
Social Security cards located at _________________________
Pay status
Base pay ___________________________
Quarters allowance ___________________________
Subsistence ___________________________
Hazardous duty pay ___________________________
Other pay ___________________________
Total ___________________________
Former service numbers ____________________________________
Entered military service on ____________ at _______________
Military service (list here or separately all military service including units, grades, and periods of service) ______________________________
____
____
____
____

II. Will

Date and location of will ____________________________________
Where made ____
Executor's name and address _________________________________
Spouse or joint will? _______________________________________
Date and location of spouse's will ____________________________
Where made ____
Executor's name and address _________________________________

III. Power of Attorney

Does a power of attorney exist? _______________________________
Type (general, limited). If limited, for what purpose? ___________
Date of execution ____________ Date of expiration ______________
Name and address of grantee _________________________________

IV. Taxes

Federal income taxes paid through calendar year _________________
State income taxes paid through calendar year ___________________
Real estate taxes paid until ___________________________________
Personal property taxes paid until ______________________________
Location of tax return records __________________________________

V. Property Ownership

1. Real estate ______________________________

Description of real estate owned ______________________________

____

____

Names in which held ______________________________

Date acquired ______________________________

Purchase price ____________ Estimated present value ____________

Mortgage amount ____________ Held by ____________

Name and address of insurance company ______________________________

____

Policy no. ____________ Expiration date ____________

in the amount of $ ______________________________

against ______________________________

(fire, damage, liability, etc.)

Lease on rented property expiration date ____________

Pertinent documents located at ____________

2. Automobile Record

Make ____________ Model ____________ Year ____________

Serial no. ____________ Motor no. ____________ Color ____________

License plate no. ____________ Year ____________ State ____________

Title no. ____________ Title state ____________ Date ____________

Insurance company ______________________________

Address ______________________________

Insurance policy no. ____________ Expiration date ____________

Insured Against:	Yes	No	Limits
Bodily injury	______	______	______
Property damage	______	______	______
Public liability	______	______	______
Collision	______	______	______
Comprehensive	______	______	______
Other (explain)	______	______	______

Name and address of finance company ______________________________

Balance due ____________ Monthly payments ____________

Automobile papers located at ______________________________

3. Other personal property (jewelry, boats, trailers, etc.)

List property of great value	Amount of lien and monthly payment	Lien held by	Insurance company, limits, policy no., exp. date)

VI. Credit Cards

Company	Card no.	No. of cards	Expiration date

Credit card insurance? ________ Amount ____________________

Name of insurance company______________ Policy no. __________

VII. Bank Accounts and Savings Deposits

Name and address of bank	Type account	Account number

Bonds are located at ______________________________

VIII. U.S. Bonds

Denomination	Number	In Name of

Bonds are located at ______________________________

IX. Stocks, Mutual Funds, and Other Securities

Company Date purchased Purchase price Certificate number

____

____

____

____

____

Carried in account number __________ maintained with _______

____

(Name and address of broker)

X. Insurance

1. I (do) (do not) have government life insurance.
   This insurance is (U.S. government life insurance)
   (Servicemembers Group Life Insurance)
   The policy number is______________ Type of insurance _______
   Amount of government insurance ________________________
   The policy is located at ______________________________
2. I have in effect the following commercial life insurance:

   Company Address Policy number Amount

   ____

   ____

   ____

   These policies are located at ___________________________
   The following loans are outstanding against these policies:

   ____

   ____
3. I have accomplished an insurance program that outlines the manner in which the proceeds of each are to be paid. It is located at __________

   ____
4. Primary beneficiary___________________________________
   Contingent beneficiaries _______________________________
5. Life insurance in effect upon the lives of my wife and children:

   Name and relationship Company policy no. Amount Premium due

   ____

   ____

   ____

6. The property and casualty insurance policies presently in effect are:

	Company	Address	Policy no.
Personal property	__________	__________	__________
Personal liability	__________	__________	__________
Hospitalization and health	__________	__________	__________

XI. Moneys Owed to Me

Amount Debtor

____

____

XII. Liabilities (Loans, notes not previously listed)

Amount Lender Date made Date due

____

____

XIII. Safe Deposit Box

Location of box ______________________________

Safe deposit box key located at ________________________

XIV. Burial

I desire to be interred at ___________________________

I desire (that the government grave marker be utilized)

(that a monument be erected at the place of my interment at a cost not to exceed $ ______________________________).

XV. Other Pertinent Information and Instructions:

____

____

____

XVI. This record was last checked on ________________________

Notes:

Birth and marriage certificates should be obtained as part of estate planning. At least fifteen copies of each should be on hand, as they are generally required for pensions, Social Security, and sometimes by commercial insurance companies.

Burial may be at a post or national cemetery. A government grave marker is furnished gratuitously.

Some rights of surviving spouses:

1. Entitled to purchase at commissary and post exchanges.
2. Entitled to medical care and hospitalization when facilities are available.
3. May be entitled to state bonus.
4. Eligible, if not remarried, for GI home or business loans to same extent as veteran.
5. Entitled to preference in federal civil service examination.
6. Entitled to transportation of self, children, and household goods to new home.
7. Entitled to GI educational benefits.

About the Authors

Professor Dean D. Dudley is an associate professor of economics at the United States Military Academy (USMA), having taught nearly every economics course offered at USMA. Previously he taught at Indiana University. He holds a B.A. from Eastern Washington University and a Ph.D. from Indiana University, Bloomington.

Major Sonya L. Finley is a comparative and international relations and financial planning instructor at USMA. She is an air defense artillery officer with previous assignments in Germany, Czech Republic, Texas, and Saudi Arabia. She has a B.A. from Emory University and an M.P.A. from Cornell University.

Major Blaire Harms is an instructor of international relations and comparative politics at USMA. She is a military intelligence officer with previous assignments at the 2nd Infantry Division in Korea and at the 82nd Airborne Division and U.S. Army Special Operations Command at Fort Bragg, North Carolina. She has a B.A. from California State University, Chico, and an M.A. in political science, from Rutgers University, where she is also working on her Ph.D.

Lieutenant Colonel Richard A. Hewitt is currently the director of the economics program at USMA. He has served as an infantry officer with the 82nd, 7th, and 2nd Infantry Divisions. He holds a B.S. from USMA and an M.B.A. from the University of Chicago Graduate School of Business and is licensed as a certified financial planner.

Major Paul D. Kucik is the deputy director of the Office of Economic and Manpower Analysis and an economics instructor at USMA. He is an aviation officer with previous assignments in the 24th and 25th Infantry Divisions. He holds a B.S. from USMA and an M.B.A. from the Sloan School of Management at MIT.

Major Joel Levesque is an air defense artillery officer who is a graduate of West Point and the Simon School of Business at the University of Rochester. He is a holder of the CFA designation and a member of the New York Society of Security Analysts and the Association of Investment Management and

Research (AIMR). He is also a partner in a real estate investment partnership. Currently, he is the air defense coordinator (ADCOORD) for the 10th Mountain Division (Light) at Fort Drum, New York.

Second Lieutenant Felisa Lewis (Medical Service Corps, USAR) is currently a medical student at the Uniformed Services University of the Health Sciences in Bethesda, Maryland. Since graduating from West Point in 1990 as a military intelligence officer, she has served in various staff and command positions, including most recently teaching international relations and economics in the Department of Social Sciences at USMA. She is also a graduate of the Johns Hopkins School of Advanced International Studies, with an M.A. in international relations.

Major J. Christopher Lover graduated from Georgetown University in 1990 with a B.S. in Finance. He was commissioned as a field artillery officer and spent his three years in Germany. After returning to the states for the field artillery advanced course, his next assignment was in Fort Lewis, Washington, from 1994-1997. There he commanded Alpha Battery, 1-37 Field Artillery. In 1999, he graduated from Columbia University with an M.B.A. He currently teaches at West Point.

Major Stephen Mannell Jr. is a special forces officer who is a graduate of the USMA and the John F. Kennedy School of Government at Harvard University. Currently, he teaches economics at the USMA at West Point.

Colonel Gregg Martin is an engineer officer currently teaching at the Army War College in the Department of Command, Leadership and Management, where he is director of leadership and command instruction. In addition to serving in a variety of command and staff assignments throughout the Army, he taught in the Department of Social Sciences at the USMA. A graduate of West Point, he holds advanced degrees from both the Army and Naval War Colleges, as well as MIT, where he earned a Ph.D. He is slated to take command of the 130th Engineer Brigade in June 2002.

Major Steven Miska is a student at the Command and General Staff College at Fort Leavenworth, Kansas. He has served as an assistant professor of economics at USMA and as an infantry officer with the 82nd Infantry Division. He has a B.S. from USMA and an M.B.A. from Cornell University's Johnson Graduate School of Management.

Major Joanne Moore is a political science and financial planning instructor at USMA. She is a military police officer with previous assignments in Korea and Fort Benning. She has a B.A. from USMA and an M.P.A. from Columbia University.

Major James O'Connor was commissioned a second lieutenant in military intelligence in May 1987 after graduating from the University of Bridgeport, Bridgeport, Connecticut. His troop assignments include the 10th Mountain Division (Light) at Fort Drum, New York, and Somalia and the 66th Military Intelligence Brigade in Germany. He attended the University of Connecticut, obtaining an M.B.A. He is currently the executive officer and assistant professor of military science at Cornell University's Army ROTC battalion in Ithaca, New York.

Major Carlos Perez Jr. is a student at the Command and General Staff College at Fort Leavenworth, Kansas. He has served as an assistant professor of economics at USMA and as an engineer officer in Europe and with the 4th Infantry Division. He holds a B.S. in economics from West Point and an M.B.A. from the Stanford University Graduate School of Business.

Major Michael Peters is an instructor of public finance and international economics at USMA. He is an infantry officer with previous command and staff assignments with the 2nd Infantry Division in Korea and the 82nd Airborne Division. He holds a B.A. in political science from Davidson College and a master's in international affairs from Columbia University.

Major Gary Pieringer teaches financial planning at USMA. He is a field artillery officer currently in the reserves, having served on active duty at Fort Lewis and in Korea. Since departing from active duty, he has worked for American Express and founded an Internet-based business. He holds a B.S. from USMA and an M.B.A. from Harvard Business School.

Captain Paul Ritkouski is currently the accounting course director at USMA. He is an aviation officer with previous assignments as an aeroscout platoon leader and staff officer at Fort Hood, Texas, and an air traffic control company commander at Fort Rucker, Alabama. He has a B.S. from USMA and an M.B.A., with distinction, from Cornell University's Johnson Graduate School of Management.

Major David Trybula is an assistant professor of economics at West Point. He has served in armor and cavalry assignments with the 24th Infantry Division, the 2nd Armor Division, and the 4th Infantry Division. He holds a B.S. from USMA and an M.S. and Ph.D. from the University of Texas at Austin.

Major Michael Wright is an armor officer/comptroller with a B.S. from West Point in 1989 and an M.B.A. from the University of Texas at Austin in 1998. He is currently assigned to the staff and faculty of the USMA as the executive officer to the dean of the Academic Board and has taught courses in economics, accounting, and finance.

Index

U

V

W